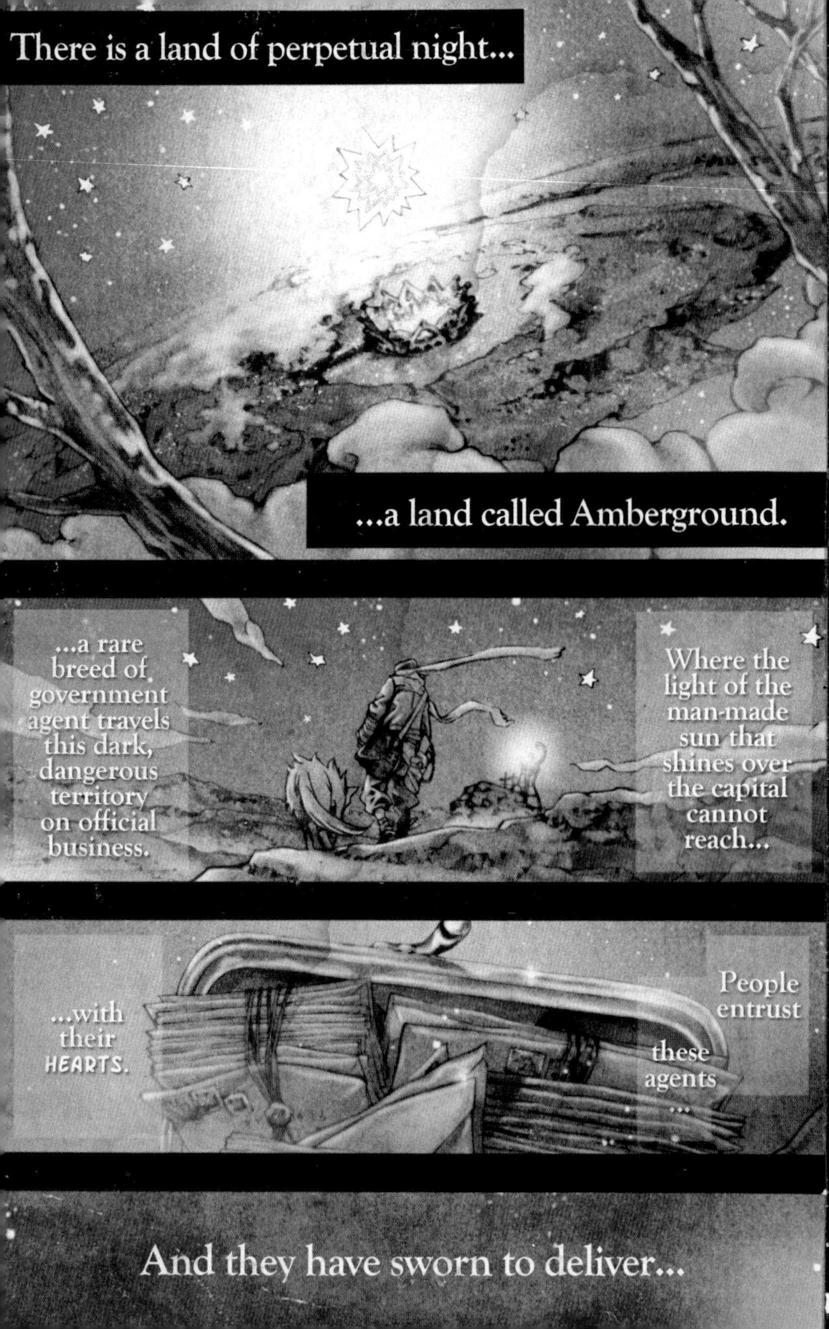
There is a land of perpetual night...
...a land called Amberground.
Where the light of the man-made sun that shines over the capital cannot reach...
...a rare breed of government agent travels this dark, dangerous territory on official business.
People entrust these agents...
...with their HEARTS.
And they have sworn to deliver...

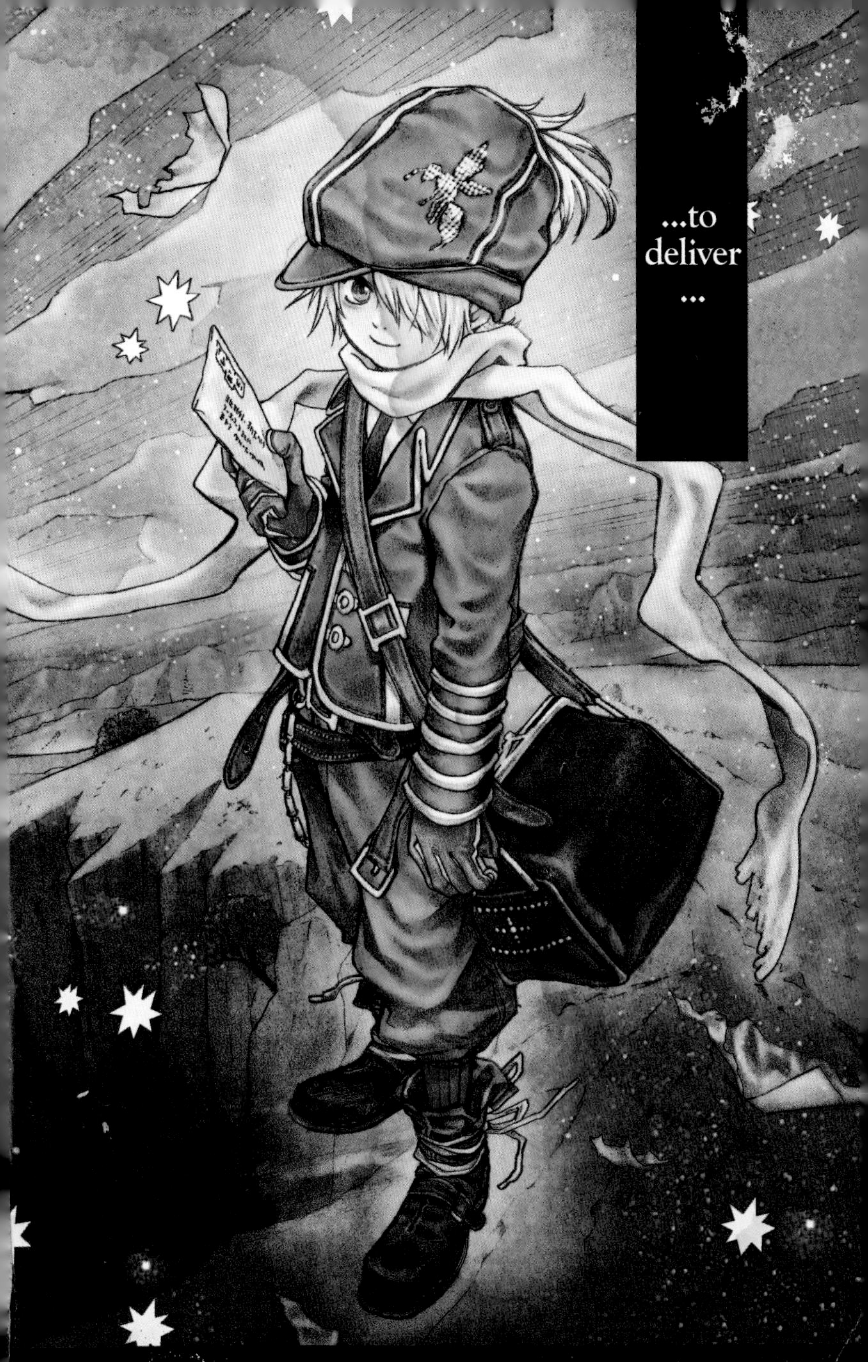
...to
deliver
...

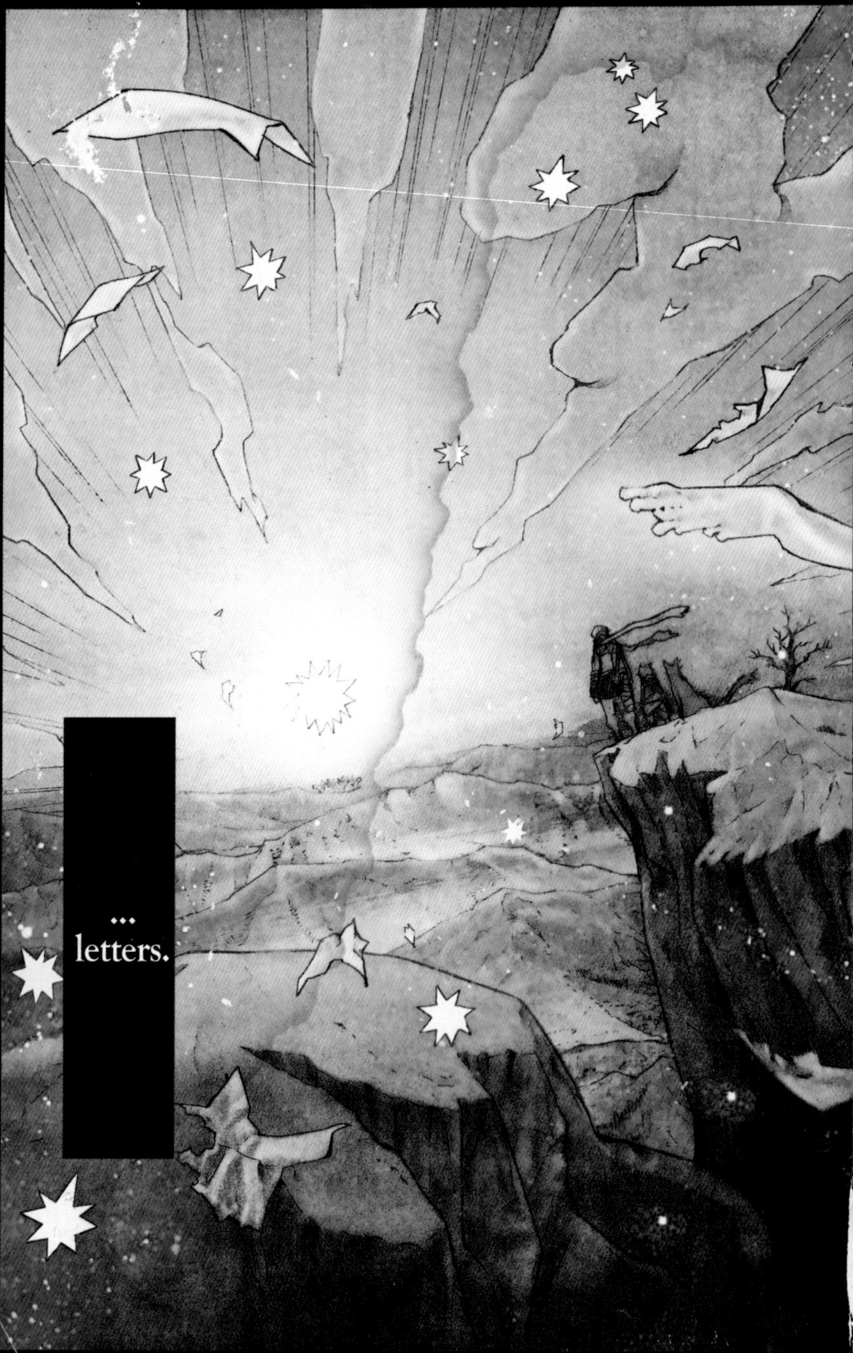
... letters.

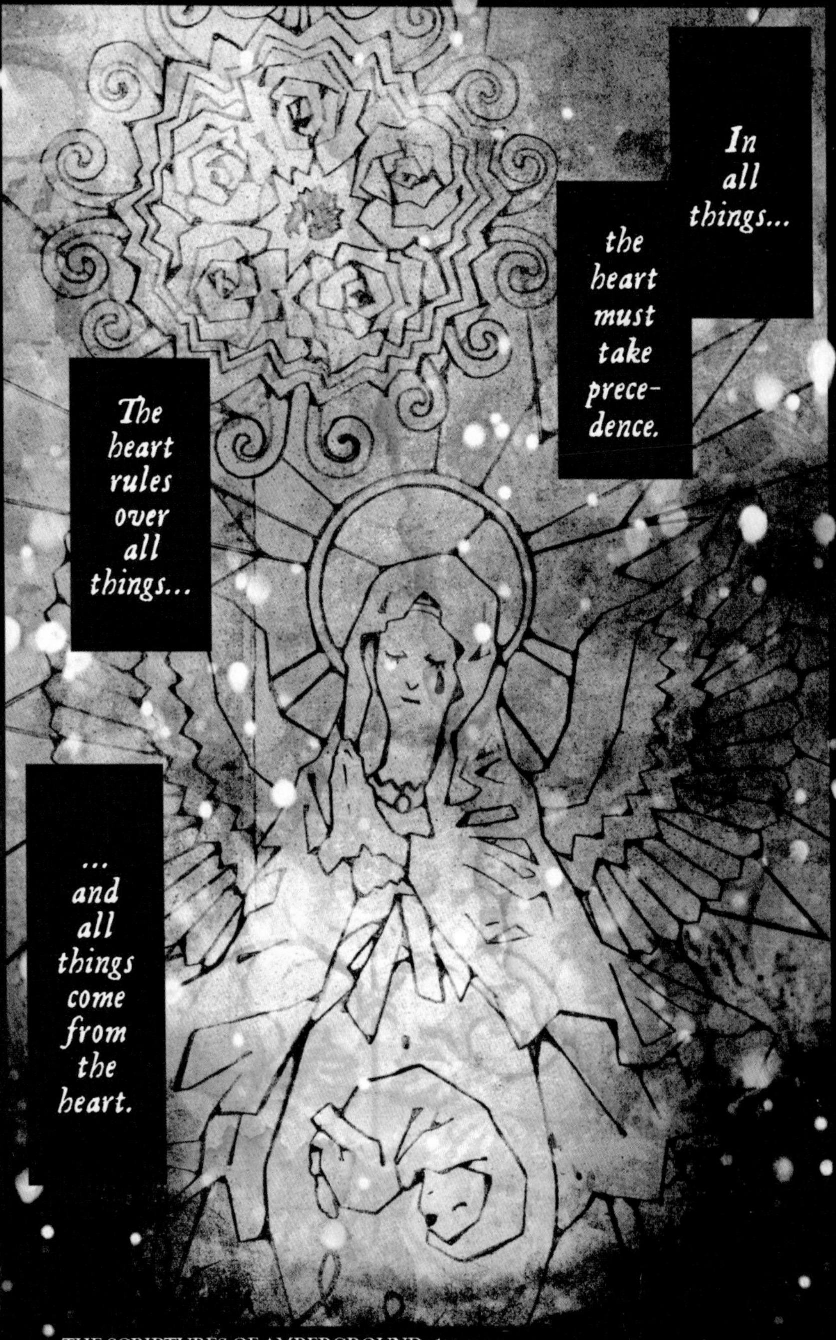
In all things...
the heart must take precedence.
The heart rules over all things...
... and all things come from the heart.

–THE SCRIPTURES OF AMBERGROUND, 1st verse

Tegami Bachi

LETTER · BEE

VOLUME 1

Letter and Letter Bee

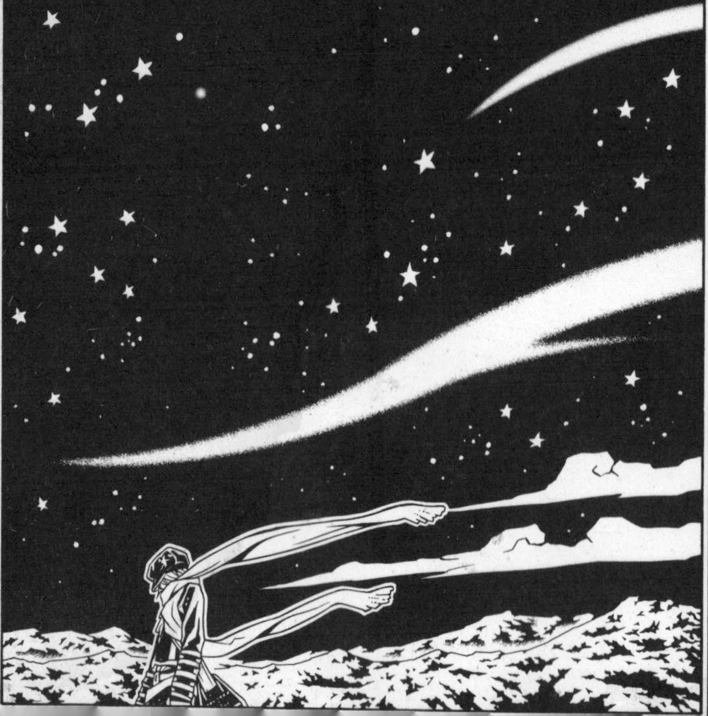

In the postscript of a previously published
collection of my artwork, I wrote that
"the pages of my favorite books are tattered."
I keep the books I love within arm's reach,
and I read them over and over. The tattered
pages show how much I love them.

I hope you wear out the pages of *Tegami Bachi*.

Another adventure is about to begin. Let's go!

—Hiroyuki Asada, 2006

Hiroyuki Asada made his debut in *Monthly Shonen
Jump* in 1986. He's best known for his basketball
manga *I'll*. He's a contributor to artist Range Murata's
quarterly manga anthology *Robot*. *Tegami Bachi:
Letter Bee* is his most recent series.

Tegami Bachi
LETTER · BEE

VOLUME 1
Letter and Letter Bee

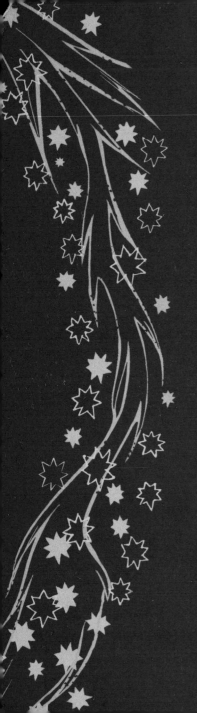

CHAPTER 1: Letter and Letter Bee

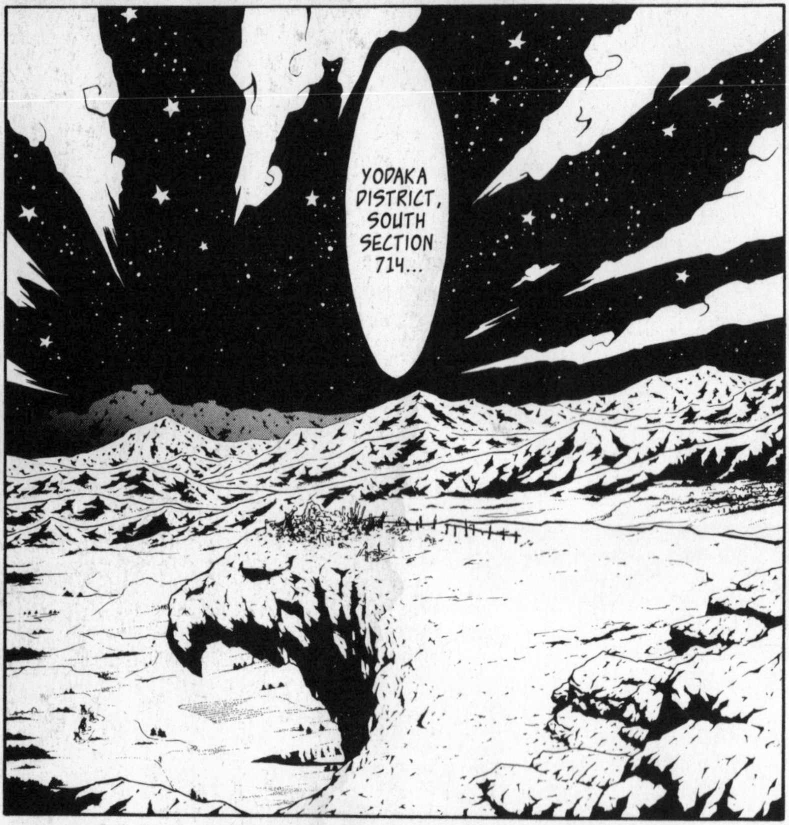
YODAKA DISTRICT, SOUTH SECTION 714...

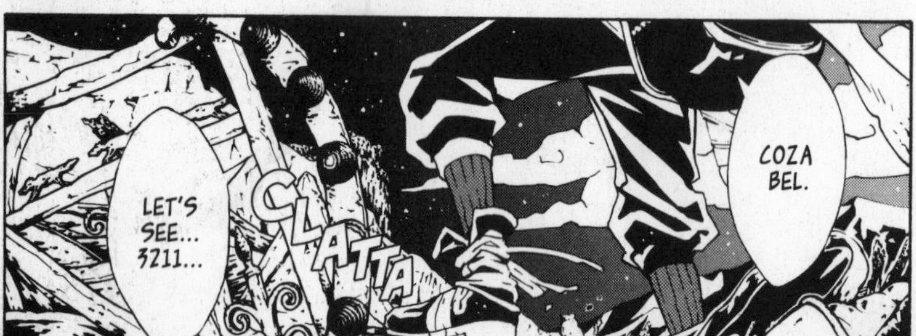
COZA BEL.
LET'S SEE... 3211...
CLATTA

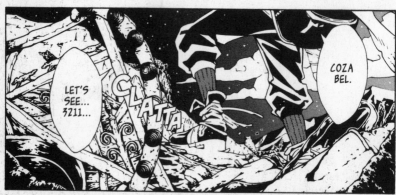

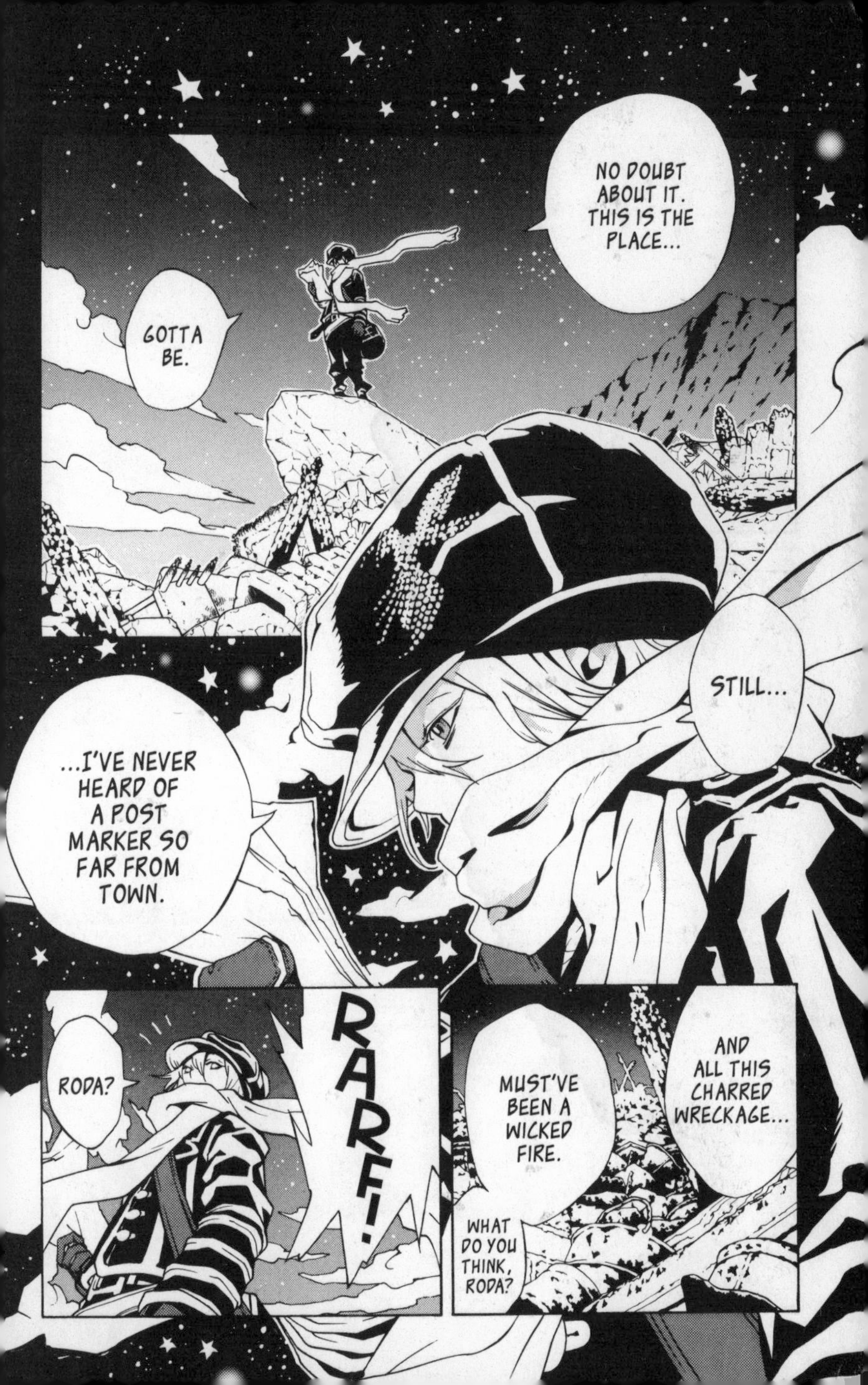
NO DOUBT ABOUT IT. THIS IS THE PLACE...
GOTTA BE.
STILL...
...I'VE NEVER HEARD OF A POST MARKER SO FAR FROM TOWN.
AND ALL THIS CHARRED WRECKAGE...
MUST'VE BEEN A WICKED FIRE.
WHAT DO YOU THINK, RODA?
RARF!
RODA?

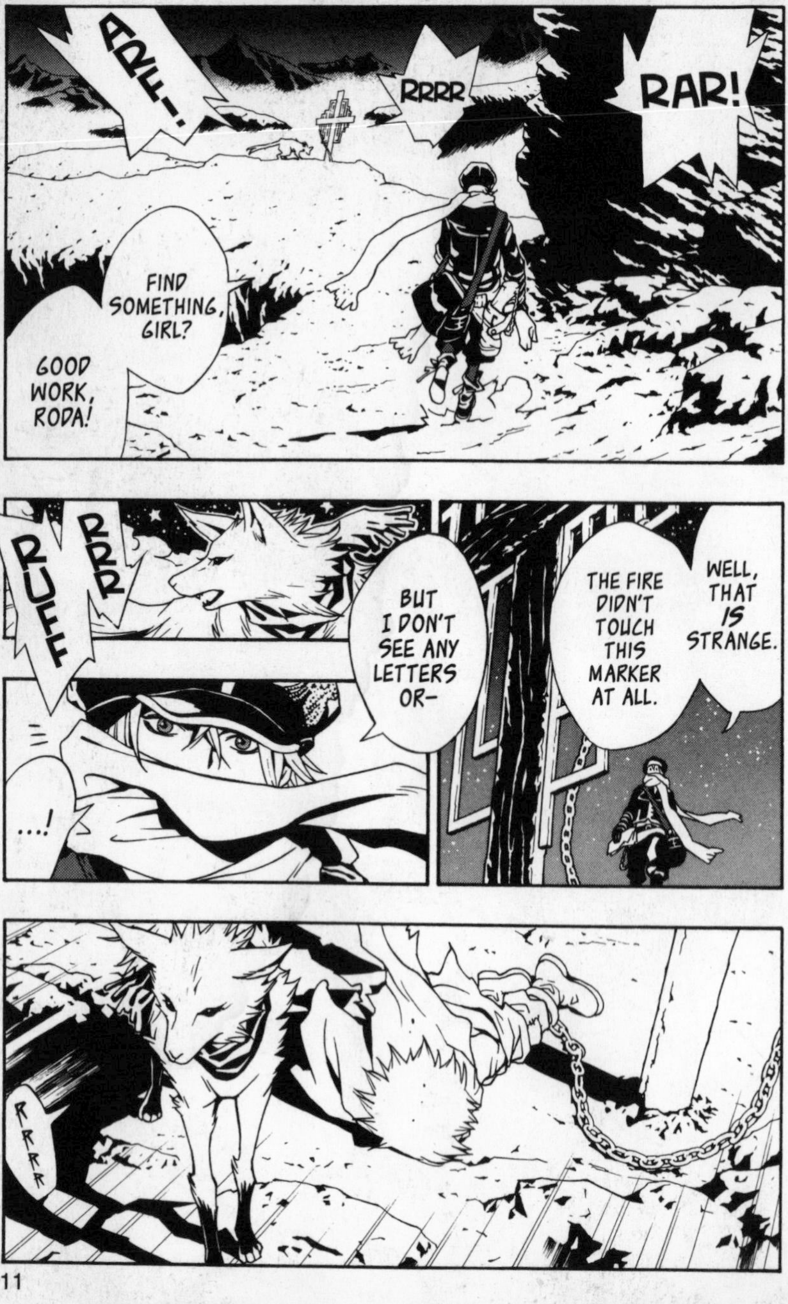

RAR!
RRRR
ARF!
FIND SOMETHING, GIRL?
GOOD WORK, RODA!
WELL, THAT *IS* STRANGE.
THE FIRE DIDN'T TOUCH THIS MARKER AT ALL.
BUT I DON'T SEE ANY LETTERS OR–
RRR
RUFF
...!
RRRR

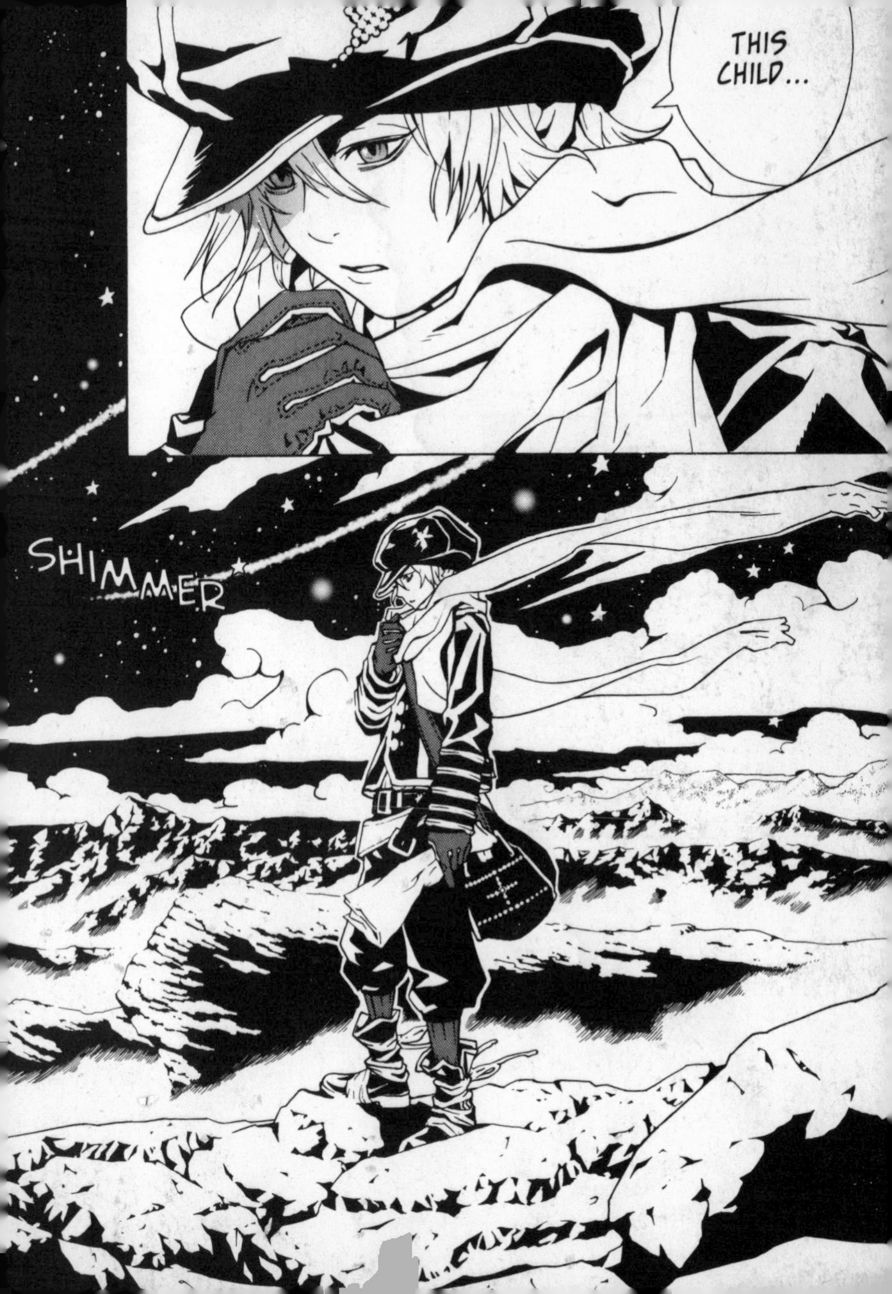
THIS CHILD...
SHIMMER

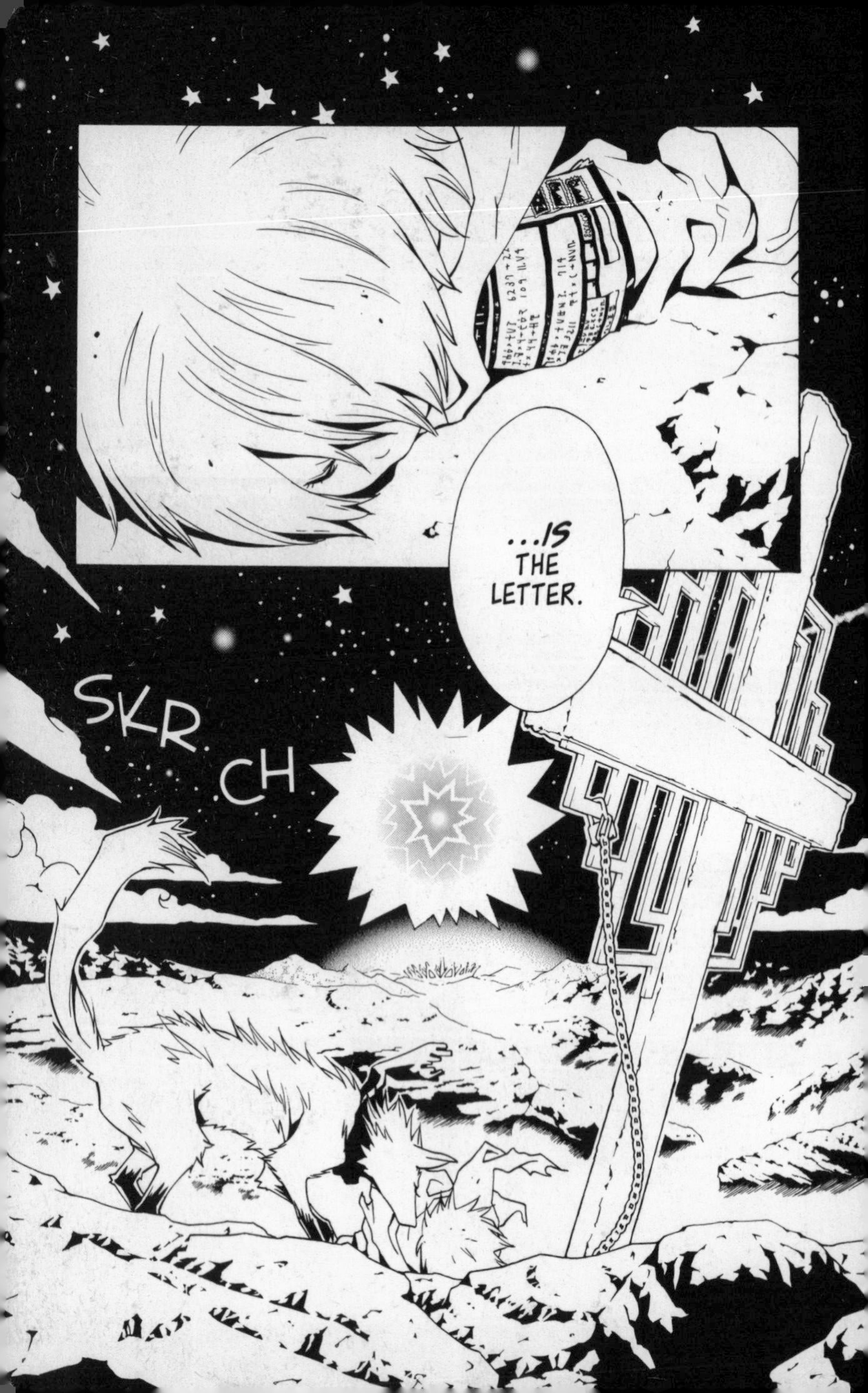
...IS THE LETTER.
SKR CH

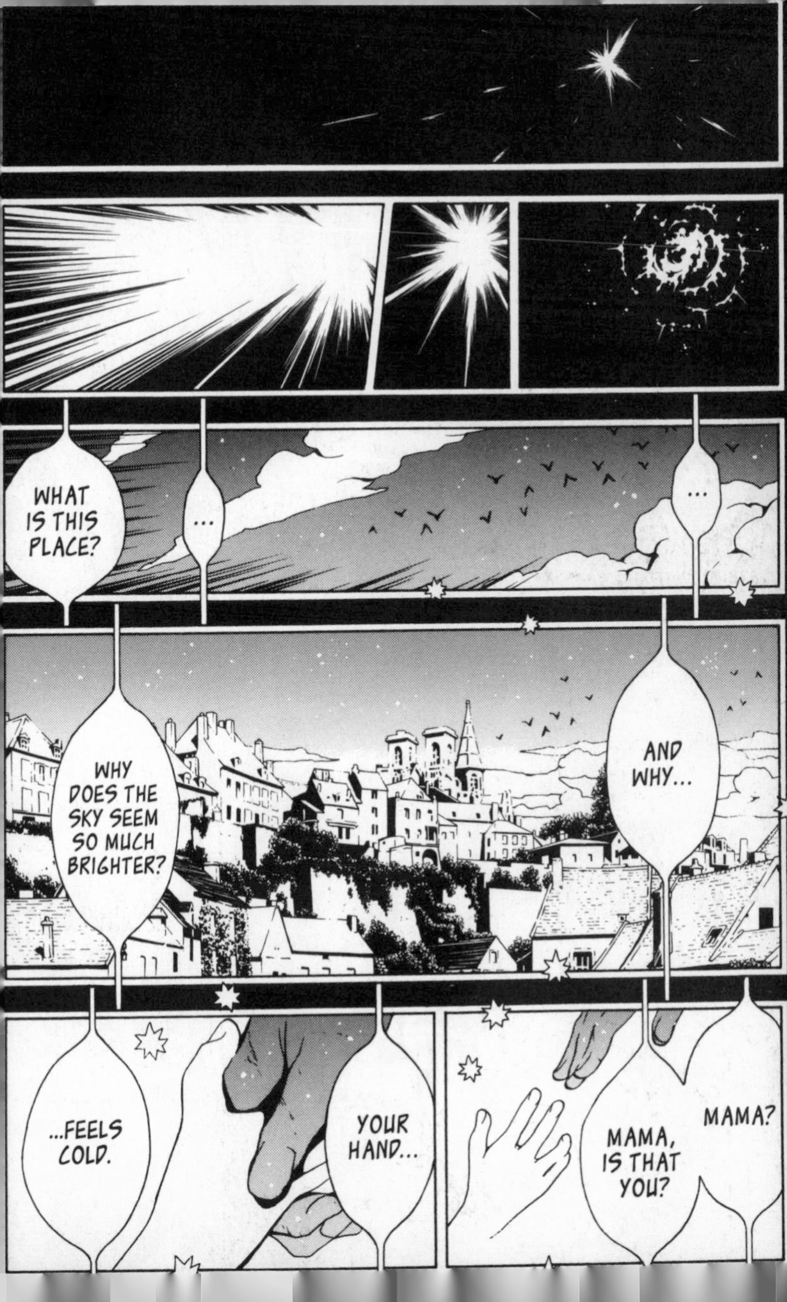
...
...
WHAT IS THIS PLACE?
AND WHY...
WHY DOES THE SKY SEEM SO MUCH BRIGHTER?
MAMA?
MAMA, IS THAT YOU?
YOUR HAND...
...FEELS COLD.

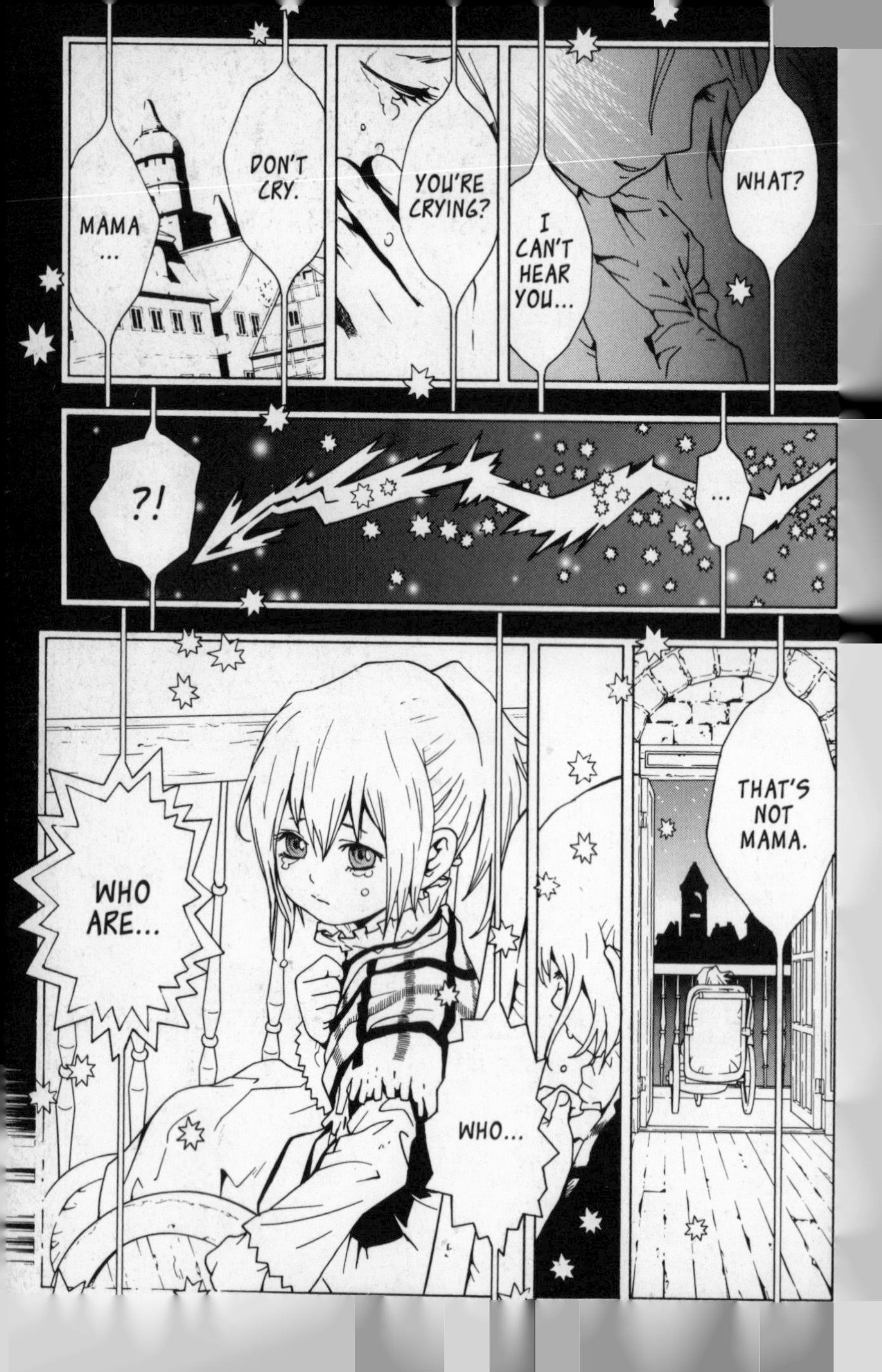

WHAT?
I CAN'T HEAR YOU...
YOU'RE CRYING?
DON'T CRY.
MAMA ...
...
?!
THAT'S NOT MAMA.
WHO...
WHO ARE...

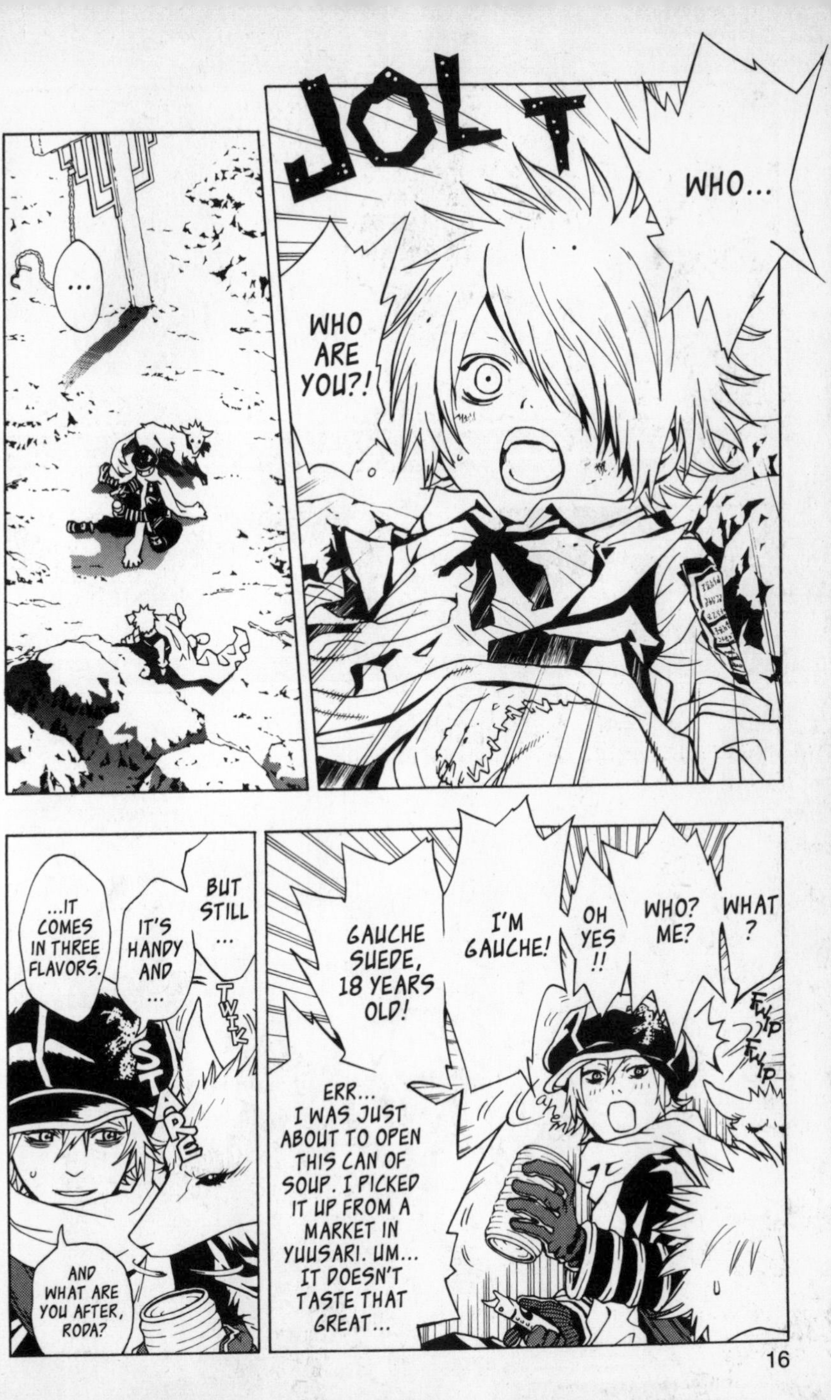
JOLT
WHO...
WHO ARE YOU?!
...
WHAT?
WHO? ME?
OH YES!!
I'M GAUCHE!
GAUCHE SUEDE, 18 YEARS OLD!
FWIP FWIP
ERR... I WAS JUST ABOUT TO OPEN THIS CAN OF SOUP. I PICKED IT UP FROM A MARKET IN YUUSARI. UM... IT DOESN'T TASTE THAT GREAT...
BUT STILL...
IT'S HANDY AND...
...IT COMES IN THREE FLAVORS.
TWIK
STARE
AND WHAT ARE YOU AFTER, RODA?

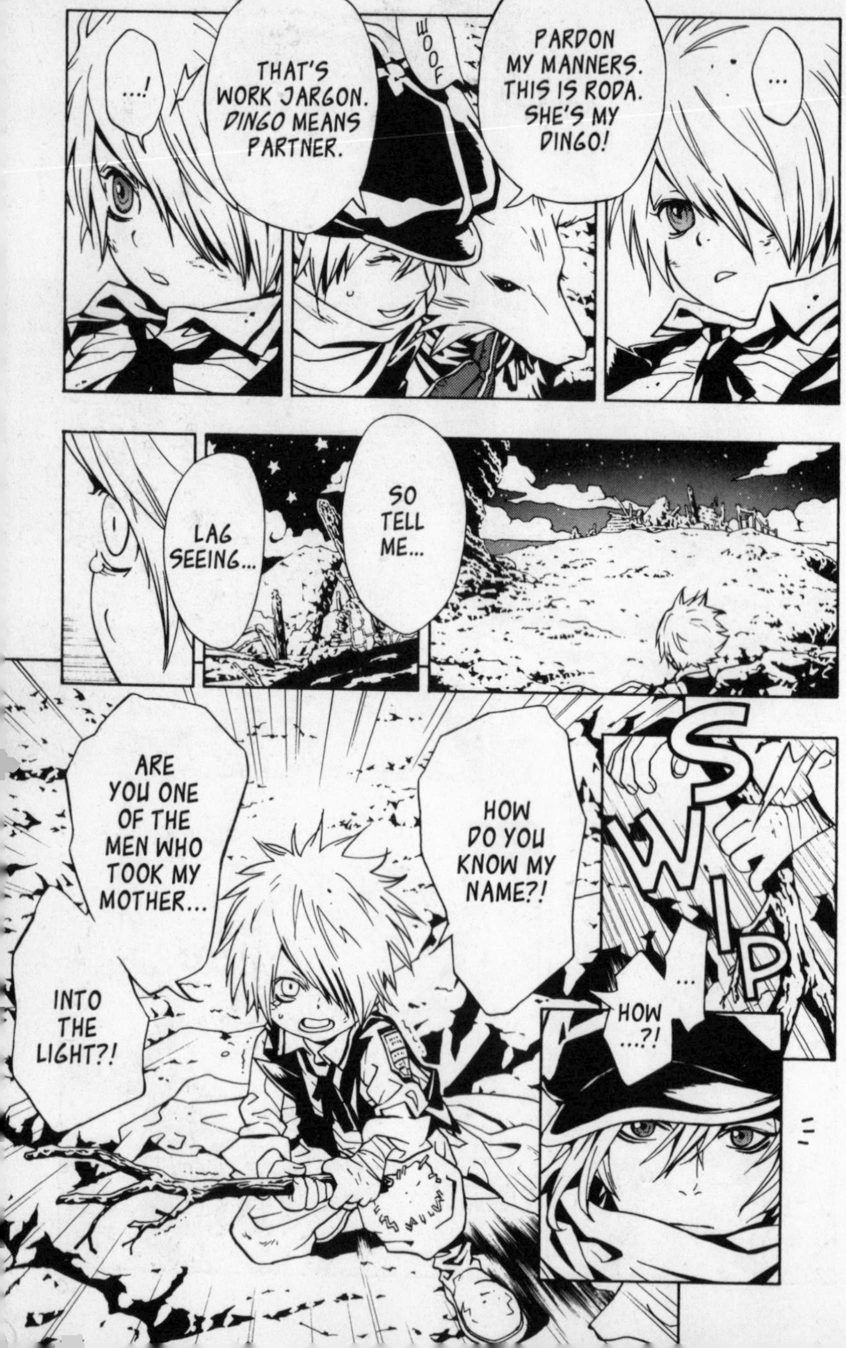
...
PARDON MY MANNERS. THIS IS RODA. SHE'S MY DINGO!
WOOF
THAT'S WORK JARGON. DINGO MEANS PARTNER.
...!
SO TELL ME...
LAG SEEING...
SWIP
...
HOW ...?!
HOW DO YOU KNOW MY NAME?!
ARE YOU ONE OF THE MEN WHO TOOK MY MOTHER...
INTO THE LIGHT?!

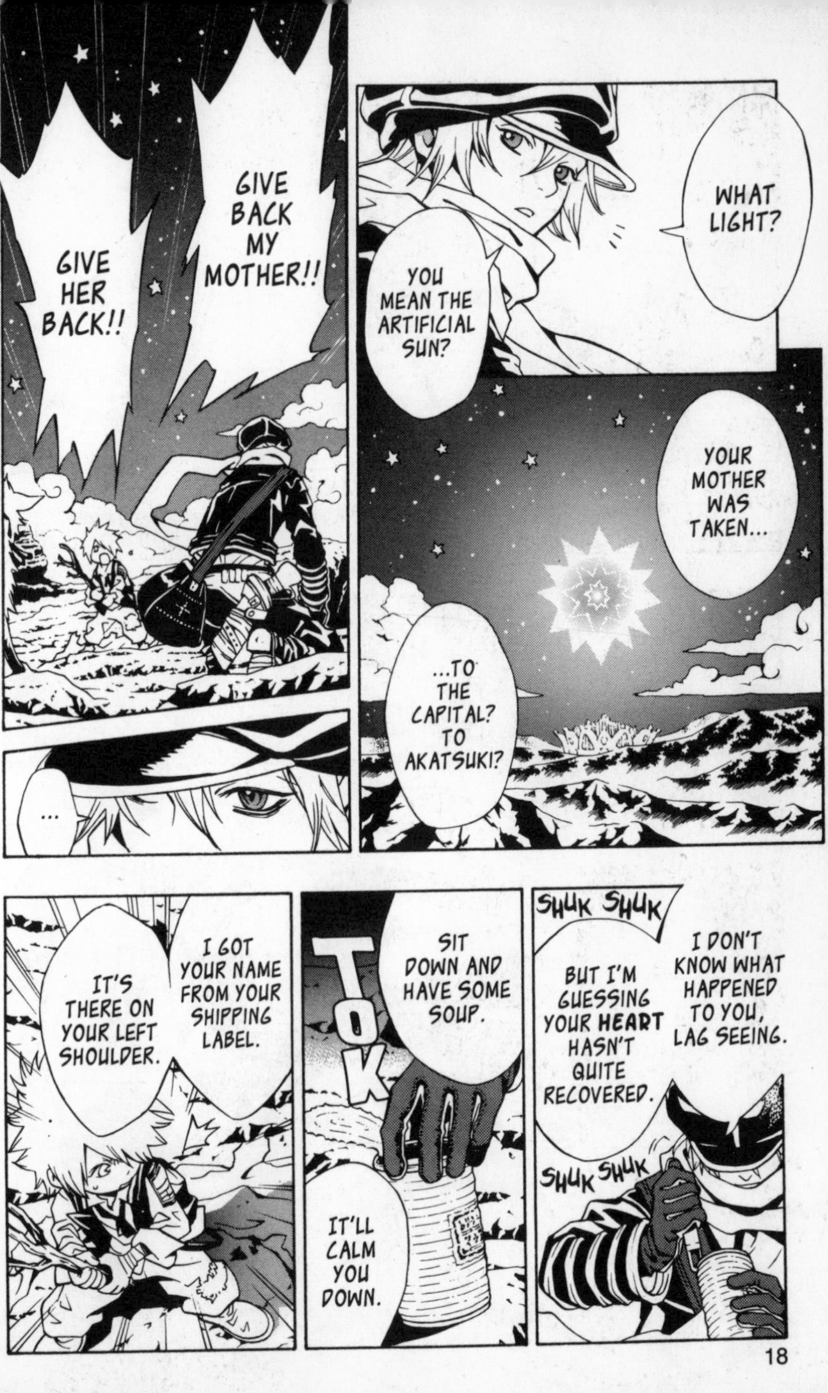
WHAT LIGHT?
YOU MEAN THE ARTIFICIAL SUN?
YOUR MOTHER WAS TAKEN...
...TO THE CAPITAL? TO AKATSUKI?
GIVE BACK MY MOTHER!!
GIVE HER BACK!!
...
SHUK SHUK
I DON'T KNOW WHAT HAPPENED TO YOU, LAG SEEING.
BUT I'M GUESSING YOUR HEART HASN'T QUITE RECOVERED.
SHUK SHUK
TOK
SIT DOWN AND HAVE SOME SOUP.
IT'LL CALM YOU DOWN.
I GOT YOUR NAME FROM YOUR SHIPPING LABEL.
IT'S THERE ON YOUR LEFT SHOULDER.

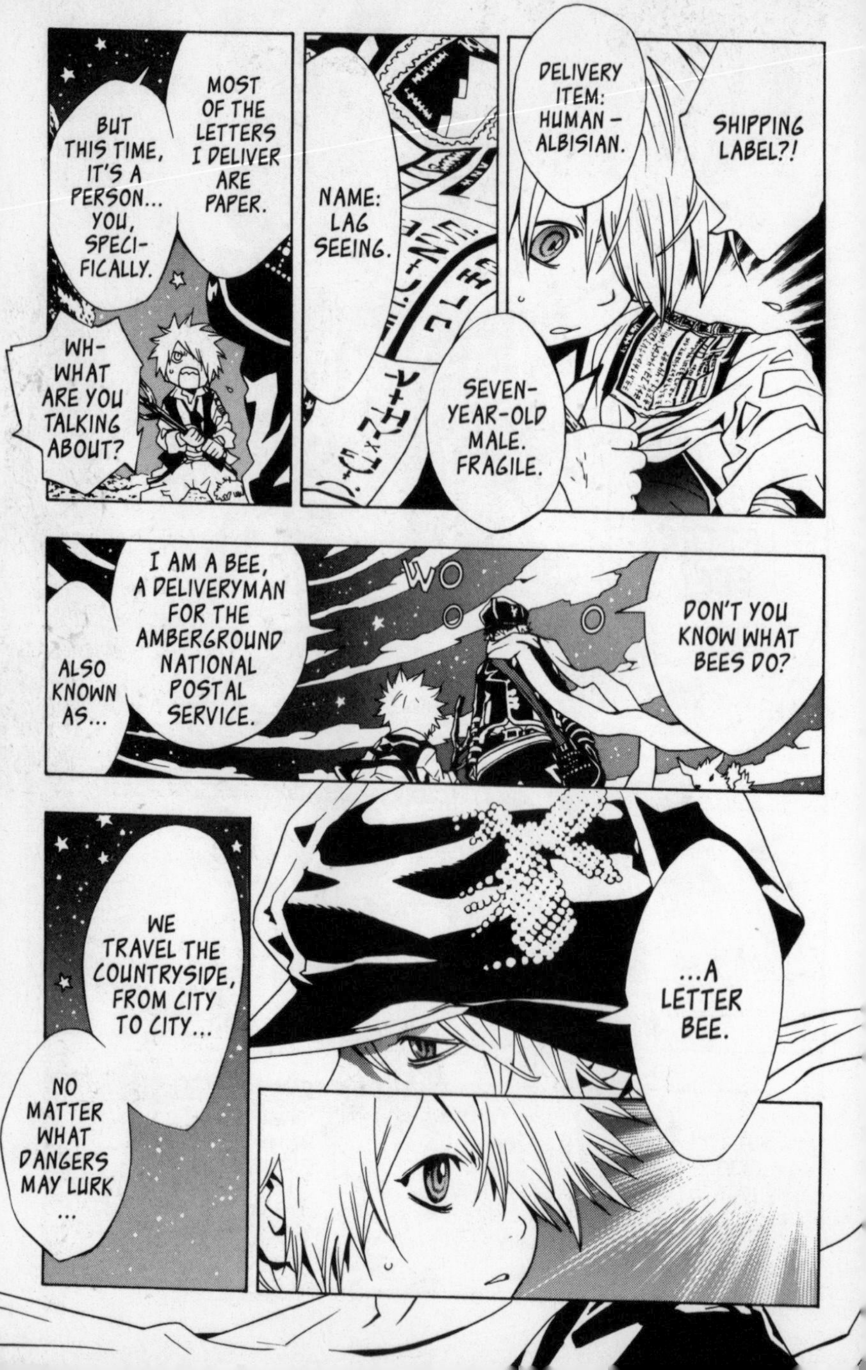
SHIPPING LABEL?!
DELIVERY ITEM: HUMAN - ALBISIAN.
NAME: LAG SEEING.
SEVEN-YEAR-OLD MALE. FRAGILE.
MOST OF THE LETTERS I DELIVER ARE PAPER.
BUT THIS TIME, IT'S A PERSON... YOU, SPECIFICALLY.
WH-WHAT ARE YOU TALKING ABOUT?
DON'T YOU KNOW WHAT BEES DO?
I AM A BEE, A DELIVERYMAN FOR THE AMBERGROUND NATIONAL POSTAL SERVICE.
ALSO KNOWN AS...
...A LETTER BEE.
WE TRAVEL THE COUNTRYSIDE, FROM CITY TO CITY...
NO MATTER WHAT DANGERS MAY LURK ...

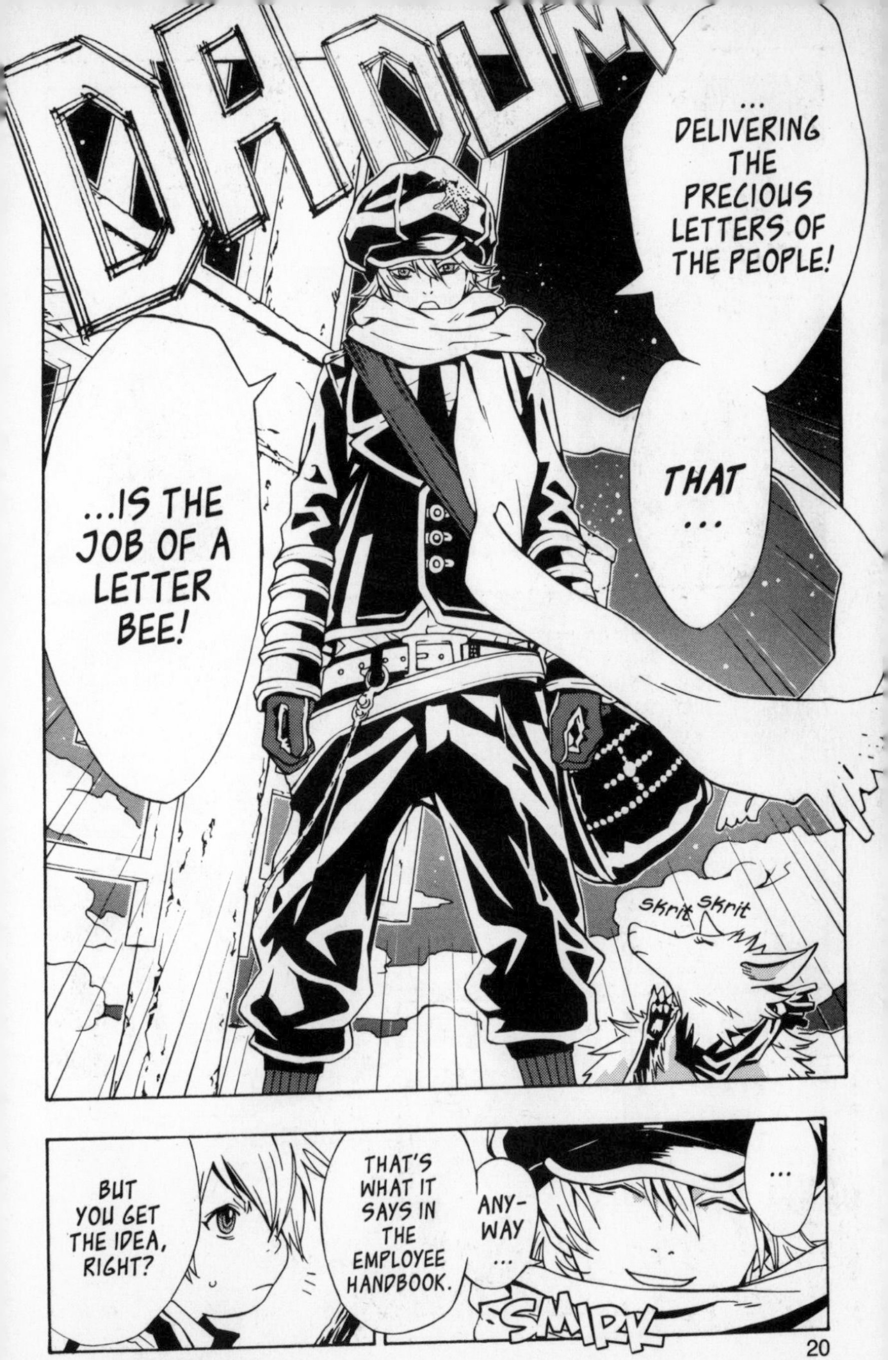
DADUM
...DELIVERING THE PRECIOUS LETTERS OF THE PEOPLE!
THAT...
...IS THE JOB OF A LETTER BEE!
Skrit Skrit
...
ANY-WAY...
SMIRK
THAT'S WHAT IT SAYS IN THE EMPLOYEE HANDBOOK.
BUT YOU GET THE IDEA, RIGHT?

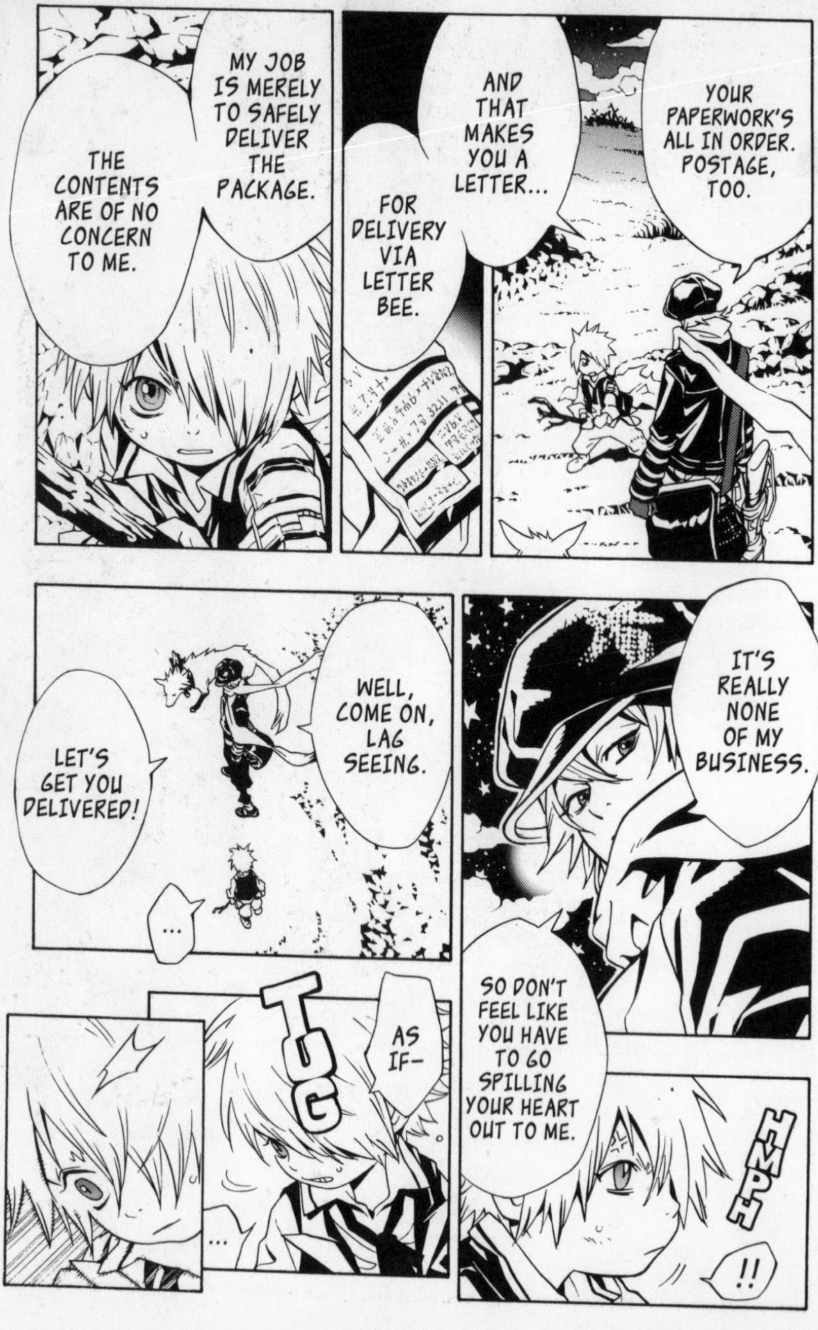
YOUR PAPERWORK'S ALL IN ORDER. POSTAGE, TOO.
AND THAT MAKES YOU A LETTER...
FOR DELIVERY VIA LETTER BEE.
MY JOB IS MERELY TO SAFELY DELIVER THE PACKAGE.
THE CONTENTS ARE OF NO CONCERN TO ME.
IT'S REALLY NONE OF MY BUSINESS.
SO DON'T FEEL LIKE YOU HAVE TO GO SPILLING YOUR HEART OUT TO ME.
WELL, COME ON, LAG SEEING.
LET'S GET YOU DELIVERED!
...
HMPH
!!
TUG
AS IF-
...

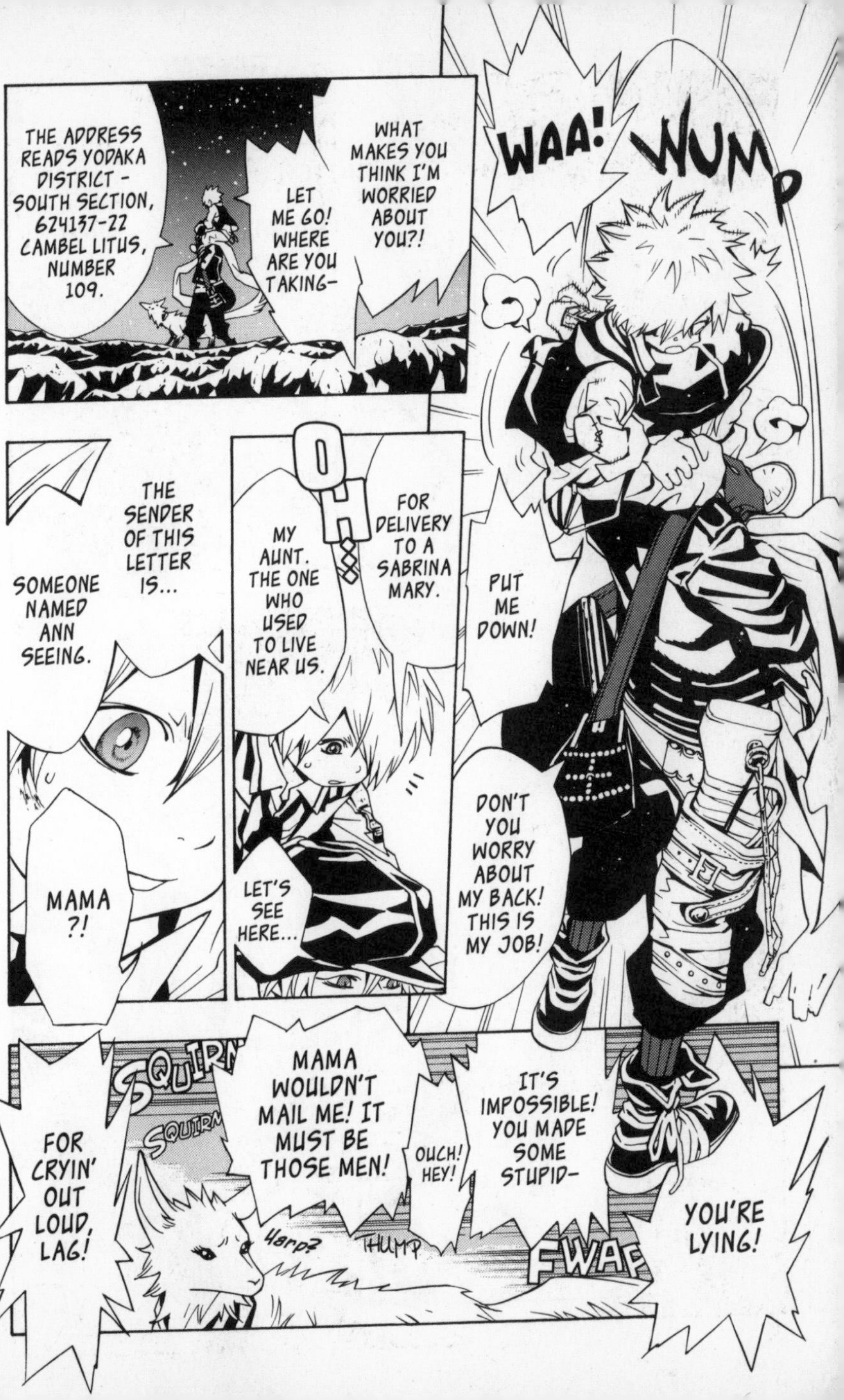
WUMP
WAA!
PUT ME DOWN!
DON'T YOU WORRY ABOUT MY BACK! THIS IS MY JOB!
WHAT MAKES YOU THINK I'M WORRIED ABOUT YOU?!
LET ME GO! WHERE ARE YOU TAKING-
THE ADDRESS READS YODAKA DISTRICT - SOUTH SECTION, 624137-22 CAMBEL LITUS, NUMBER 109.
OH
FOR DELIVERY TO A SABRINA MARY.
MY AUNT. THE ONE WHO USED TO LIVE NEAR US.
LET'S SEE HERE...
THE SENDER OF THIS LETTER IS...
SOMEONE NAMED ANN SEEING.
MAMA ?!
YOU'RE LYING!
FWAP
IT'S IMPOSSIBLE! YOU MADE SOME STUPID-
OUCH! HEY!
THUMP
MAMA WOULDN'T MAIL ME! IT MUST BE THOSE MEN!
SQUIRM
SQUIRM
Uarp?
FOR CRYIN' OUT LOUD, LAG!

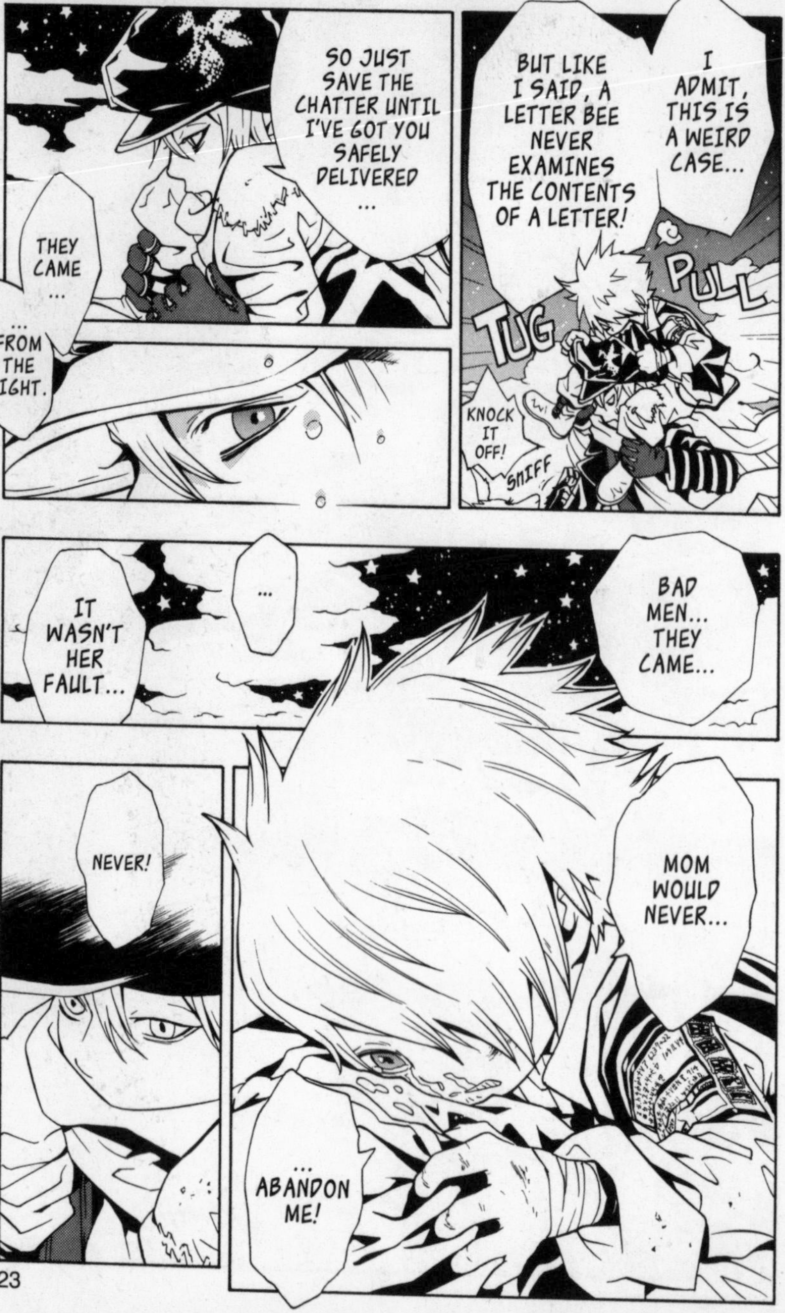
I ADMIT, THIS IS A WEIRD CASE...
BUT LIKE I SAID, A LETTER BEE NEVER EXAMINES THE CONTENTS OF A LETTER!
PULL
TUG
KNOCK IT OFF!
SNIFF
SO JUST SAVE THE CHATTER UNTIL I'VE GOT YOU SAFELY DELIVERED ...
THEY CAME ...
... FROM THE LIGHT.
BAD MEN... THEY CAME...
...
IT WASN'T HER FAULT...
MOM WOULD NEVER...
... ABANDON ME!
NEVER!

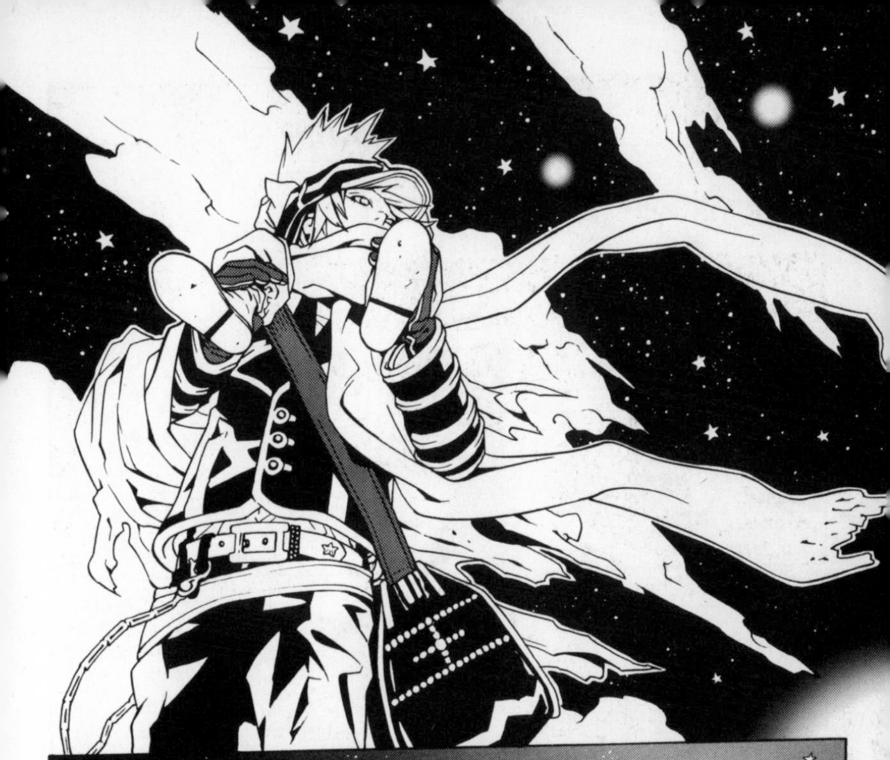

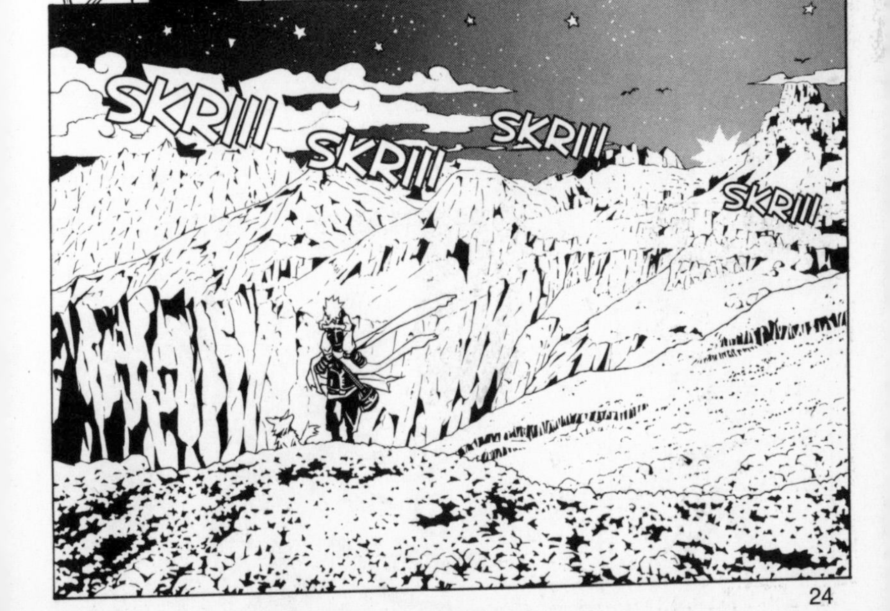
SKRIII
SKRIII
SKRIII
SKRIII

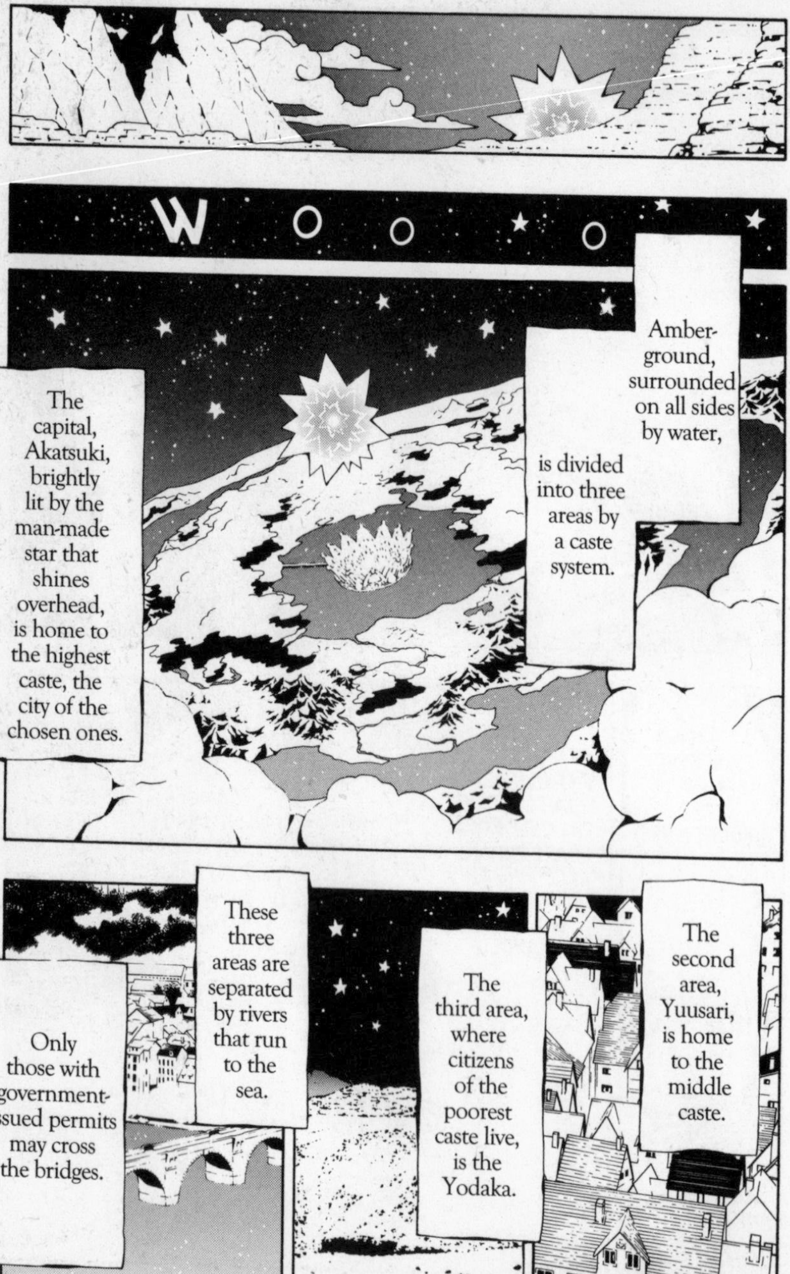
WOOO
Amber-ground, surrounded on all sides by water,
is divided into three areas by a caste system.
The capital, Akatsuki, brightly lit by the man-made star that shines overhead, is home to the highest caste, the city of the chosen ones.
The second area, Yuusari, is home to the middle caste.
The third area, where citizens of the poorest caste live, is the Yodaka.
These three areas are separated by rivers that run to the sea.
Only those with government-issued permits may cross the bridges.

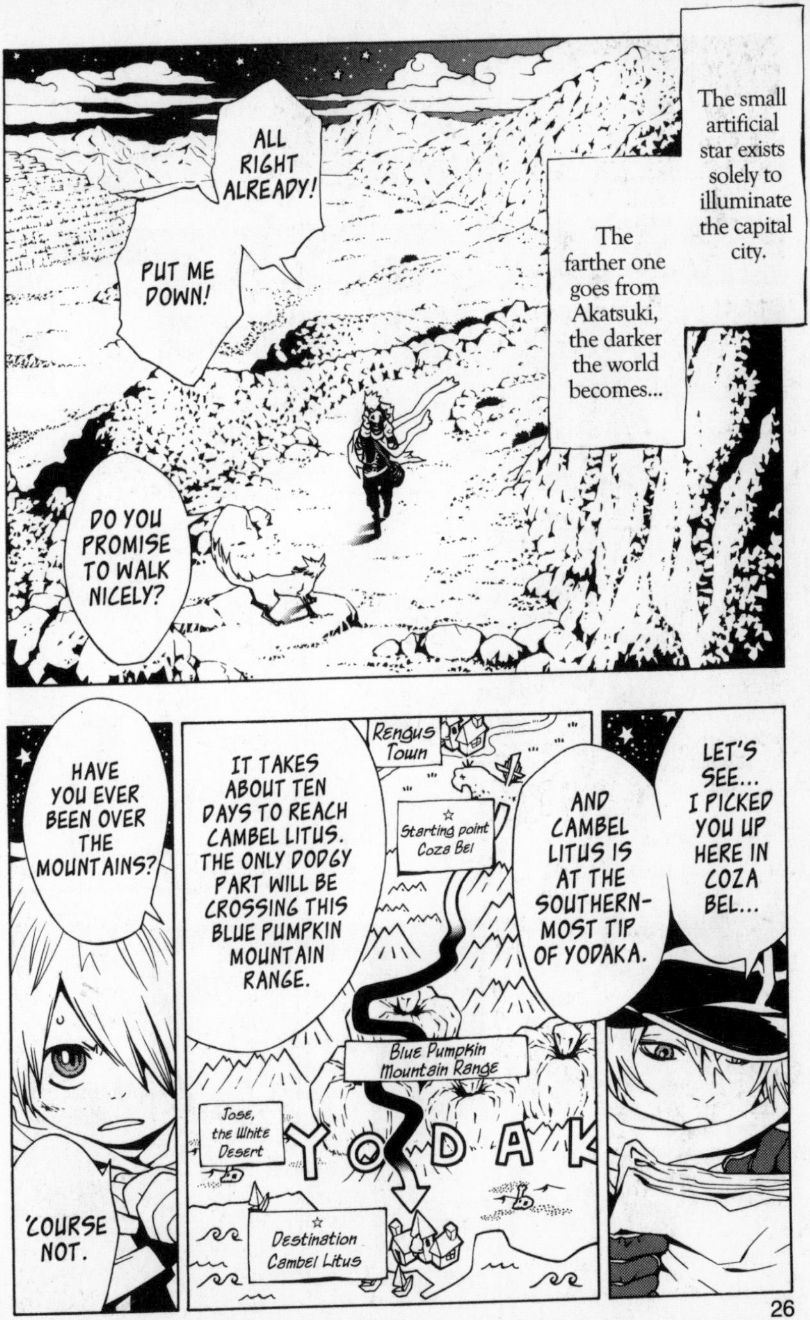
The small artificial star exists solely to illuminate the capital city.
The farther one goes from Akatsuki, the darker the world becomes...
ALL RIGHT ALREADY!
PUT ME DOWN!
DO YOU PROMISE TO WALK NICELY?
LET'S SEE... I PICKED YOU UP HERE IN COZA BEL...
AND CAMBEL LITUS IS AT THE SOUTHERN-MOST TIP OF YODAKA.
IT TAKES ABOUT TEN DAYS TO REACH CAMBEL LITUS. THE ONLY DODGY PART WILL BE CROSSING THIS BLUE PUMPKIN MOUNTAIN RANGE.
Rengus Town
☆ Starting point Coza Bel
Blue Pumpkin Mountain Range
Jose, the White Desert
YODAK
☆ Destination Cambel Litus
HAVE YOU EVER BEEN OVER THE MOUNTAINS?
'COURSE NOT.

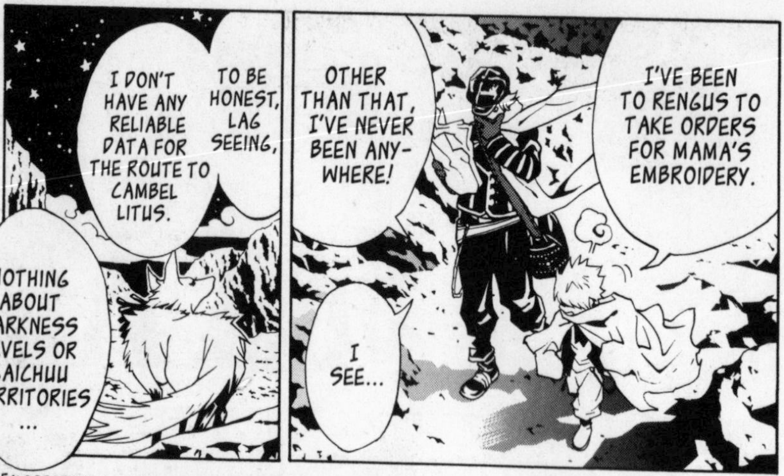
I'VE BEEN TO RENGUS TO TAKE ORDERS FOR MAMA'S EMBROIDERY.
OTHER THAN THAT, I'VE NEVER BEEN ANY-WHERE!
I SEE...
TO BE HONEST, LAG SEEING,
I DON'T HAVE ANY RELIABLE DATA FOR THE ROUTE TO CAMBEL LITUS.
NOTHING ABOUT DARKNESS LEVELS OR GAICHUU TERRITORIES...

[GLOSSARY: 鎧虫 =GAICHUU = ARMOR + INSECT/BUG]

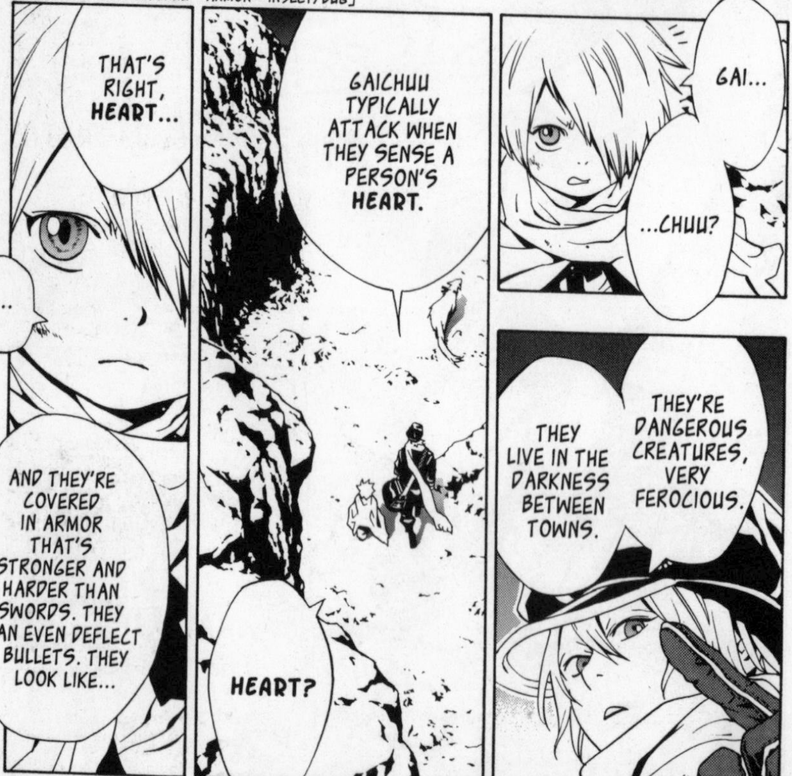
GAI...
...CHUU?
THEY'RE DANGEROUS CREATURES, VERY FEROCIOUS.
THEY LIVE IN THE DARKNESS BETWEEN TOWNS.
GAICHUU TYPICALLY ATTACK WHEN THEY SENSE A PERSON'S **HEART**.
HEART?
THAT'S RIGHT, **HEART**...
...
AND THEY'RE COVERED IN ARMOR THAT'S STRONGER AND HARDER THAN SWORDS. THEY CAN EVEN DEFLECT BULLETS. THEY LOOK LIKE...

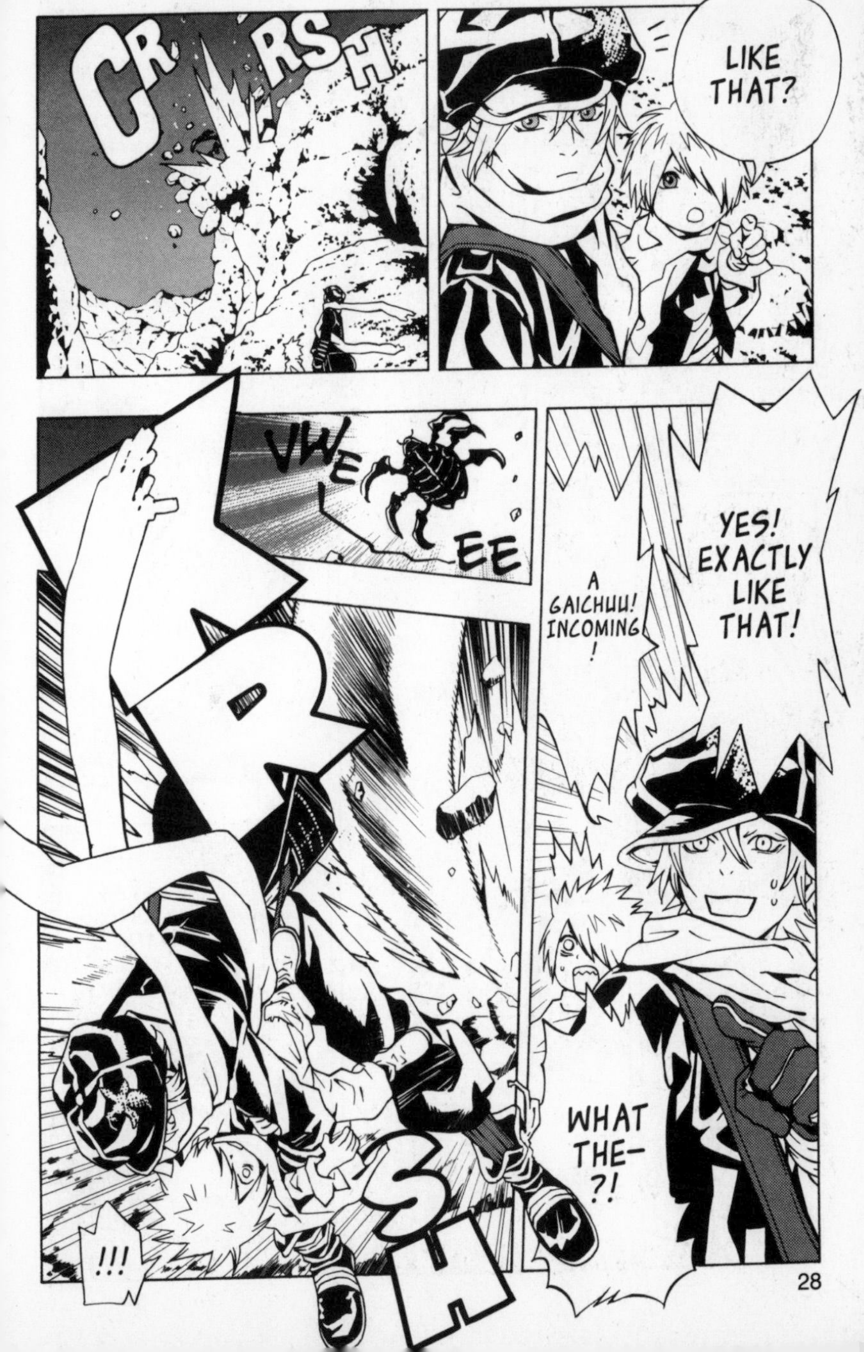
LIKE THAT?
CRSH
YES! EXACTLY LIKE THAT!
A GAICHUU! INCOMING!
WHAT THE-?!
VWEEE
!!!

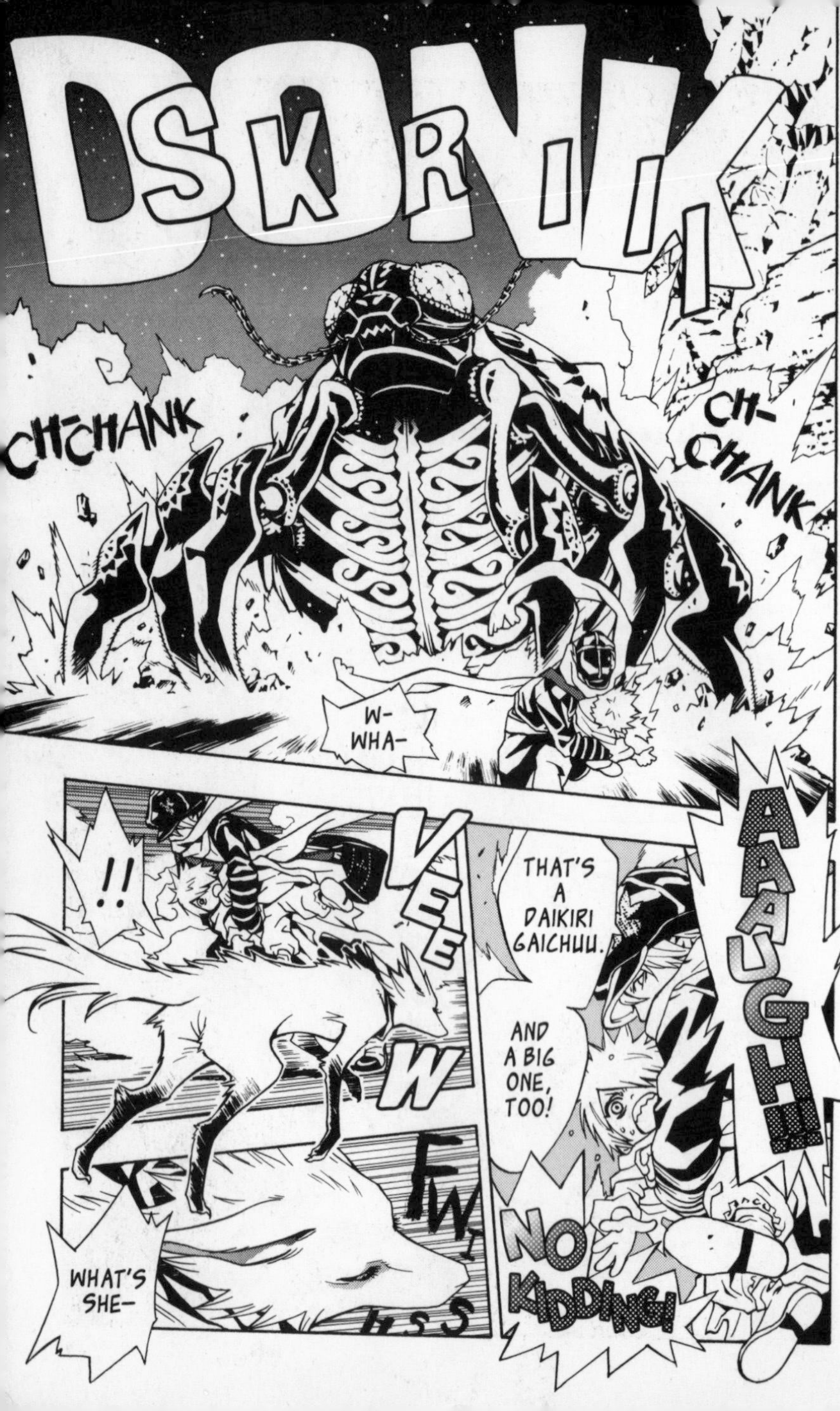
DSKRIIIK
CH-CHANK
CHCHANK
W- WHA-
AAAUGH!!!
THAT'S A DAIKIRI GAICHUU.
AND A BIG ONE, TOO!
NO KIDDING!
VEEEW
!!
FWI
HSS
WHAT'S SHE-

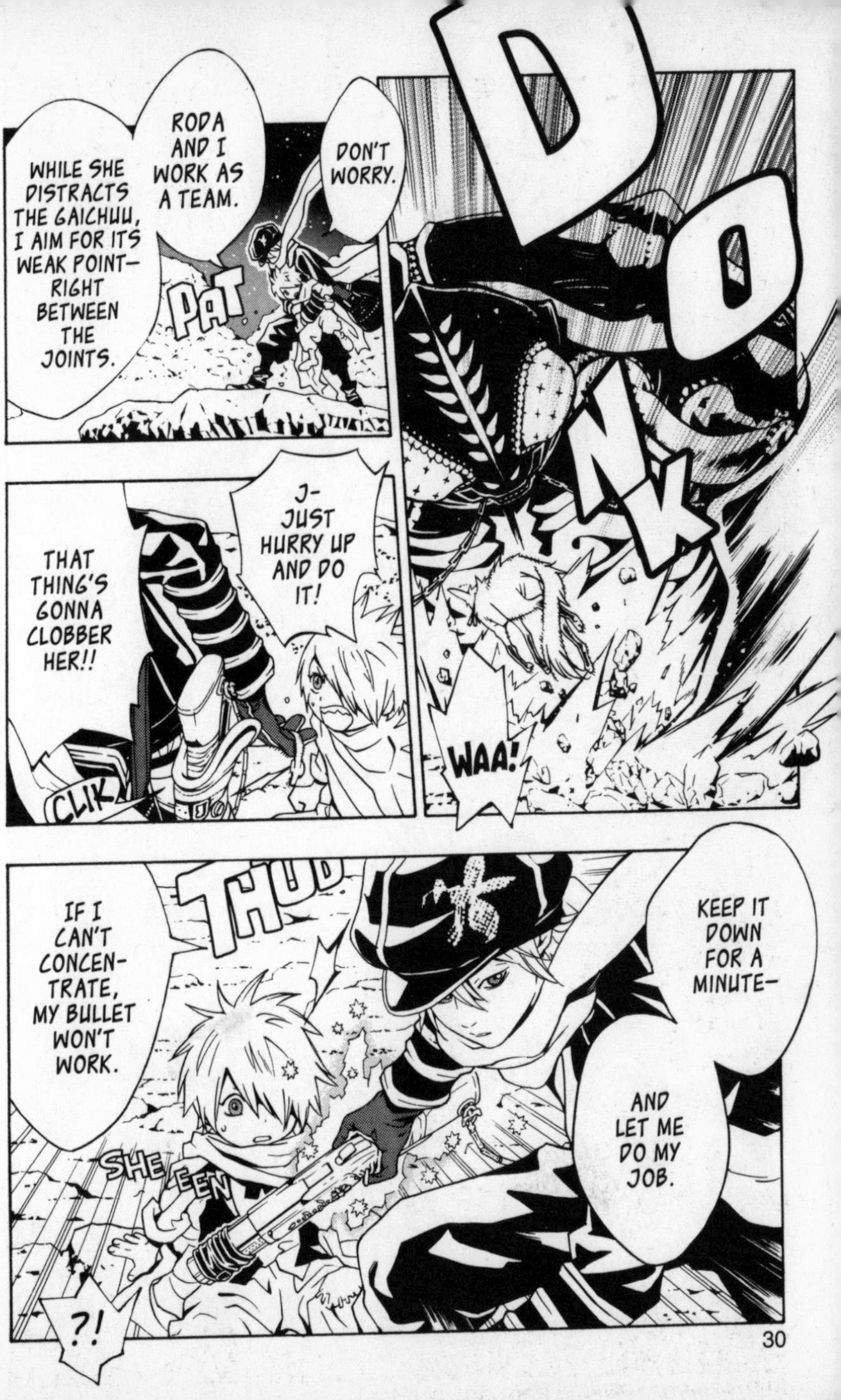
DONK
WAA!
DON'T WORRY.
RODA AND I WORK AS A TEAM.
WHILE SHE DISTRACTS THE GAICHUU, I AIM FOR ITS WEAK POINT—RIGHT BETWEEN THE JOINTS.
PAT
J-JUST HURRY UP AND DO IT!
THAT THING'S GONNA CLOBBER HER!!
CLIK
KEEP IT DOWN FOR A MINUTE—
AND LET ME DO MY JOB.
THUD
IF I CAN'T CONCENTRATE, MY BULLET WON'T WORK.
SHEEEN
?!

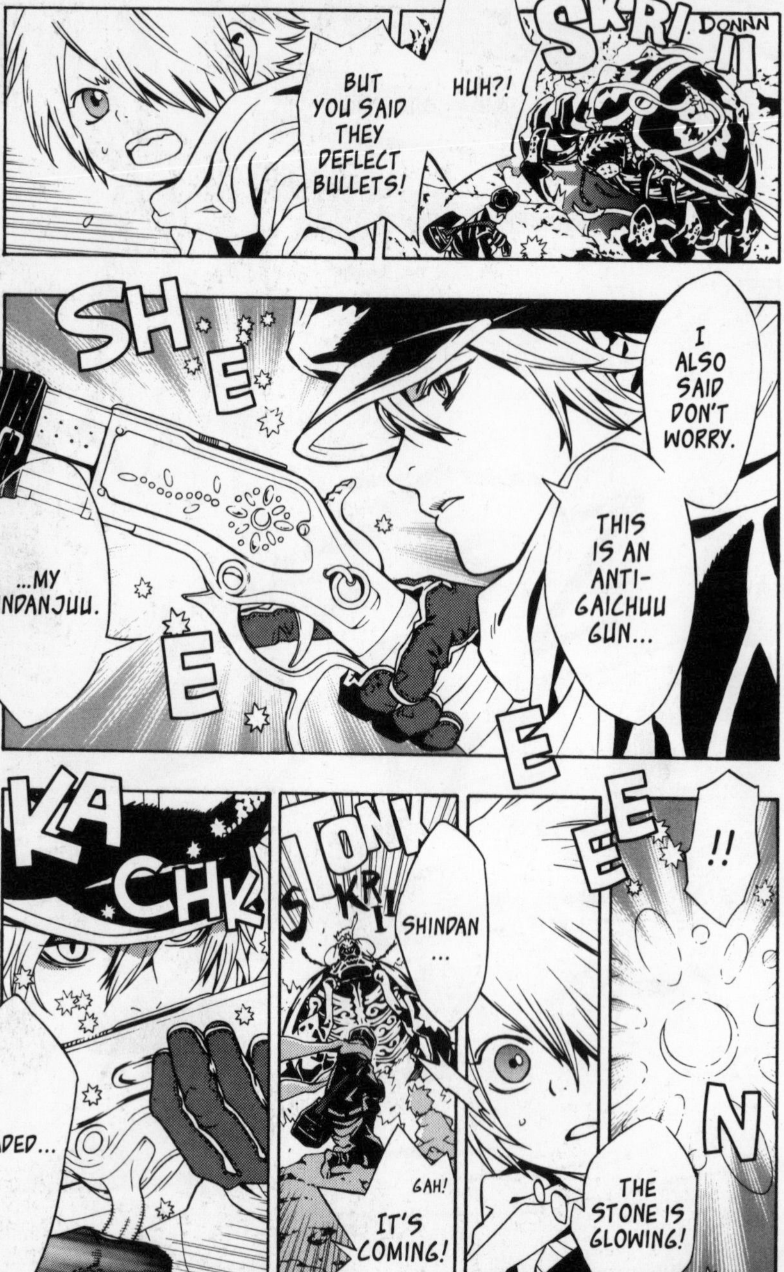
SKRIII
DONNN
HUH?!
BUT YOU SAID THEY DEFLECT BULLETS!
SHEEEE
I ALSO SAID DON'T WORRY.
THIS IS AN ANTI-GAICHUU GUN...
...MY SHINDANJUU.
!!
EEEN
THE STONE IS GLOWING!
TONK
SKRII
SHINDAN ...
GAH!
IT'S COMING!
KACHK
LOADED...

[GLOSSARY: 心弾銃 = SHINDANJUU = HEART+BULLET+GUN/PISTOL]

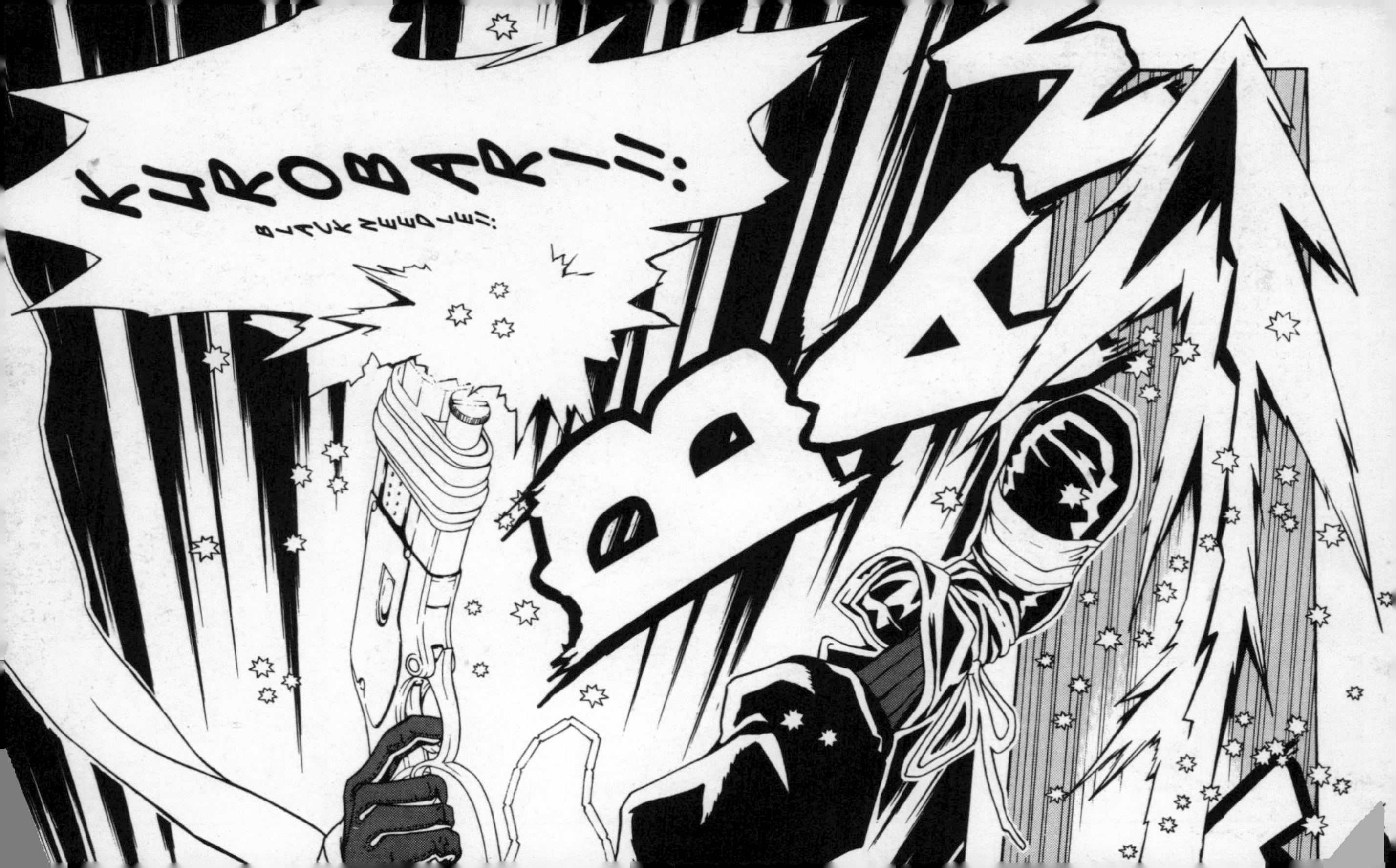
KUROBARI!!
BLACK NEEDLE!!
BAM

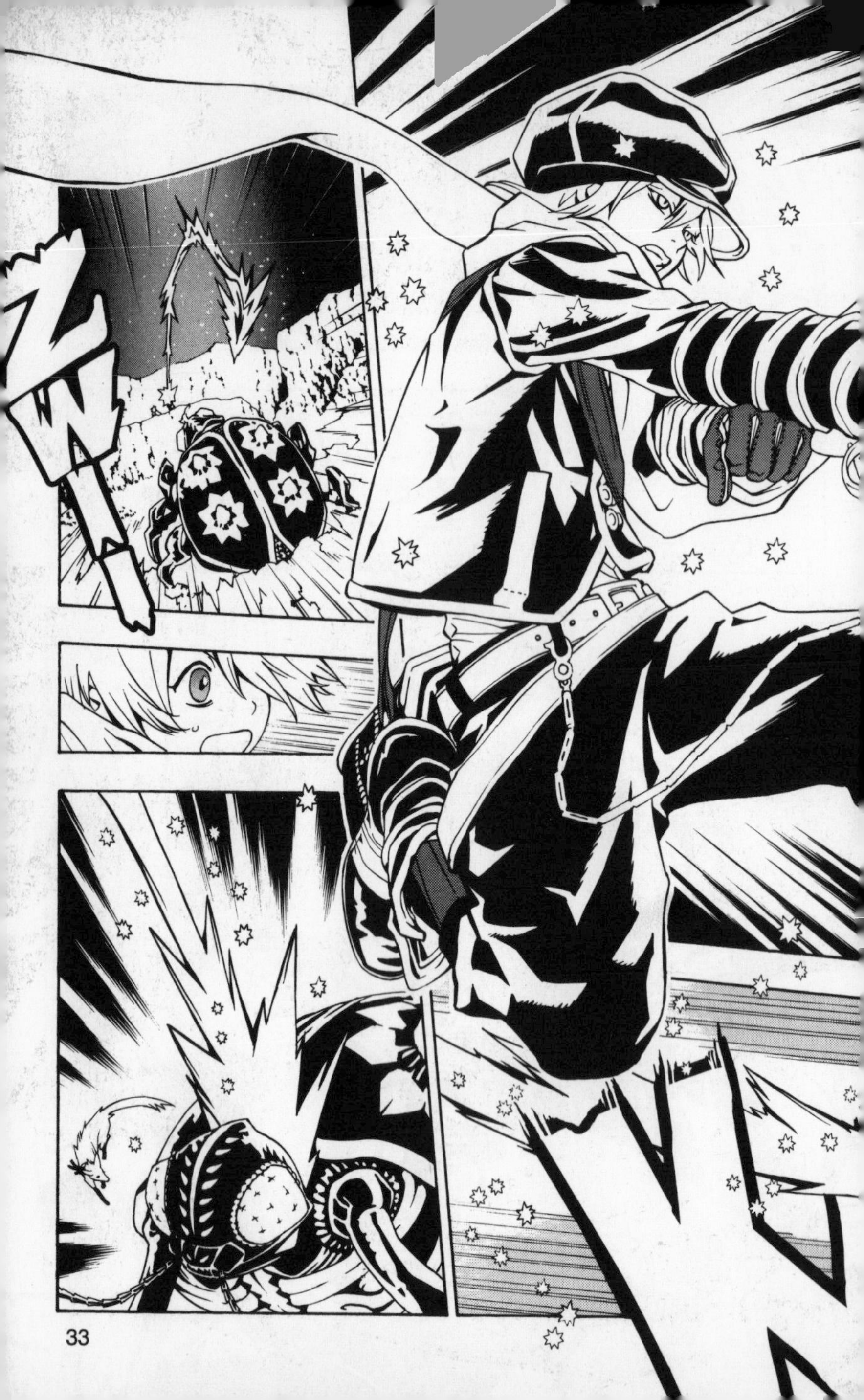

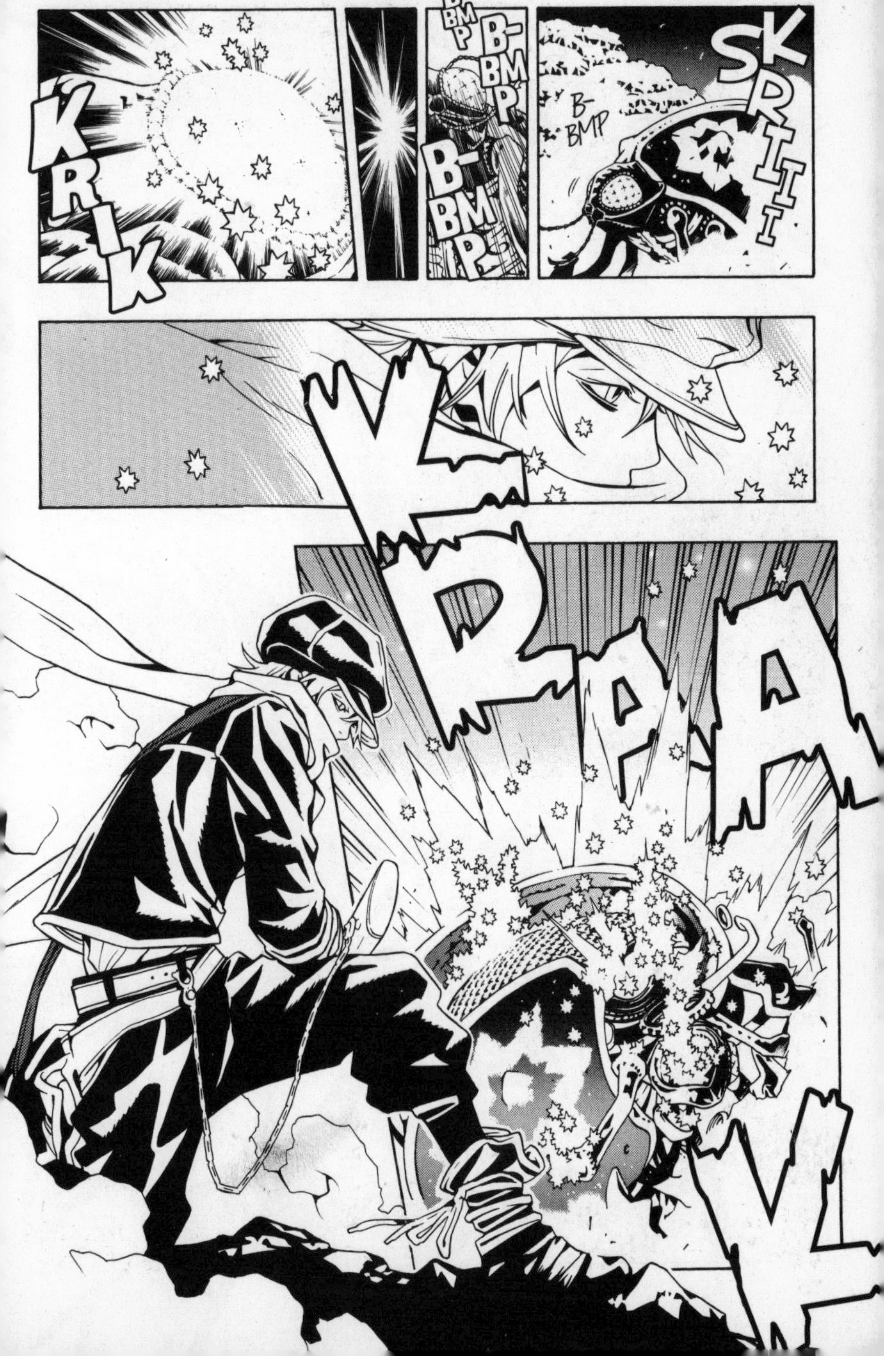
SKRIII
B-BMP
B-BMP
B-BMP
B-BMP
KRIK
KRAAK

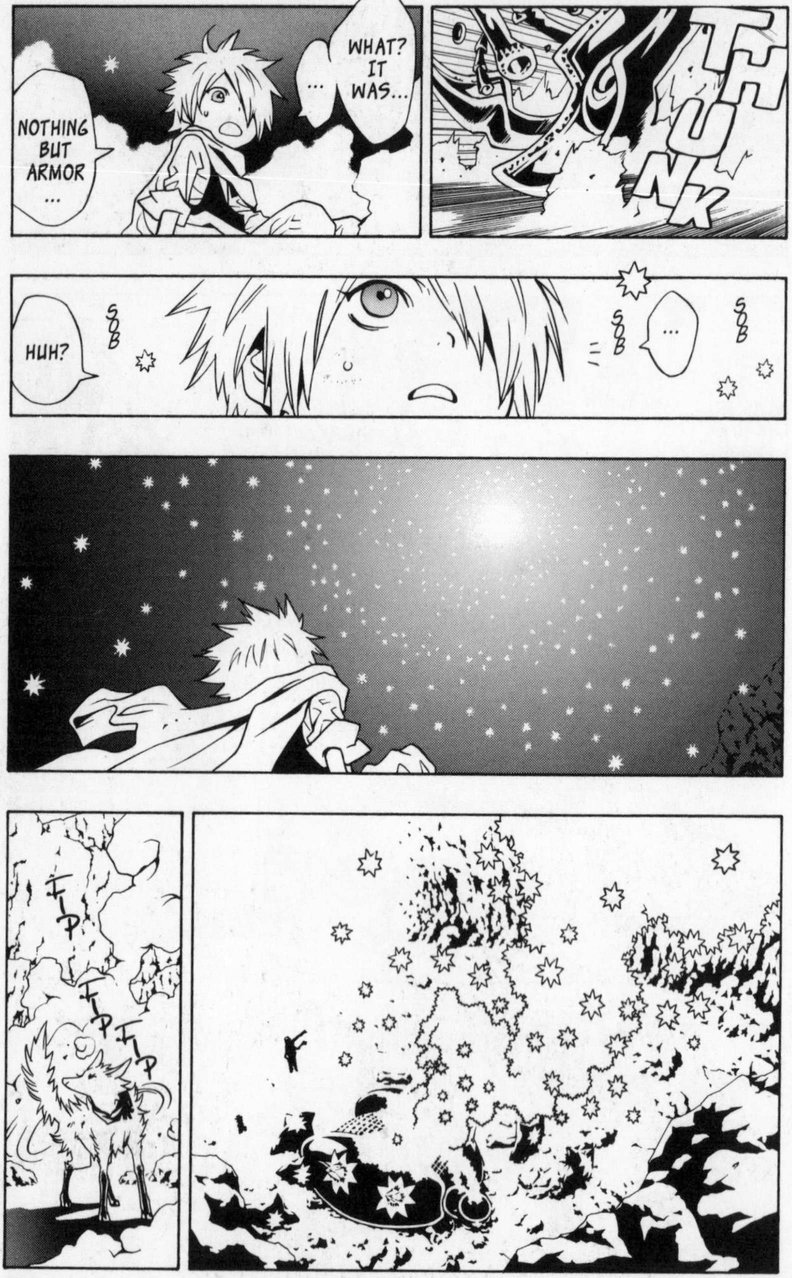
THUNK
WHAT? IT WAS...
...
NOTHING BUT ARMOR ...
SOB
...
SOB
HUH?
SOB
FIP
FIP
FIP

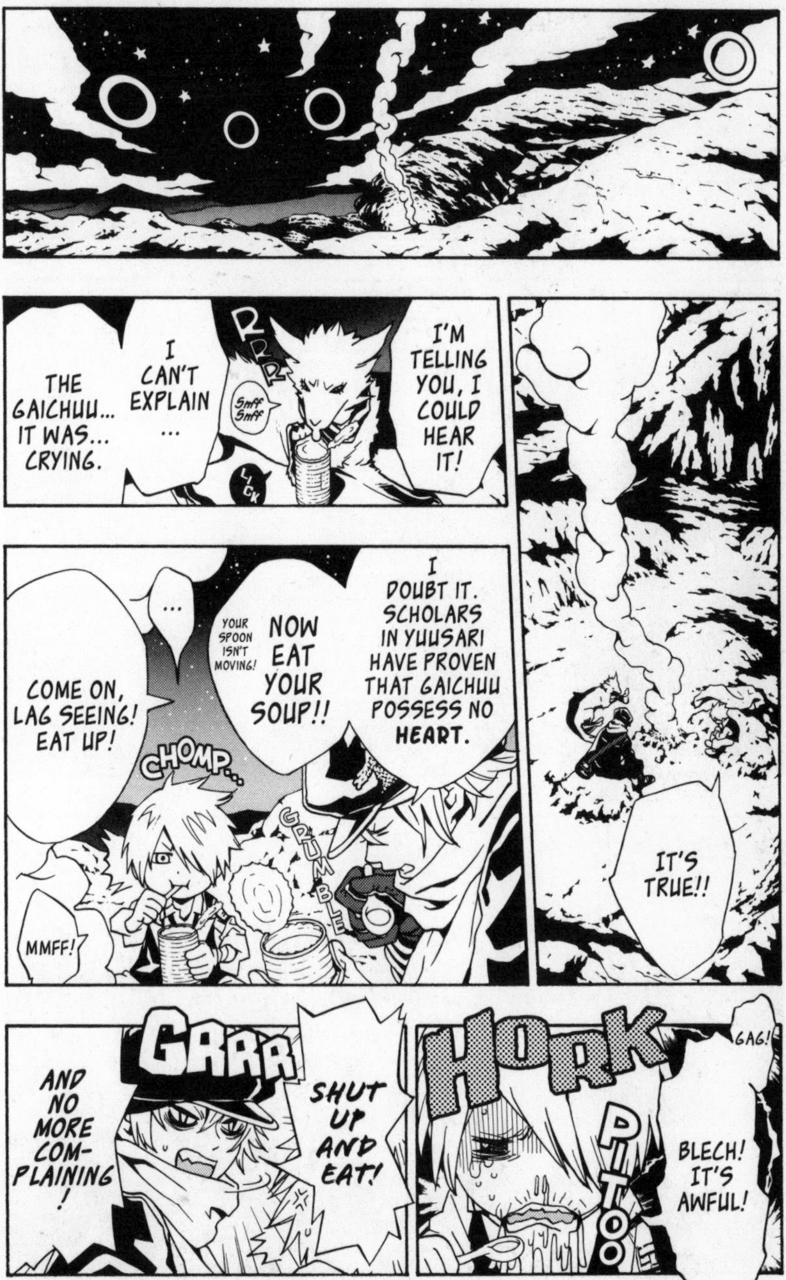
IT'S TRUE!!
RRRR
I'M TELLING YOU, I COULD HEAR IT!
Smff Smff
I CAN'T EXPLAIN...
LICK
THE GAICHUU... IT WAS... CRYING.
I DOUBT IT. SCHOLARS IN YUUSARI HAVE PROVEN THAT GAICHUU POSSESS NO HEART.
NOW EAT YOUR SOUP!!
YOUR SPOON ISN'T MOVING!
...
COME ON, LAG SEEING! EAT UP!
CHOMP...
GRUMBLE
MMFF!
GAG!
HORK
BLECH! IT'S AWFUL!
PITOO
SHUT UP AND EAT!
GRRR
AND NO MORE COM-PLAINING!

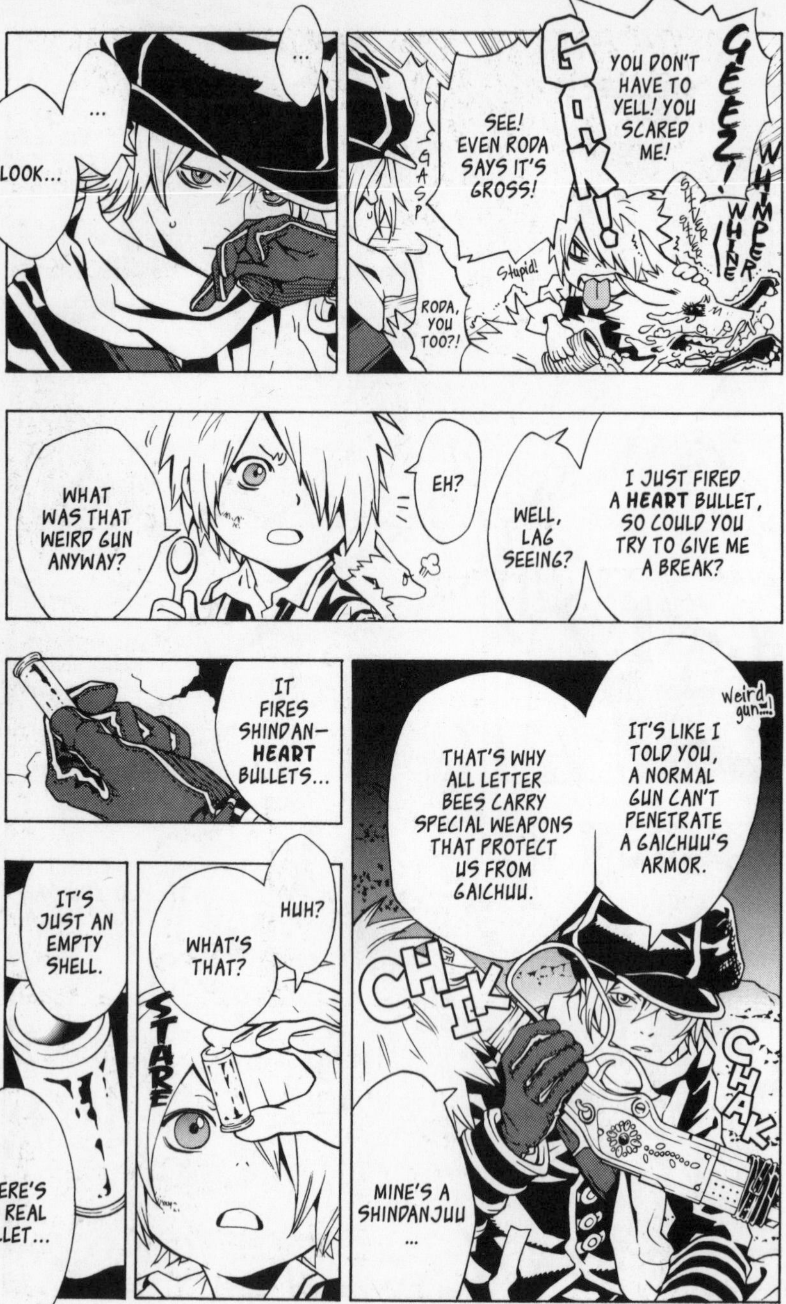
GAK!
YOU DON'T HAVE TO YELL! YOU SCARED ME!
GEEZ!
WHIMPER
WHINE
SHIVER SHIVER
SEE! EVEN RODA SAYS IT'S GROSS!
GASP
Stupid!
RODA, YOU TOO?!
...
...
LOOK...
I JUST FIRED A **HEART** BULLET, SO COULD YOU TRY TO GIVE ME A BREAK?
WELL, LAG SEEING?
EH?
WHAT WAS THAT WEIRD GUN ANYWAY?
Weird gun...!
IT'S LIKE I TOLD YOU, A NORMAL GUN CAN'T PENETRATE A GAICHUU'S ARMOR.
THAT'S WHY ALL LETTER BEES CARRY SPECIAL WEAPONS THAT PROTECT US FROM GAICHUU.
CHIK
CHAK
MINE'S A SHINDANJUU ...
IT FIRES SHINDAN-**HEART** BULLETS...
HUH?
WHAT'S THAT?
STARE
IT'S JUST AN EMPTY SHELL.
THERE'S NO REAL BULLET...

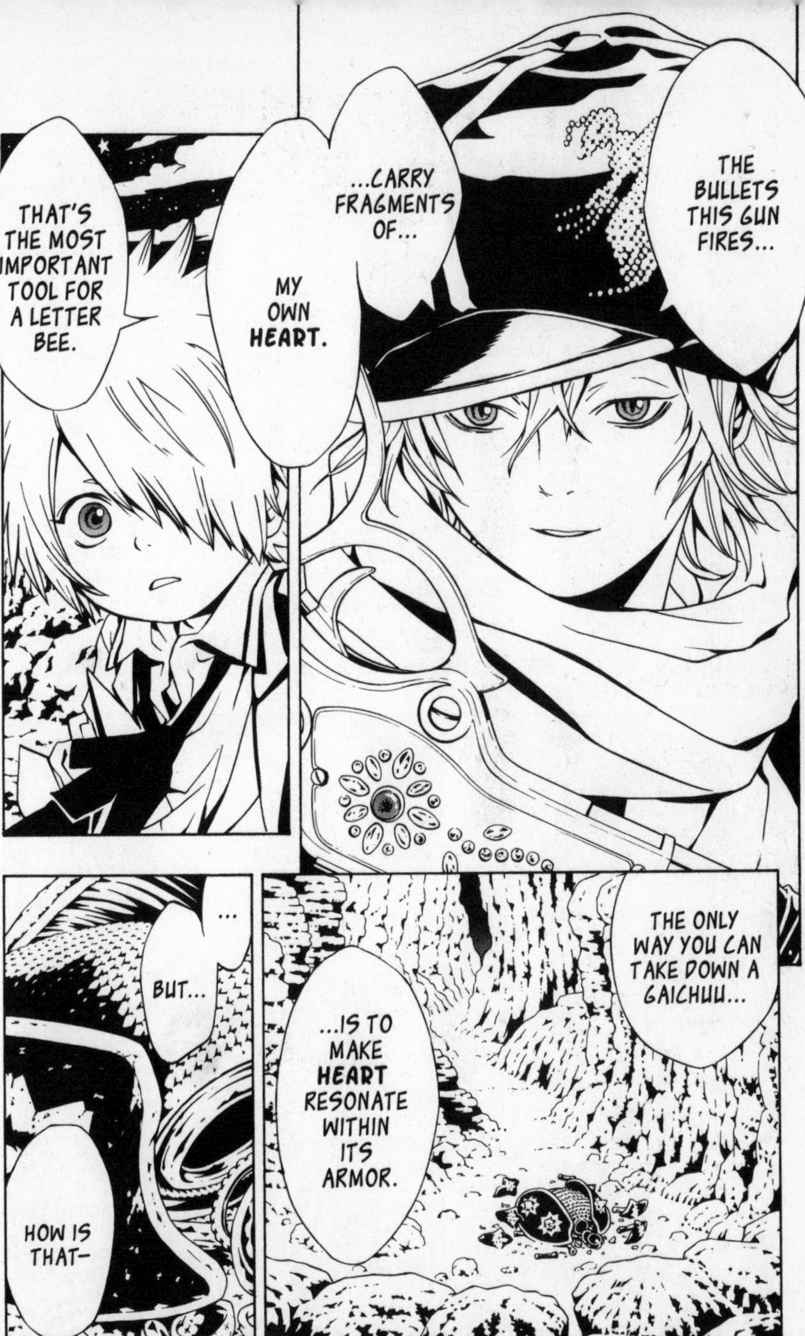
THE BULLETS THIS GUN FIRES...
...CARRY FRAGMENTS OF...
MY OWN **HEART**.
THAT'S THE MOST IMPORTANT TOOL FOR A LETTER BEE.
THE ONLY WAY YOU CAN TAKE DOWN A GAICHUU...
...IS TO MAKE **HEART** RESONATE WITHIN ITS ARMOR.
...
BUT...
HOW IS THAT-

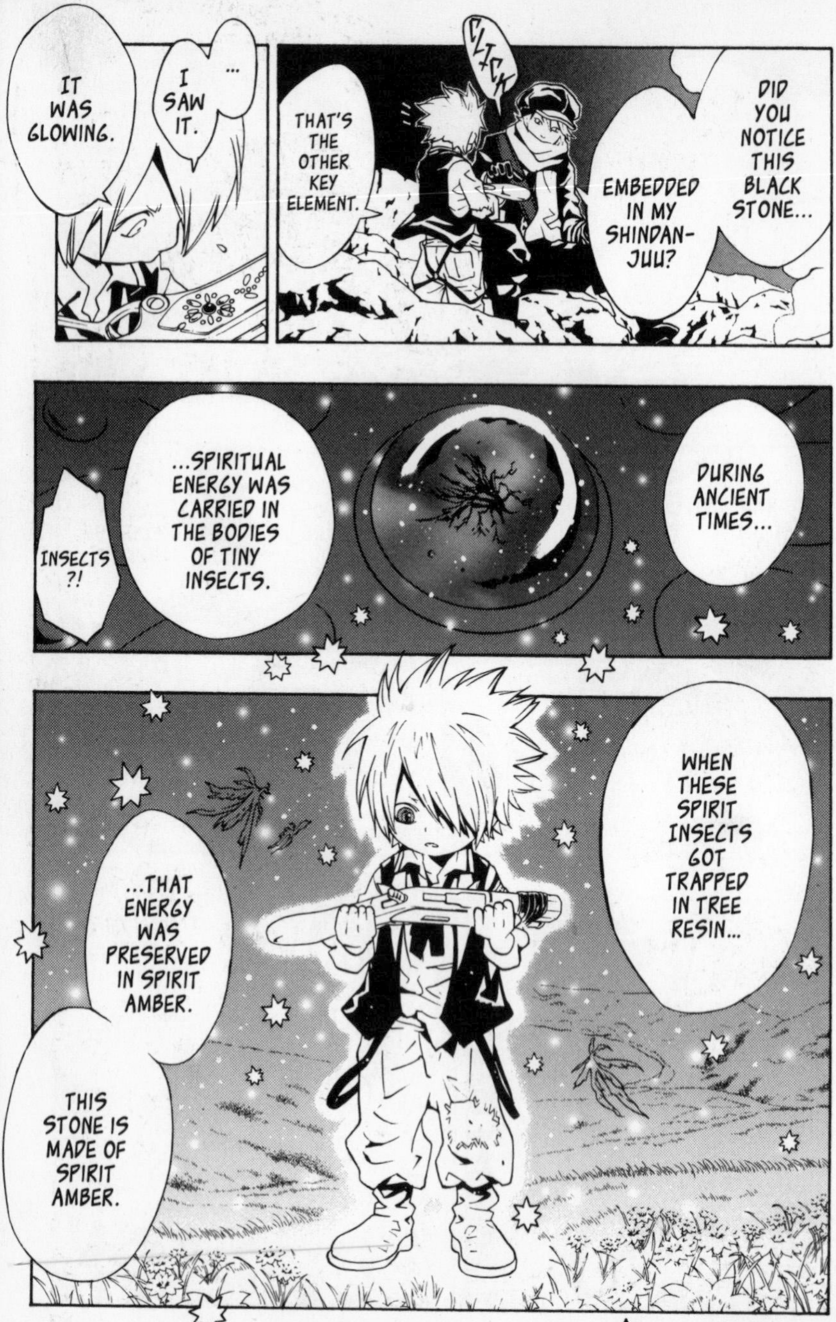

DID YOU NOTICE THIS BLACK STONE...
EMBEDDED IN MY SHINDAN-JUU?
CLICK
THAT'S THE OTHER KEY ELEMENT.
...
I SAW IT.
IT WAS GLOWING.
DURING ANCIENT TIMES...
...SPIRITUAL ENERGY WAS CARRIED IN THE BODIES OF TINY INSECTS.
INSECTS?!
WHEN THESE SPIRIT INSECTS GOT TRAPPED IN TREE RESIN...
...THAT ENERGY WAS PRESERVED IN SPIRIT AMBER.
THIS STONE IS MADE OF SPIRIT AMBER.

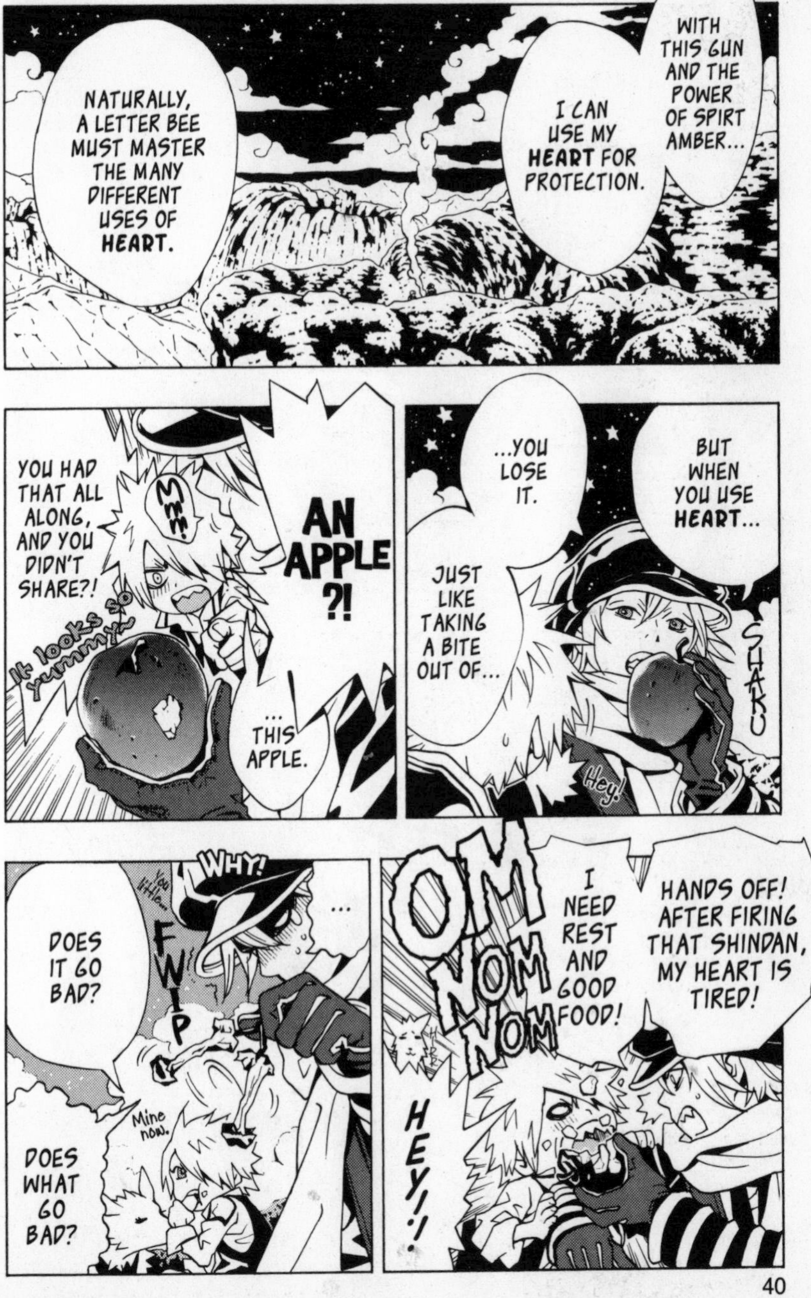
WITH THIS GUN AND THE POWER OF SPIRT AMBER...
I CAN USE MY HEART FOR PROTECTION.
NATURALLY, A LETTER BEE MUST MASTER THE MANY DIFFERENT USES OF HEART.
BUT WHEN YOU USE HEART...
...YOU LOSE IT.
JUST LIKE TAKING A BITE OUT OF...
SHAKU
Hey!
...THIS APPLE.
AN APPLE?!
Mmm!
YOU HAD THAT ALL ALONG, AND YOU DIDN'T SHARE?!
It looks so yummy~
HANDS OFF! AFTER FIRING THAT SHINDAN, MY HEART IS TIRED!
I NEED REST AND GOOD FOOD!
OM NOM NOM NOM
HEY!!
...
WHY!
You little...
DOES IT GO BAD?
FWIP
Mine now.
DOES WHAT GO BAD?

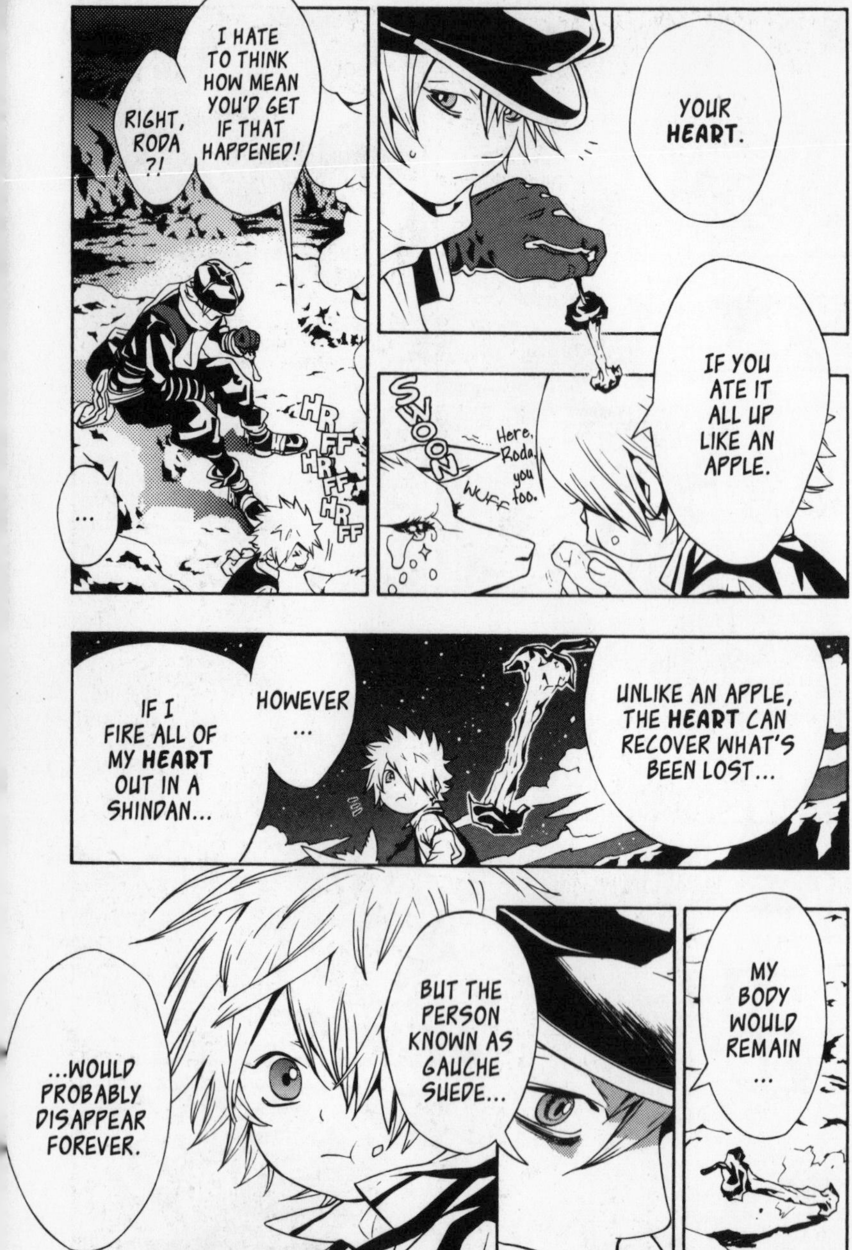
YOUR HEART.
IF YOU ATE IT ALL UP LIKE AN APPLE.
SWOON
Here, Roda, you too.
WUFF
I HATE TO THINK HOW MEAN YOU'D GET IF THAT HAPPENED!
RIGHT, RODA?!
HRFF HRFF HRFF
...
UNLIKE AN APPLE, THE HEART CAN RECOVER WHAT'S BEEN LOST...
HOWEVER...
IF I FIRE ALL OF MY HEART OUT IN A SHINDAN...
MY BODY WOULD REMAIN...
BUT THE PERSON KNOWN AS GAUCHE SUEDE...
...WOULD PROBABLY DISAPPEAR FOREVER.

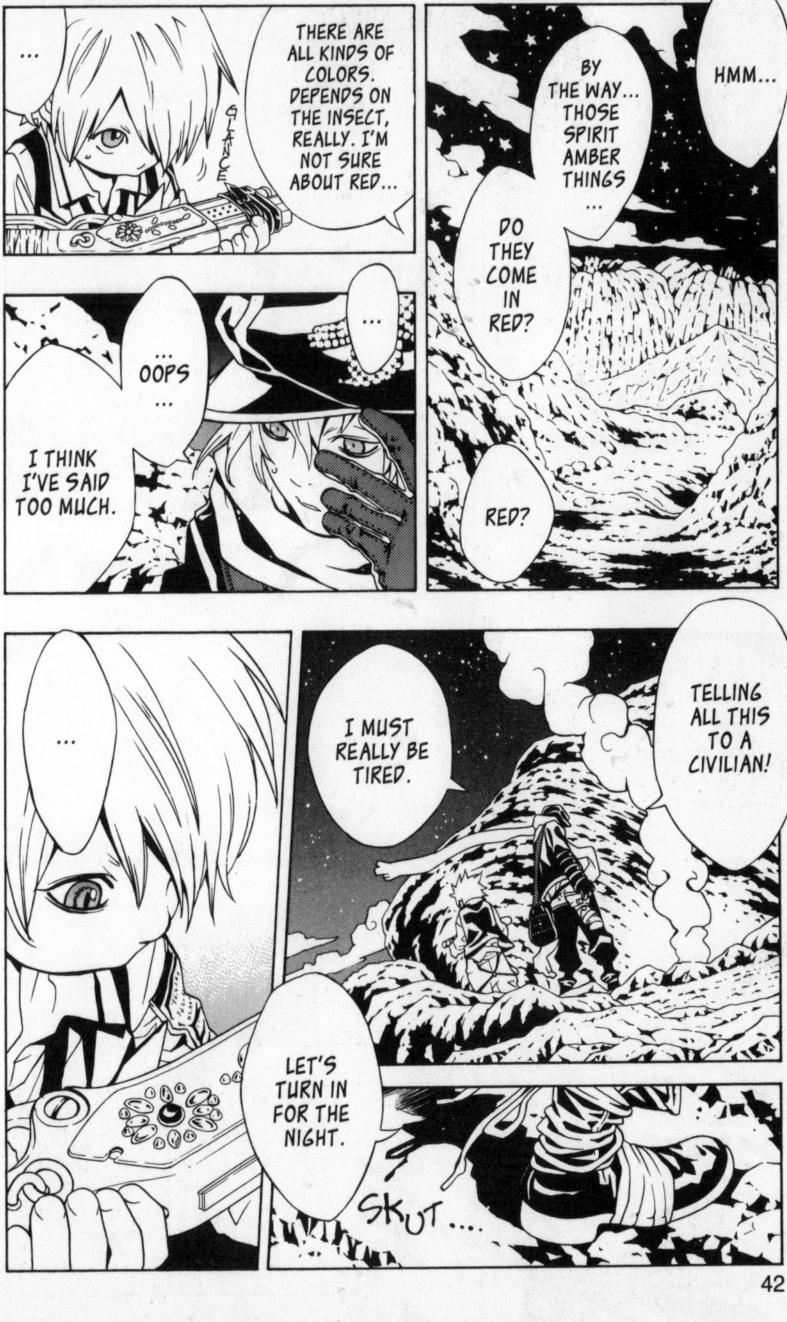
HMM...
BY THE WAY... THOSE SPIRIT AMBER THINGS...
DO THEY COME IN RED?
RED?
THERE ARE ALL KINDS OF COLORS. DEPENDS ON THE INSECT, REALLY. I'M NOT SURE ABOUT RED...
GLANCE
...
...
... OOPS ...
I THINK I'VE SAID TOO MUCH.
TELLING ALL THIS TO A CIVILIAN!
I MUST REALLY BE TIRED.
LET'S TURN IN FOR THE NIGHT.
SKUT....
...

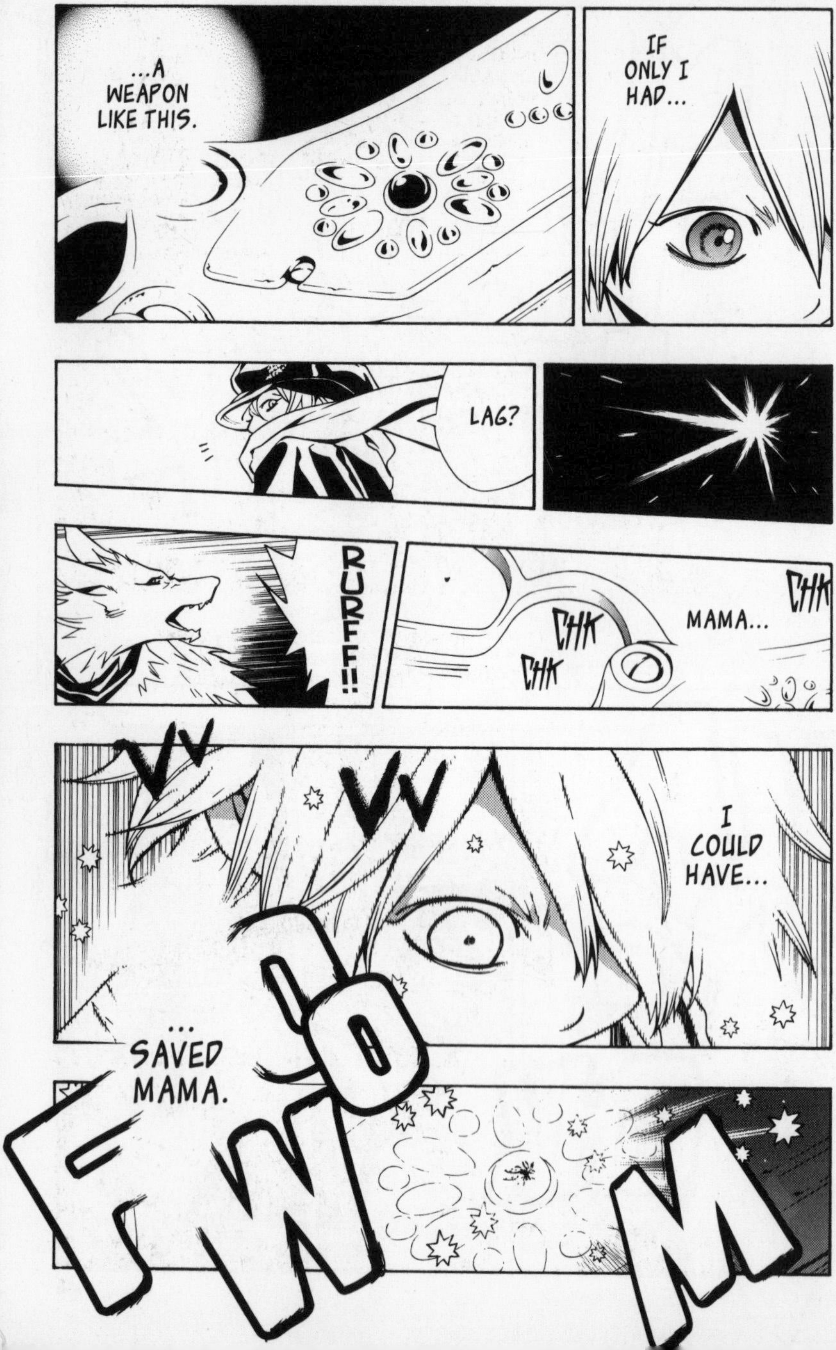
IF ONLY I HAD...
...A WEAPON LIKE THIS.
LAG?
CHK
MAMA...
CHK
CHK
RURFF!!
I COULD HAVE...
... SAVED MAMA.
FWOOM

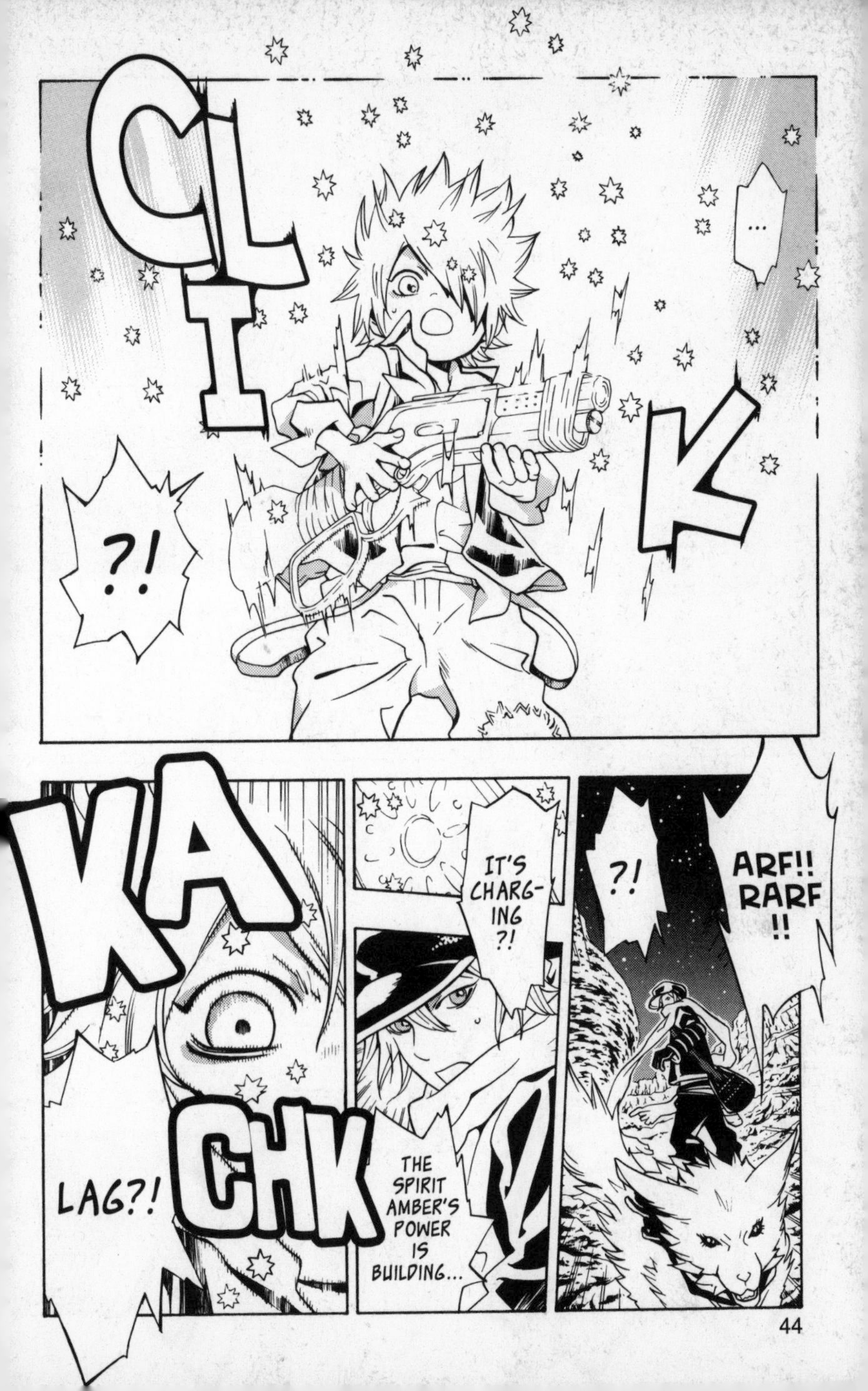
...
CLICK
?!
ARF!! RARF!!
?!
IT'S CHARG-ING?!
THE SPIRIT AMBER'S POWER IS BUILDING...
KA-CHK
LAG?!

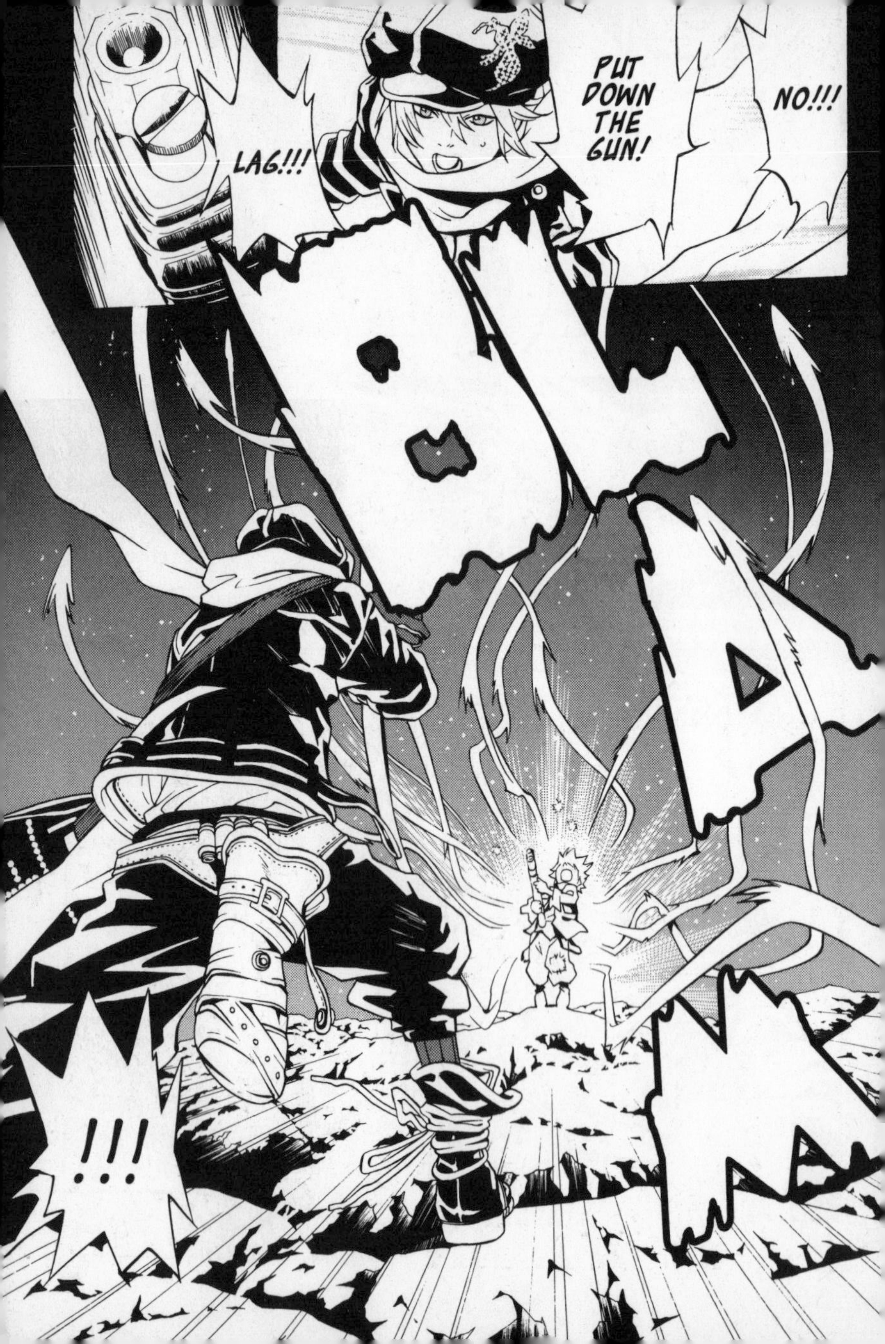
NO!!!
PUT DOWN THE GUN!
LAG!!!
!!!

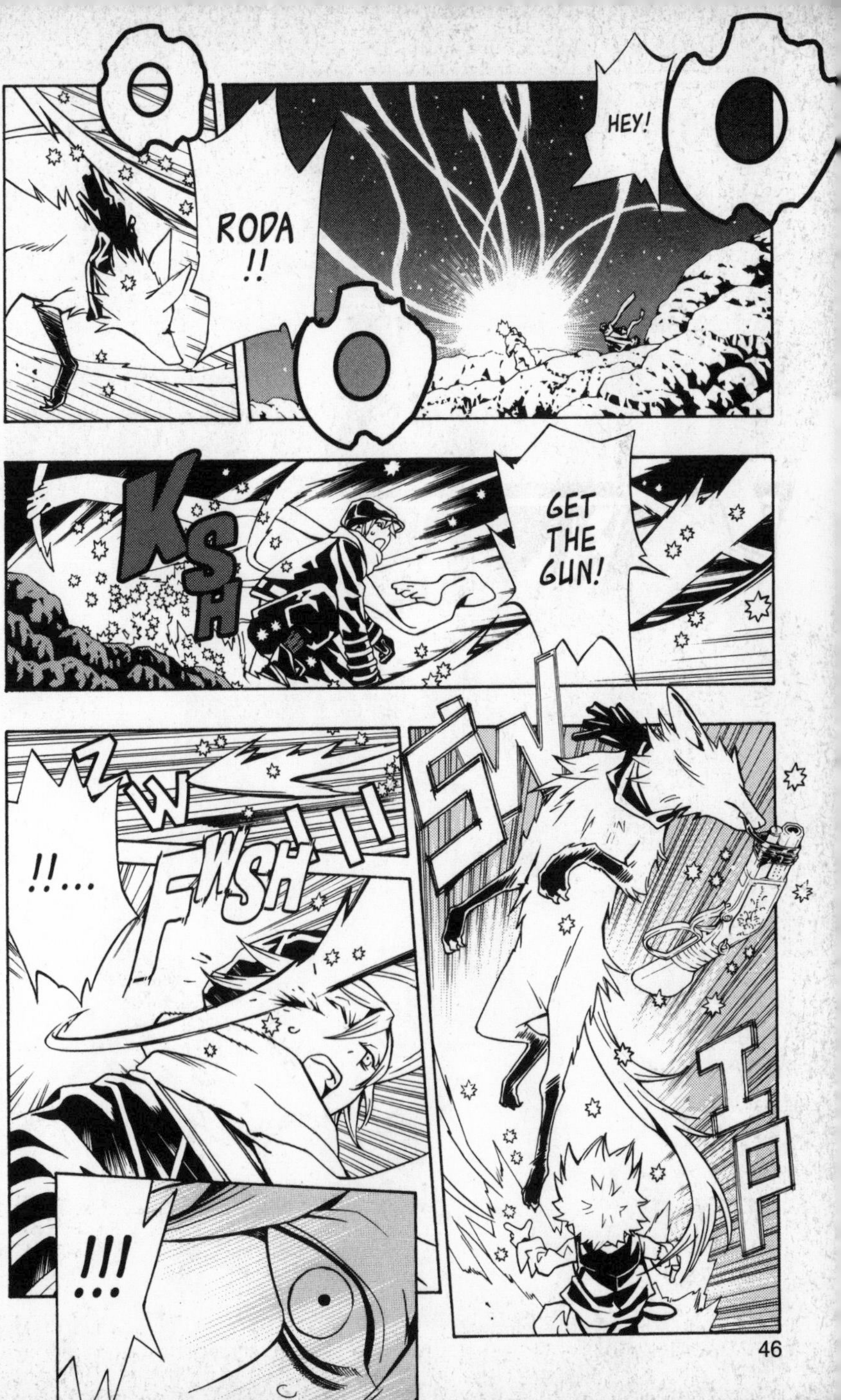
HEY!
RODA !!
GET THE GUN!
KSH
FWSH
!!...
!!!

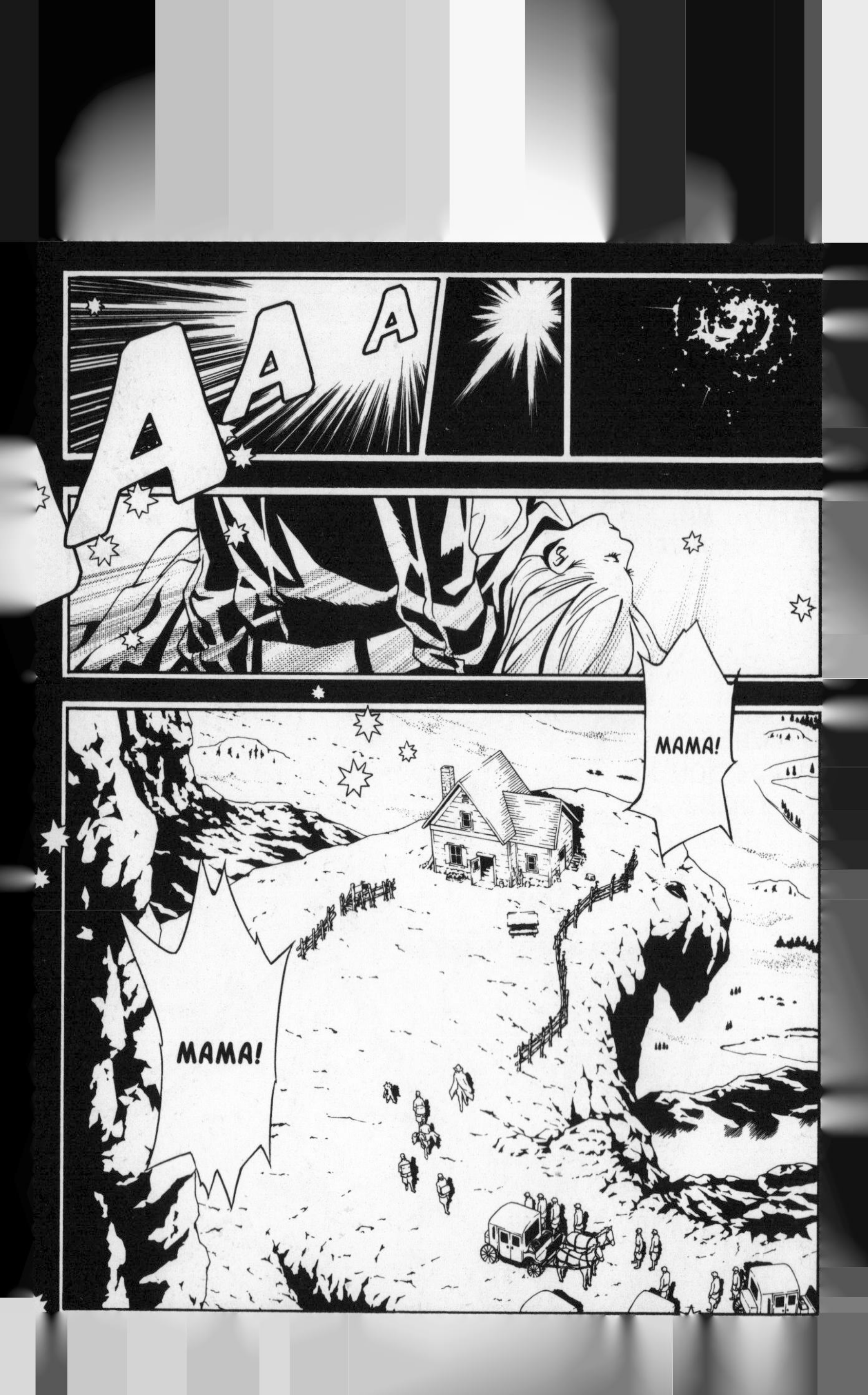
AAAA
MAMA!
MAMA!

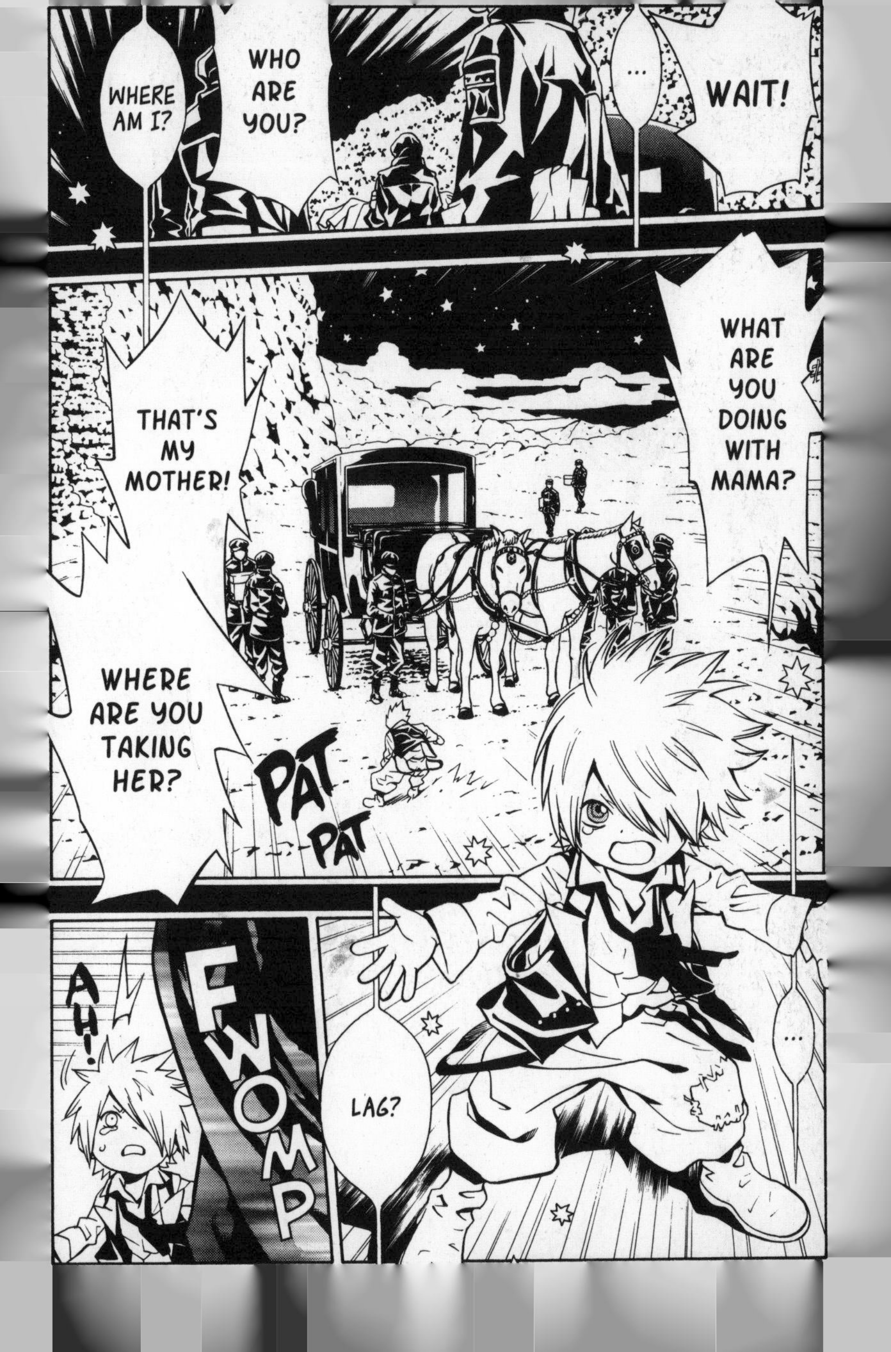
WAIT!
...
WHO ARE YOU?
WHERE AM I?
WHAT ARE YOU DOING WITH MAMA?
THAT'S MY MOTHER!
WHERE ARE YOU TAKING HER?
PAT PAT
...
LAG?
FWOMP
AH!

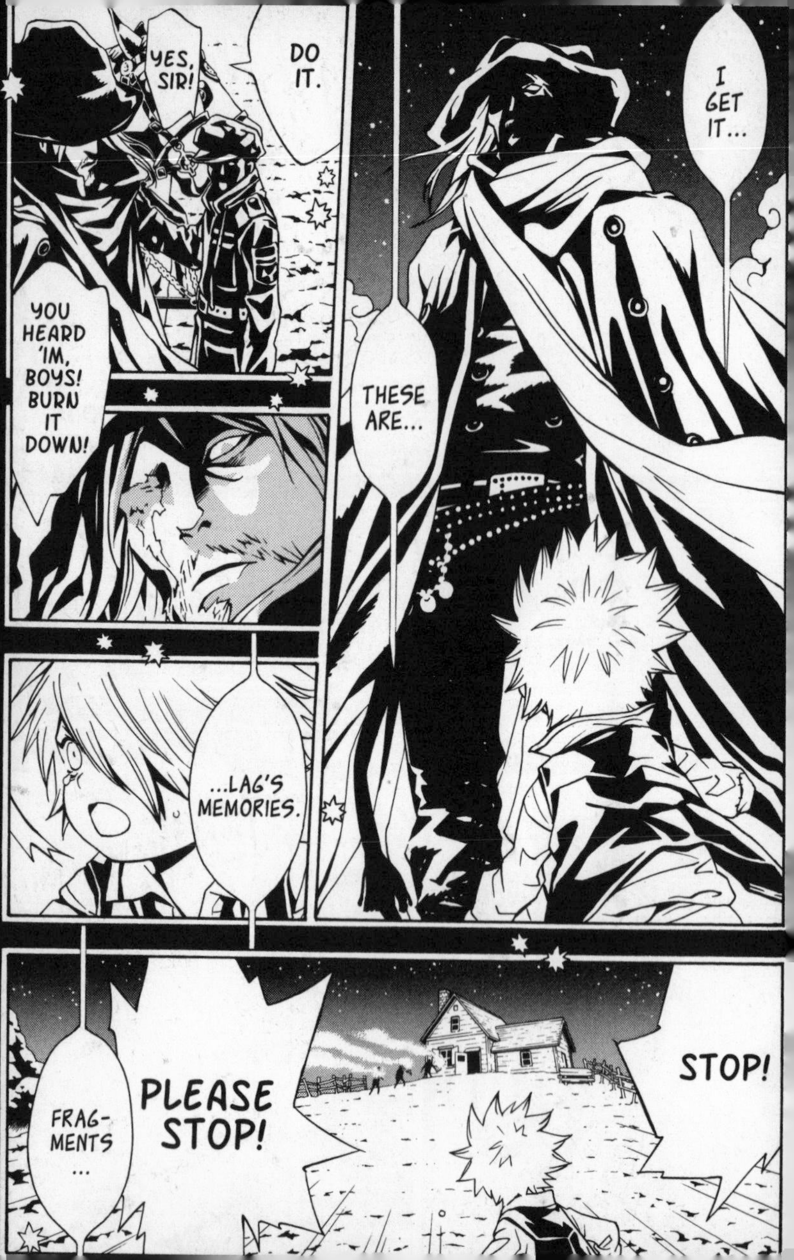
I GET IT...
THESE ARE...
DO IT.
YES, SIR!
YOU HEARD 'IM, BOYS! BURN IT DOWN!
...LAG'S MEMORIES.
STOP!
PLEASE STOP!
FRAG-MENTS ...

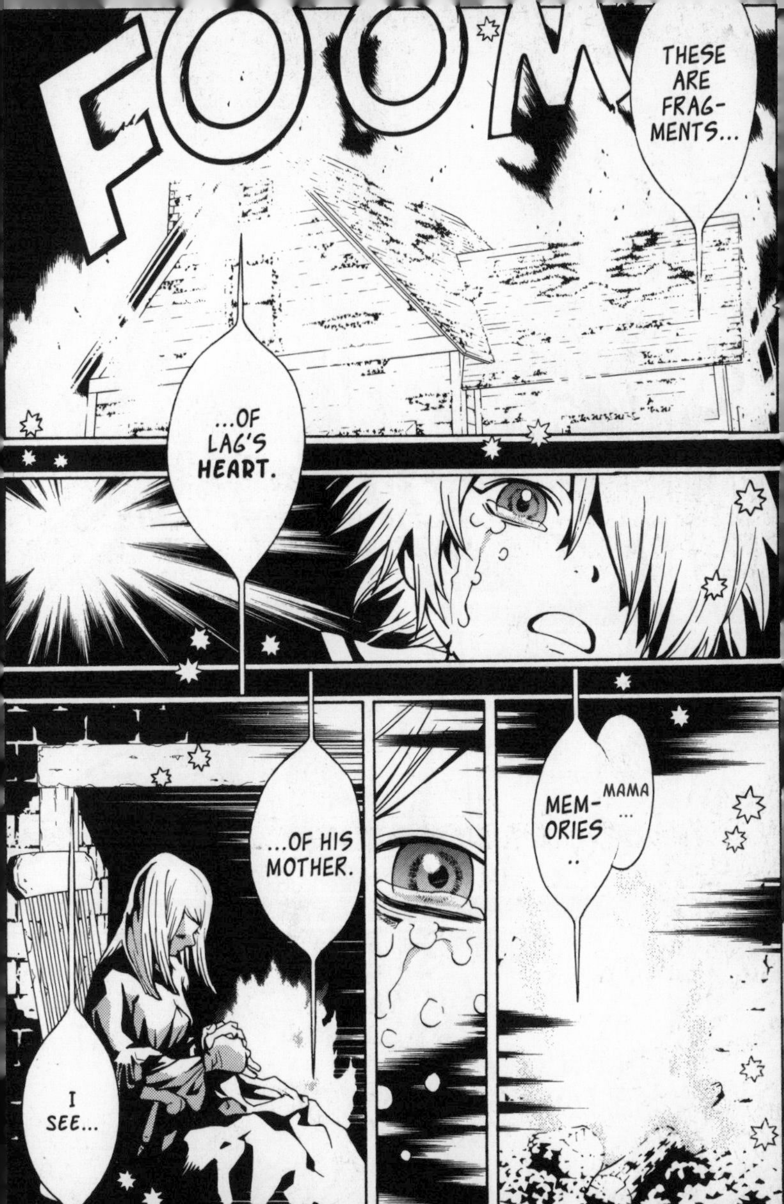
THESE ARE FRAGMENTS...
FOOM
...OF LAG'S HEART.
MAMA...
MEMORIES...
...OF HIS MOTHER.
I SEE...

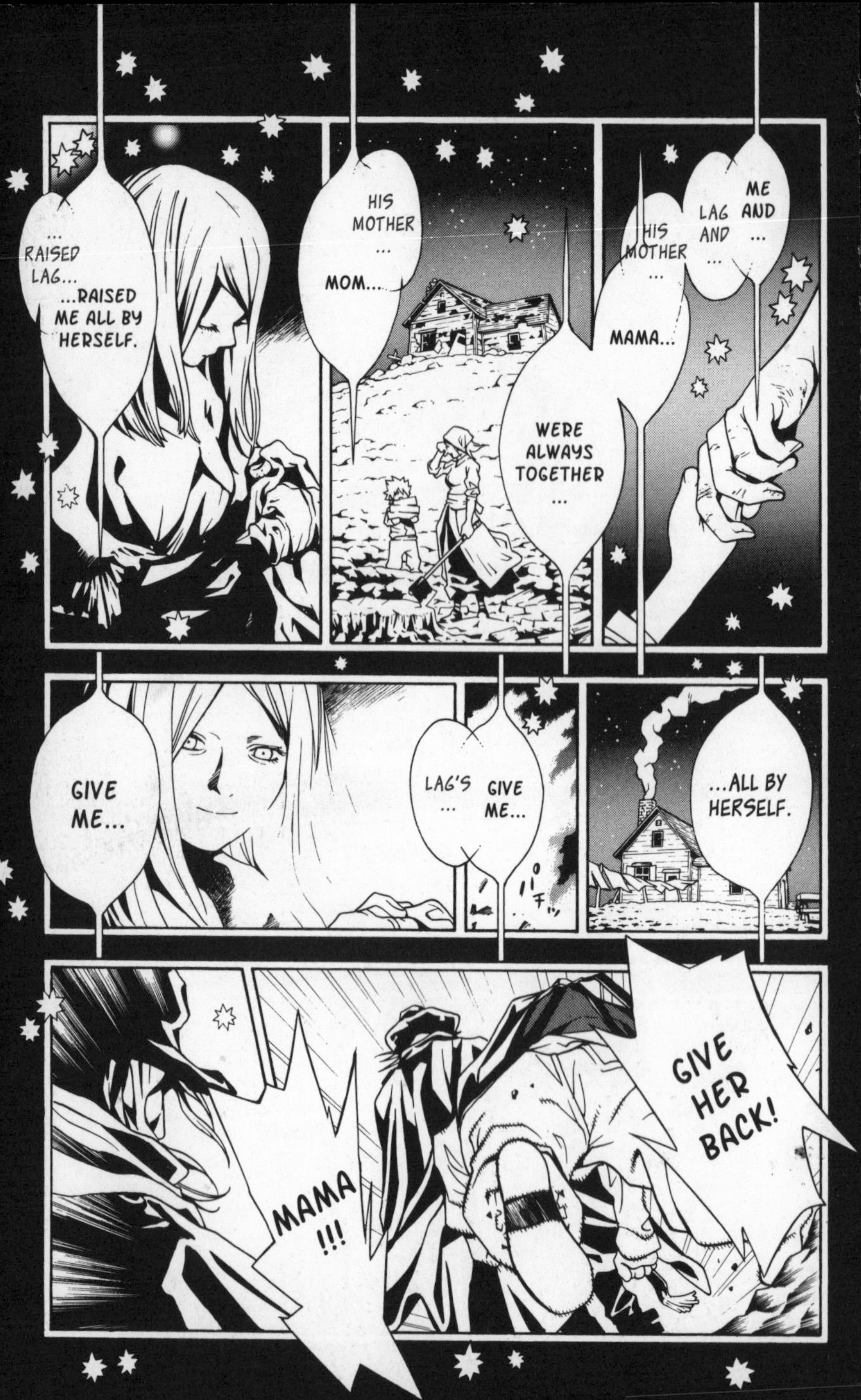
ME AND ...
LAG AND ...
HIS MOTHER ...
MAMA...
WERE ALWAYS TOGETHER ...
HIS MOTHER ...
MOM...
... RAISED LAG...
...RAISED ME ALL BY HERSELF.
...ALL BY HERSELF.
GIVE ME...
LAG'S ...
GIVE ME...
GIVE HER BACK!
MAMA !!!

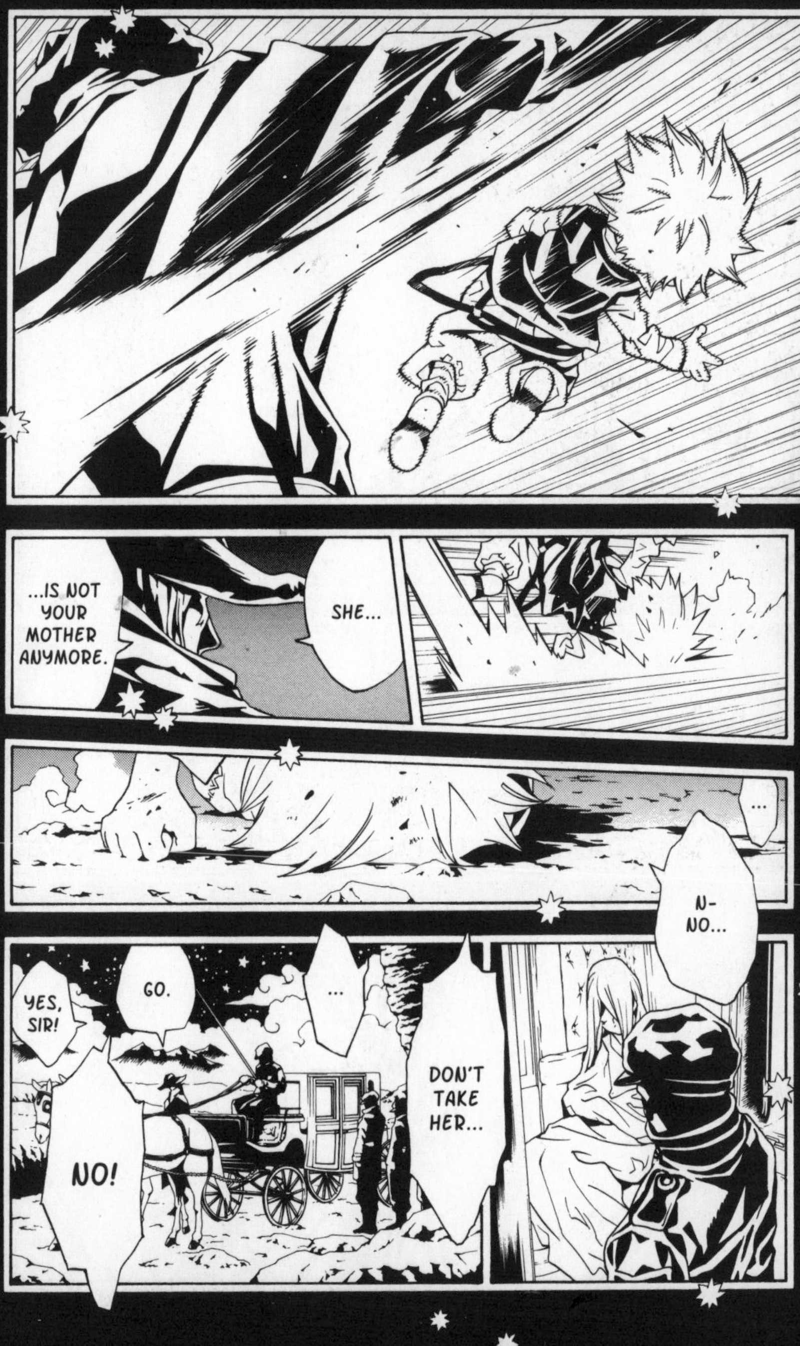
SHE...
...IS NOT YOUR MOTHER ANYMORE.
...
N- NO...
DON'T TAKE HER...
...
GO.
YES, SIR!
NO!

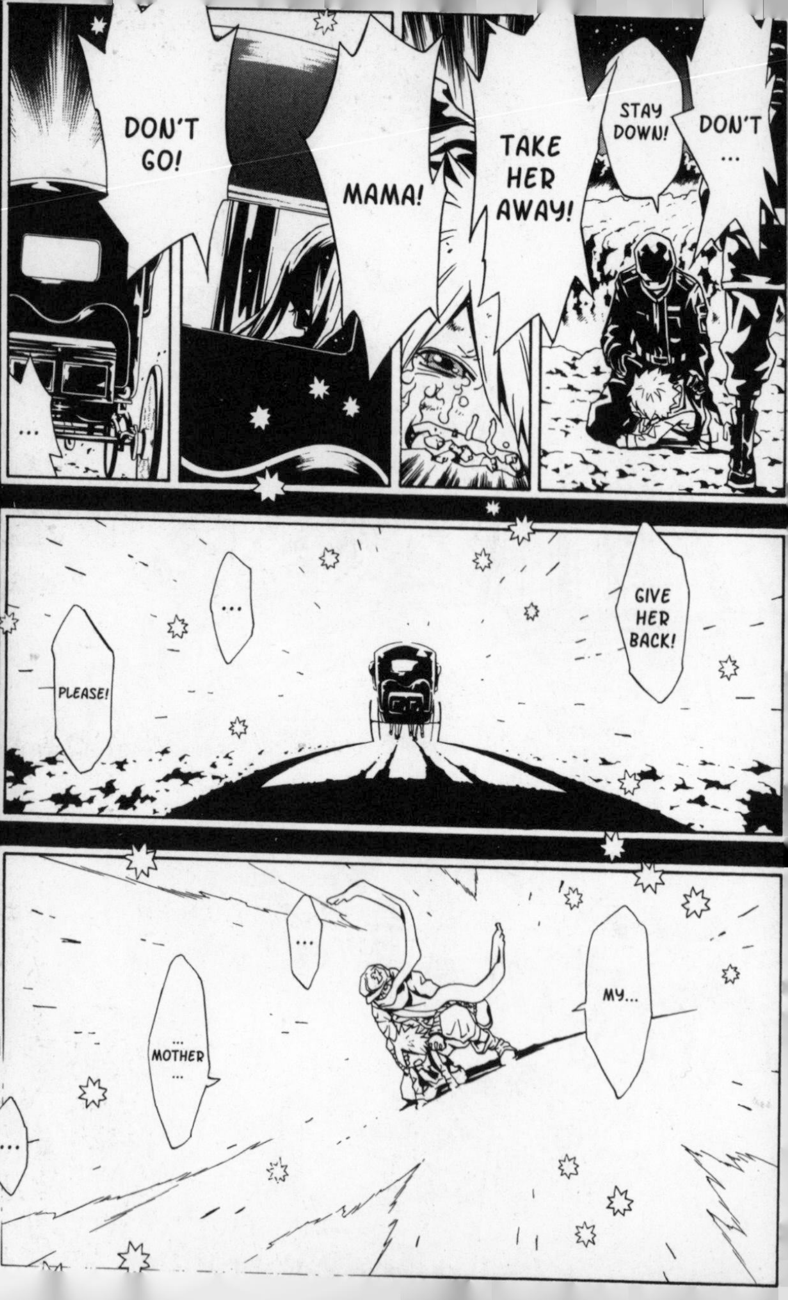
DON'T ...
STAY DOWN!
TAKE HER AWAY!
MAMA!
DON'T GO!
...
GIVE HER BACK!
...
PLEASE!
MY...
...
... MOTHER ...
...

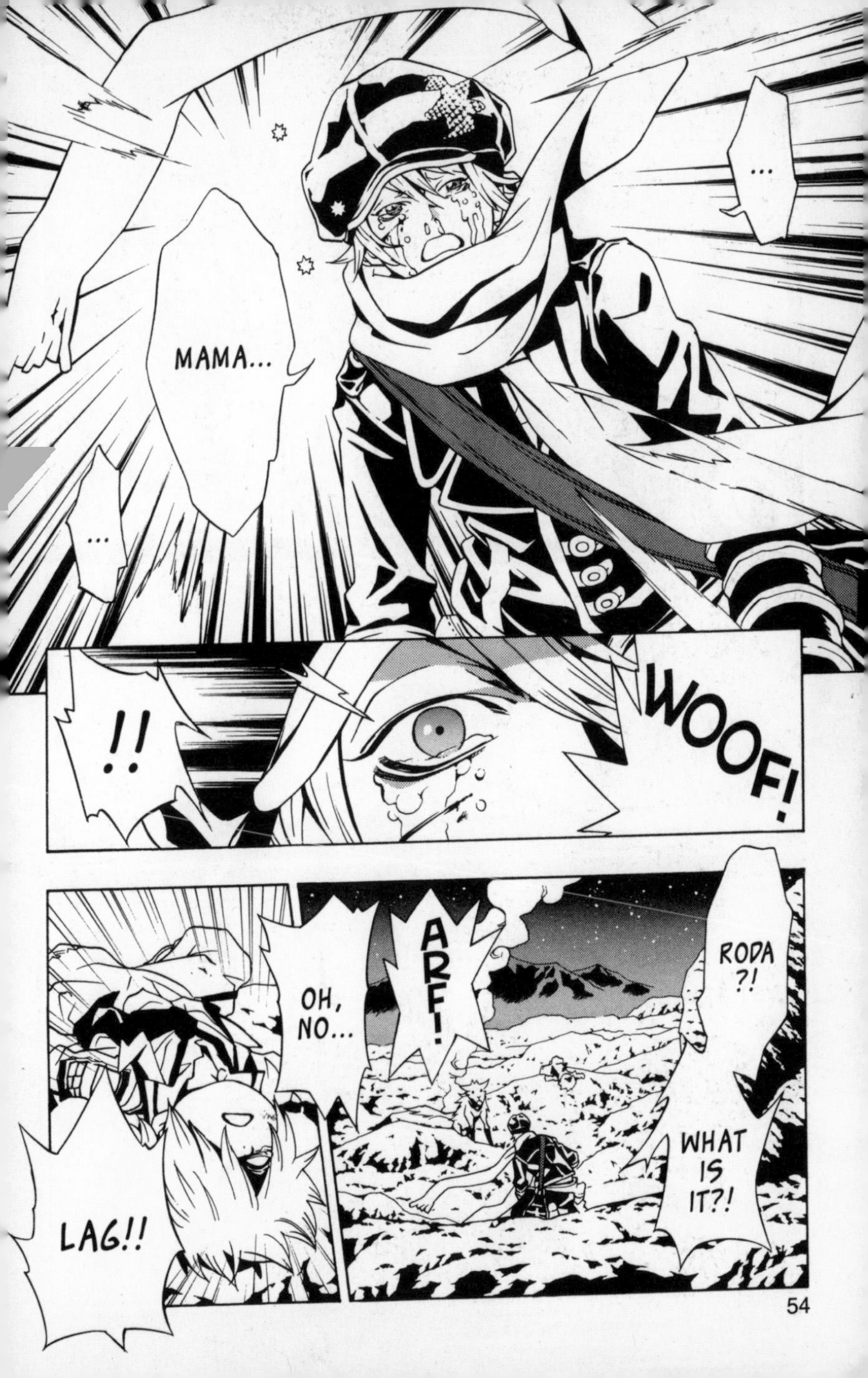
...
MAMA...
...
WOOF!
!!
RODA ?!
WHAT IS IT?!
ARF!
OH, NO...
LAG!!

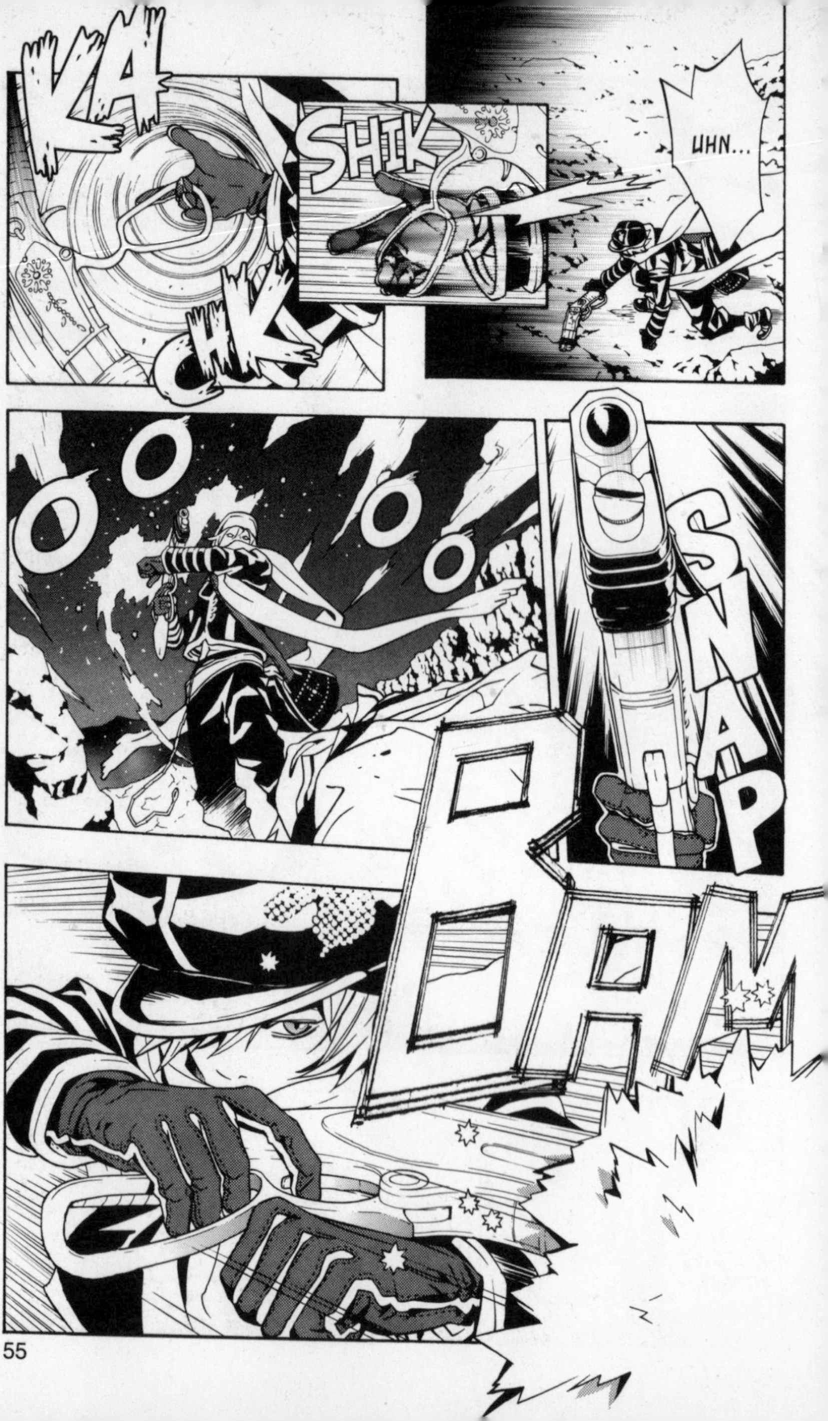
UHN...
KA
SHIK
CHK
SNAP
OOOOO
BAM

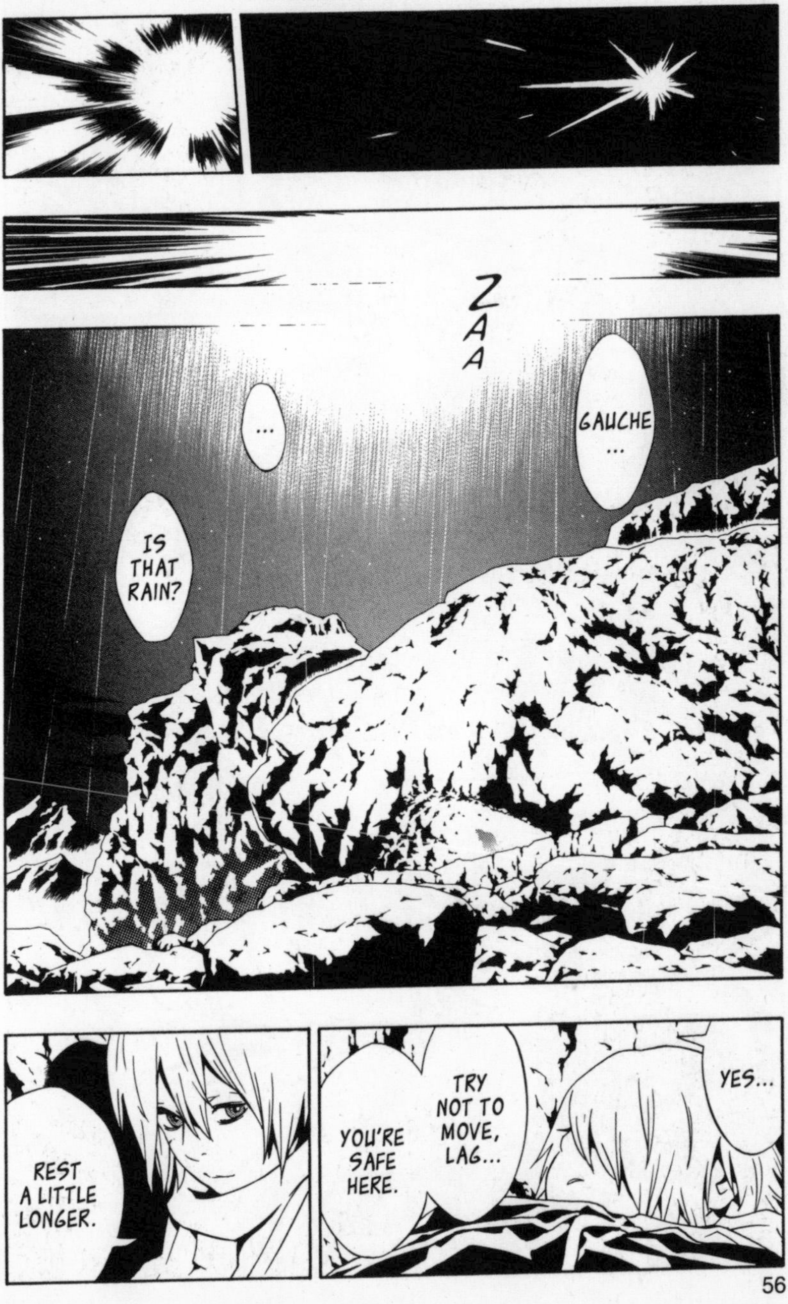
ZAA
GAUCHE ...
...
IS THAT RAIN?
YES...
TRY NOT TO MOVE, LAG...
YOU'RE SAFE HERE.
REST A LITTLE LONGER.

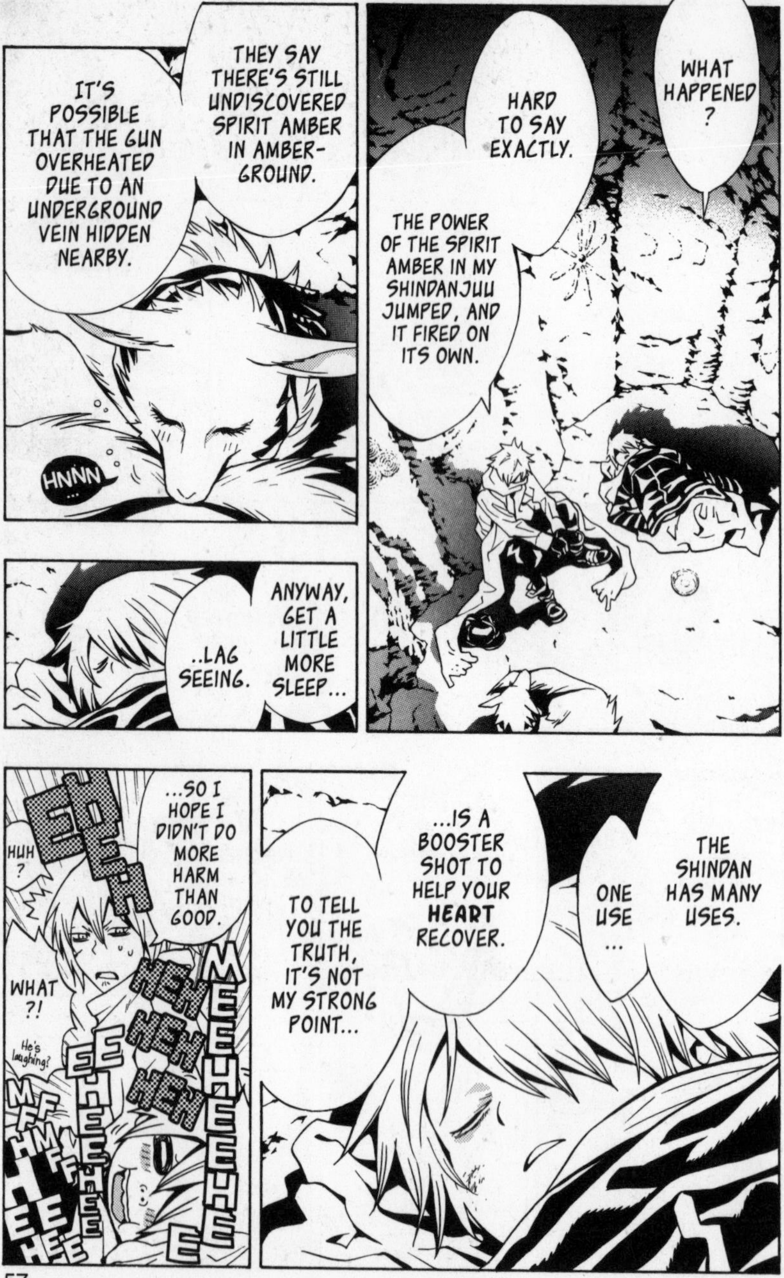
WHAT HAPPENED?
HARD TO SAY EXACTLY.
THE POWER OF THE SPIRIT AMBER IN MY SHINDANJUU JUMPED, AND IT FIRED ON ITS OWN.
THEY SAY THERE'S STILL UNDISCOVERED SPIRIT AMBER IN AMBERGROUND.
IT'S POSSIBLE THAT THE GUN OVERHEATED DUE TO AN UNDERGROUND VEIN HIDDEN NEARBY.
HNNN...
ANYWAY, GET A LITTLE MORE SLEEP...
..LAG SEEING.
THE SHINDAN HAS MANY USES.
ONE USE...
...IS A BOOSTER SHOT TO HELP YOUR **HEART** RECOVER.
TO TELL YOU THE TRUTH, IT'S NOT MY STRONG POINT...
...SO I HOPE I DIDN'T DO MORE HARM THAN GOOD.
HUH?
WHAT?!
He's laughing?
MEEHEHEHEHE
HEH HEH HEH
EEHEHEHEE
MFF HMFF HEHEHEE

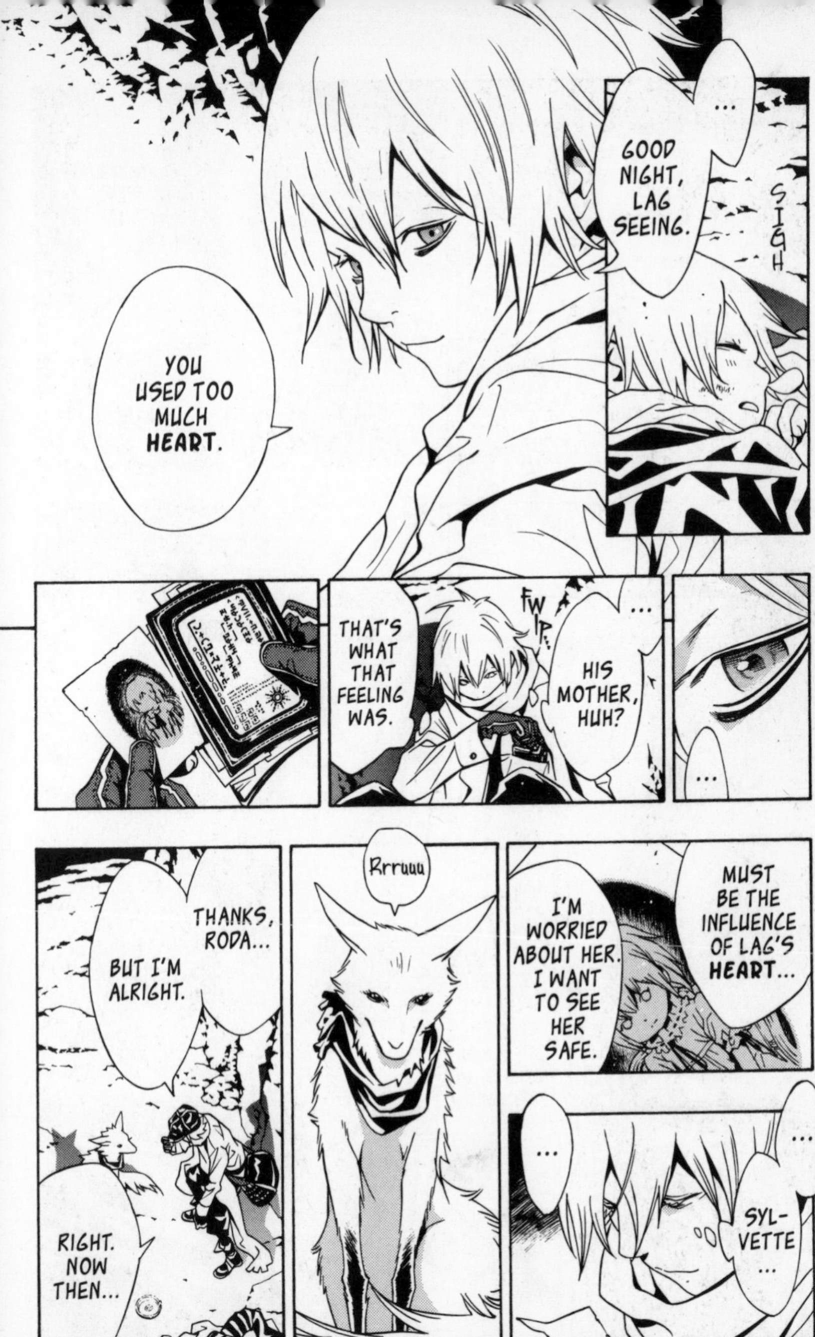
...
GOOD NIGHT, LAG SEEING.
SIGH
YOU USED TOO MUCH HEART.
...
...
HIS MOTHER, HUH?
FWIP...
THAT'S WHAT THAT FEELING WAS.
MUST BE THE INFLUENCE OF LAG'S HEART...
I'M WORRIED ABOUT HER. I WANT TO SEE HER SAFE.
...
SYLVETTE...
...
Rrruuu
THANKS, RODA...
BUT I'M ALRIGHT.
RIGHT. NOW THEN...

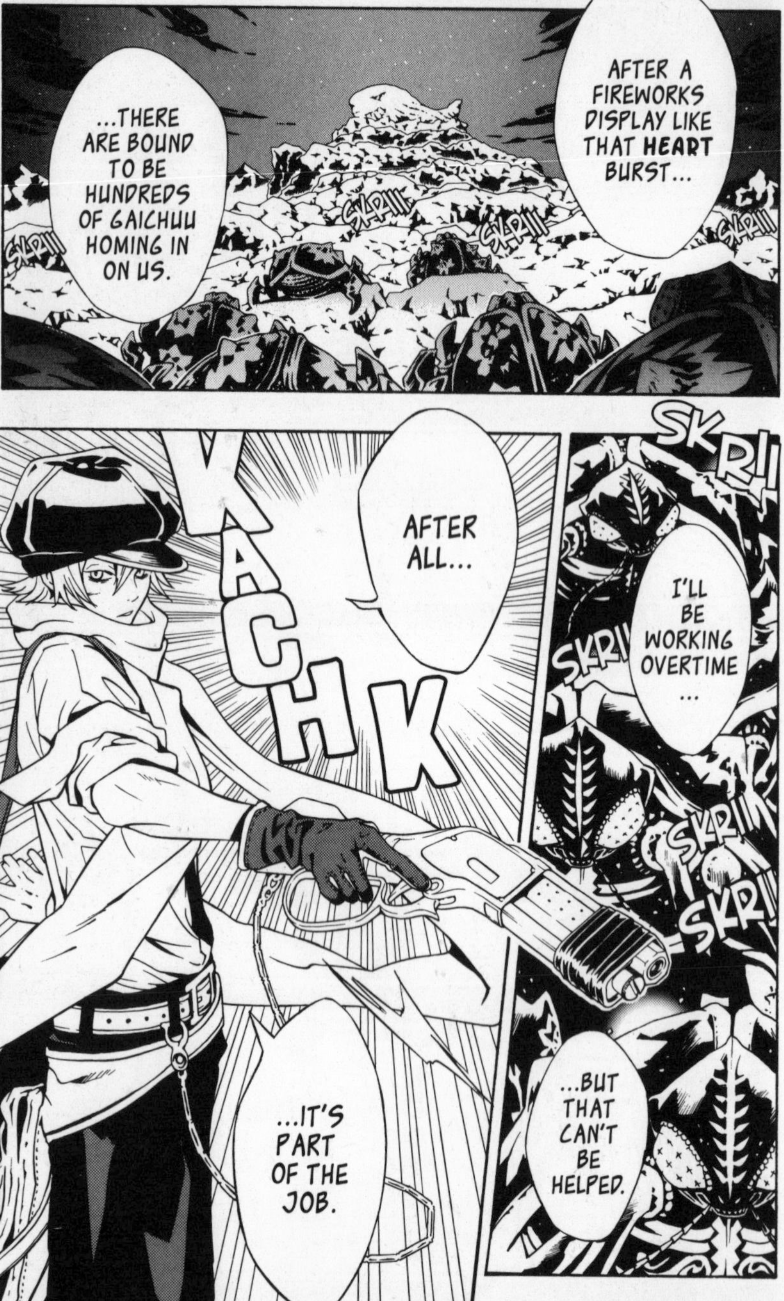
AFTER A FIREWORKS DISPLAY LIKE THAT **HEART** BURST...
SKRIII
SKRIII
SKRIII
...THERE ARE BOUND TO BE HUNDREDS OF GAICHUU HOMING IN ON US.
SKRIII
SKRII
I'LL BE WORKING OVERTIME...
SKRII
SKRII
SKRII
...BUT THAT CAN'T BE HELPED.
KACHK
AFTER ALL...
...IT'S PART OF THE JOB.

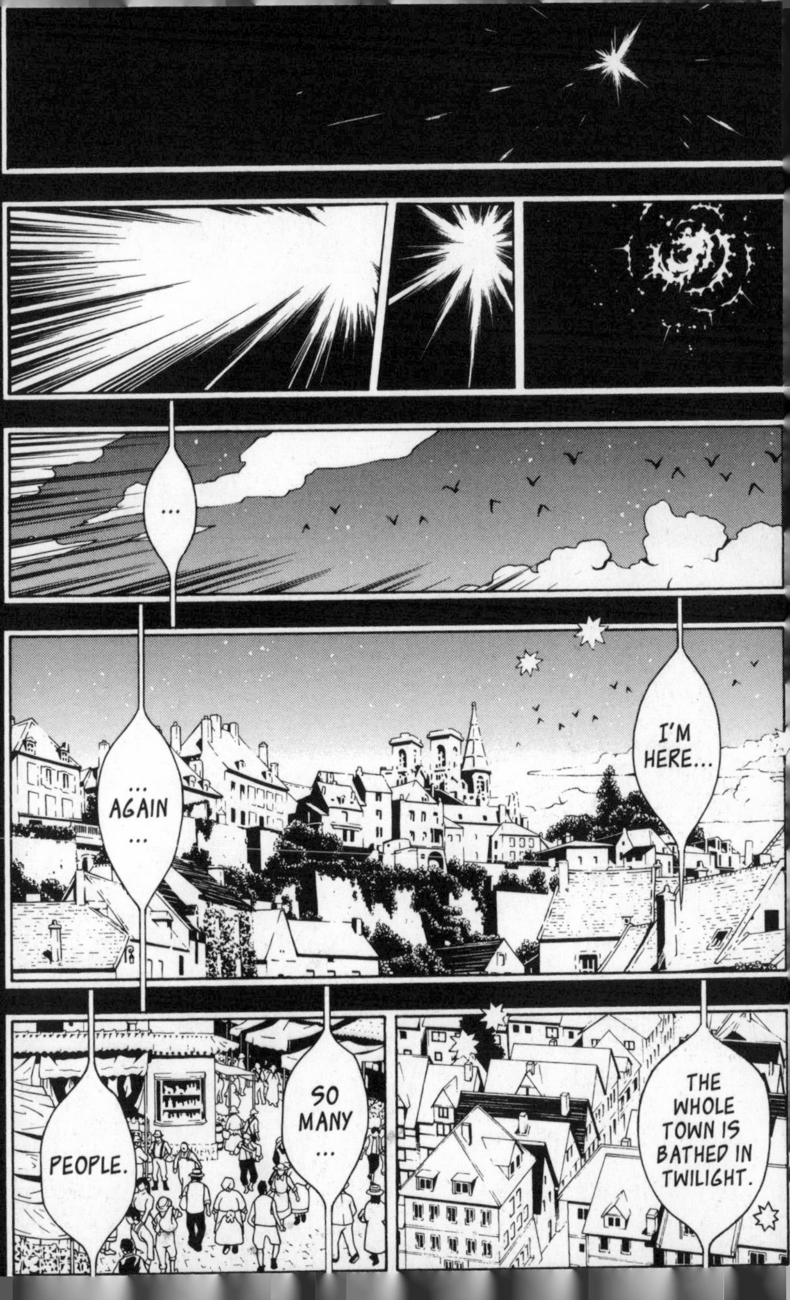
...
I'M HERE...
...AGAIN...
THE WHOLE TOWN IS BATHED IN TWILIGHT.
SO MANY...
PEOPLE.

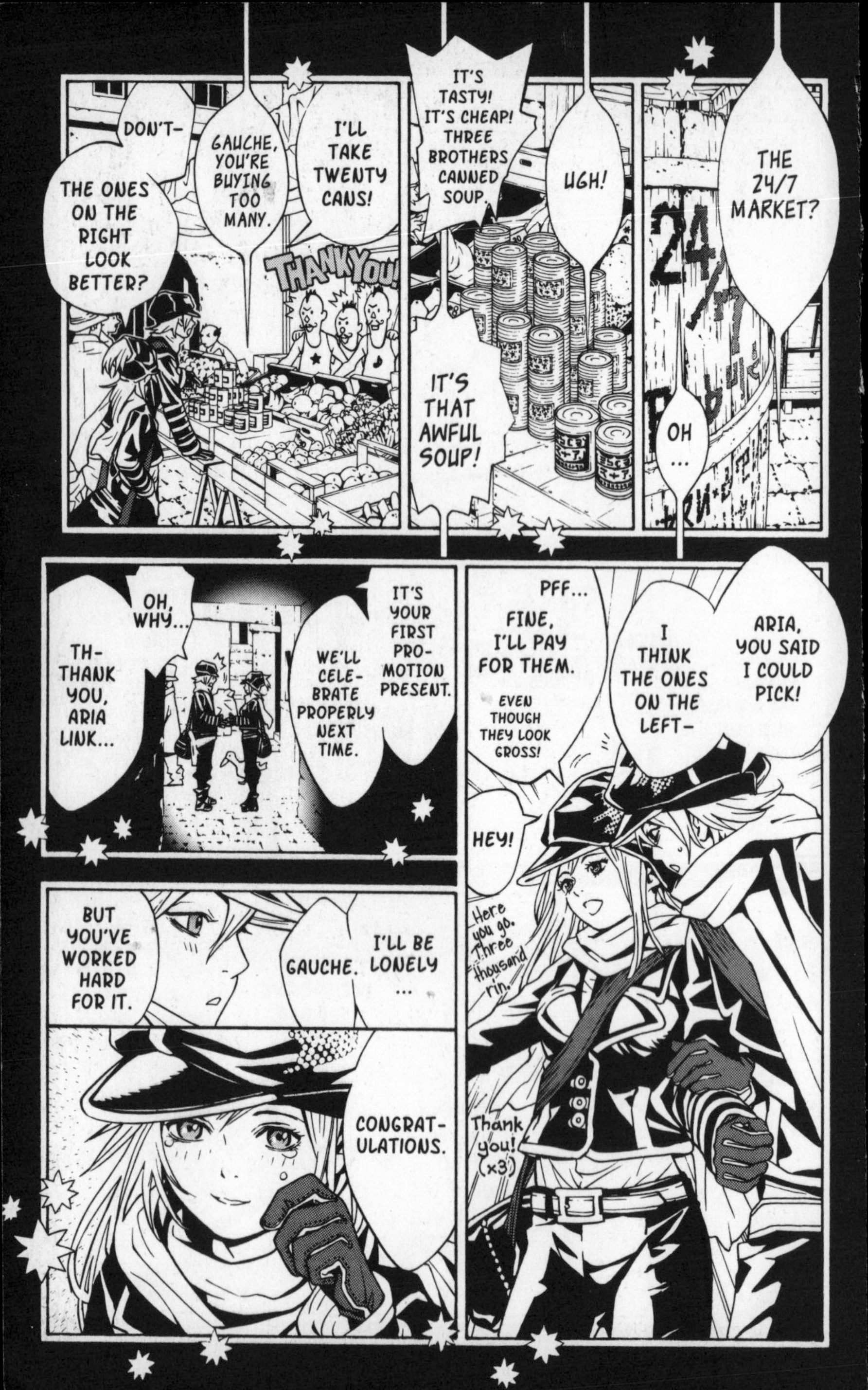

THE 24/7 MARKET?
OH ...
UGH!
IT'S TASTY! IT'S CHEAP! THREE BROTHERS CANNED SOUP.
IT'S THAT AWFUL SOUP!
I'LL TAKE TWENTY CANS!
THANKYOU!
GAUCHE, YOU'RE BUYING TOO MANY.
DON'T-
THE ONES ON THE RIGHT LOOK BETTER?
ARIA, YOU SAID I COULD PICK!
I THINK THE ONES ON THE LEFT-
PFF...
FINE, I'LL PAY FOR THEM.
EVEN THOUGH THEY LOOK GROSS!
HEY!
Here you go. Three thousand rin.
Thank you! (x3)
IT'S YOUR FIRST PROMOTION PRESENT.
WE'LL CELEBRATE PROPERLY NEXT TIME.
OH, WHY...
TH-THANK YOU, ARIA LINK...
I'LL BE LONELY ...
GAUCHE.
BUT YOU'VE WORKED HARD FOR IT.
CONGRATULATIONS.

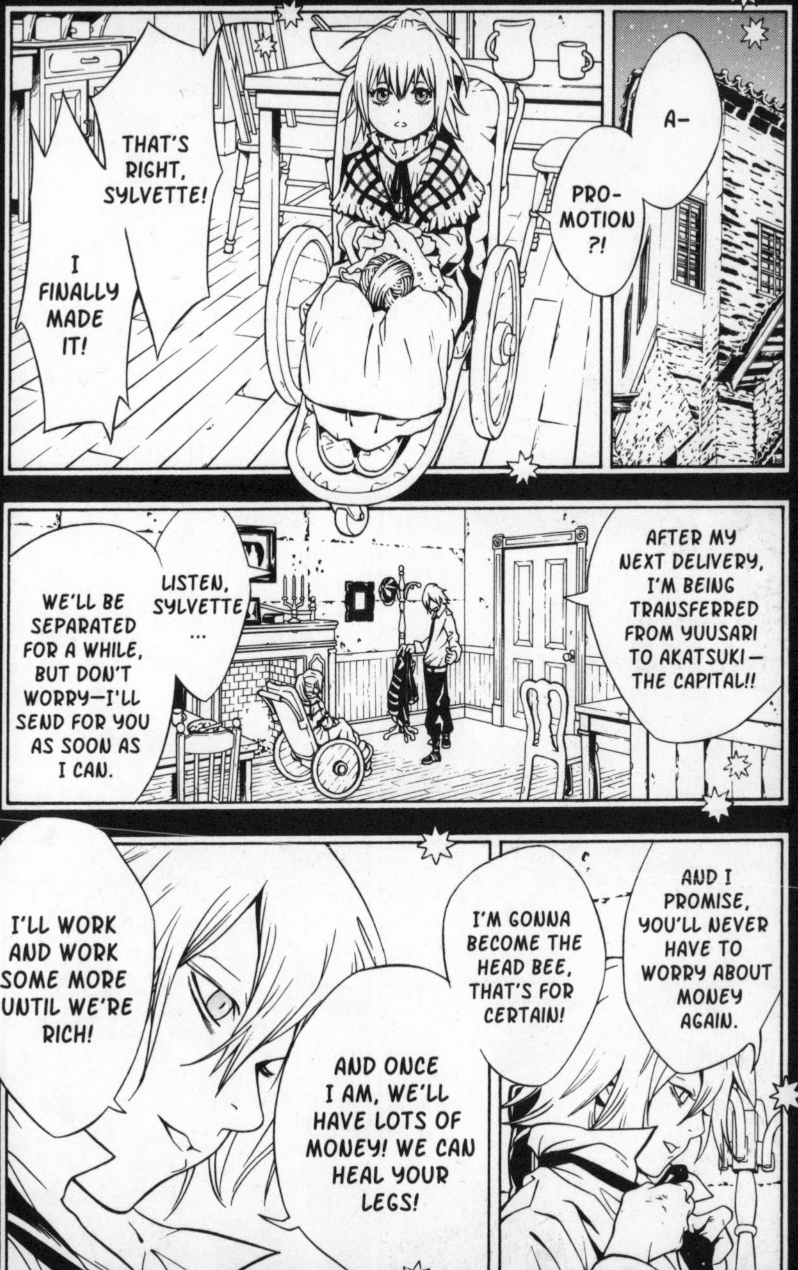
A-
PRO-MOTION?!
THAT'S RIGHT, SYLVETTE!
I FINALLY MADE IT!
AFTER MY NEXT DELIVERY, I'M BEING TRANSFERRED FROM YUUSARI TO AKATSUKI—THE CAPITAL!!
LISTEN, SYLVETTE...
WE'LL BE SEPARATED FOR A WHILE, BUT DON'T WORRY—I'LL SEND FOR YOU AS SOON AS I CAN.
AND I PROMISE, YOU'LL NEVER HAVE TO WORRY ABOUT MONEY AGAIN.
I'M GONNA BECOME THE HEAD BEE, THAT'S FOR CERTAIN!
I'LL WORK AND WORK SOME MORE UNTIL WE'RE RICH!
AND ONCE I AM, WE'LL HAVE LOTS OF MONEY! WE CAN HEAL YOUR LEGS!

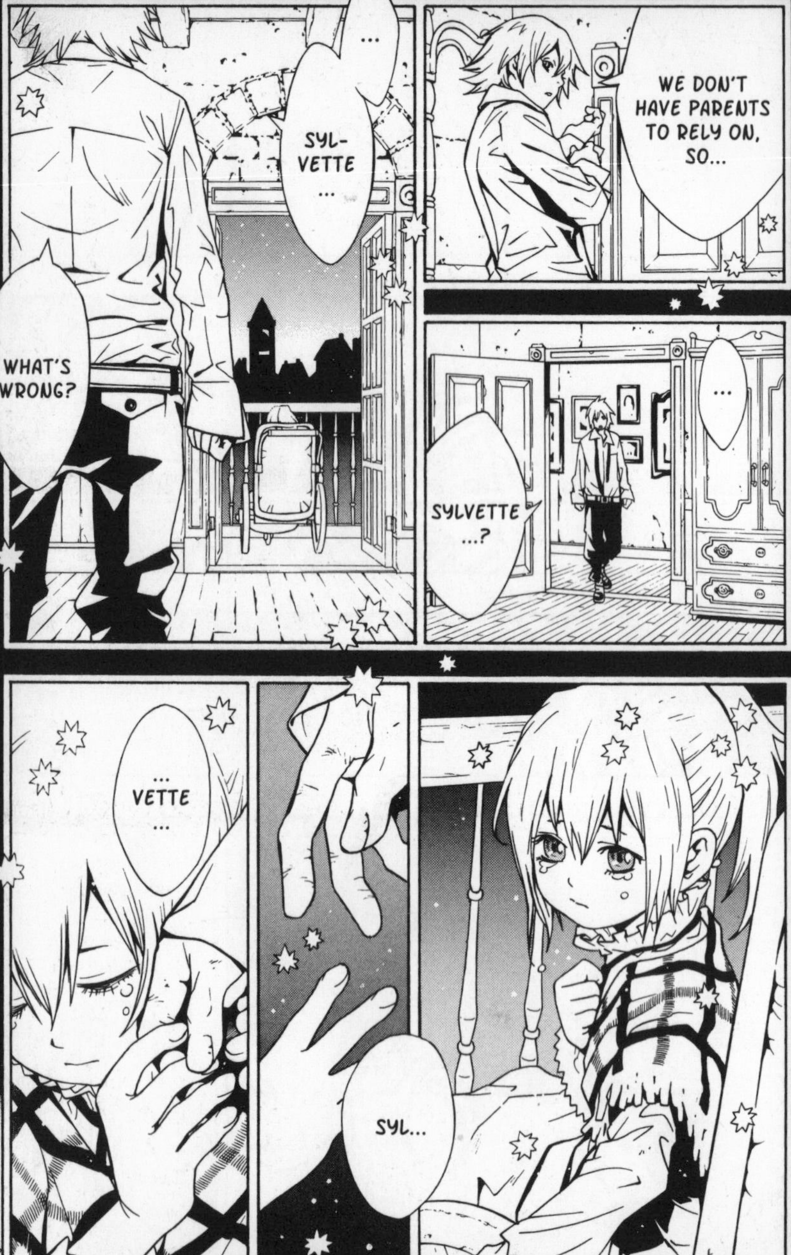
WE DON'T HAVE PARENTS TO RELY ON, SO...
...
SYLVETTE ...?
... SYL-VETTE ...
WHAT'S WRONG?
SYL...
... VETTE ...

Fsssh

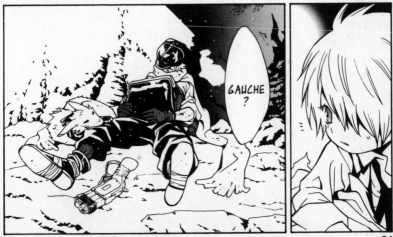

GAUCHE
?

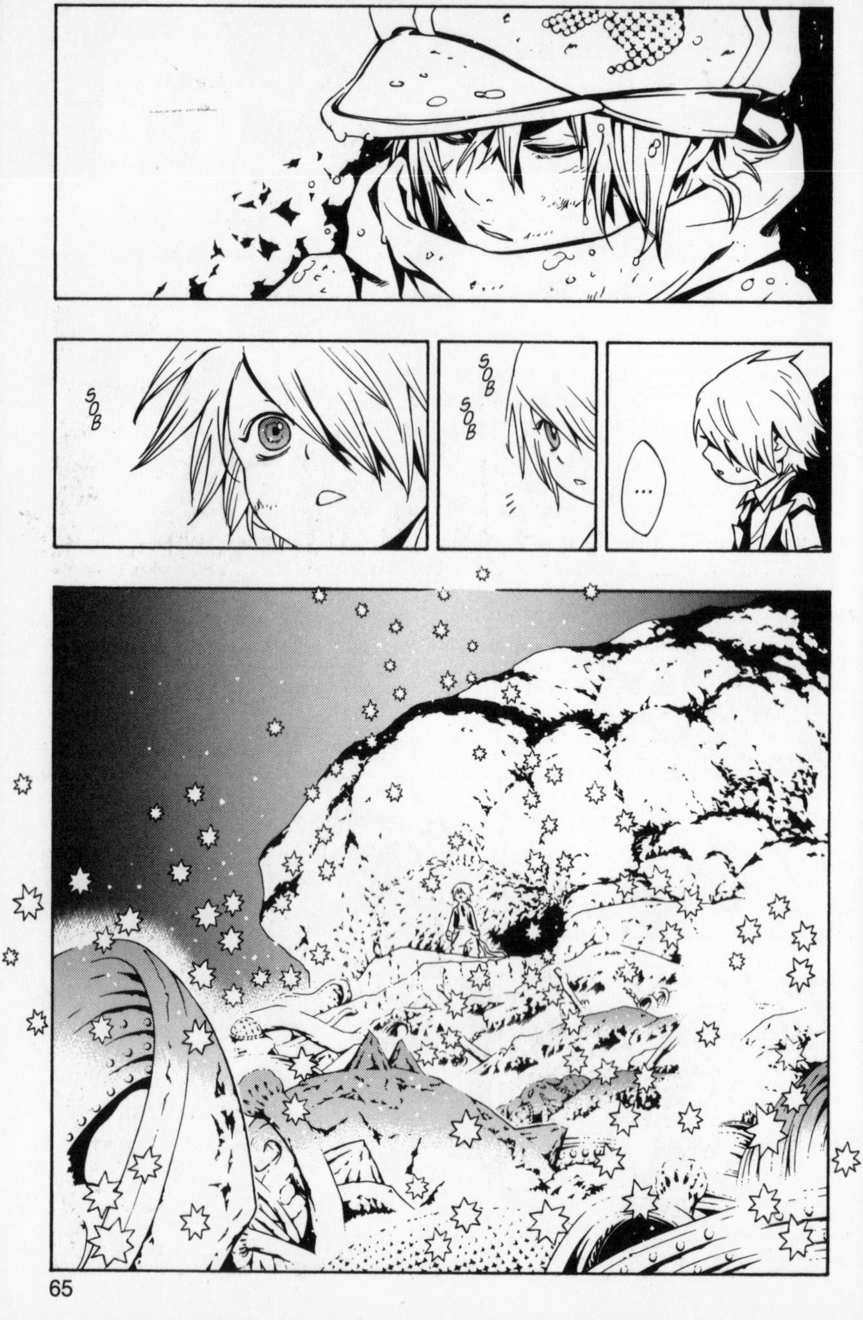
...
SOB
SOB
SOB

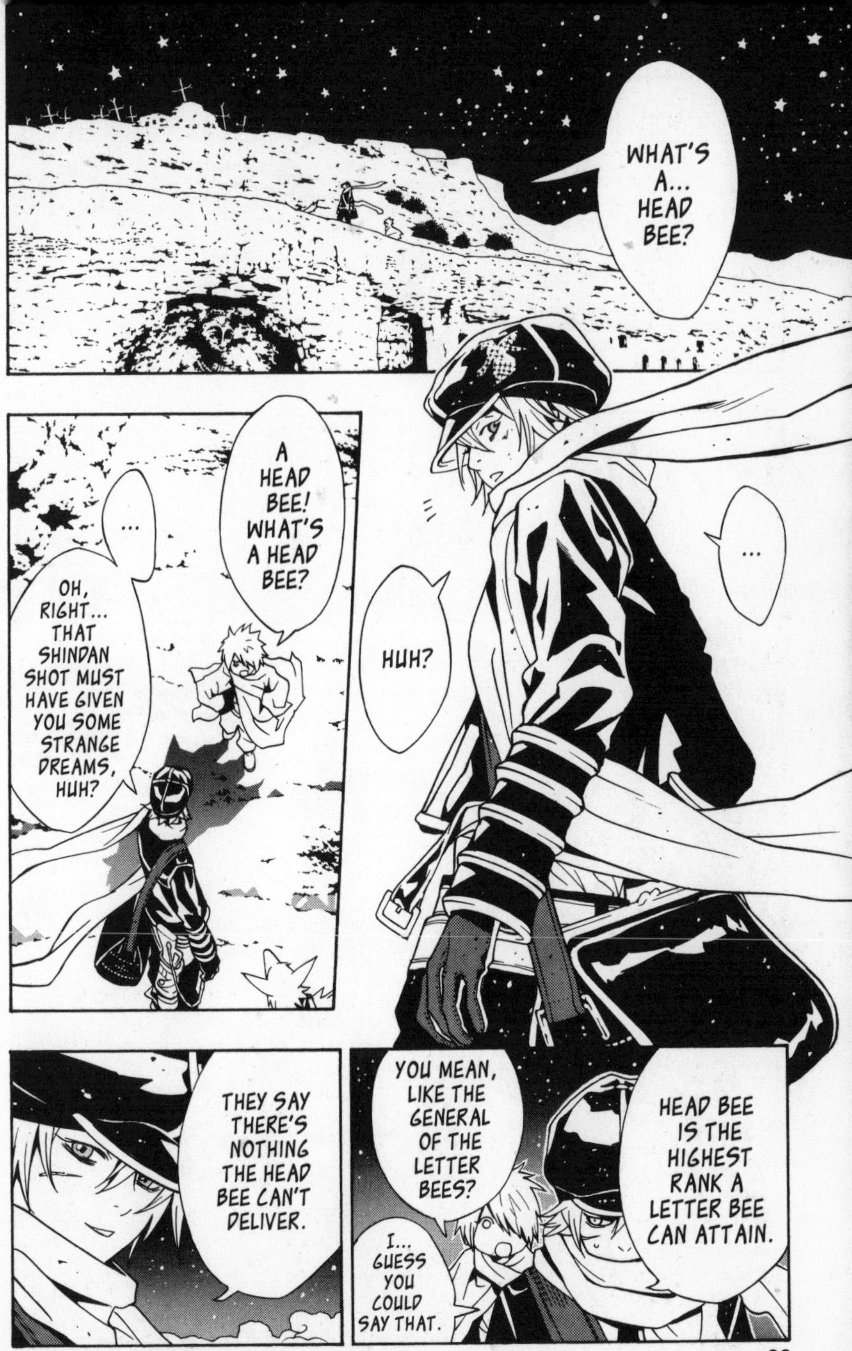

WHAT'S A... HEAD BEE?
...
HUH?
A HEAD BEE! WHAT'S A HEAD BEE?
...
OH, RIGHT... THAT SHINDAN SHOT MUST HAVE GIVEN YOU SOME STRANGE DREAMS, HUH?
HEAD BEE IS THE HIGHEST RANK A LETTER BEE CAN ATTAIN.
YOU MEAN, LIKE THE GENERAL OF THE LETTER BEES?
I... GUESS YOU COULD SAY THAT.
THEY SAY THERE'S NOTHING THE HEAD BEE CAN'T DELIVER.

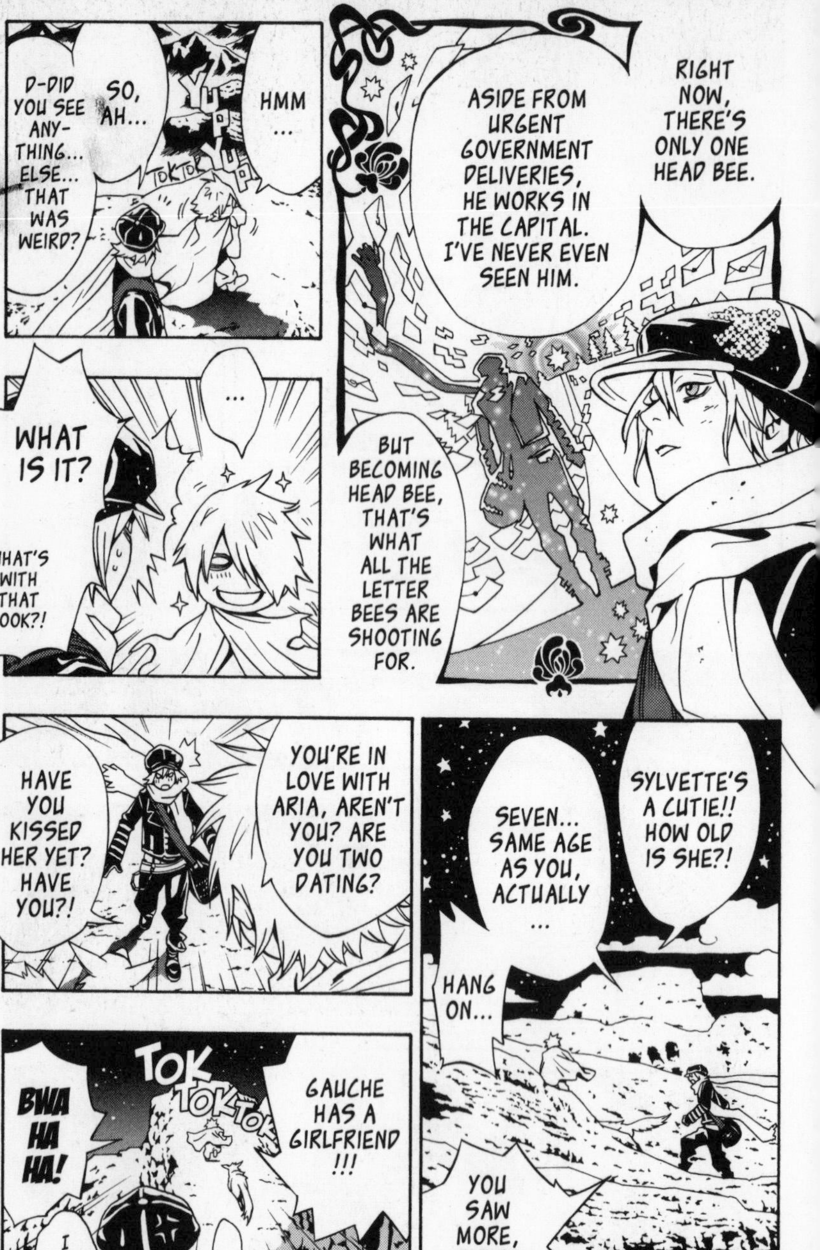
RIGHT NOW, THERE'S ONLY ONE HEAD BEE.
ASIDE FROM URGENT GOVERNMENT DELIVERIES, HE WORKS IN THE CAPITAL. I'VE NEVER EVEN SEEN HIM.
BUT BECOMING HEAD BEE, THAT'S WHAT ALL THE LETTER BEES ARE SHOOTING FOR.
HMM ...
YUP YUP
SO, AH...
D-DID YOU SEE ANYTHING... ELSE... THAT WAS WEIRD?
TOK TOK
...
WHAT IS IT?
WHAT'S WITH THAT LOOK?!
SYLVETTE'S A CUTIE!! HOW OLD IS SHE?!
SEVEN... SAME AGE AS YOU, ACTUALLY ...
HANG ON...
YOU SAW MORE, DIDN'T YOU?!
YOU'RE IN LOVE WITH ARIA, AREN'T YOU? ARE YOU TWO DATING?
HAVE YOU KISSED HER YET? HAVE YOU?!
TOK TOK TOK
GAUCHE HAS A GIRLFRIEND !!!
BWA HA HA!
...
I HATE KIDS.

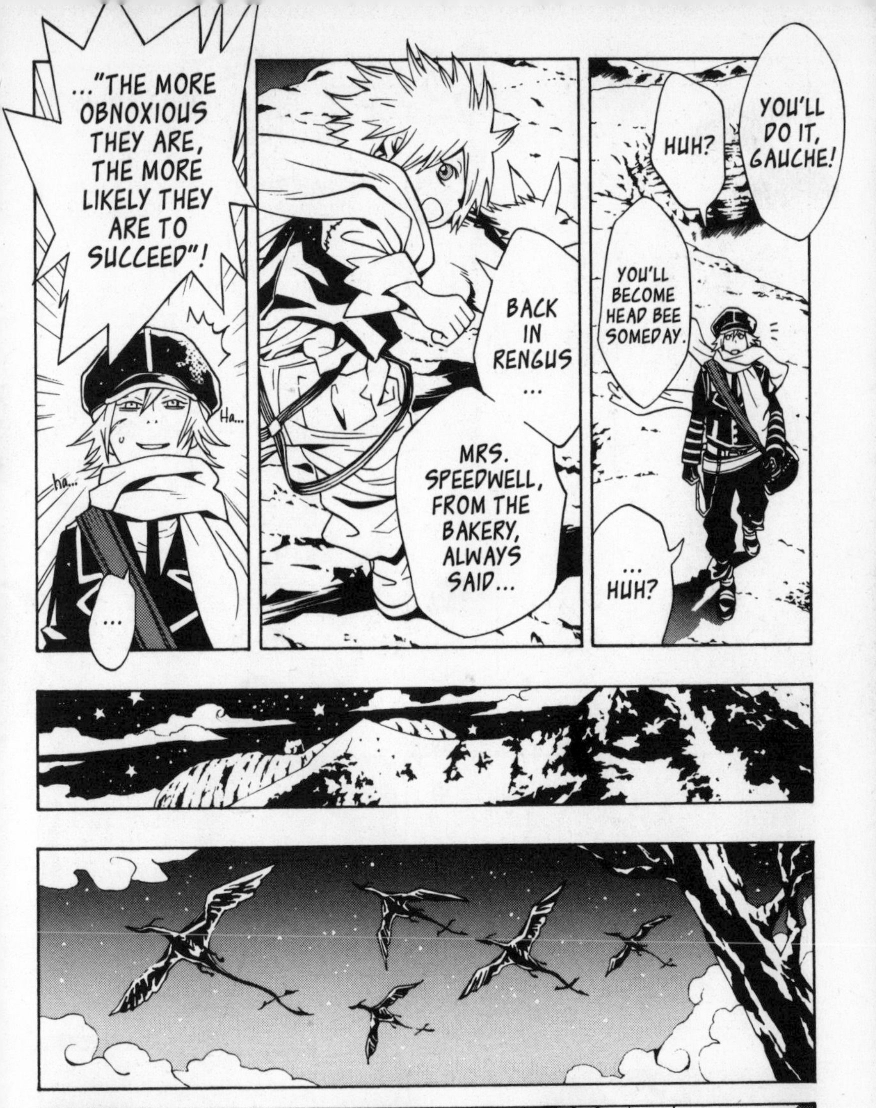
YOU'LL DO IT, GAUCHE!
HUH?
YOU'LL BECOME HEAD BEE SOMEDAY.
... HUH?
BACK IN RENGUS ...
MRS. SPEEDWELL, FROM THE BAKERY, ALWAYS SAID...
..."THE MORE OBNOXIOUS THEY ARE, THE MORE LIKELY THEY ARE TO SUCCEED"!
Ha...
ha...
...

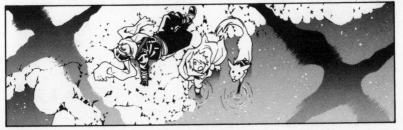

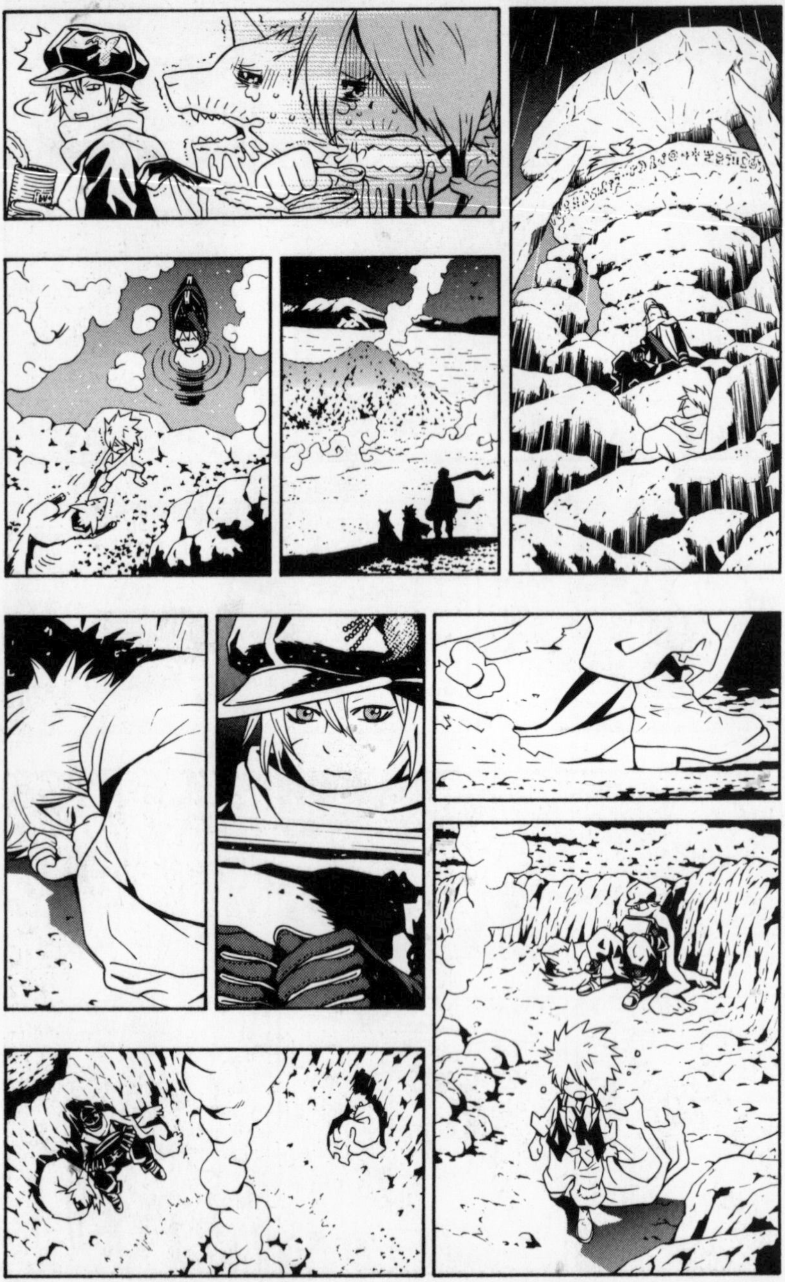

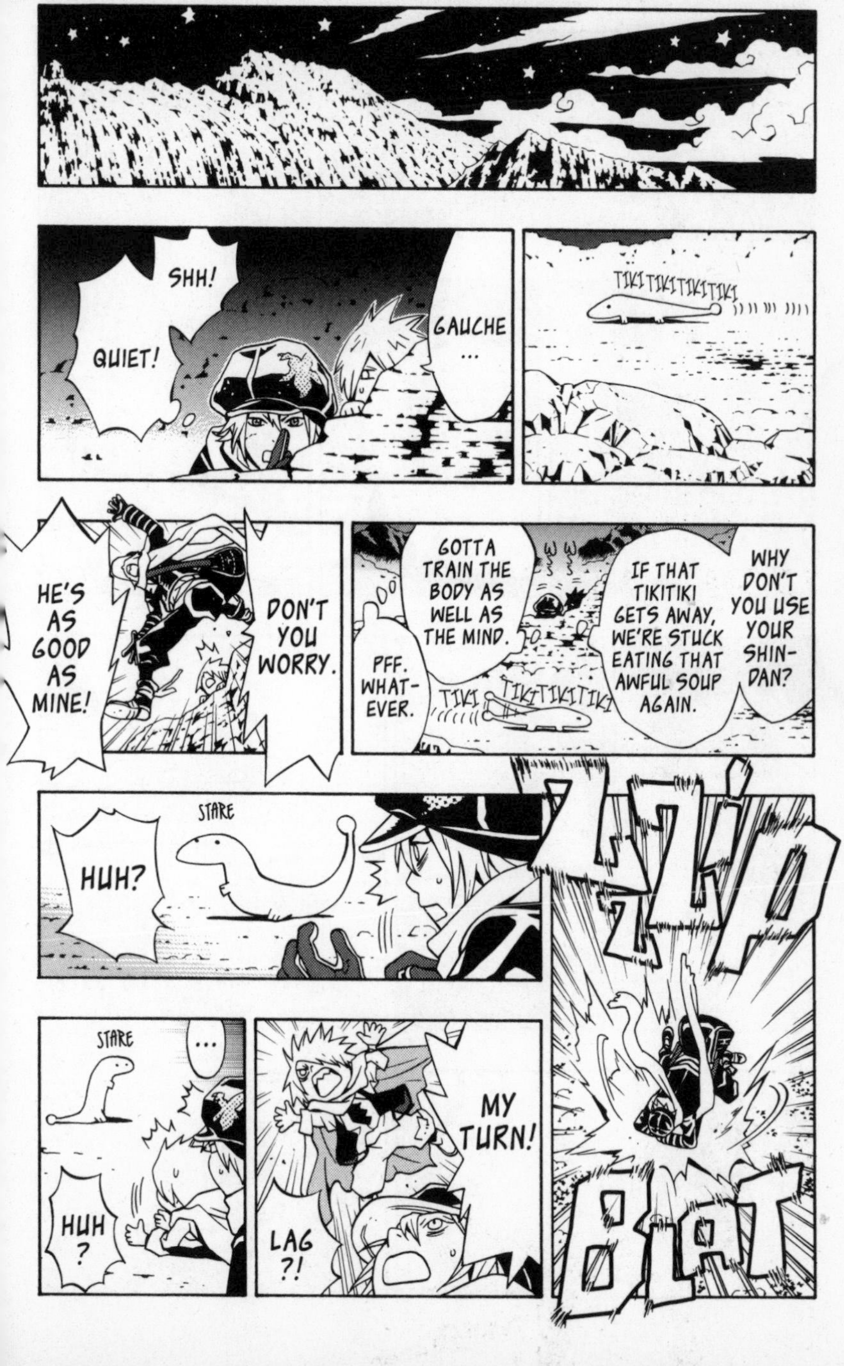
TIKITIKITIKITIKI
GAUCHE ...
SHH!
QUIET!
WHY DON'T YOU USE YOUR SHIN-DAN?
IF THAT TIKITIKI GETS AWAY, WE'RE STUCK EATING THAT AWFUL SOUP AGAIN.
GOTTA TRAIN THE BODY AS WELL AS THE MIND.
TIKITIKITIKI
TIKI
PFF. WHATEVER.
DON'T YOU WORRY.
HE'S AS GOOD AS MINE!
ZZIP
BLAT
STARE
HUH?
MY TURN!
LAG ?!
...
STARE
HUH ?

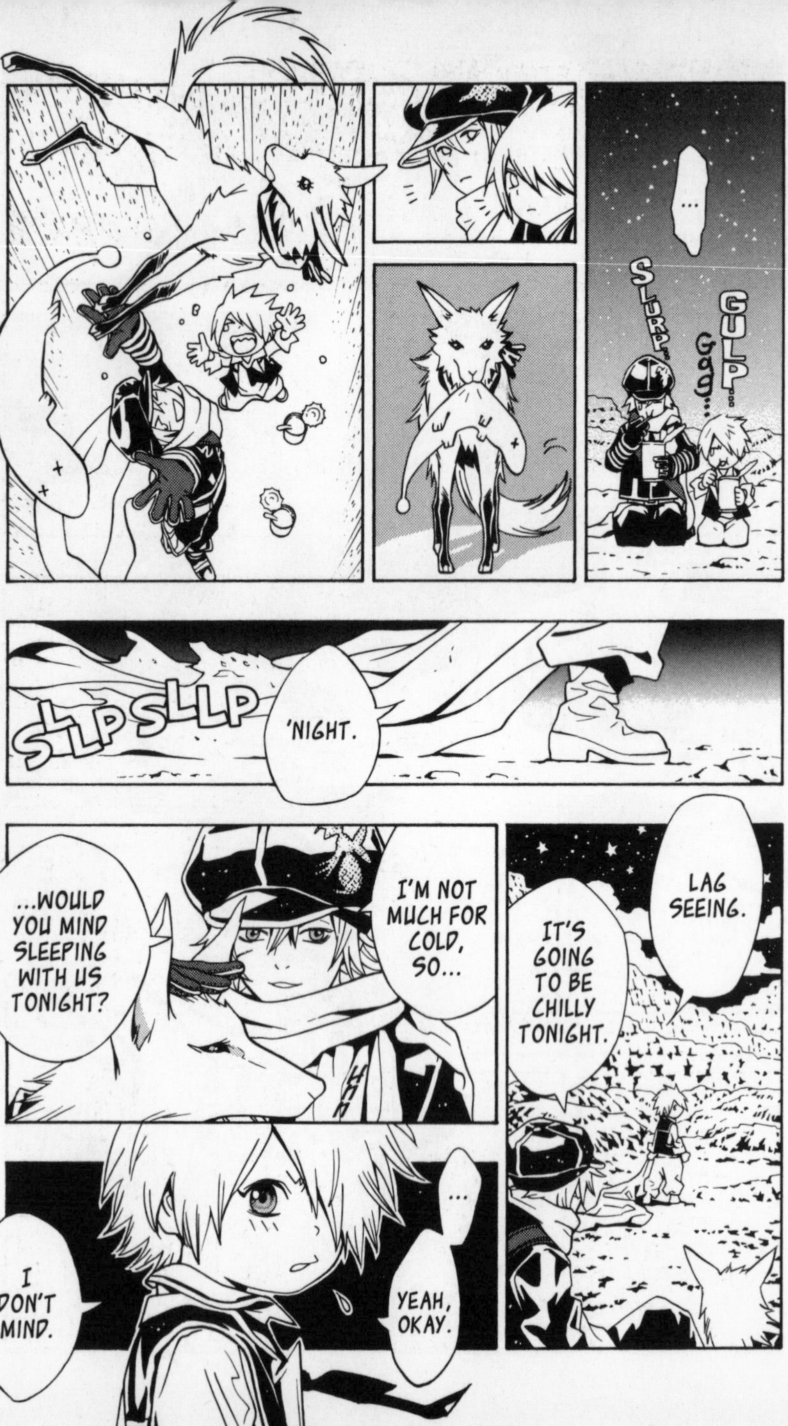
...
GULP...
Ggg...
SLURP...
SLLP SLLP
'NIGHT.
LAG SEEING.
IT'S GOING TO BE CHILLY TONIGHT.
I'M NOT MUCH FOR COLD, SO...
...WOULD YOU MIND SLEEPING WITH US TONIGHT?
...
YEAH, OKAY.
I DON'T MIND.

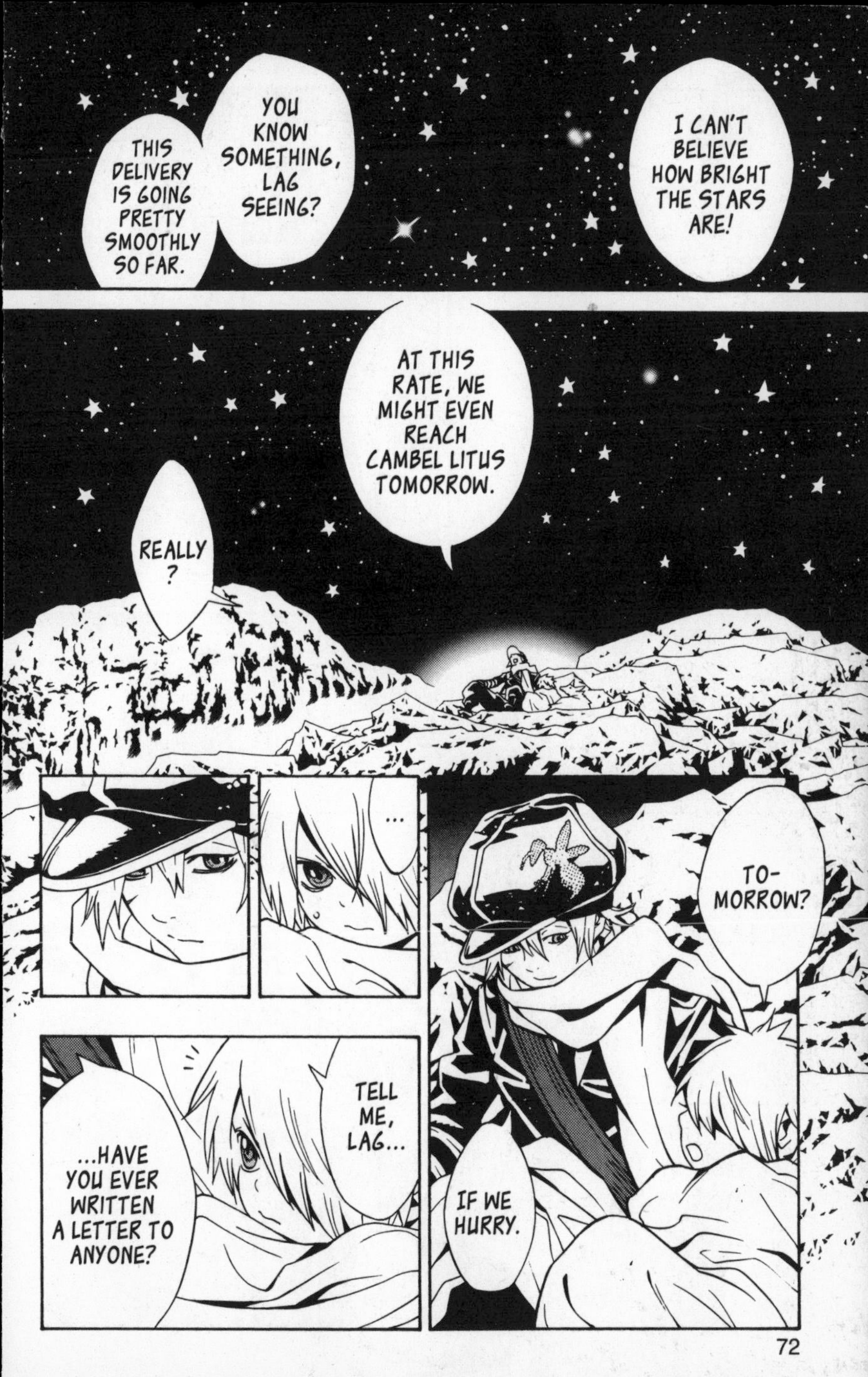
I CAN'T BELIEVE HOW BRIGHT THE STARS ARE!
YOU KNOW SOMETHING, LAG SEEING?
THIS DELIVERY IS GOING PRETTY SMOOTHLY SO FAR.
AT THIS RATE, WE MIGHT EVEN REACH CAMBEL LITUS TOMORROW.
REALLY?
TO-MORROW?
IF WE HURRY.
...
TELL ME, LAG...
...HAVE YOU EVER WRITTEN A LETTER TO ANYONE?

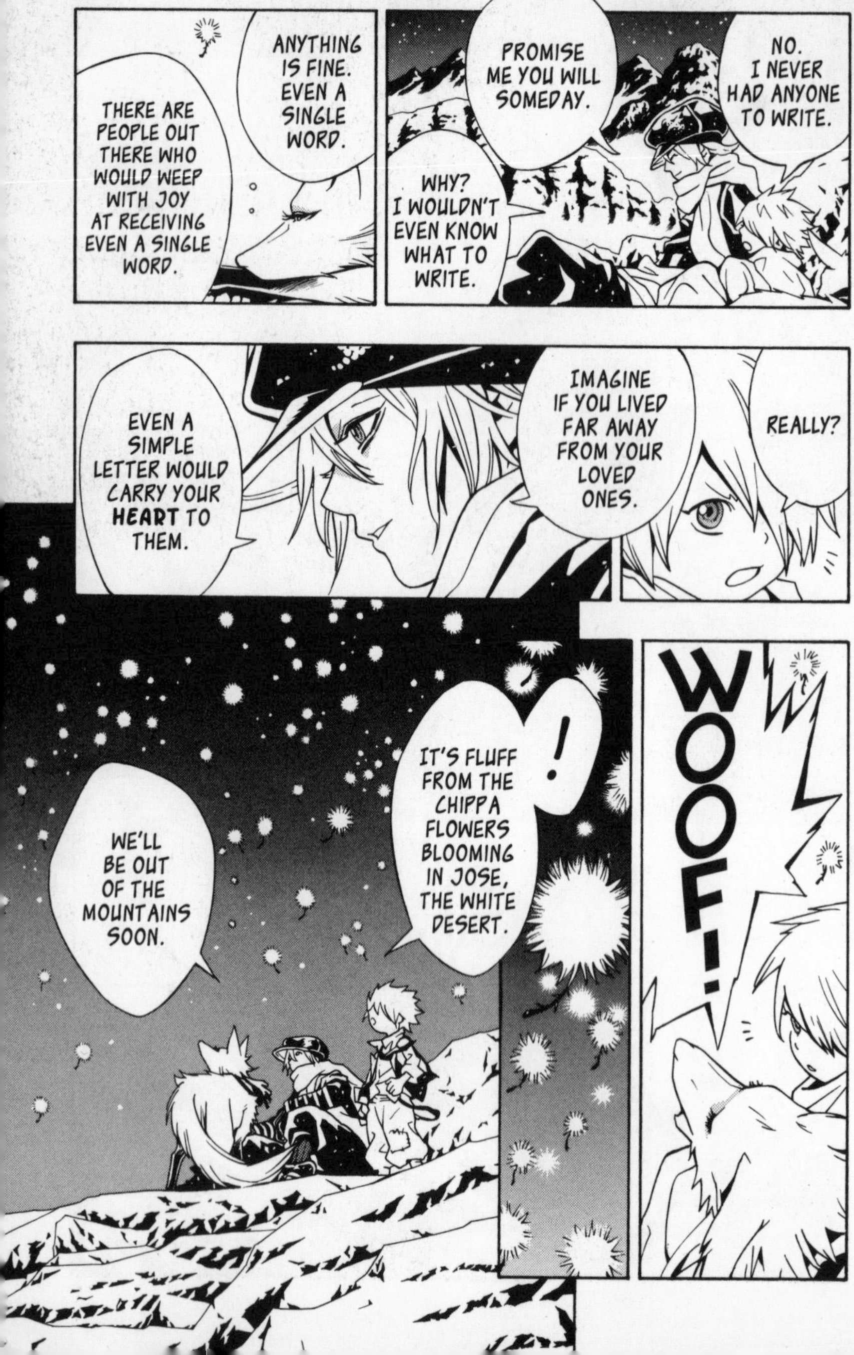
NO. I NEVER HAD ANYONE TO WRITE.
PROMISE ME YOU WILL SOMEDAY.
WHY? I WOULDN'T EVEN KNOW WHAT TO WRITE.
ANYTHING IS FINE. EVEN A SINGLE WORD.
THERE ARE PEOPLE OUT THERE WHO WOULD WEEP WITH JOY AT RECEIVING EVEN A SINGLE WORD.
REALLY?
IMAGINE IF YOU LIVED FAR AWAY FROM YOUR LOVED ONES.
EVEN A SIMPLE LETTER WOULD CARRY YOUR **HEART** TO THEM.
WOOF!!
!
IT'S FLUFF FROM THE CHIPPA FLOWERS BLOOMING IN JOSE, THE WHITE DESERT.
WE'LL BE OUT OF THE MOUNTAINS SOON.

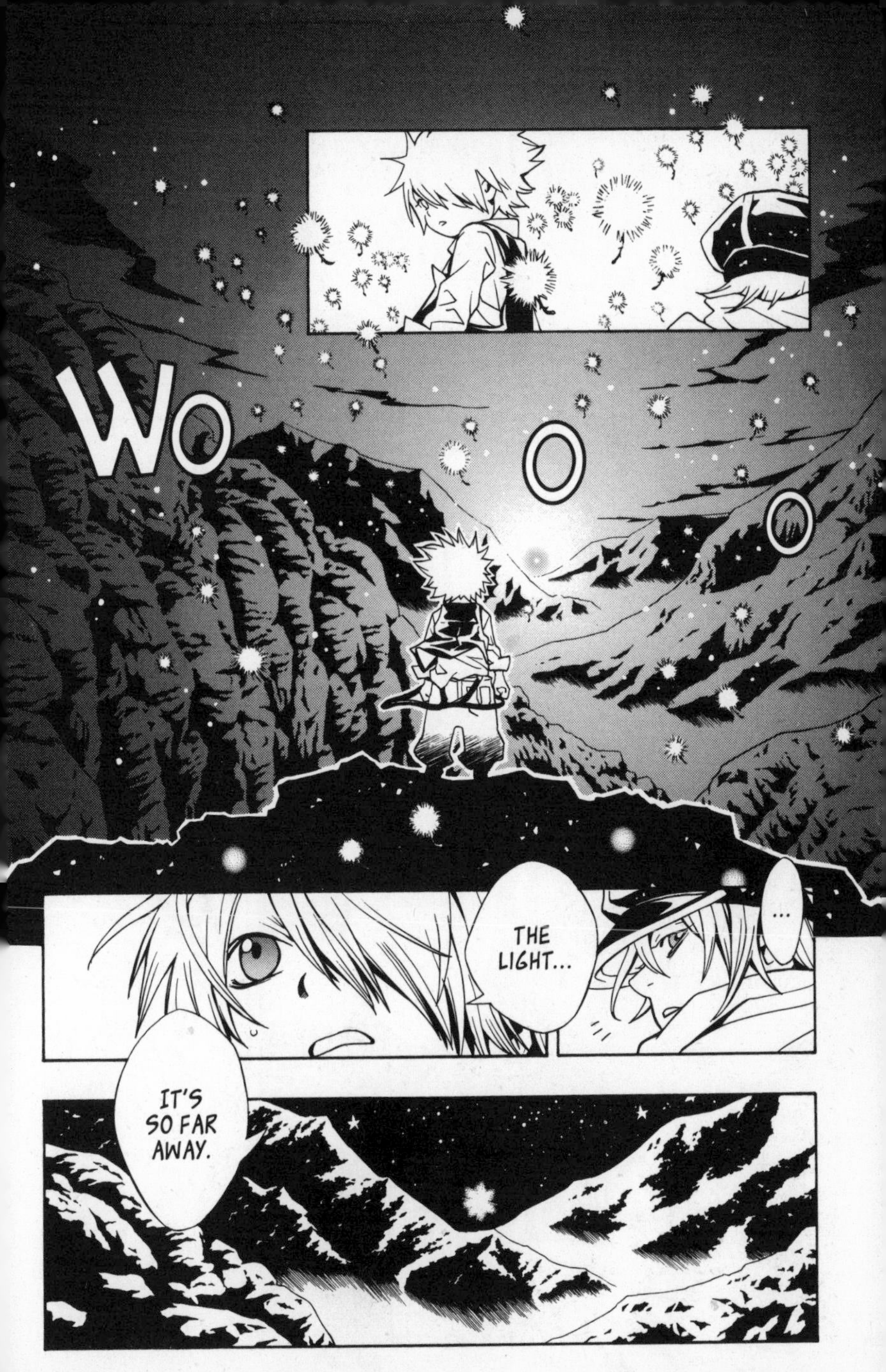
WOOO
...
THE LIGHT...
IT'S SO FAR AWAY.

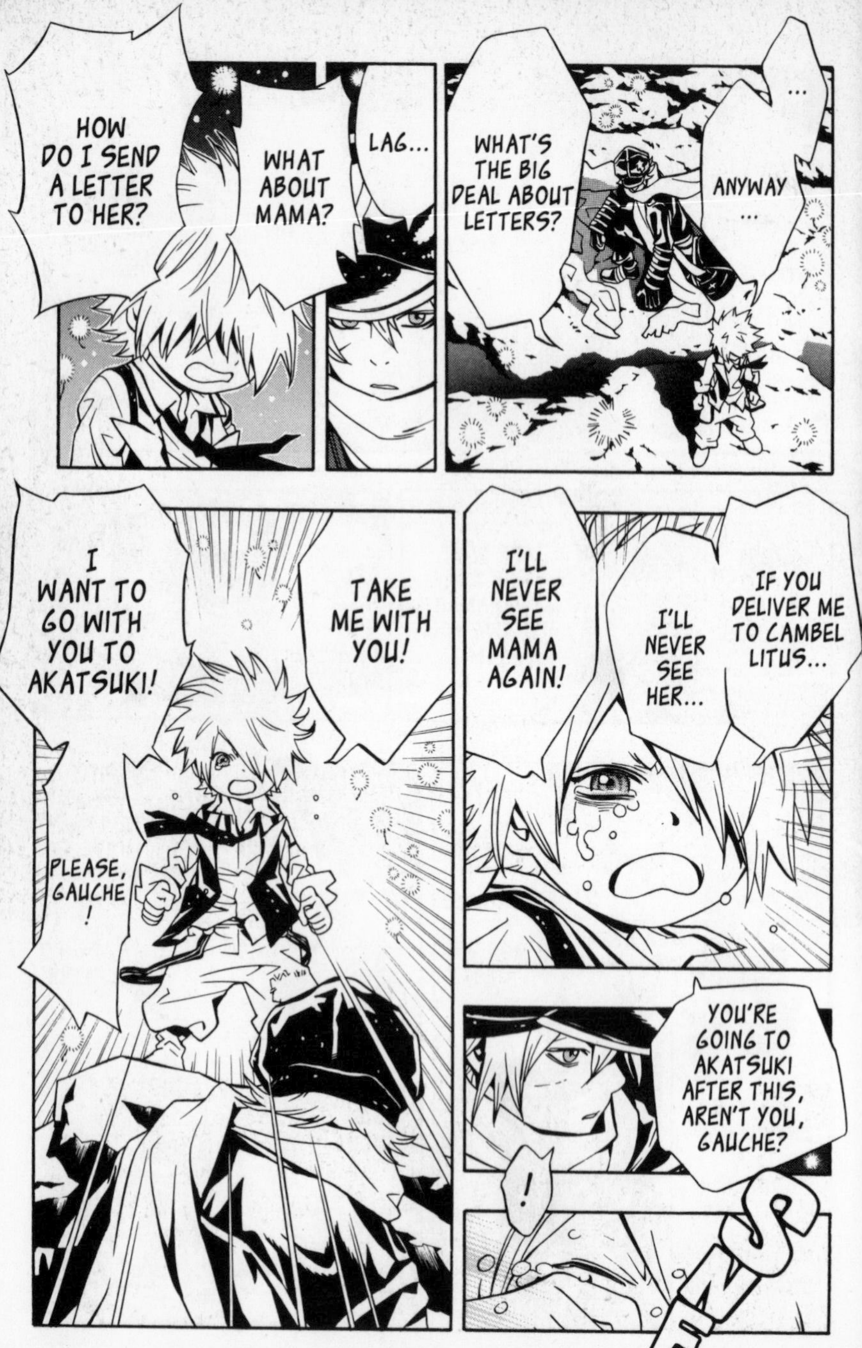
...
ANYWAY ...
WHAT'S THE BIG DEAL ABOUT LETTERS?
LAG...
WHAT ABOUT MAMA?
HOW DO I SEND A LETTER TO HER?
IF YOU DELIVER ME TO CAMBEL LITUS...
I'LL NEVER SEE HER...
I'LL NEVER SEE MAMA AGAIN!
YOU'RE GOING TO AKATSUKI AFTER THIS, AREN'T YOU, GAUCHE?
!
FZSP
TAKE ME WITH YOU!
I WANT TO GO WITH YOU TO AKATSUKI!
PLEASE, GAUCHE!

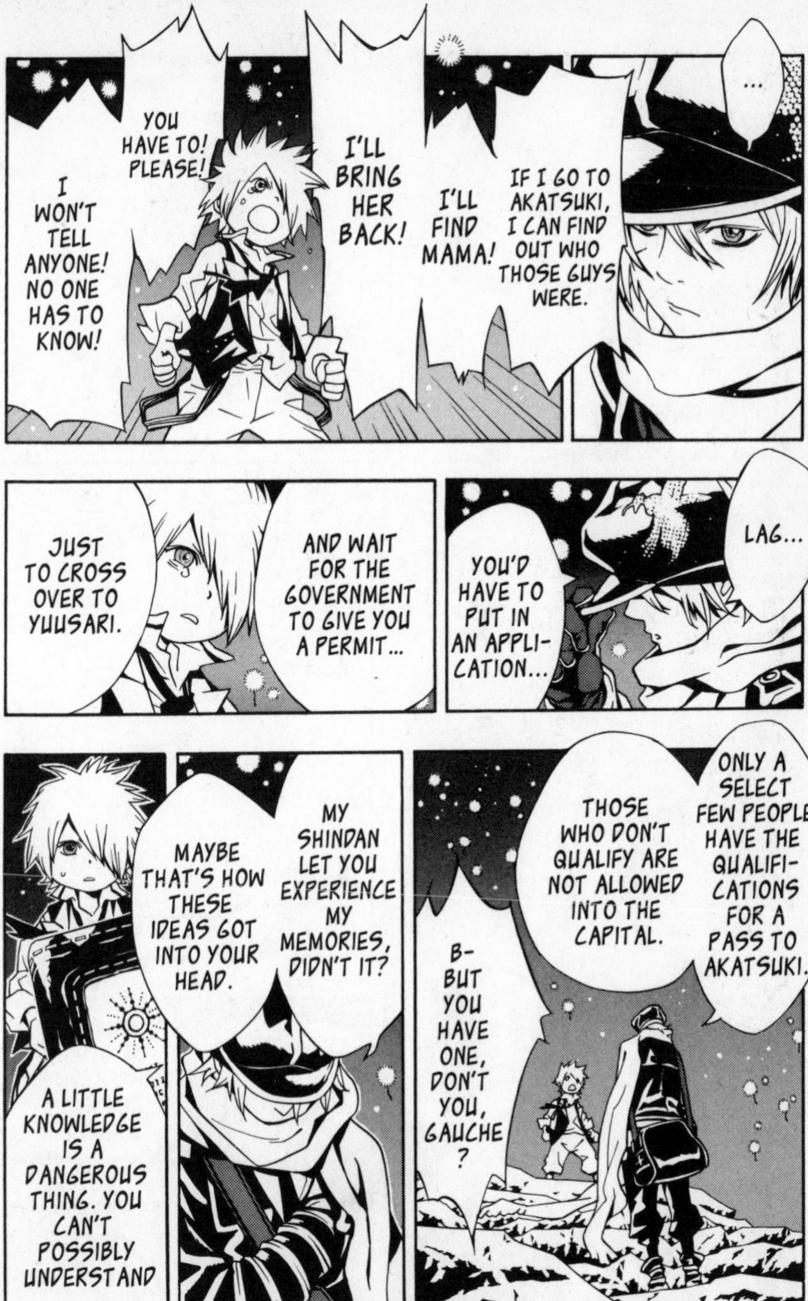
...
IF I GO TO AKATSUKI, I CAN FIND OUT WHO THOSE GUYS WERE.
I'LL FIND MAMA!
I'LL BRING HER BACK!
YOU HAVE TO! PLEASE!
I WON'T TELL ANYONE! NO ONE HAS TO KNOW!
LAG...
YOU'D HAVE TO PUT IN AN APPLI-CATION...
AND WAIT FOR THE GOVERNMENT TO GIVE YOU A PERMIT...
JUST TO CROSS OVER TO YUUSARI.
ONLY A SELECT FEW PEOPLE HAVE THE QUALIFI-CATIONS FOR A PASS TO AKATSUKI.
THOSE WHO DON'T QUALIFY ARE NOT ALLOWED INTO THE CAPITAL.
B- BUT YOU HAVE ONE, DON'T YOU, GAUCHE?
MY SHINDAN LET YOU EXPERIENCE MY MEMORIES, DIDN'T IT?
MAYBE THAT'S HOW THESE IDEAS GOT INTO YOUR HEAD.
A LITTLE KNOWLEDGE IS A DANGEROUS THING. YOU CAN'T POSSIBLY UNDERSTAND ...

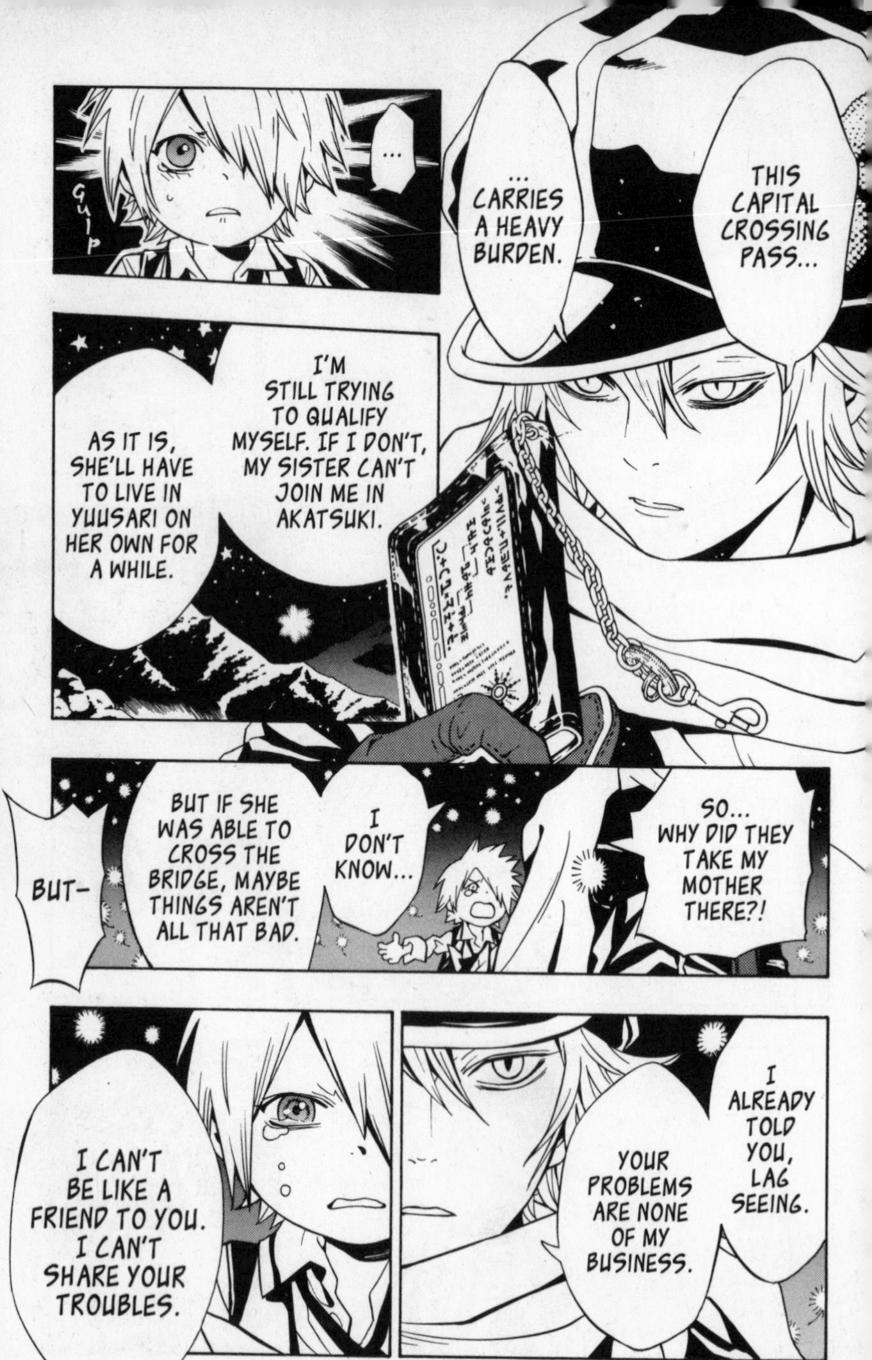
THIS CAPITAL CROSSING PASS...
... CARRIES A HEAVY BURDEN.
...
GULP
I'M STILL TRYING TO QUALIFY MYSELF. IF I DON'T, MY SISTER CAN'T JOIN ME IN AKATSUKI.
AS IT IS, SHE'LL HAVE TO LIVE IN YUUSARI ON HER OWN FOR A WHILE.
SO... WHY DID THEY TAKE MY MOTHER THERE?!
I DON'T KNOW...
BUT IF SHE WAS ABLE TO CROSS THE BRIDGE, MAYBE THINGS AREN'T ALL THAT BAD.
BUT–
I ALREADY TOLD YOU, LAG SEEING.
YOUR PROBLEMS ARE NONE OF MY BUSINESS.
I CAN'T BE LIKE A FRIEND TO YOU. I CAN'T SHARE YOUR TROUBLES.

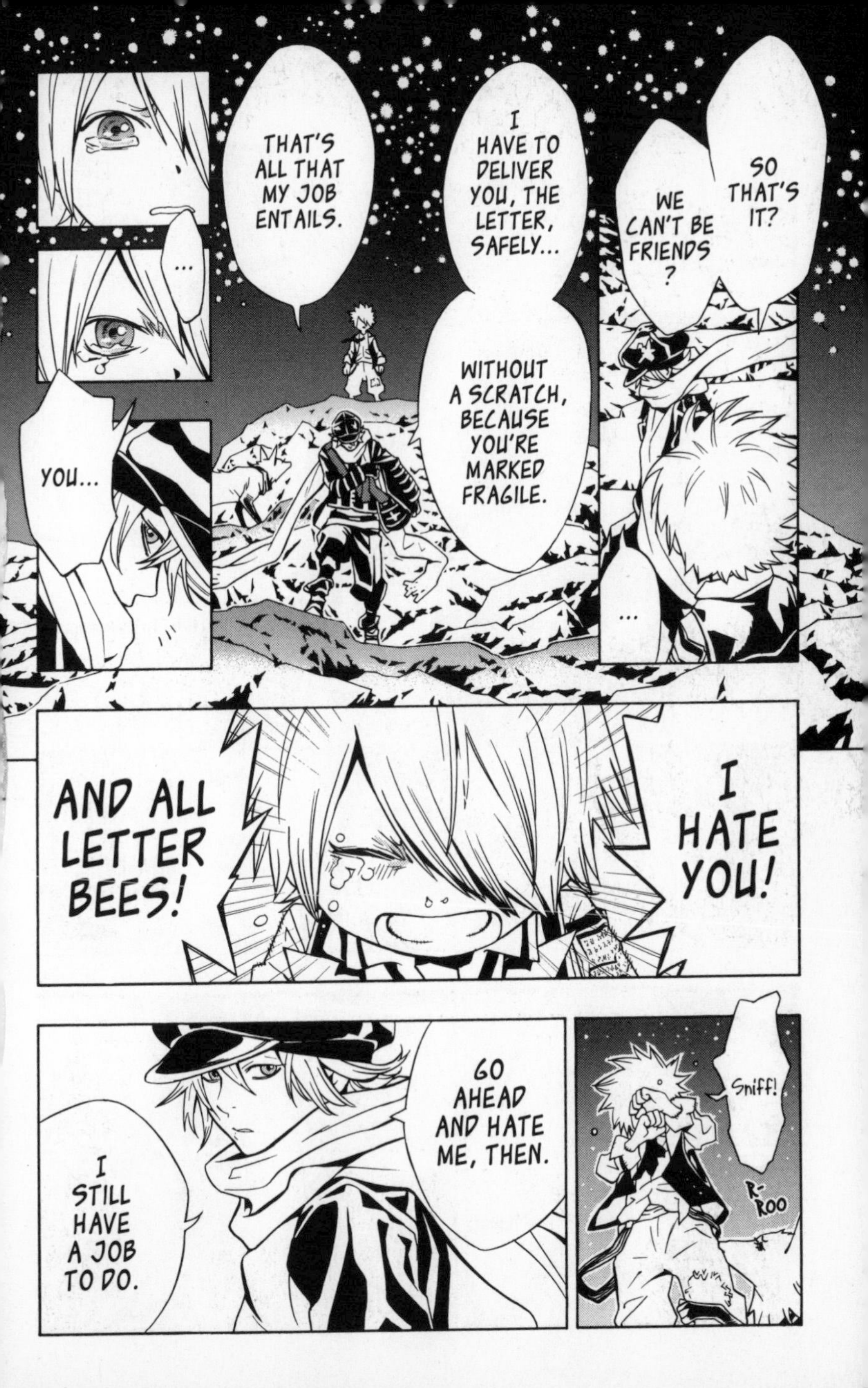
SO THAT'S IT?
WE CAN'T BE FRIENDS?
...
I HAVE TO DELIVER YOU, THE LETTER, SAFELY...
WITHOUT A SCRATCH, BECAUSE YOU'RE MARKED FRAGILE.
THAT'S ALL THAT MY JOB ENTAILS.
...
YOU...
I HATE YOU!
AND ALL LETTER BEES!
Sniff!
R-ROO
GO AHEAD AND HATE ME, THEN.
I STILL HAVE A JOB TO DO.

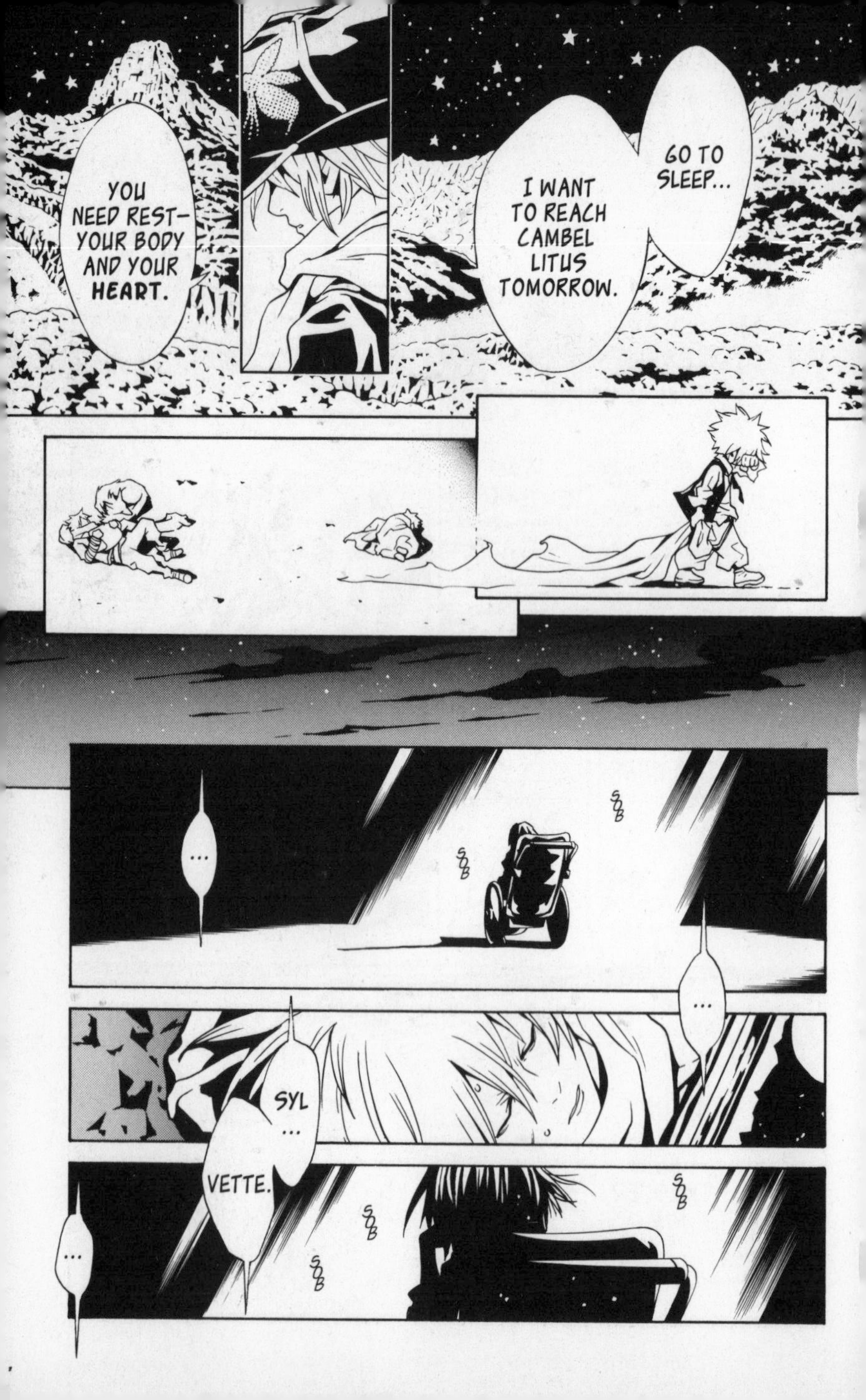
GO TO SLEEP...
I WANT TO REACH CAMBEL LITUS TOMORROW.
YOU NEED REST—YOUR BODY AND YOUR **HEART.**
SOB
SOB
...
...
SYL ...
VETTE.
SOB
SOB
SOB
...

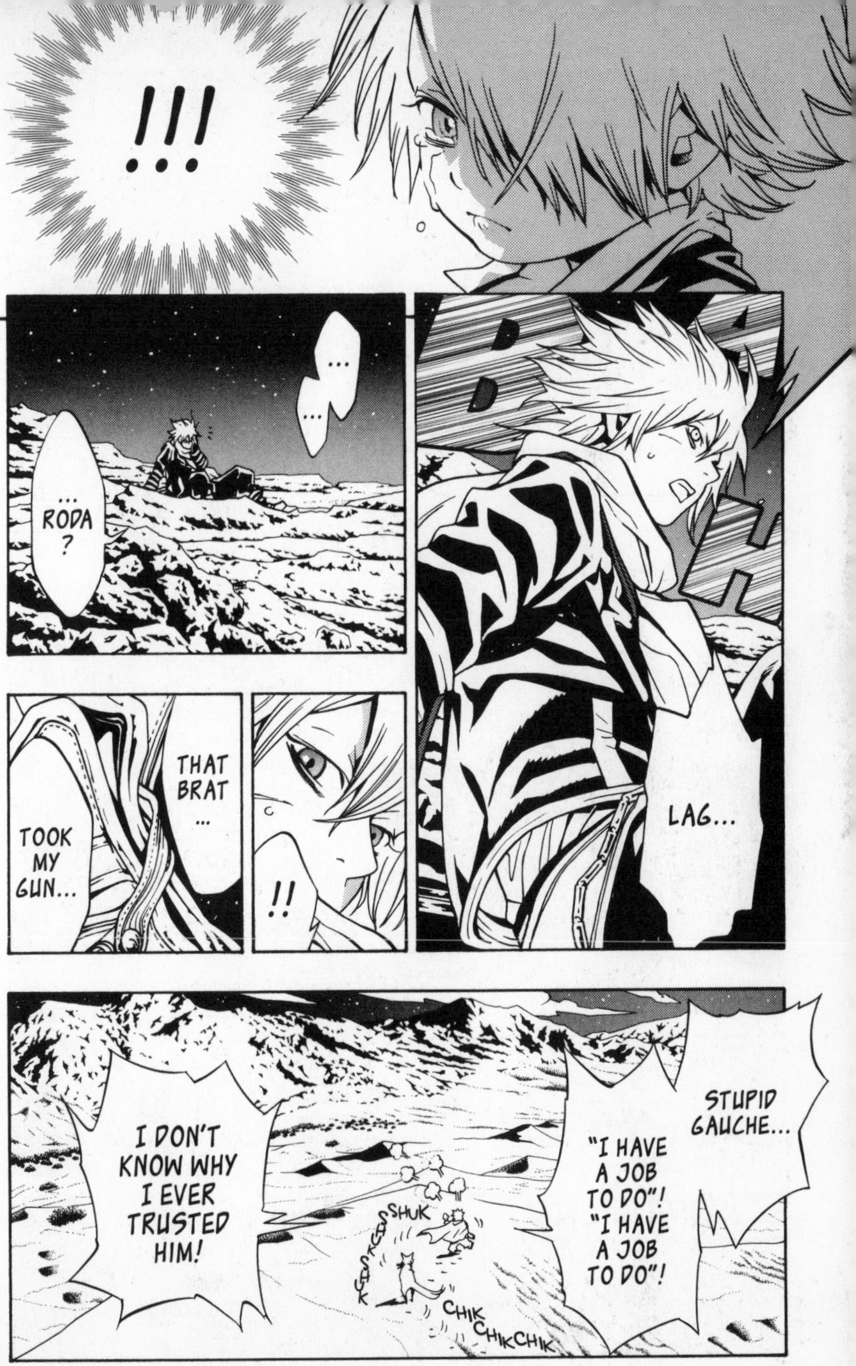
!!!
LAG...
...
...
...RODA?
!!
THAT BRAT ...
TOOK MY GUN...
STUPID GAUCHE...
"I HAVE A JOB TO DO"! "I HAVE A JOB TO DO"!
CHIK CHIKCHIK
SHUK
I DON'T KNOW WHY I EVER TRUSTED HIM!

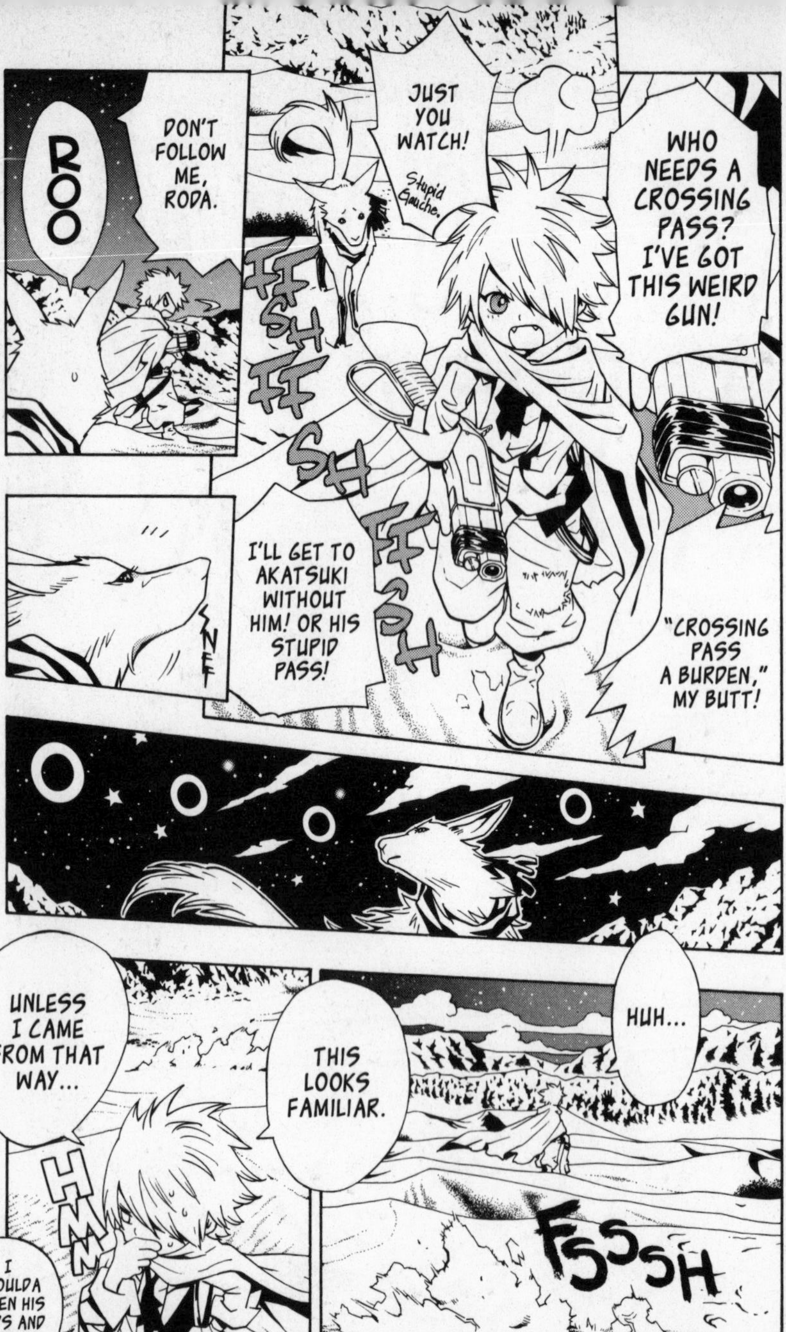
WHO NEEDS A CROSSING PASS? I'VE GOT THIS WEIRD GUN!
JUST YOU WATCH!
Stupid Gauche.
FFSH FFSH FFSH
I'LL GET TO AKATSUKI WITHOUT HIM! OR HIS STUPID PASS!
"CROSSING PASS A BURDEN," MY BUTT!
DON'T FOLLOW ME, RODA.
ROO
SNFF
HUH...
FSSSH
THIS LOOKS FAMILIAR.
UNLESS I CAME FROM THAT WAY...
HMMM
I SHOULDA TAKEN HIS MAPS AND COMPASS, TOO.

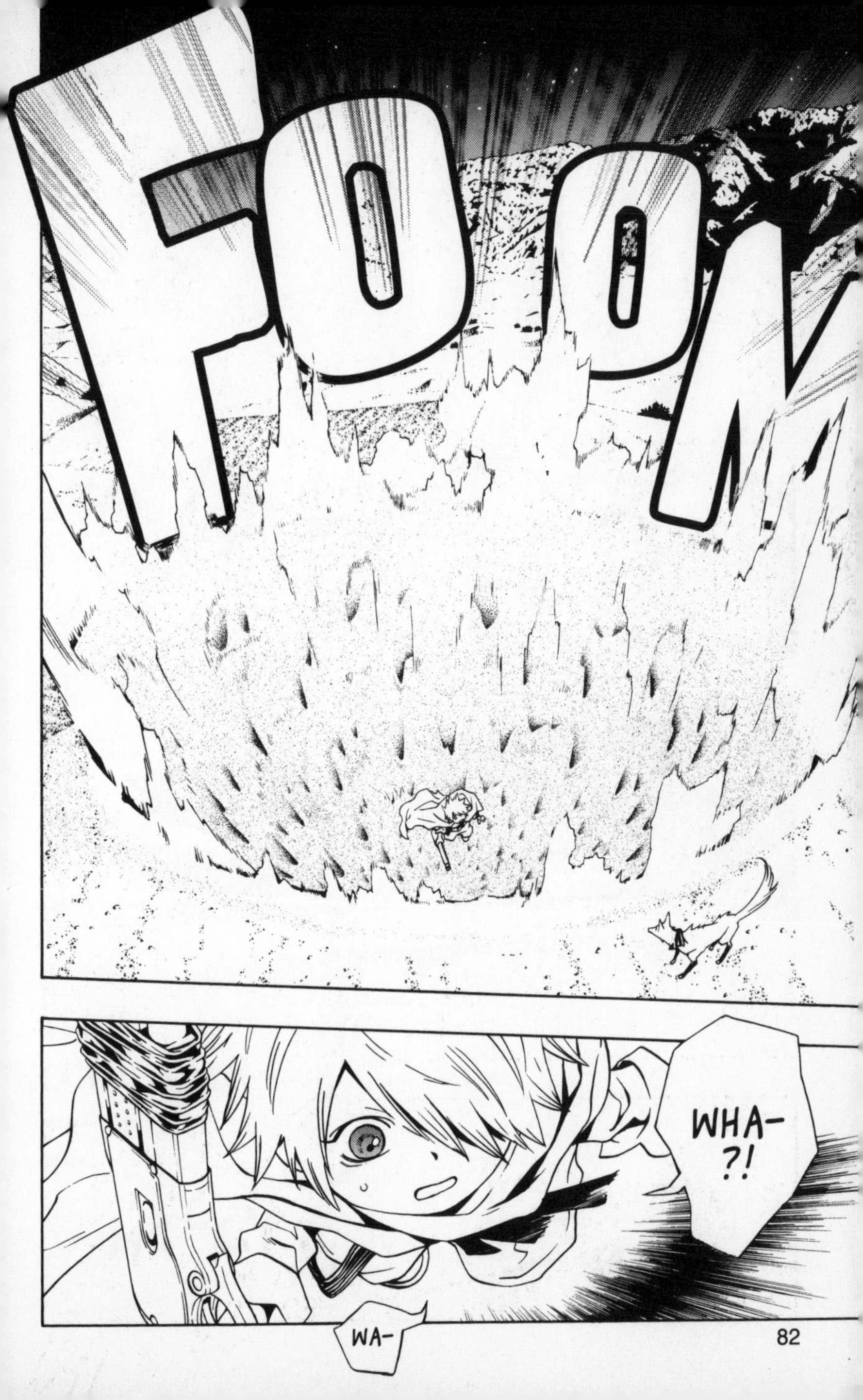
FOOM
WHA-?!
WA-

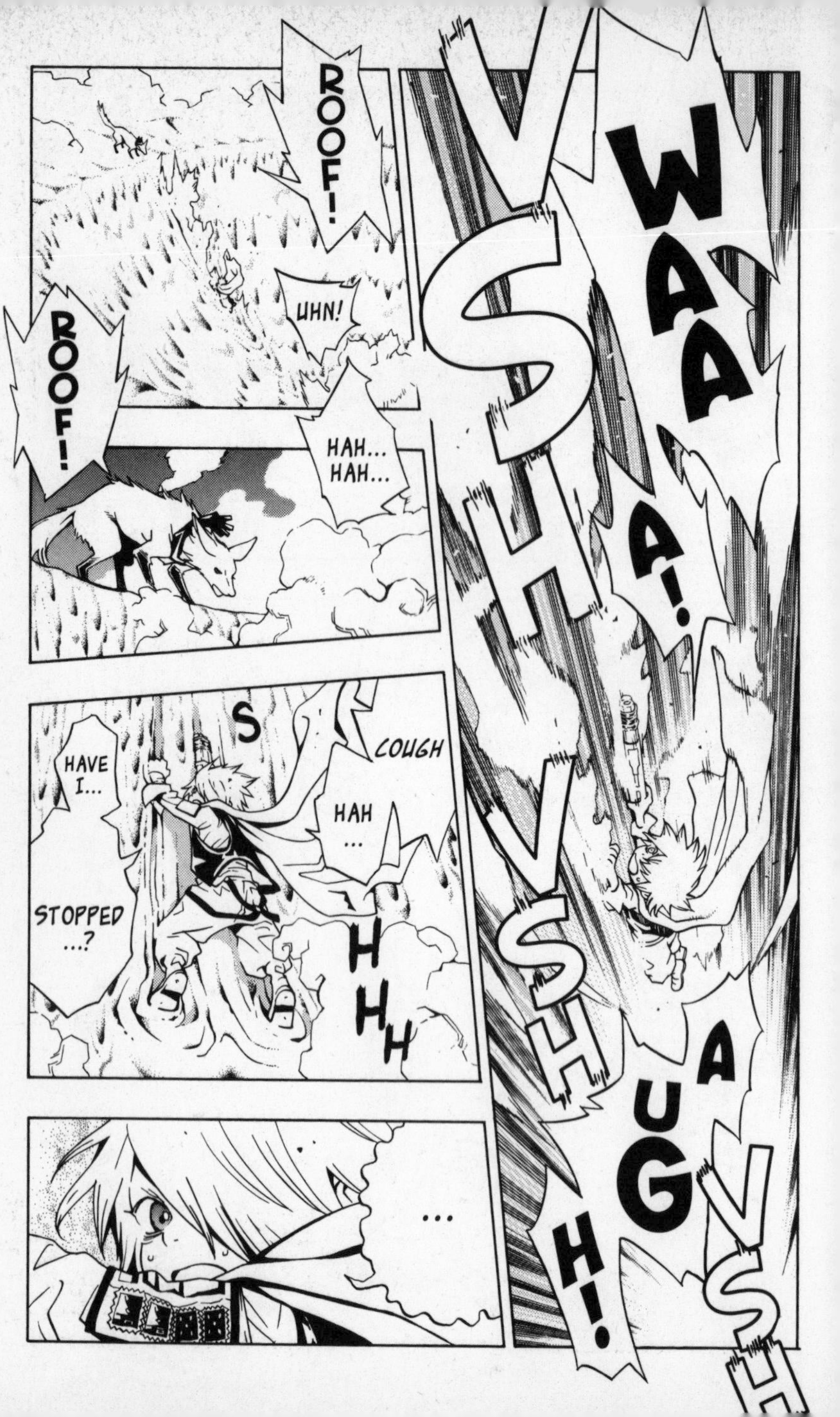
WAAA!
VSHHVSH
AUGH!
VSH
ROOF!
ROOF!
UHN!
HAH... HAH...
S
COUGH
HAH ...
HHH
HAVE I...
STOPPED ...?
...

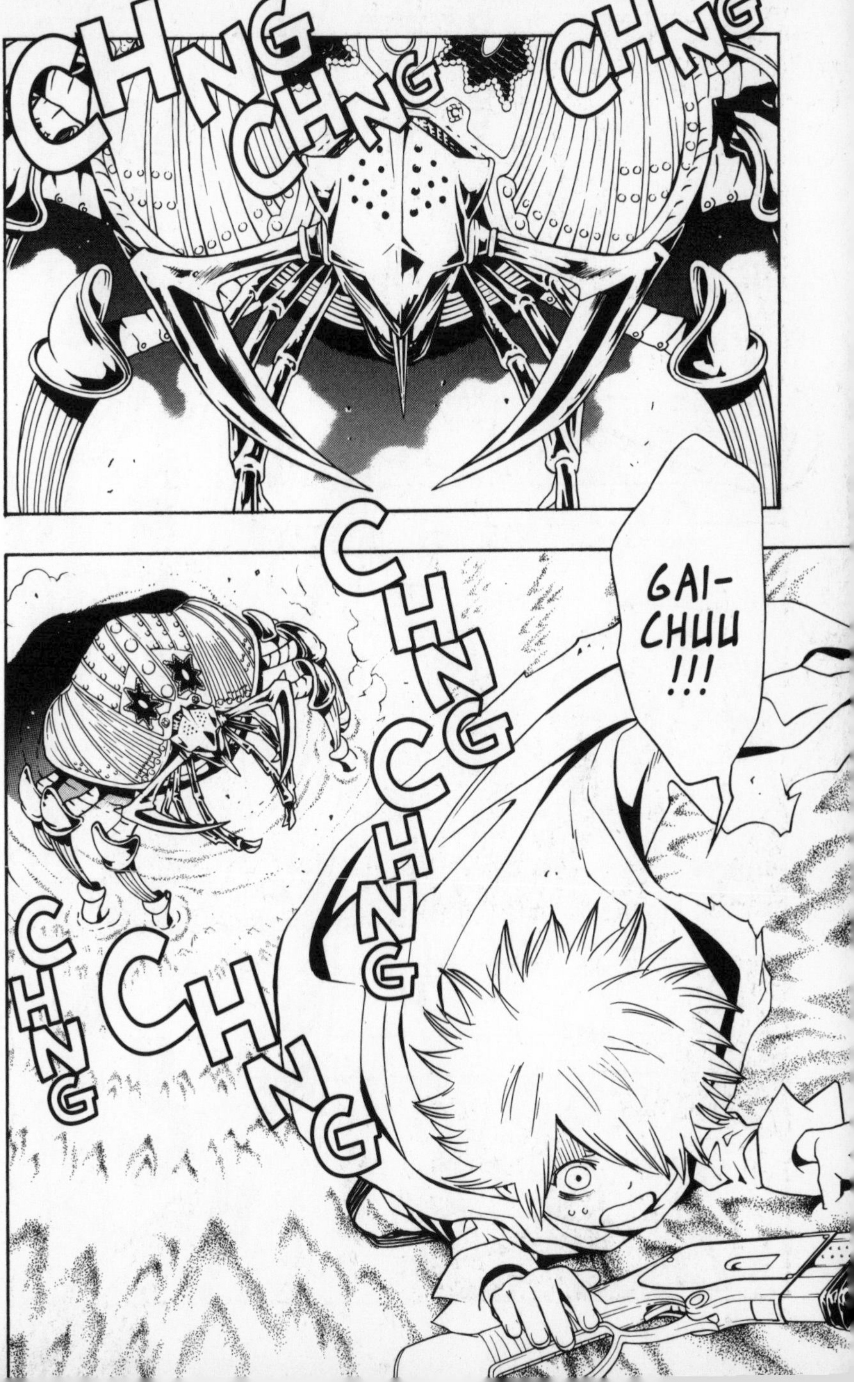
CHNG
CHNG
CHNG
CHNG
GAI-CHUU!!!
CHNG
CHNG
CHNG

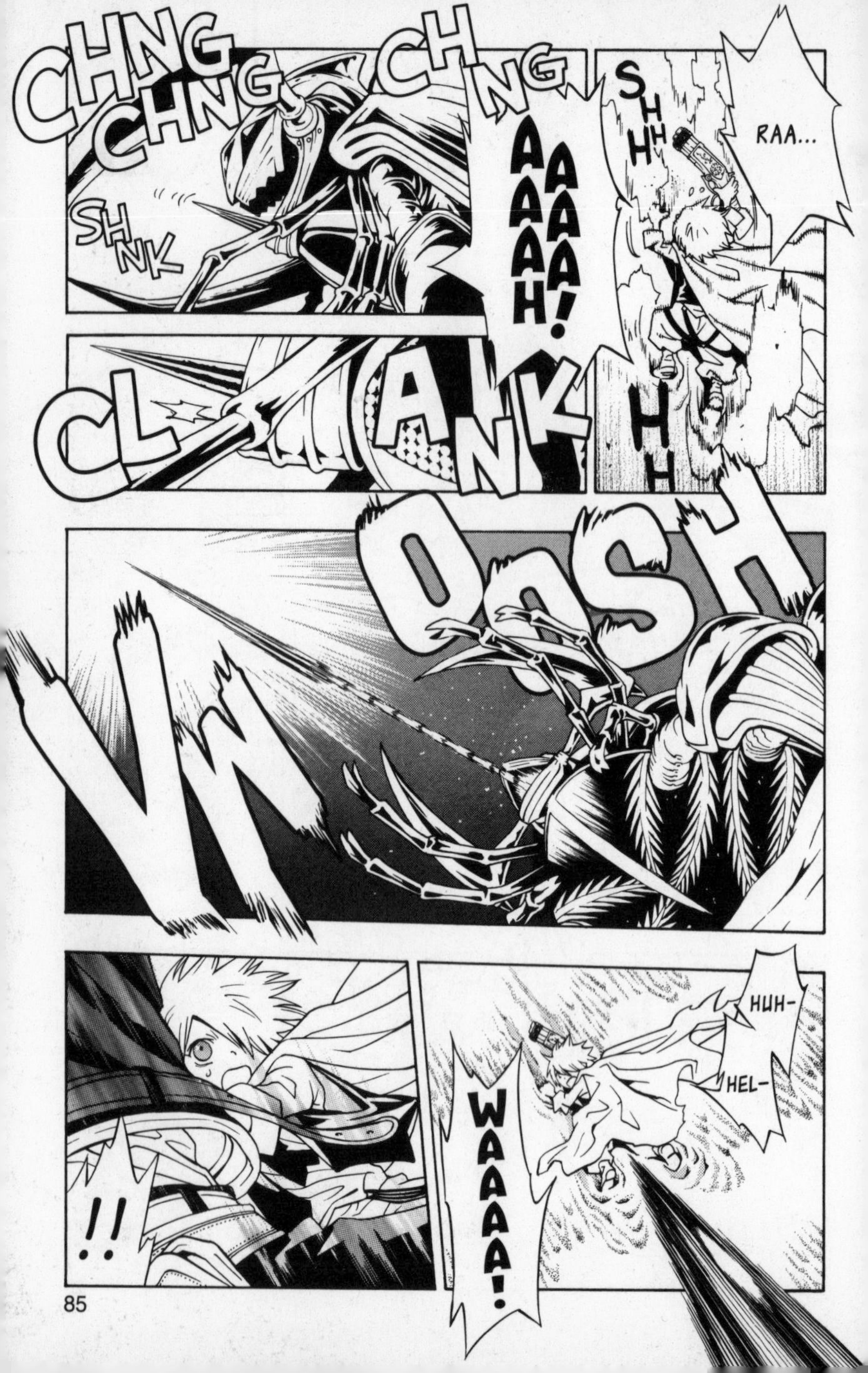
RAA...
SHHHHHH
CHNG CHNG CHNG CHNG
SHNK
AAAAAAAAAH!
CLANK
WOOSH
HUH-
HEL-
WAAAAA!
!!

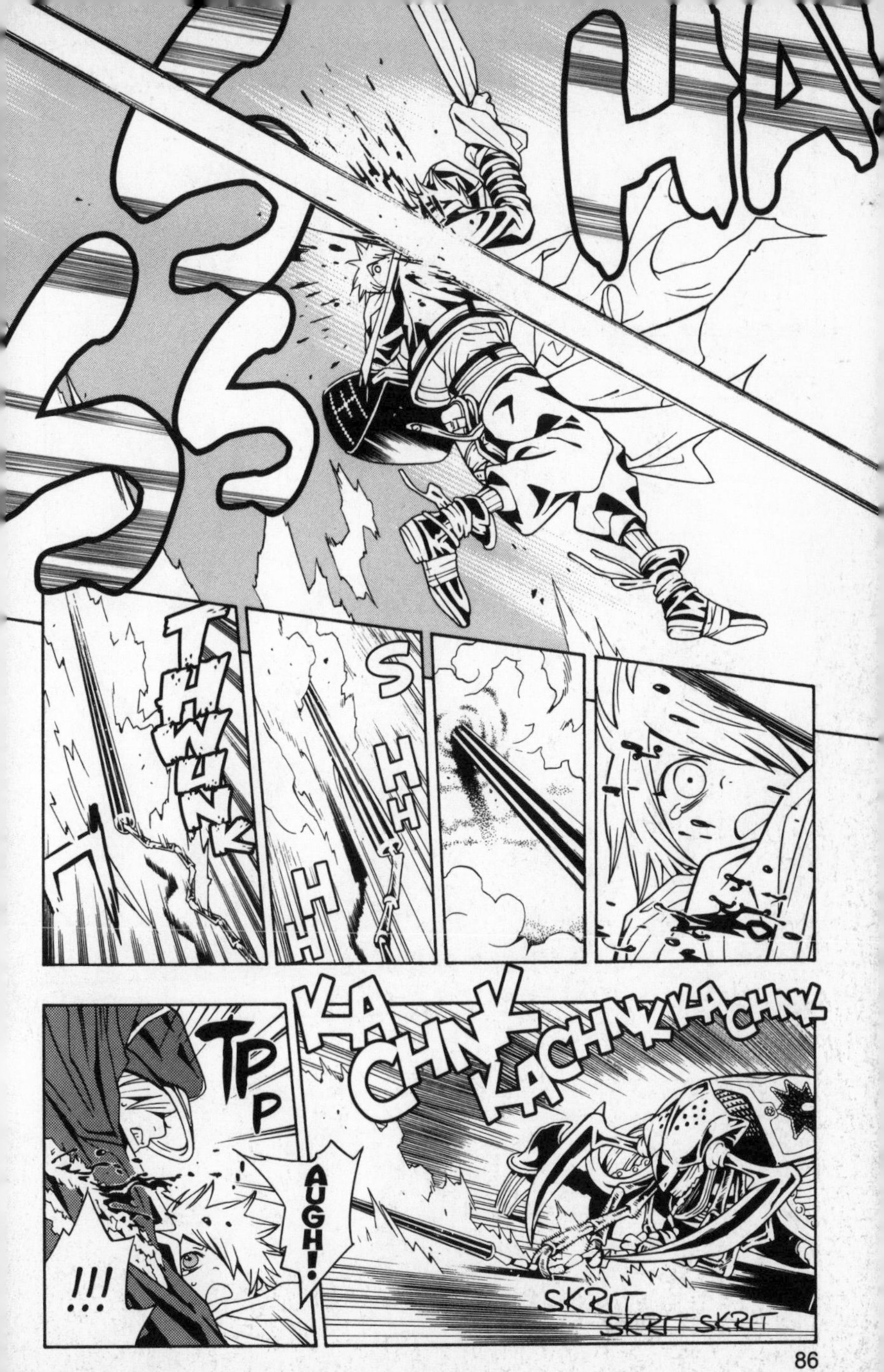
SHHHHHH
THWUNK
KACHNK KACHNK KACHNK
SKRIT SKRIT SKRIT
AUGH!
TPP
!!!

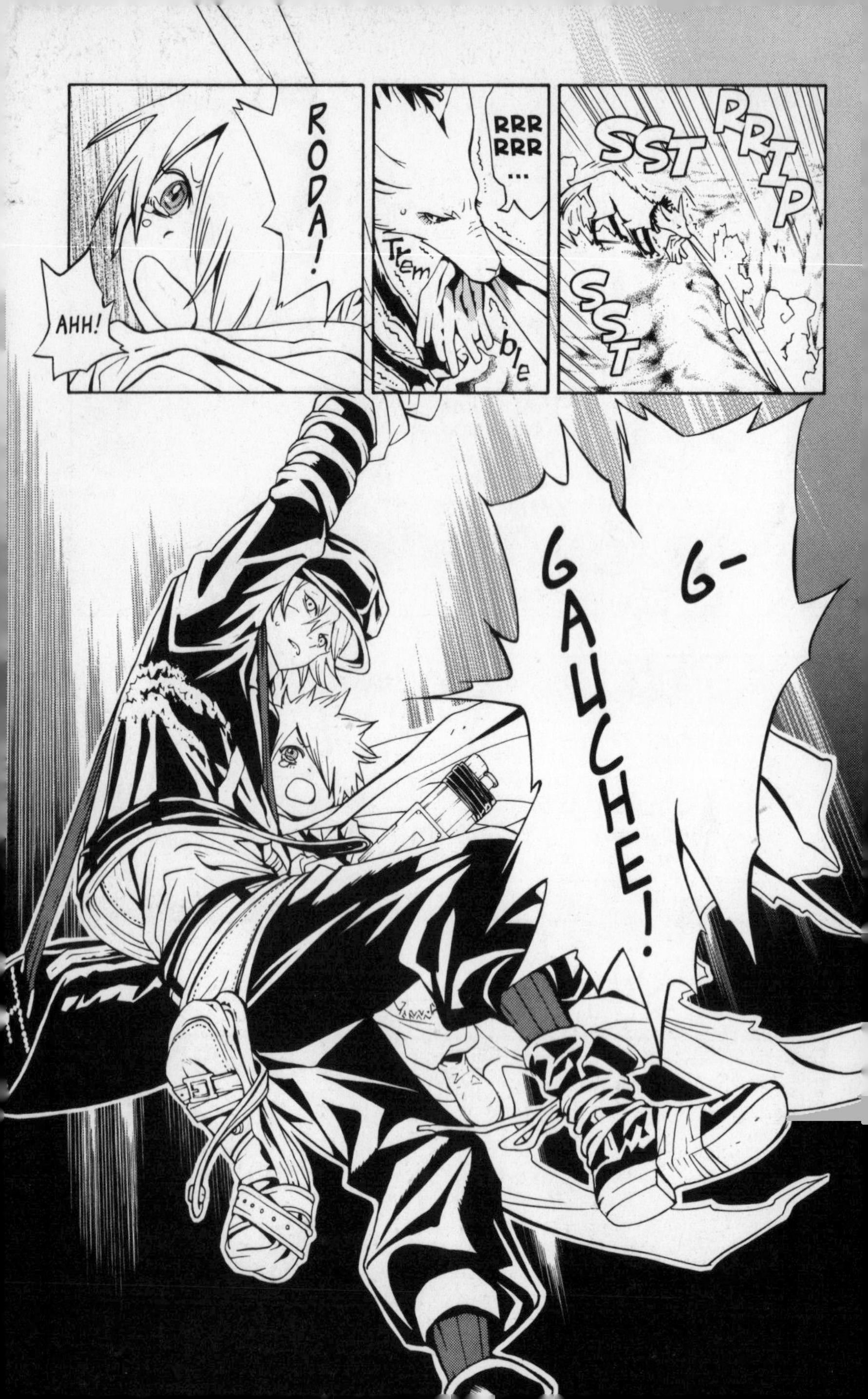
RRIP
SST
SST
RRR RRR ...
Tremble
RODA!
AHH!
G-
GAUCHE!

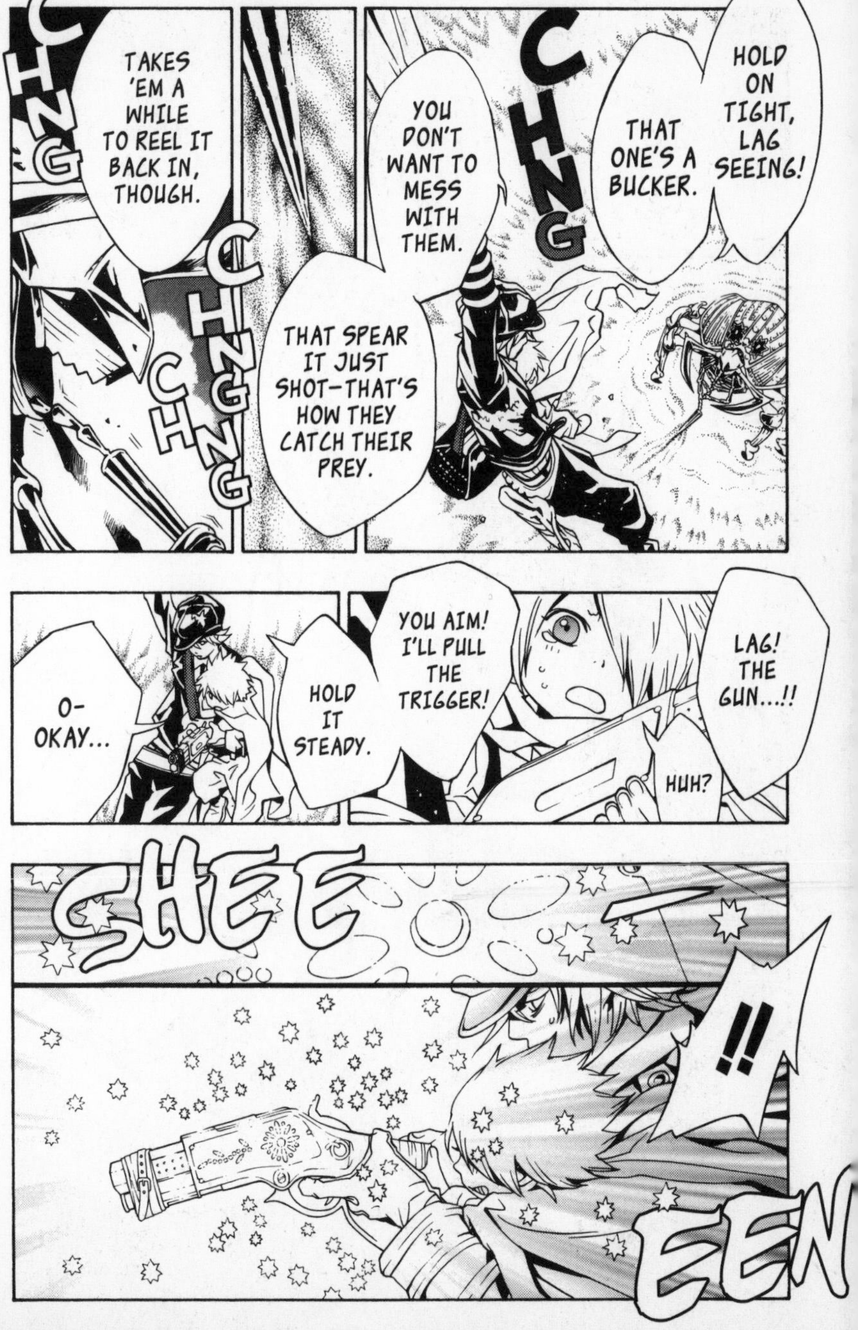
HOLD ON TIGHT, LAG SEEING!
THAT ONE'S A BUCKER.
CHNG
YOU DON'T WANT TO MESS WITH THEM.
THAT SPEAR IT JUST SHOT—THAT'S HOW THEY CATCH THEIR PREY.
CHNG
CHNG
CHNG
TAKES 'EM A WHILE TO REEL IT BACK IN, THOUGH.
CHNG
LAG! THE GUN...!!
HUH?
YOU AIM! I'LL PULL THE TRIGGER!
HOLD IT STEADY.
O-OKAY...
SHEE
EEN
!!

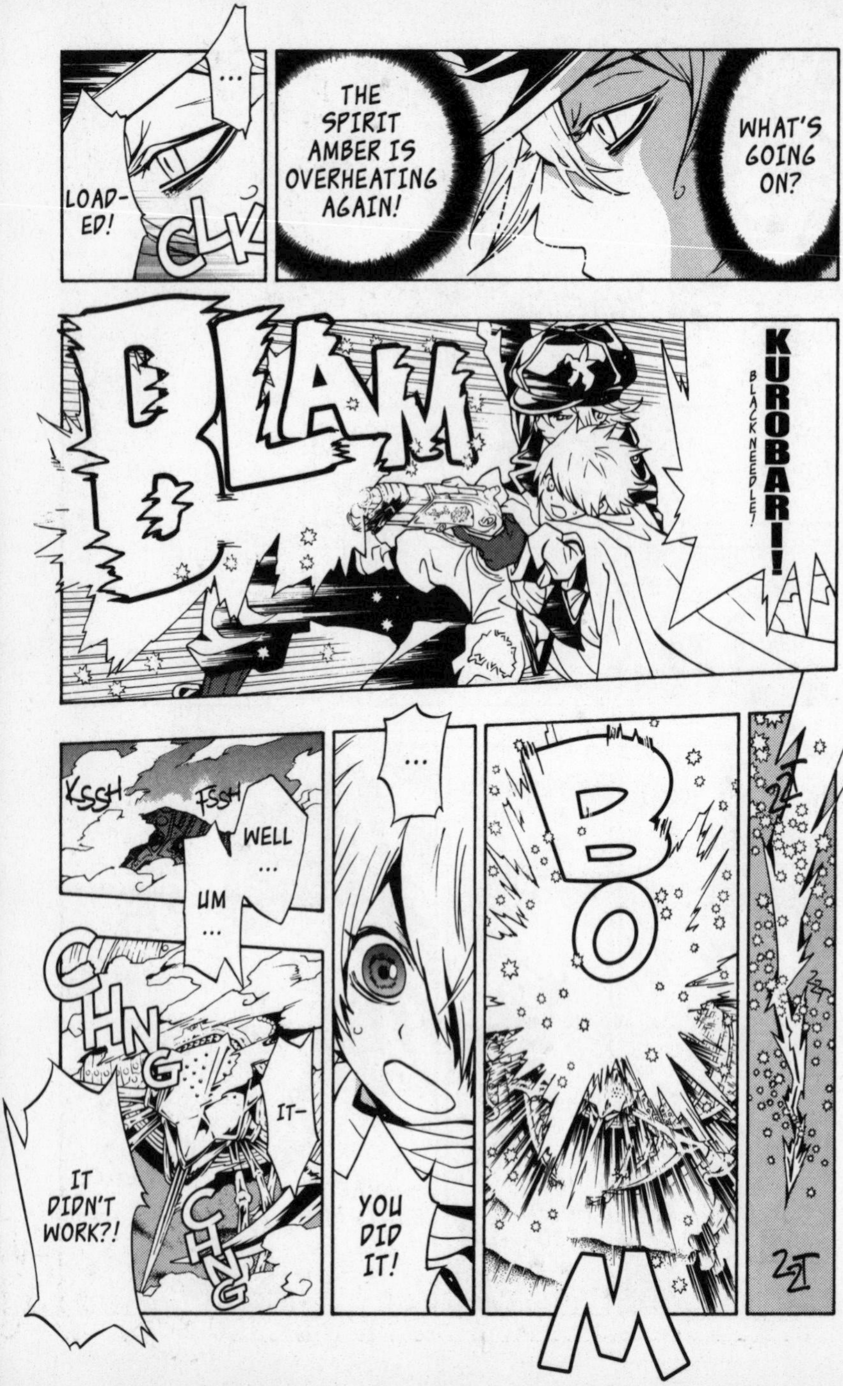

WHAT'S GOING ON?
THE SPIRIT AMBER IS OVERHEATING AGAIN!
...
LOADED!
CLK
KUROBARI!
BLACK NEEDLE!
BLAM
BOOM
...
YOU DID IT!
KSSH
FSSH
WELL ...
UM ...
CHNG
IT–
IT DIDN'T WORK?!
CHNG

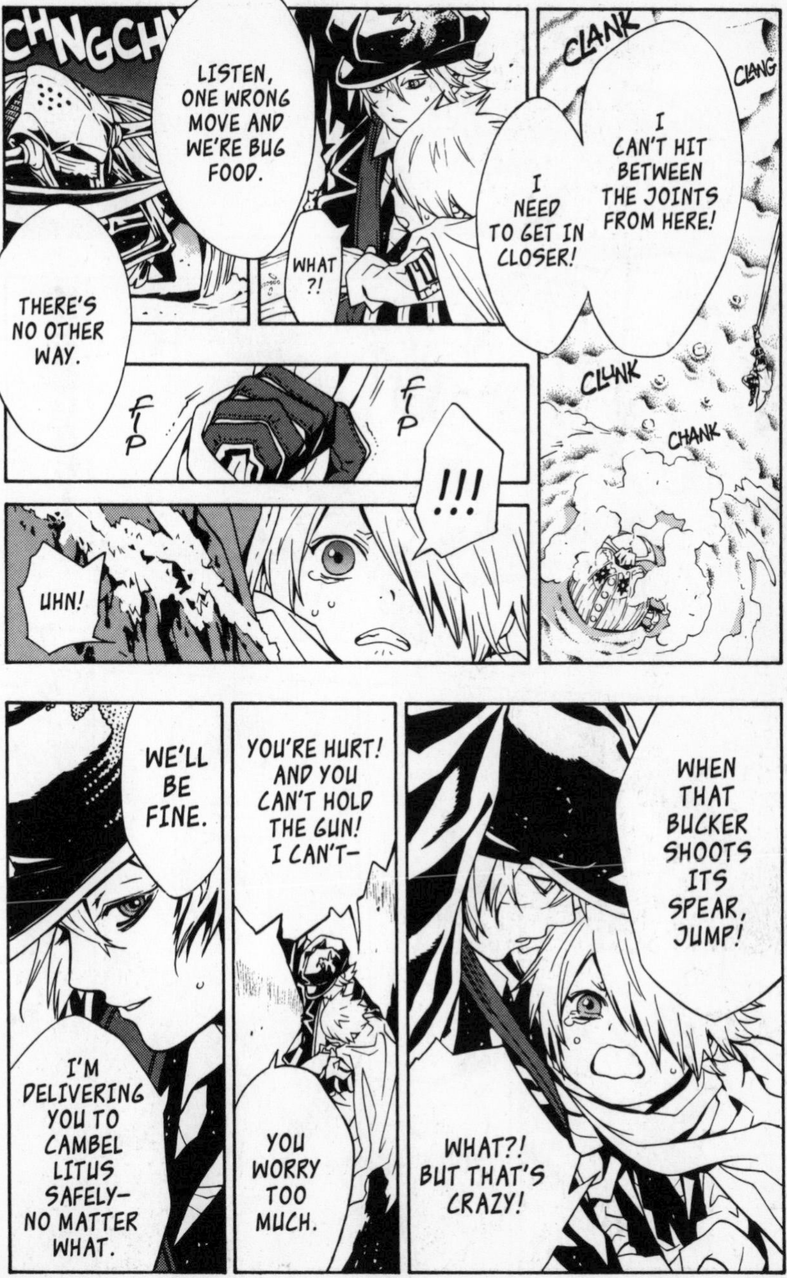
CLANK
CLANG
I CAN'T HIT BETWEEN THE JOINTS FROM HERE!
I NEED TO GET IN CLOSER!
CLUNK
CHANK
LISTEN, ONE WRONG MOVE AND WE'RE BUG FOOD.
WHAT?!
CHNGCH
THERE'S NO OTHER WAY.
FIP
FIP
!!!
UHN!
WHEN THAT BUCKER SHOOTS ITS SPEAR, JUMP!
WHAT?! BUT THAT'S CRAZY!
YOU'RE HURT! AND YOU CAN'T HOLD THE GUN! I CAN'T-
YOU WORRY TOO MUCH.
WE'LL BE FINE.
I'M DELIVERING YOU TO CAMBEL LITUS SAFELY- NO MATTER WHAT.

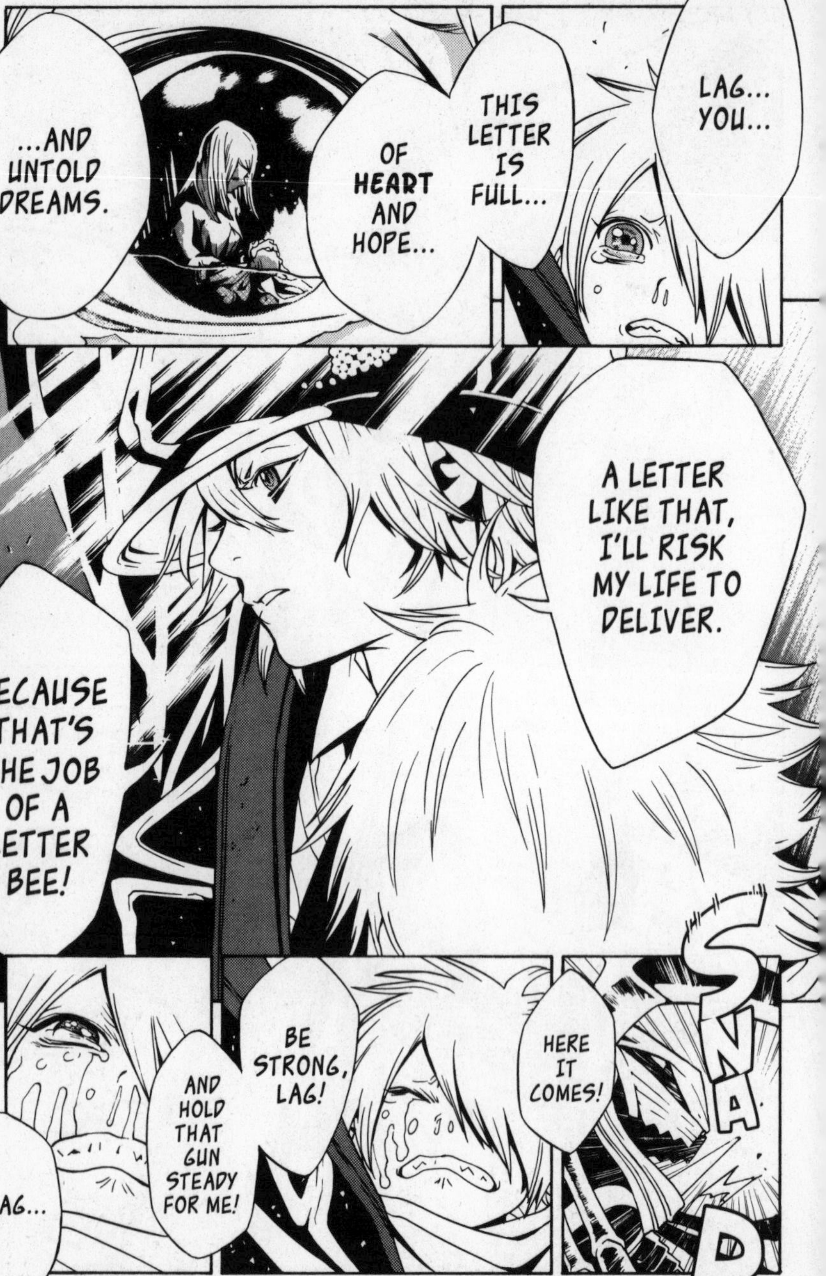
LAG... YOU...
THIS LETTER IS FULL...
OF HEART AND HOPE...
...AND UNTOLD DREAMS.
A LETTER LIKE THAT, I'LL RISK MY LIFE TO DELIVER.
BECAUSE THAT'S THE JOB OF A LETTER BEE!
SNAP
HERE IT COMES!
BE STRONG, LAG!
AND HOLD THAT GUN STEADY FOR ME!
LAG...

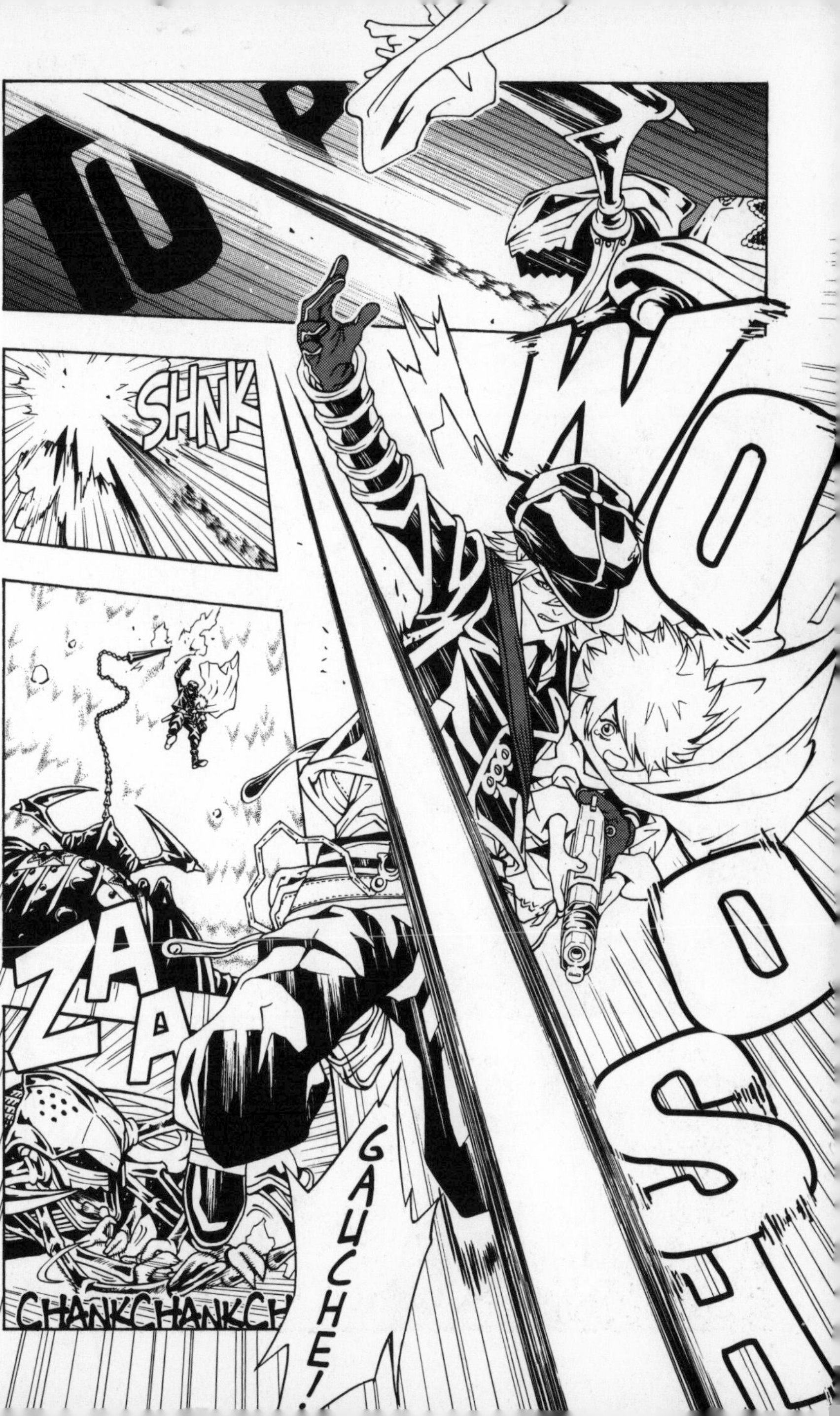
TUP
WOOSH
SHNK
ZAAP
GAUCHE!
CHANKCHANKCH

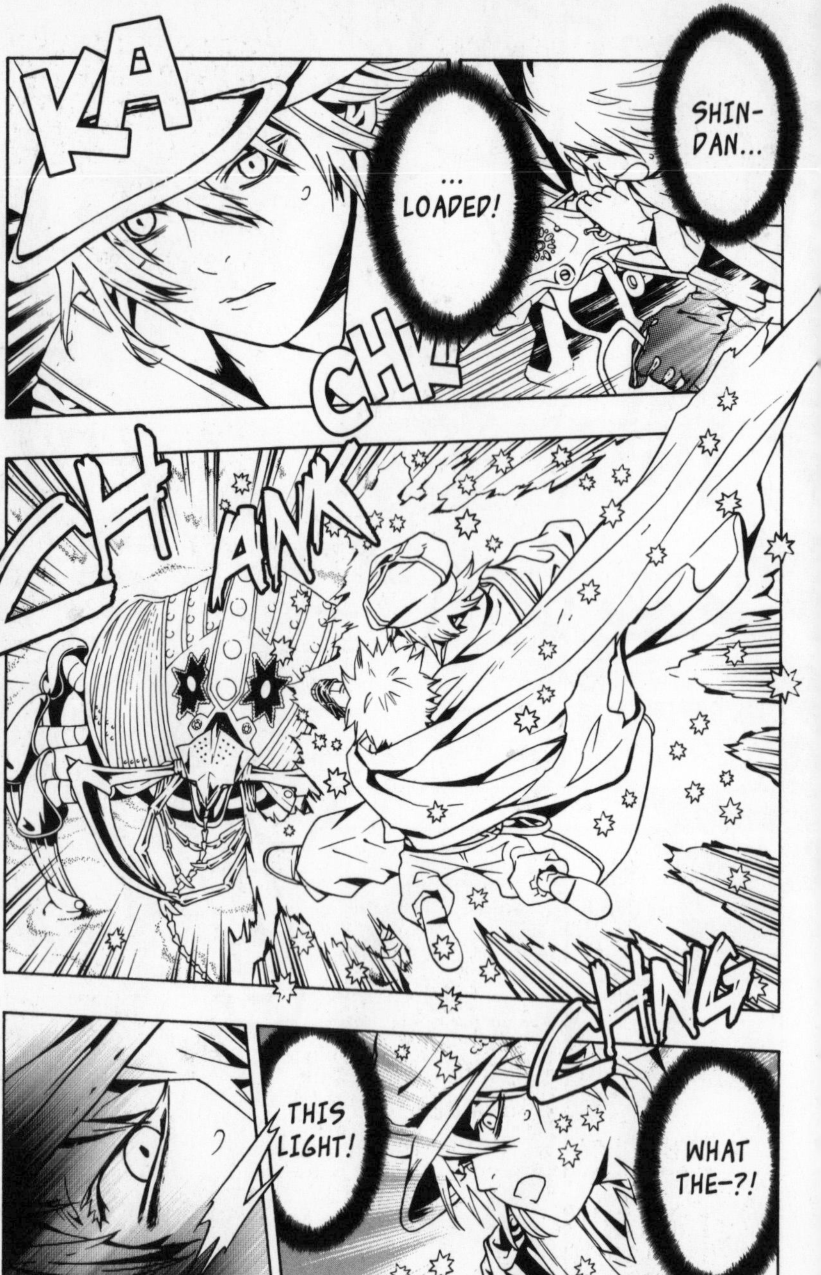
SHIN-DAN...
...LOADED!
KA
CHK
CHANK
CHING
WHAT THE-?!
THIS LIGHT!

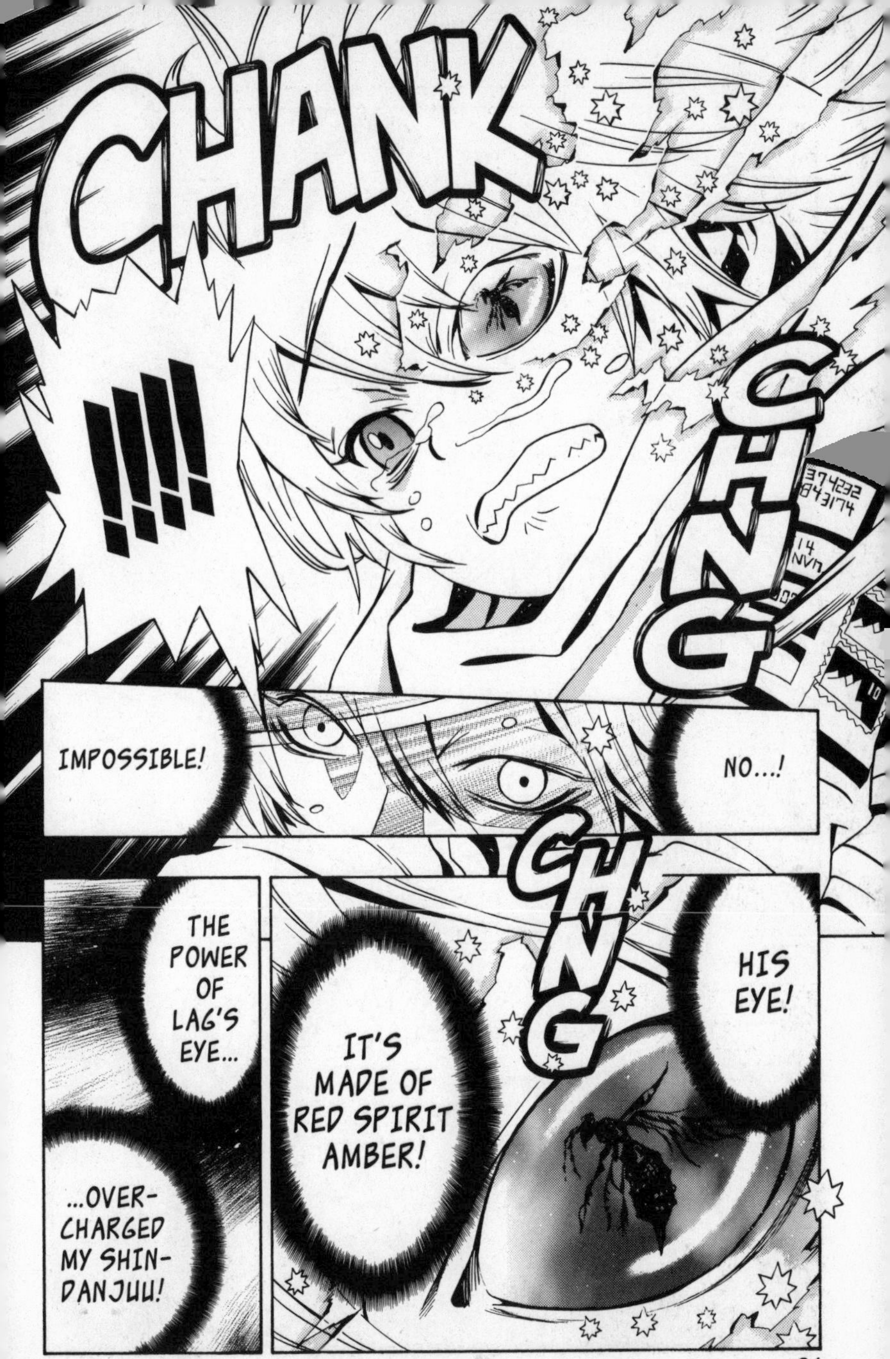
CHANK
CHNG
!!!!
NO...!
IMPOSSIBLE!
CHNG
HIS EYE!
IT'S MADE OF RED SPIRIT AMBER!
THE POWER OF LAG'S EYE...
...OVER-CHARGED MY SHIN-DANJUU!

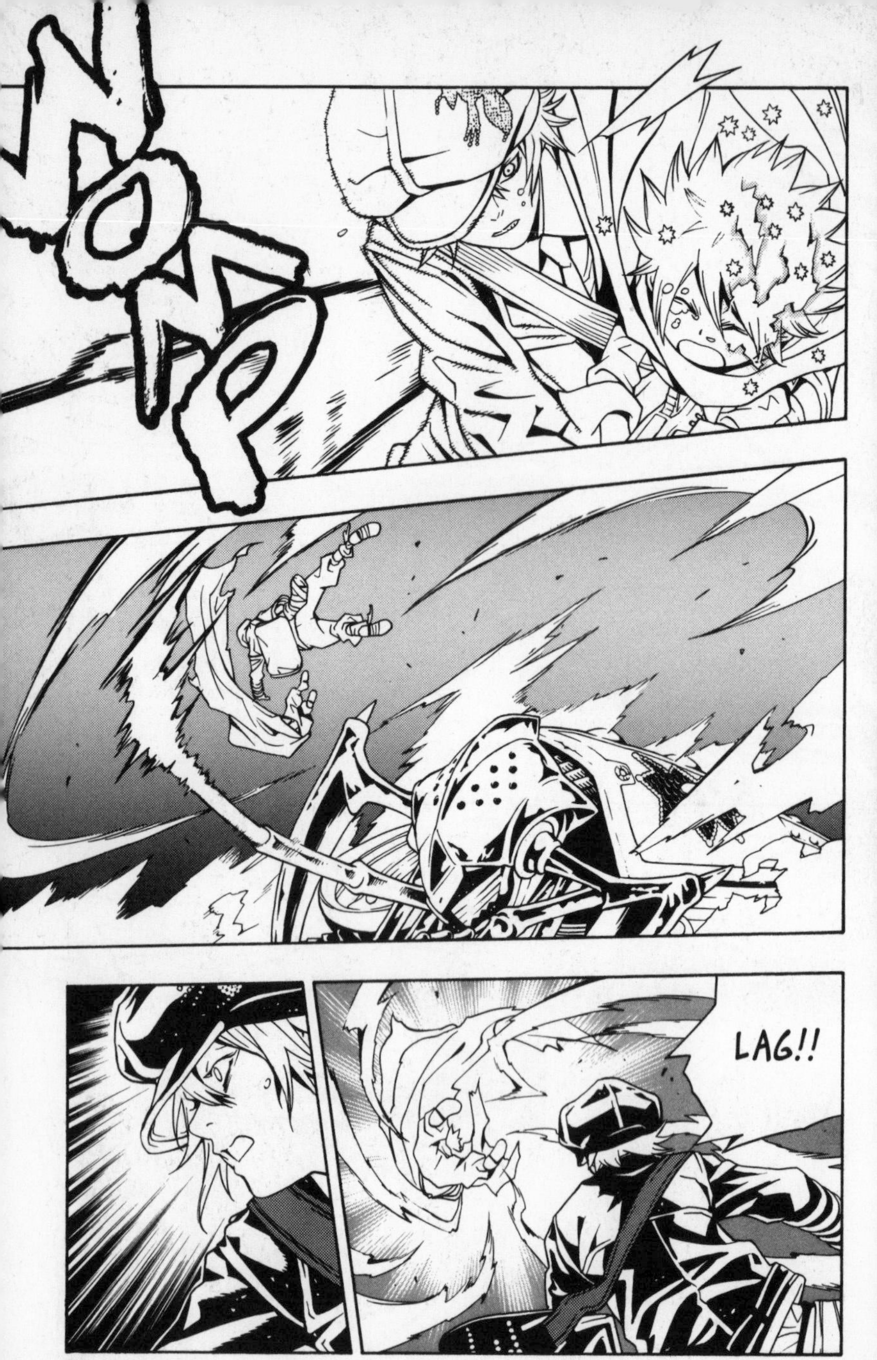
ZOMP
LAG!!

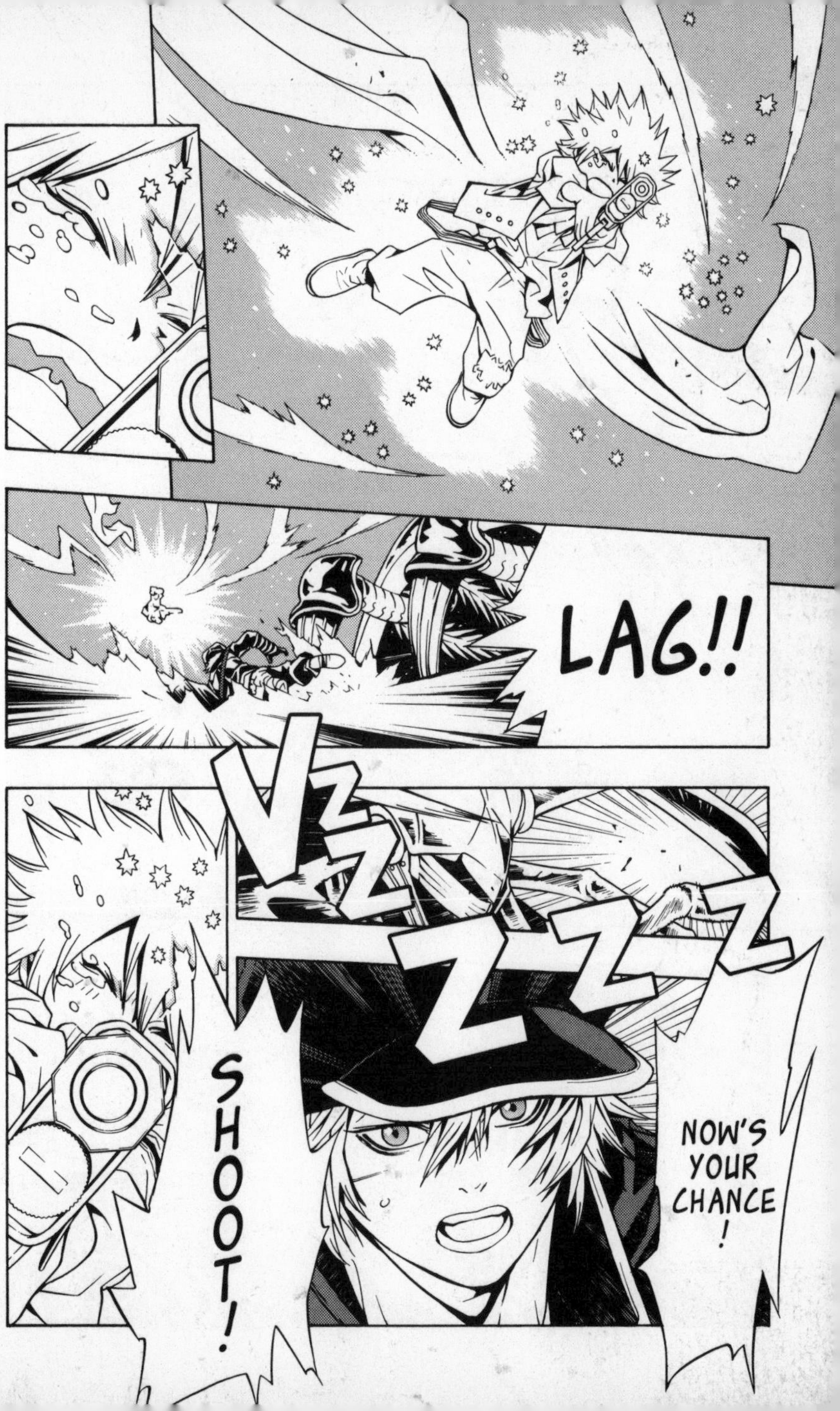
LAG!!
VZZZZZZ
NOW'S YOUR CHANCE!
SHOOT!

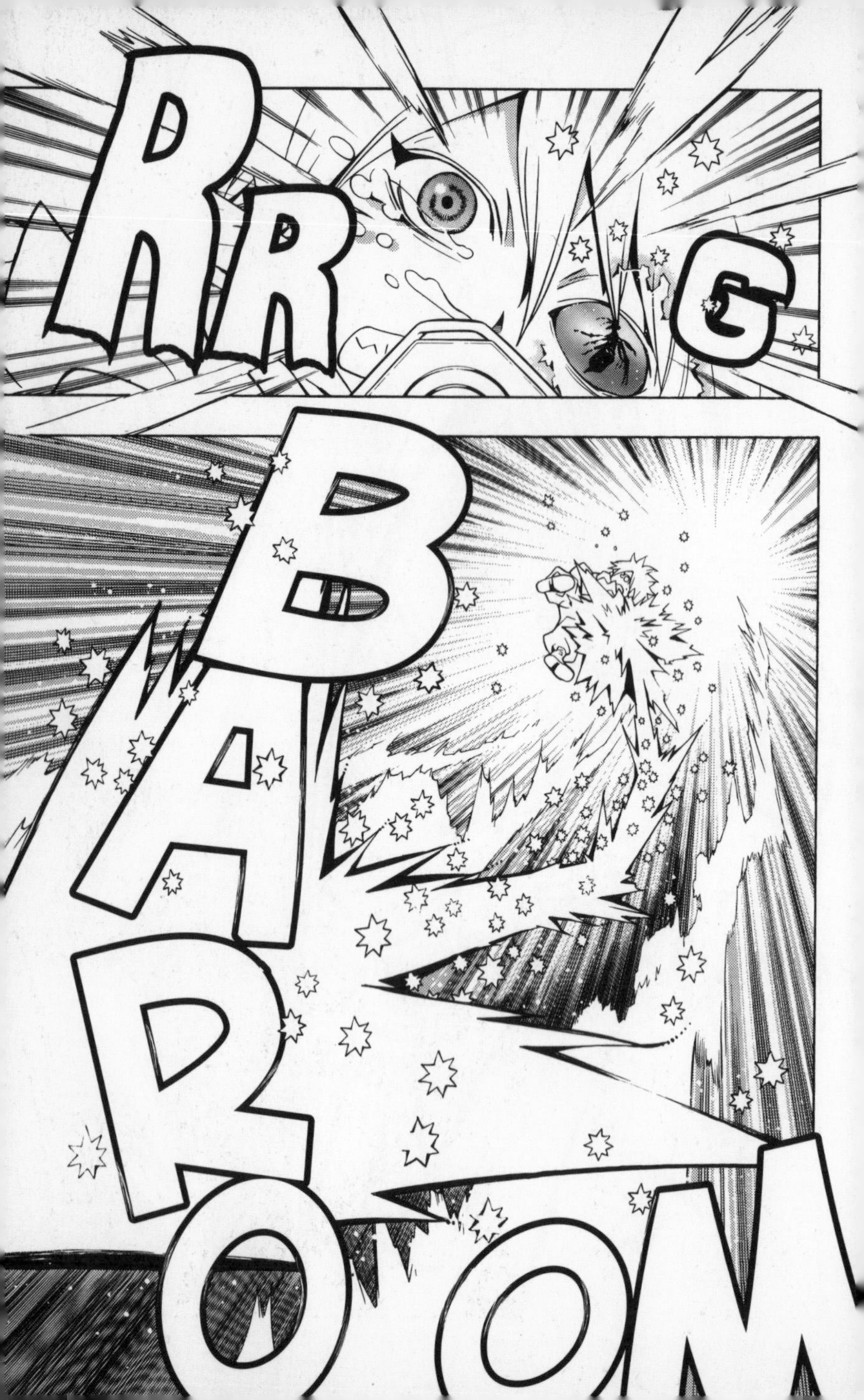
RRG
BAROOM

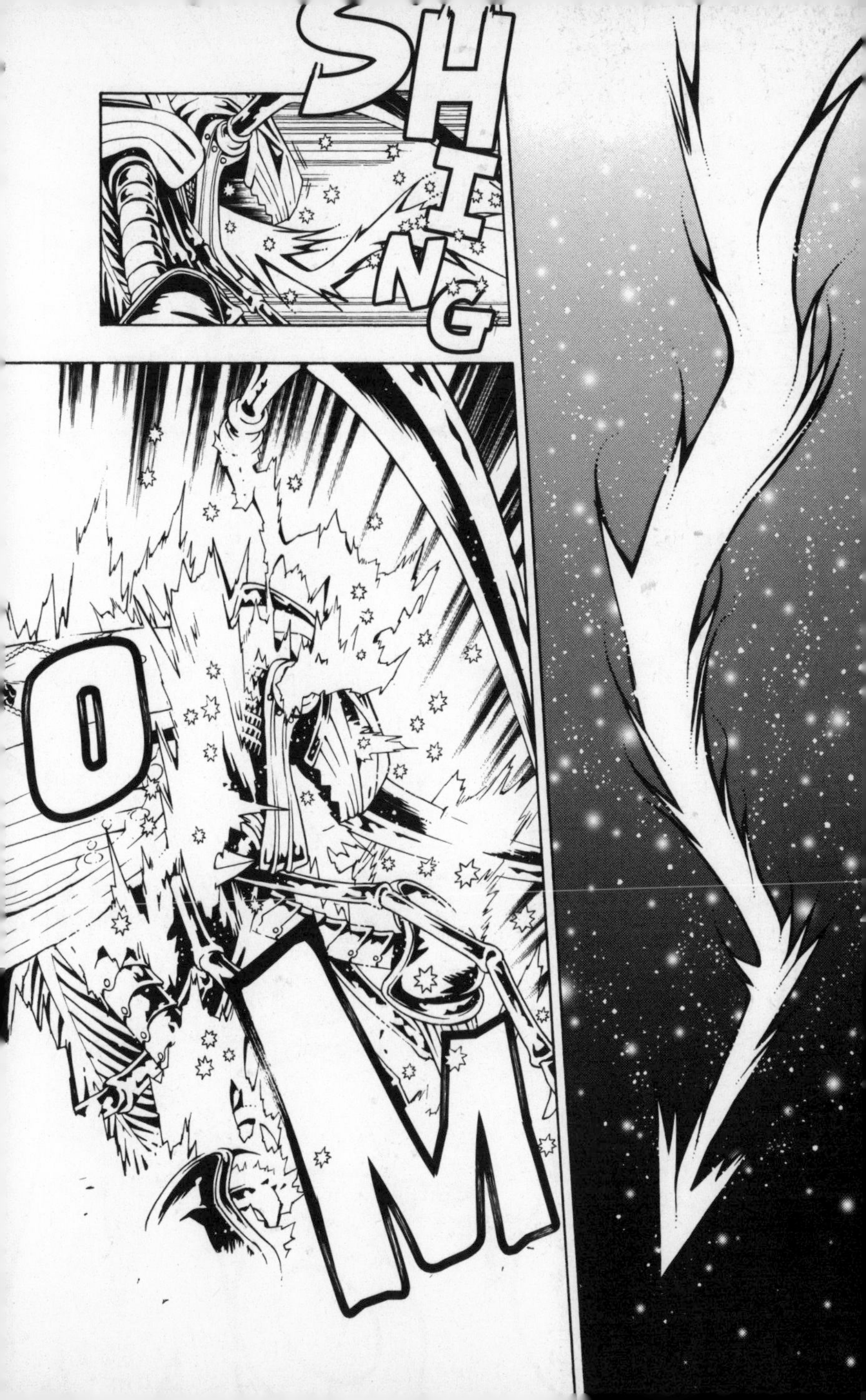
SHING
OOM

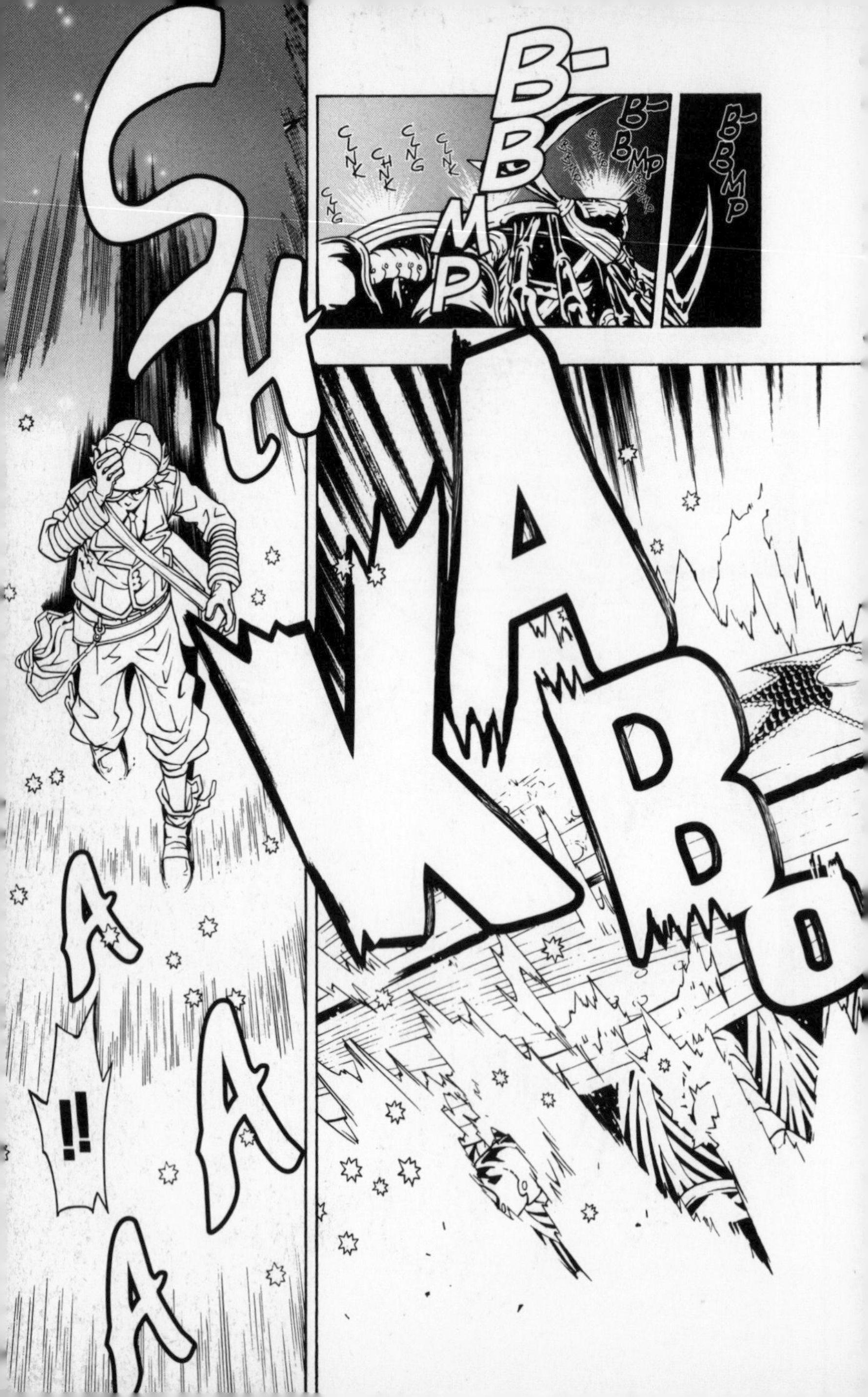
B-B-BMP
B-BMP
CLNK
CLNG
CHNK
CLNG
B-BMP
SH
WAB
AAA
!!

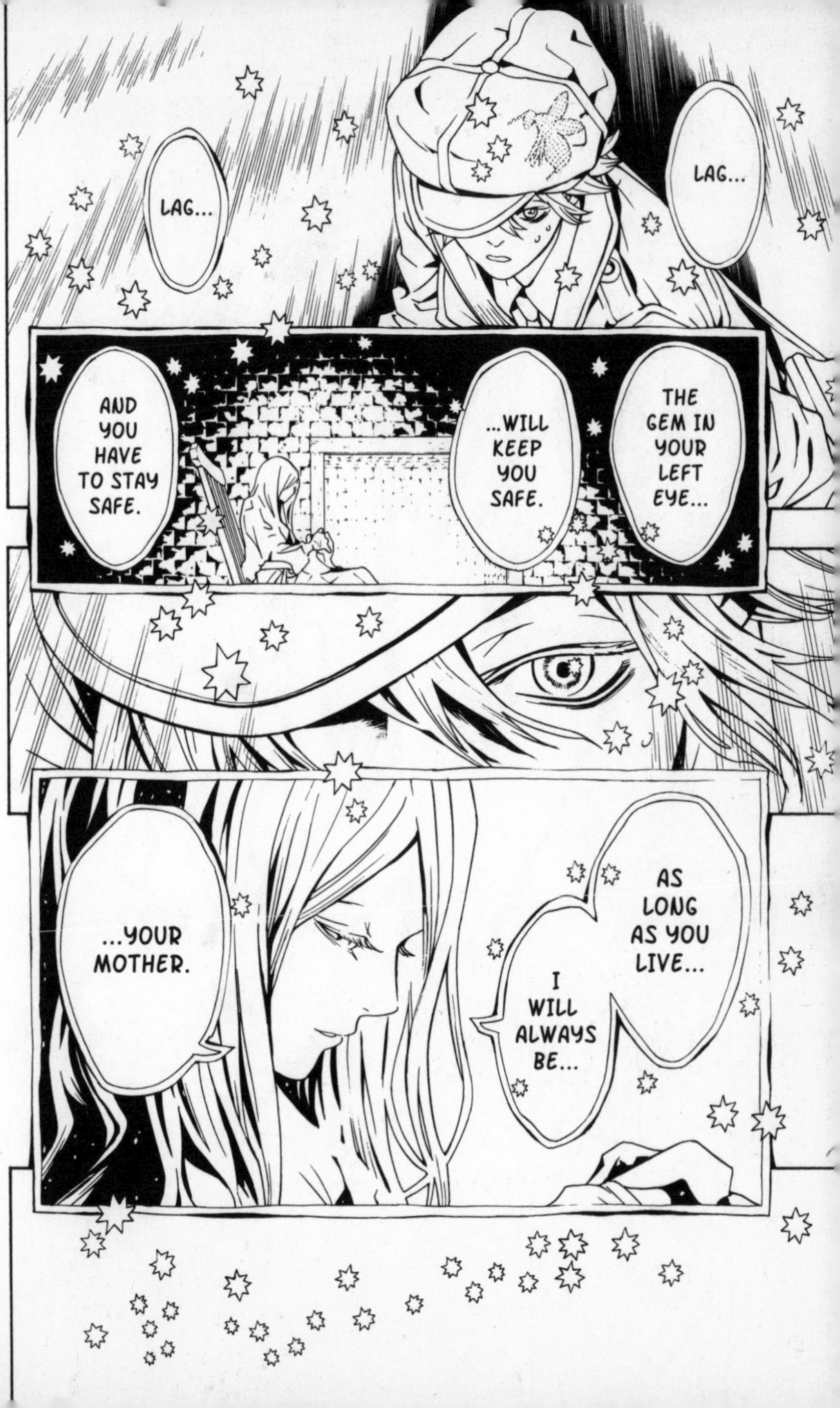
LAG...
LAG...
THE GEM IN YOUR LEFT EYE...
...WILL KEEP YOU SAFE.
AND YOU HAVE TO STAY SAFE.
AS LONG AS YOU LIVE...
I WILL ALWAYS BE...
...YOUR MOTHER.

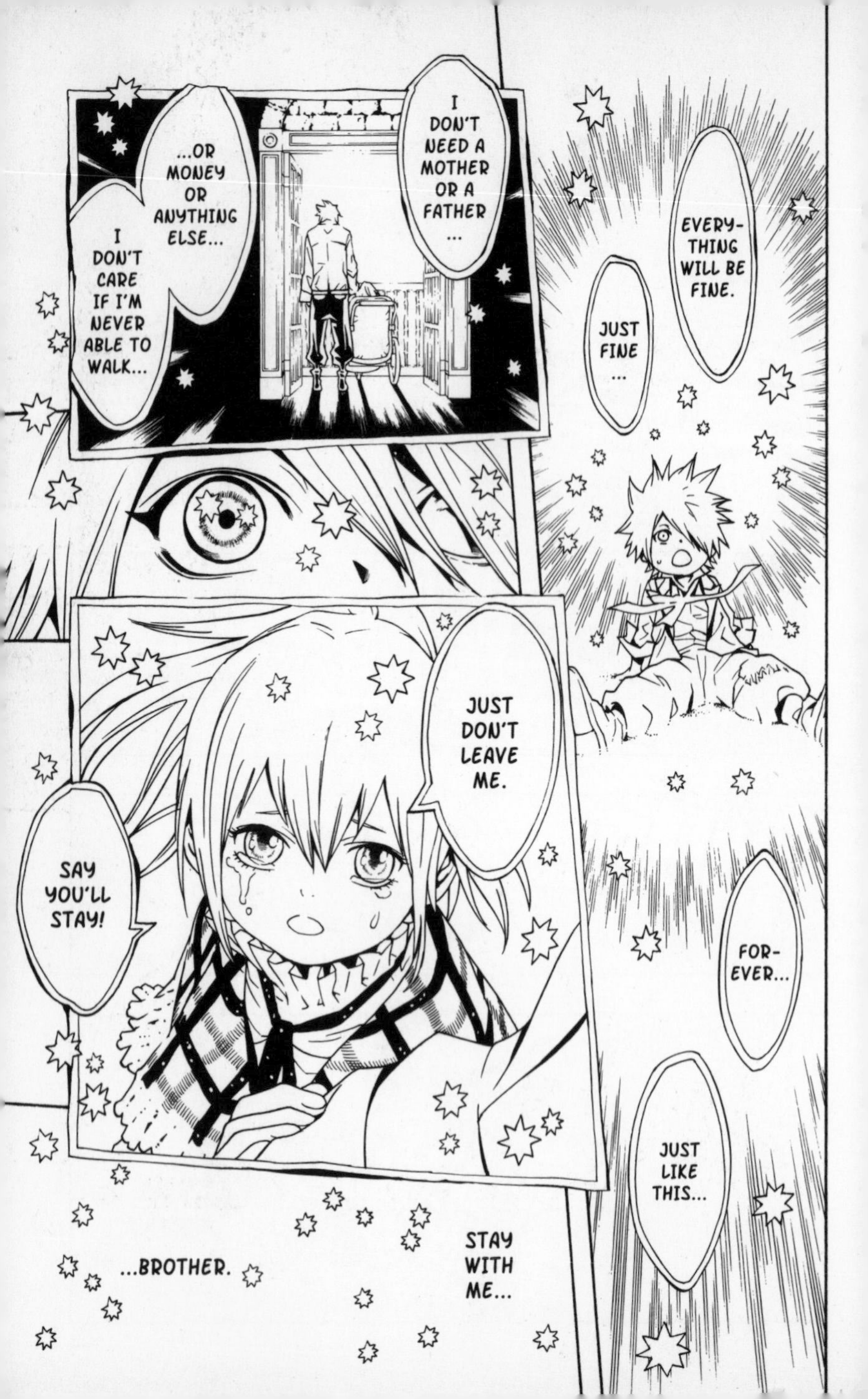
EVERY-THING WILL BE FINE.
JUST FINE ...
I DON'T NEED A MOTHER OR A FATHER ...
...OR MONEY OR ANYTHING ELSE...
I DON'T CARE IF I'M NEVER ABLE TO WALK...
JUST DON'T LEAVE ME.
SAY YOU'LL STAY!
FOR-EVER...
JUST LIKE THIS...
STAY WITH ME...
...BROTHER.

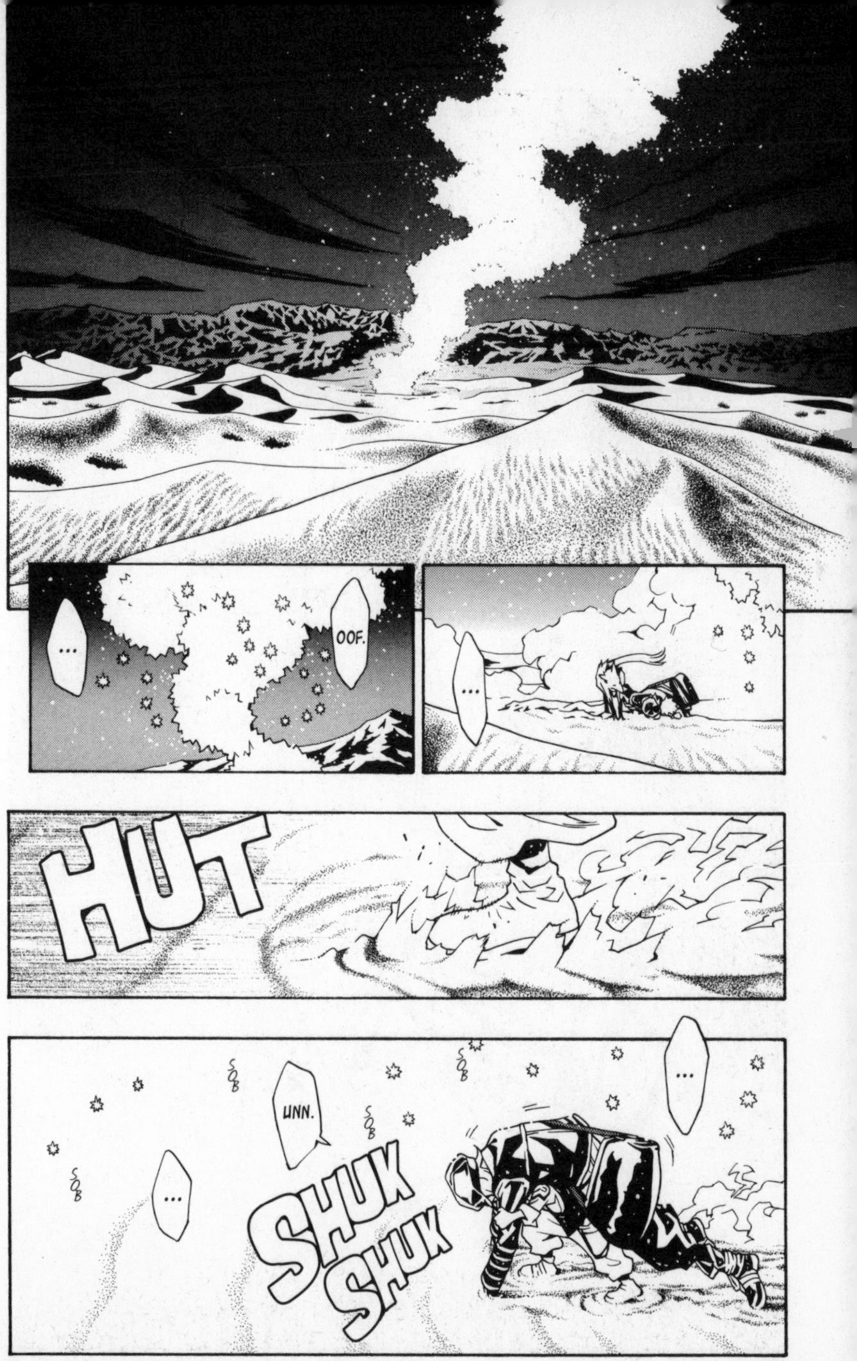
...
OOF.
...
HUT
...
SOB
UNN.
SOB
SHUK SHUK
...
SOB

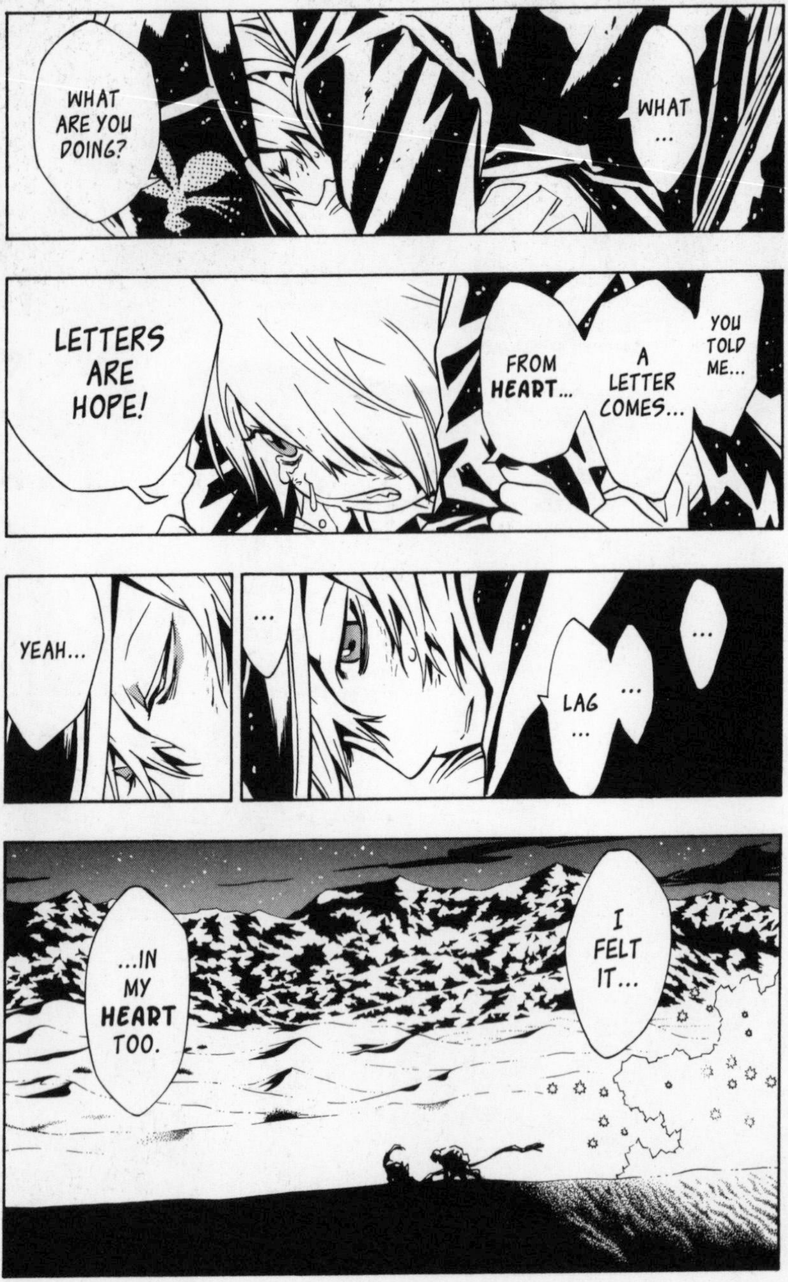
WHAT ...
WHAT ARE YOU DOING?
YOU TOLD ME...
A LETTER COMES...
FROM HEART...
LETTERS ARE HOPE!
...
...
LAG ...
...
YEAH...
I FELT IT...
...IN MY HEART TOO.

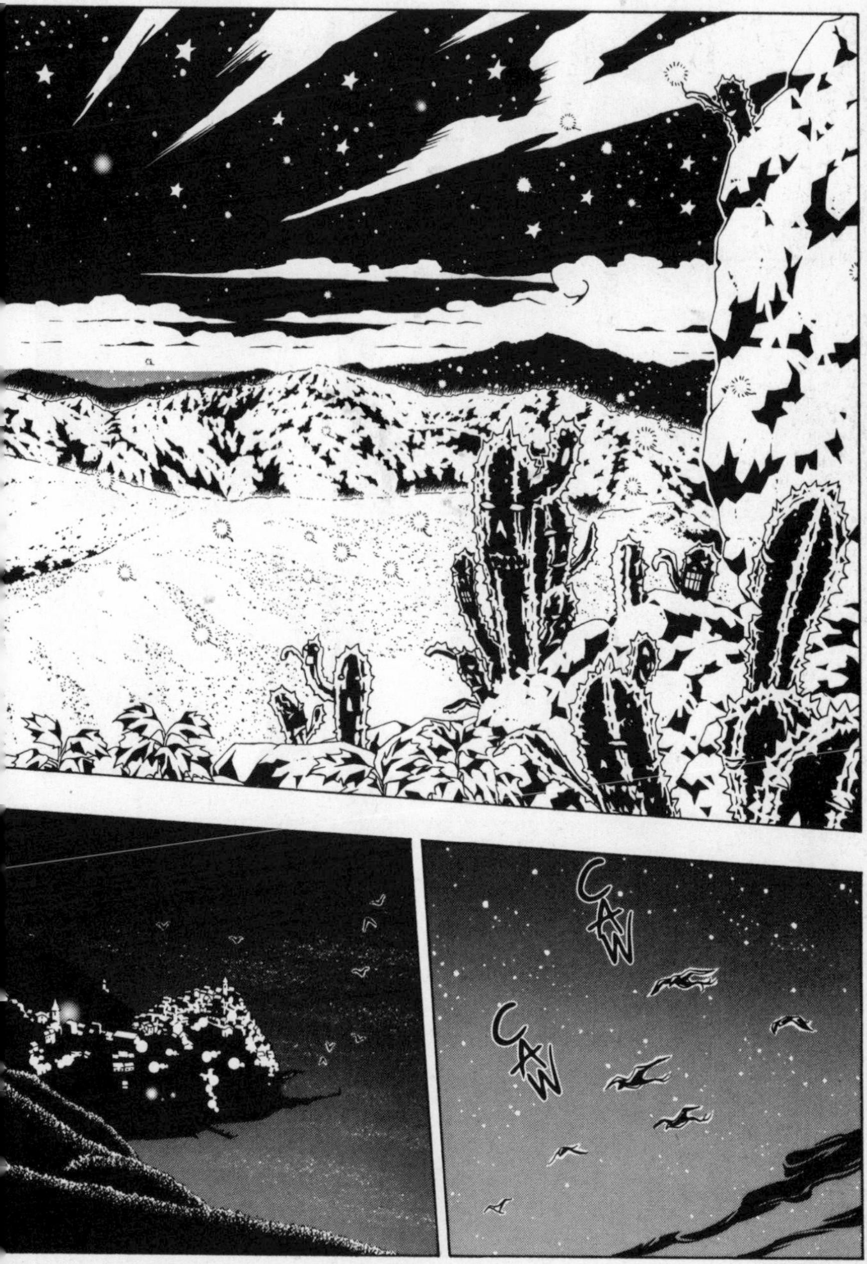
CAW
CAW

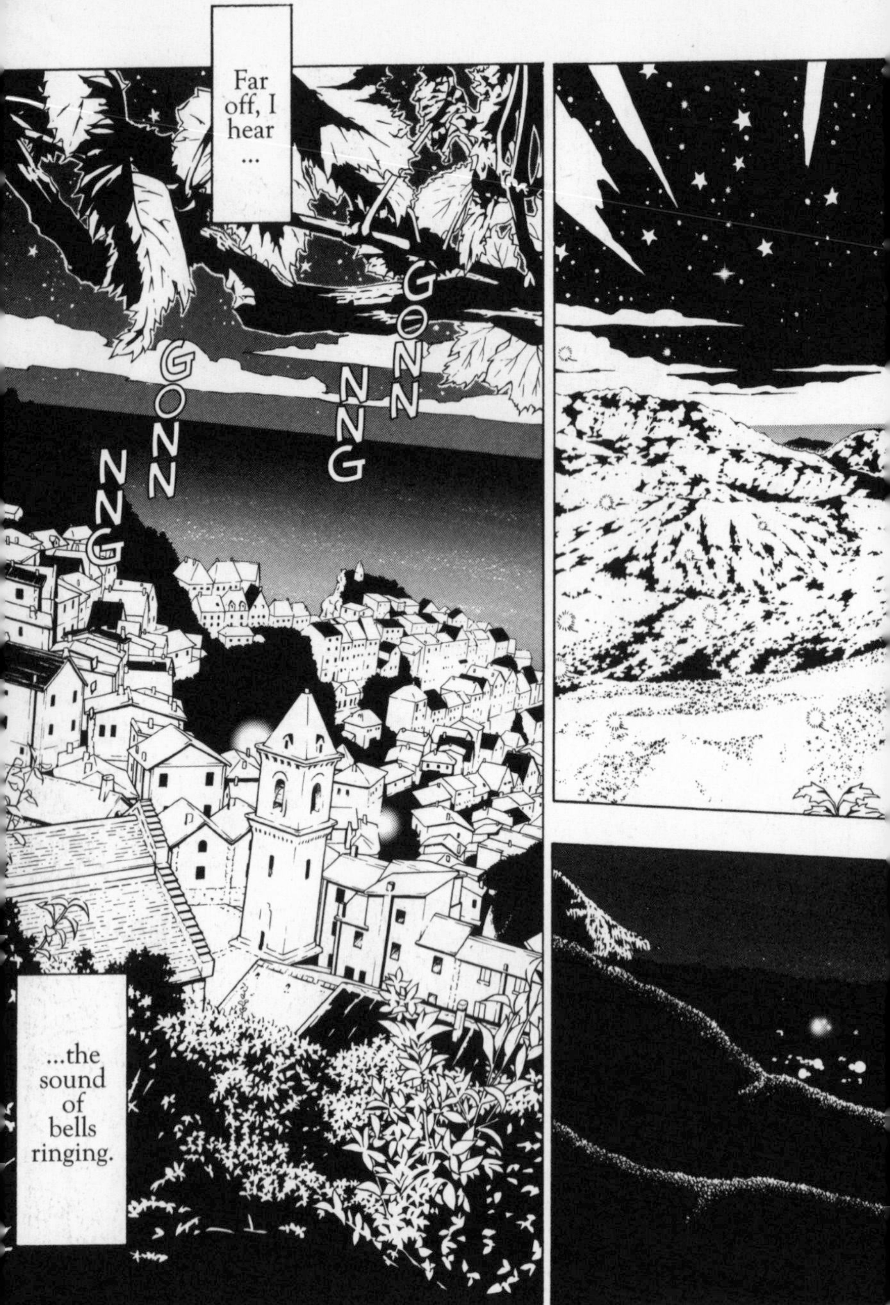
Far off, I hear ...
GONNNG
GONNNG
...the sound of bells ringing.

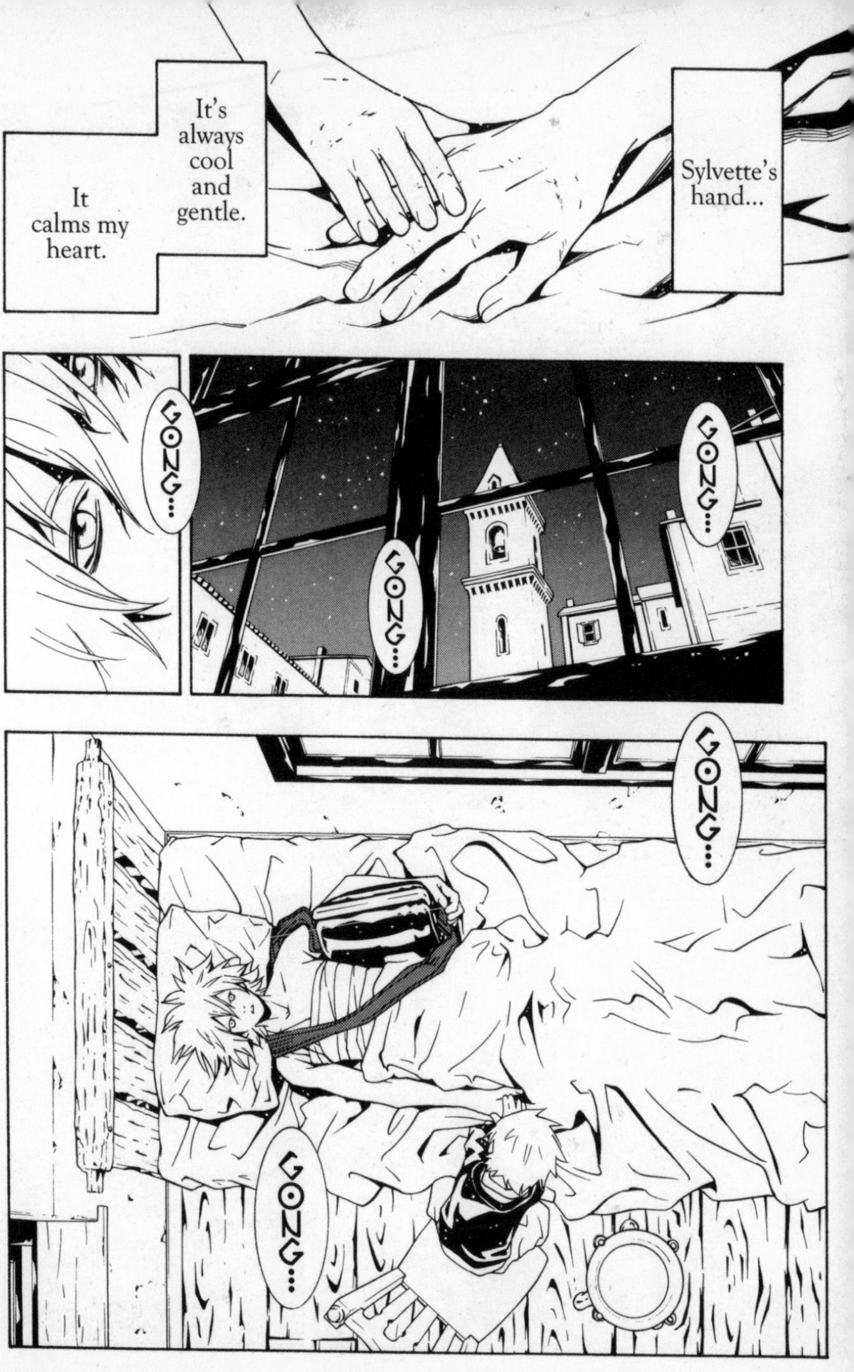
Sylvette's hand...
It's always cool and gentle.
It calms my heart.
GONG...
GONG...
GONG...
GONG...
GONG...

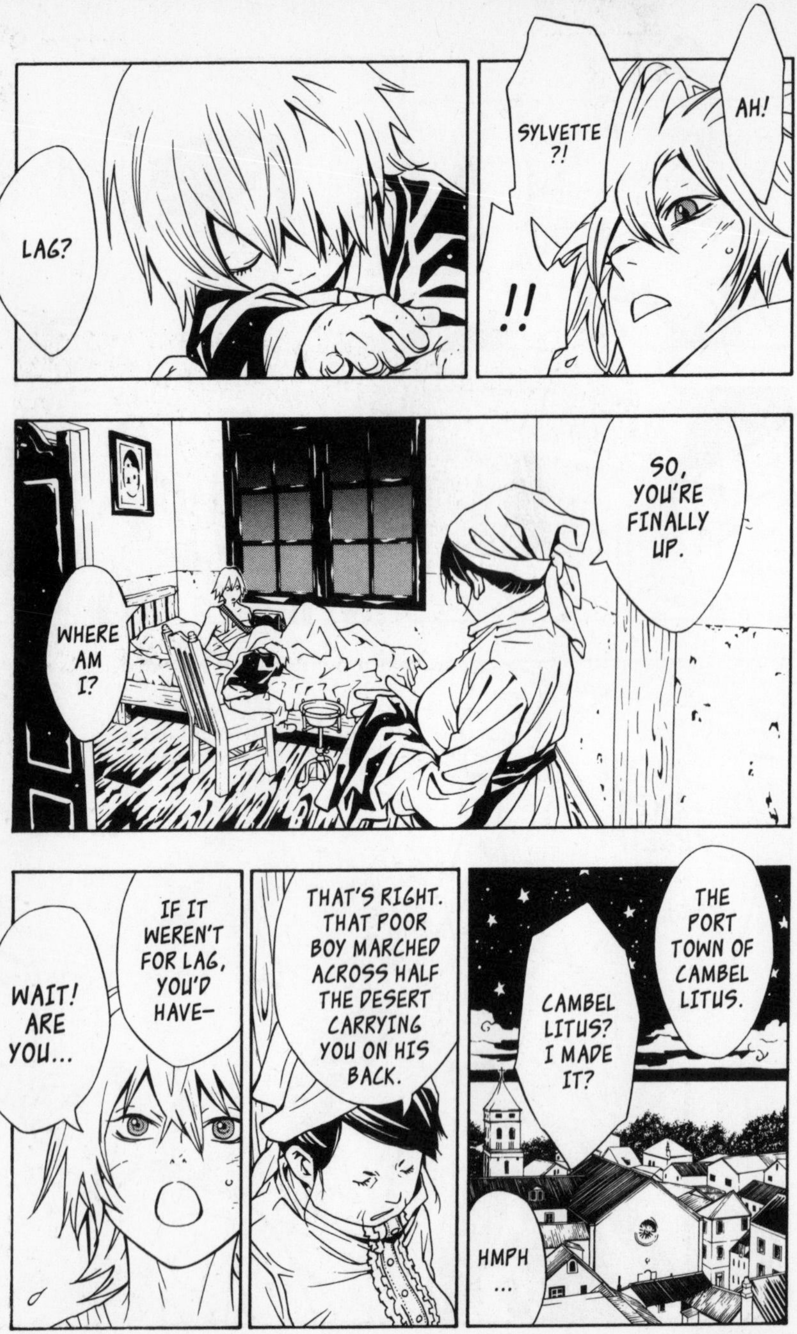
AH!
SYLVETTE ?!
!!
LAG?
SO, YOU'RE FINALLY UP.
WHERE AM I?
THE PORT TOWN OF CAMBEL LITUS.
CAMBEL LITUS? I MADE IT?
HMPH ...
THAT'S RIGHT. THAT POOR BOY MARCHED ACROSS HALF THE DESERT CARRYING YOU ON HIS BACK.
IF IT WEREN'T FOR LAG, YOU'D HAVE—
WAIT! ARE YOU...

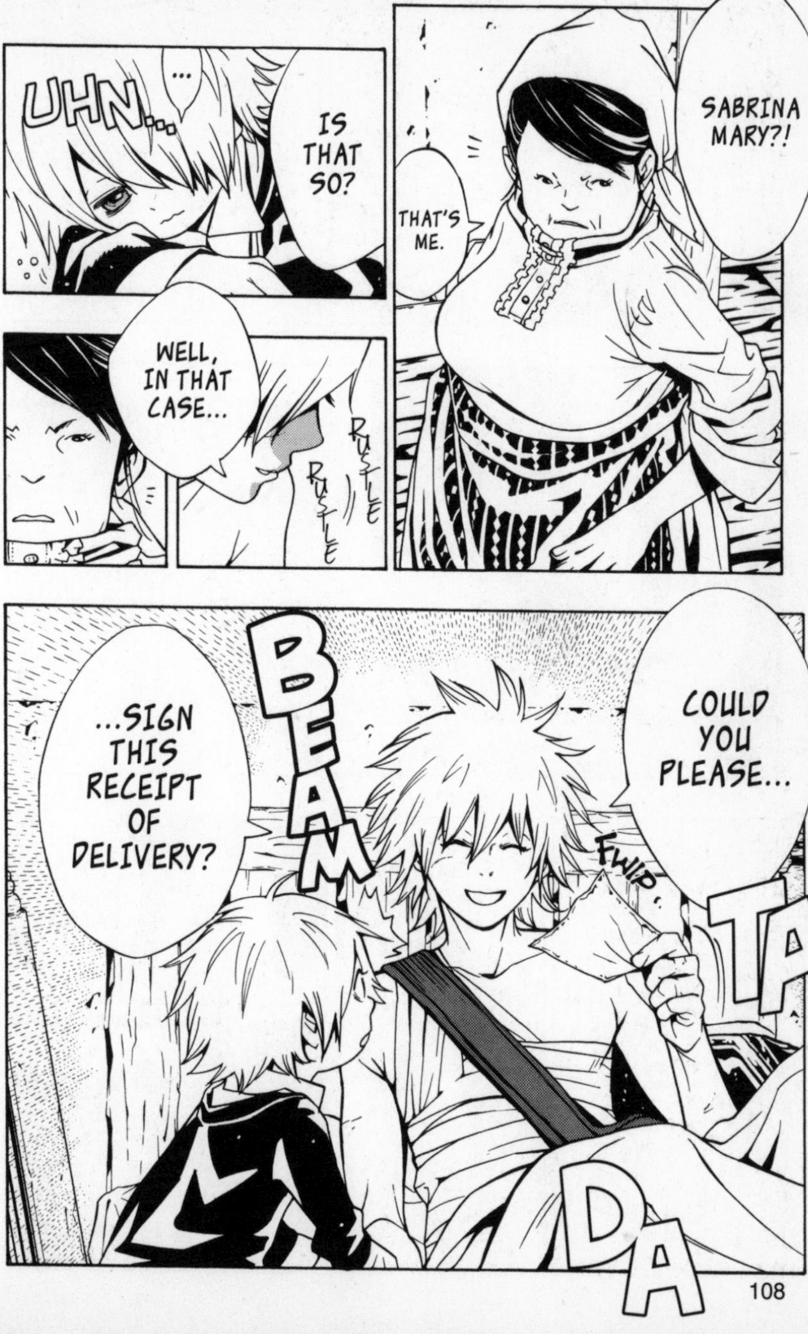
SABRINA MARY?!
THAT'S ME.
IS THAT SO?
...
UHN...
WELL, IN THAT CASE...
RUSTLE RUSTLE
COULD YOU PLEASE...
BEAM
...SIGN THIS RECEIPT OF DELIVERY?
FWIP
TA
DA

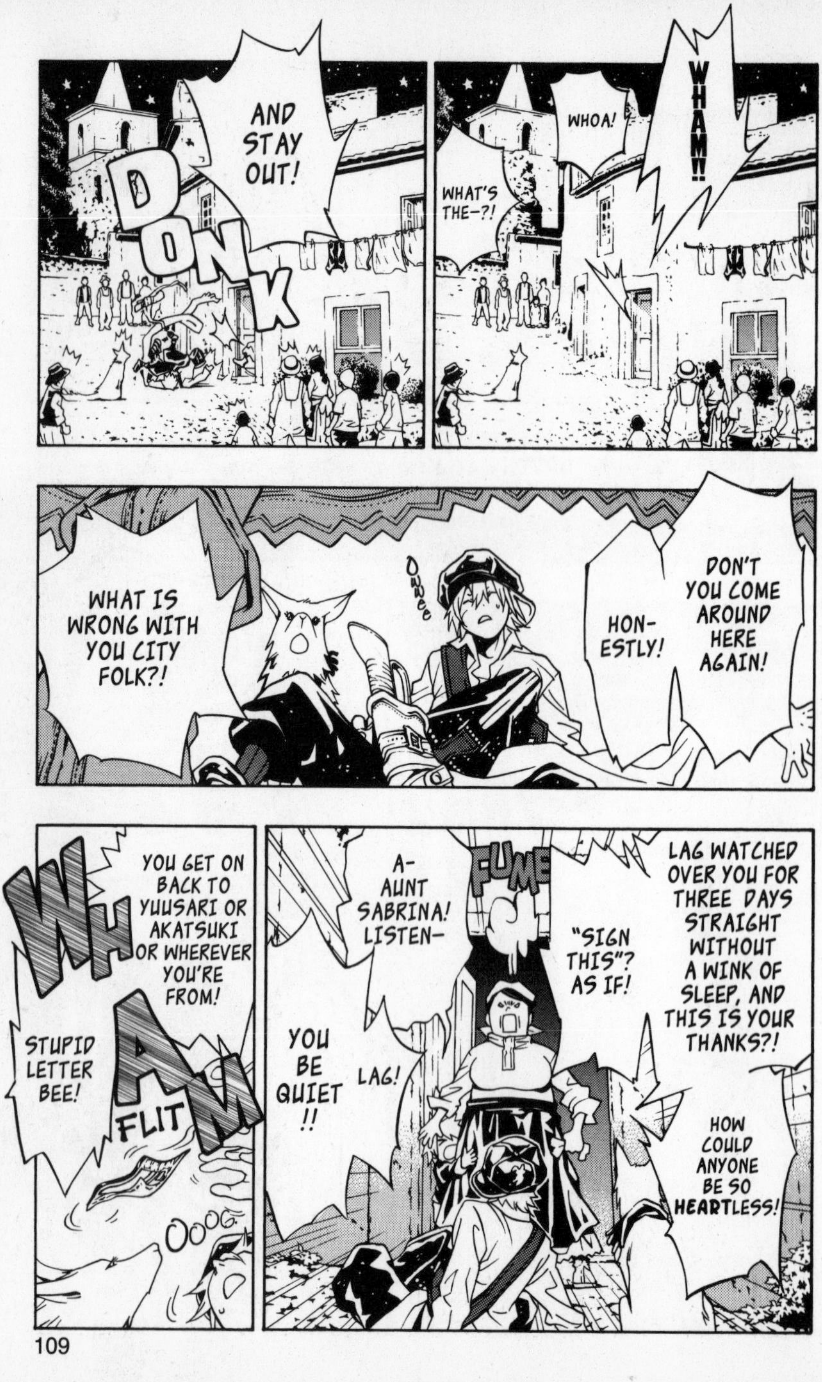
WHAM!
WHOA!
WHAT'S THE–?!
AND STAY OUT!
DONK
DON'T YOU COME AROUND HERE AGAIN!
HON-ESTLY!
Owee
WHAT IS WRONG WITH YOU CITY FOLK?!
LAG WATCHED OVER YOU FOR THREE DAYS STRAIGHT WITHOUT A WINK OF SLEEP, AND THIS IS YOUR THANKS?!
"SIGN THIS"? AS IF!
FUME
A-AUNT SABRINA! LISTEN–
HOW COULD ANYONE BE SO **HEARTLESS**!
LAG!
YOU BE QUIET!!
YOU GET ON BACK TO YUUSARI OR AKATSUKI OR WHEREVER YOU'RE FROM!
WHAM
STUPID LETTER BEE!
FLIT
OOOG.

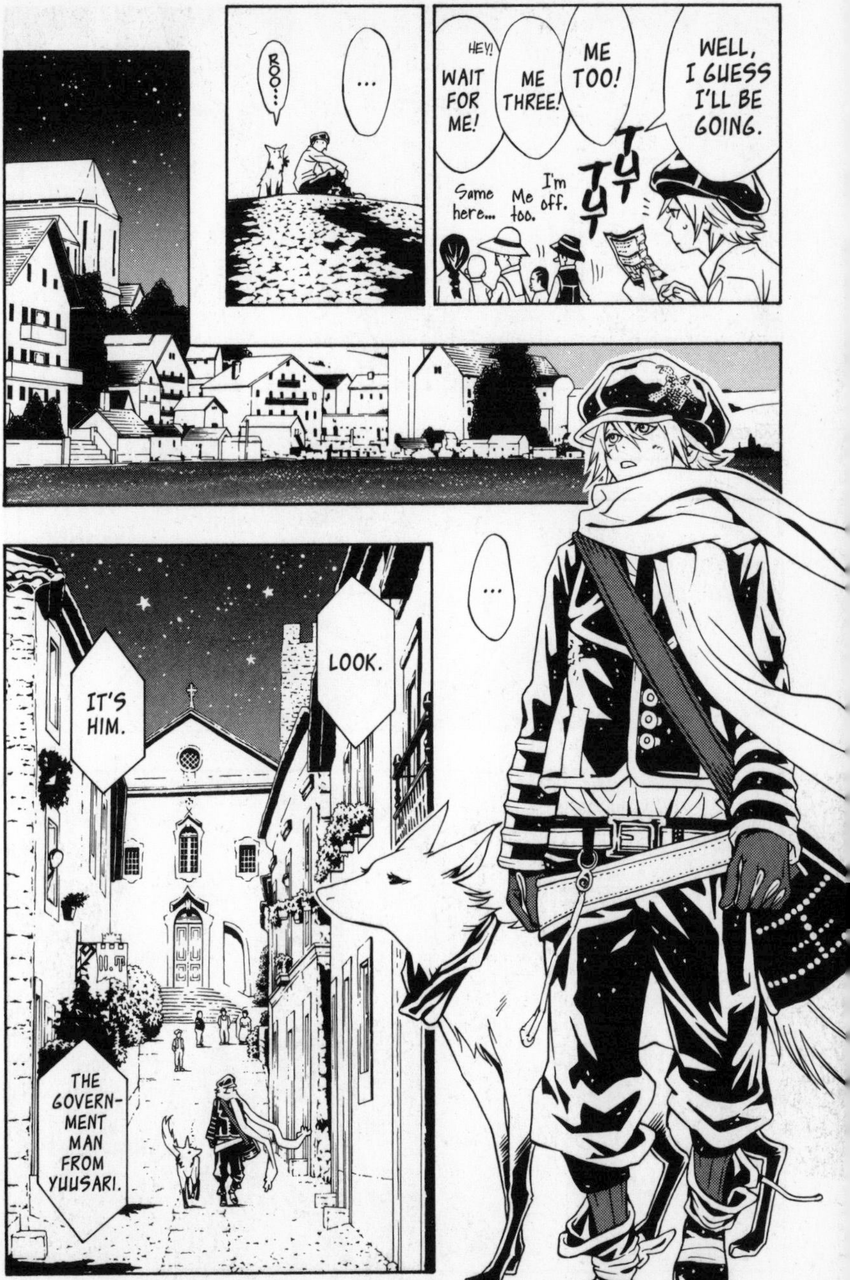
WELL, I GUESS I'LL BE GOING.
ME TOO!
ME THREE!
HEY! WAIT FOR ME!
TUT
TUT
I'm off.
Me too.
Same here...
...
ROO...
...
LOOK.
IT'S HIM.
THE GOVERNMENT MAN FROM YUUSARI.

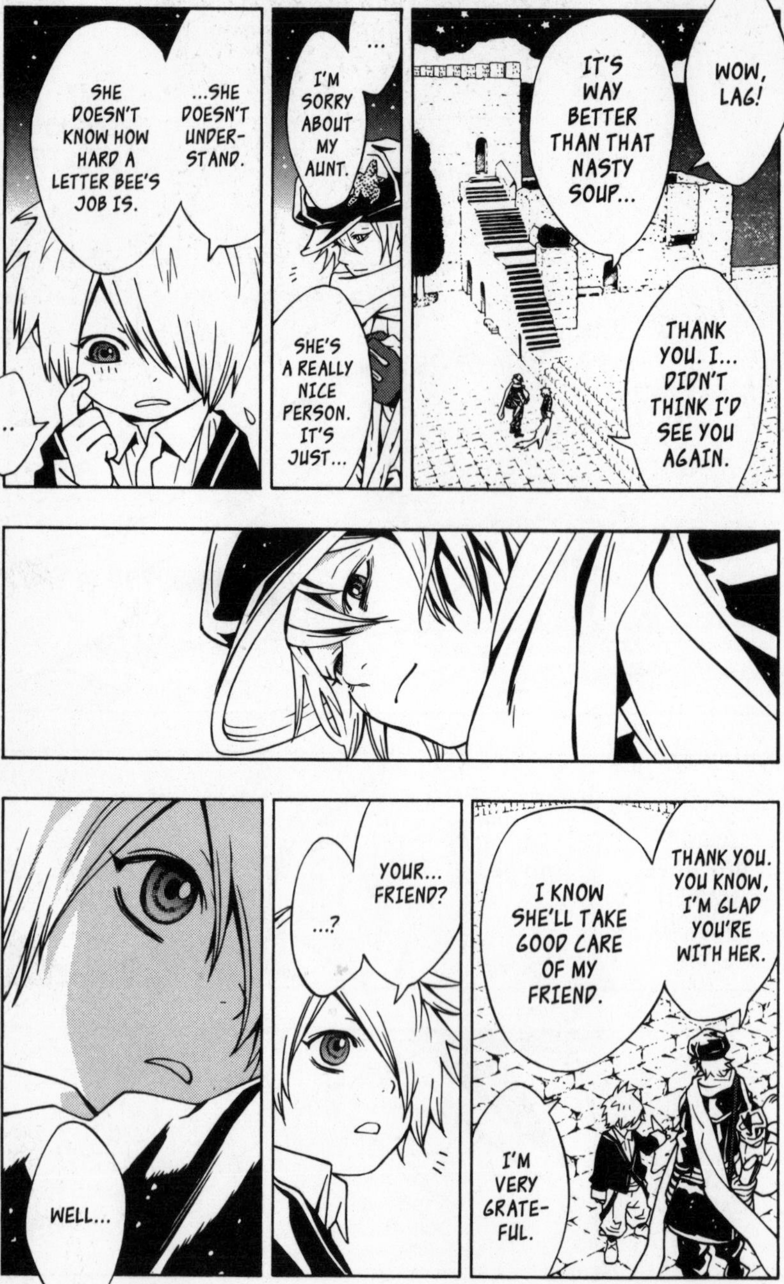
WOW, LAG!
IT'S WAY BETTER THAN THAT NASTY SOUP...
THANK YOU. I... DIDN'T THINK I'D SEE YOU AGAIN.
...
I'M SORRY ABOUT MY AUNT.
SHE'S A REALLY NICE PERSON. IT'S JUST...
...SHE DOESN'T UNDERSTAND.
SHE DOESN'T KNOW HOW HARD A LETTER BEE'S JOB IS.
...
THANK YOU. YOU KNOW, I'M GLAD YOU'RE WITH HER.
I KNOW SHE'LL TAKE GOOD CARE OF MY FRIEND.
I'M VERY GRATE-FUL.
YOUR... FRIEND?
...?
WELL...

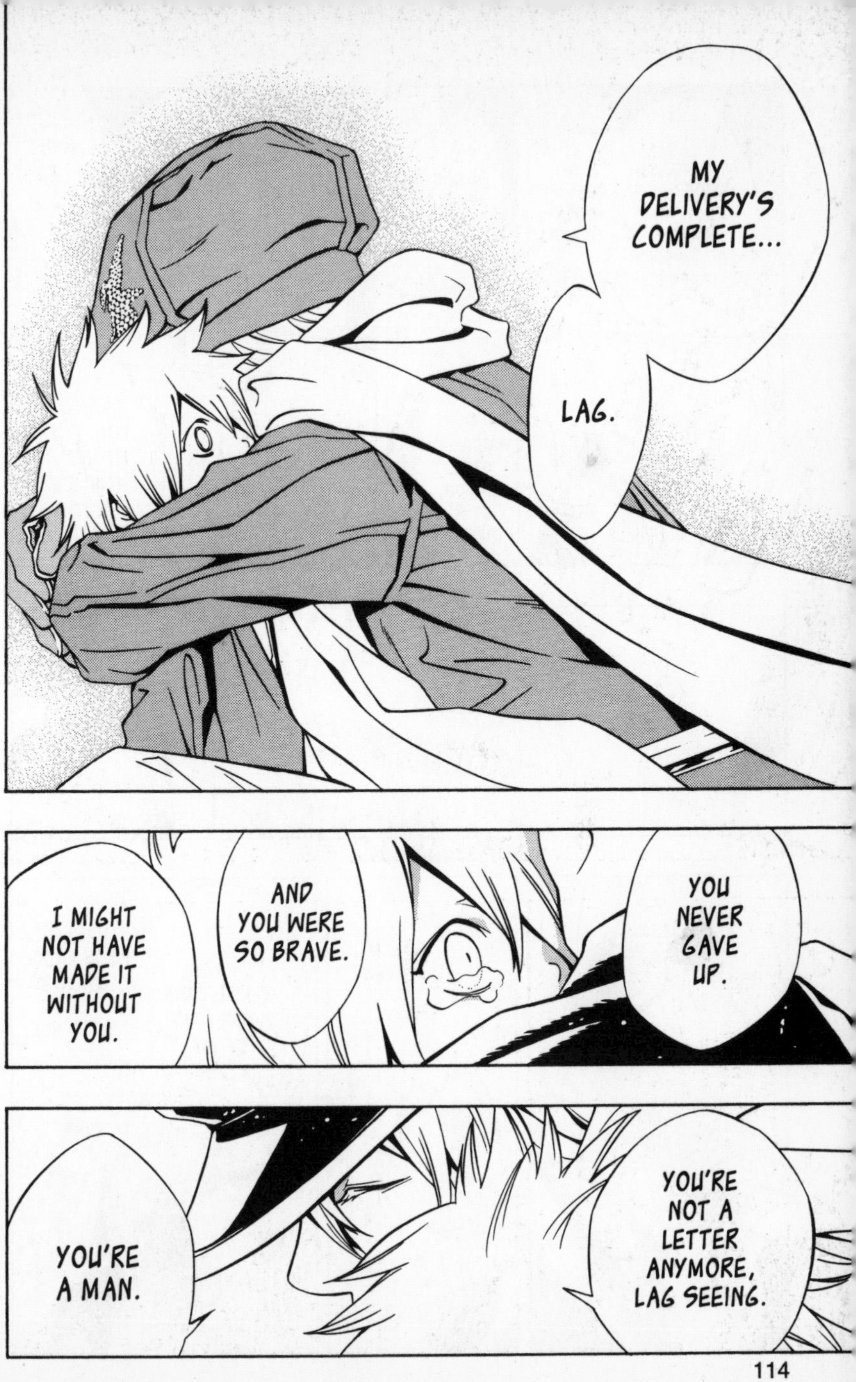
MY DELIVERY'S COMPLETE...
LAG.
YOU NEVER GAVE UP.
AND YOU WERE SO BRAVE.
I MIGHT NOT HAVE MADE IT WITHOUT YOU.
YOU'RE NOT A LETTER ANYMORE, LAG SEEING.
YOU'RE A MAN.

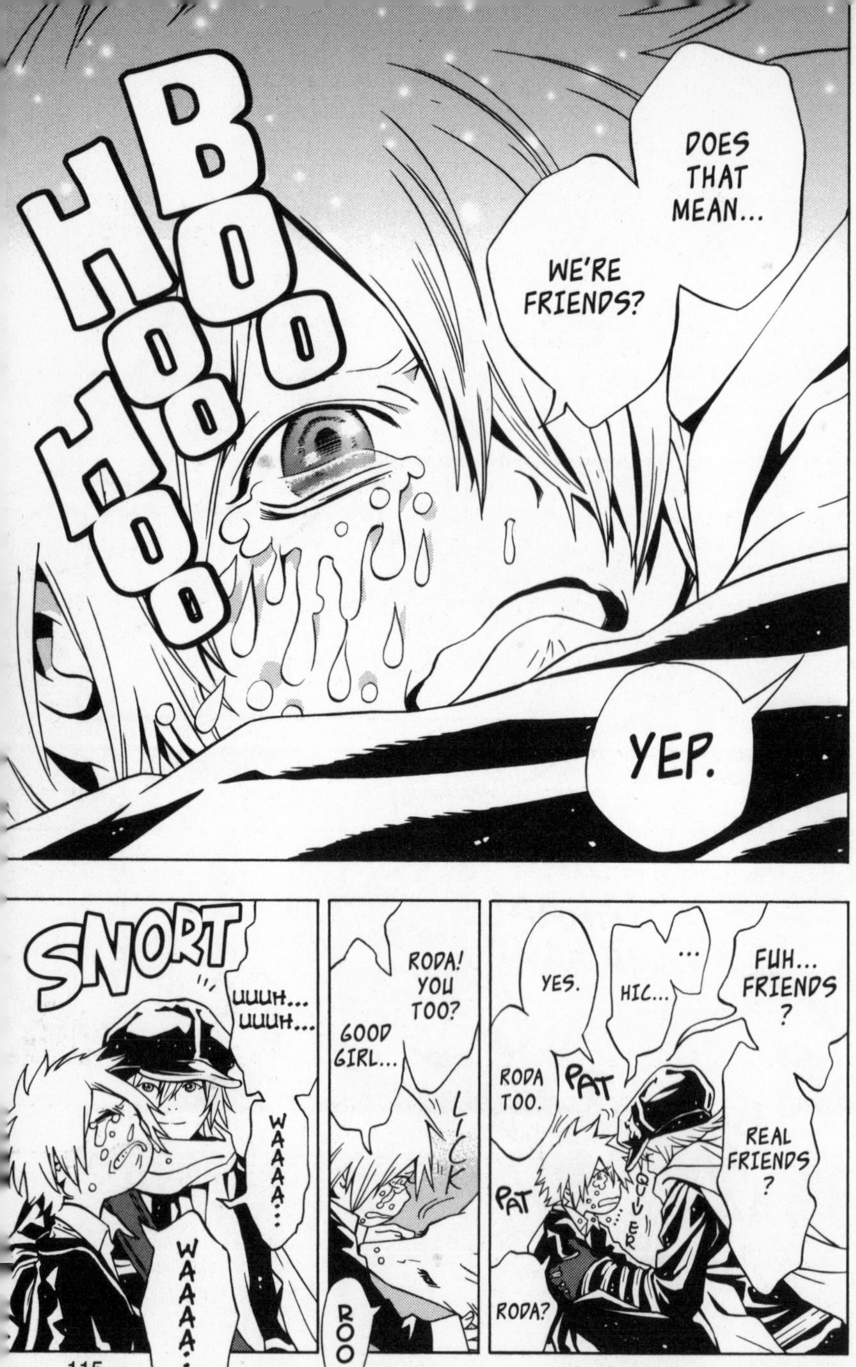
DOES THAT MEAN...
WE'RE FRIENDS?
BOO HOO HOO
YEP.
FUH... FRIENDS?
...
HIC...
YES.
RODA TOO.
PAT
REAL FRIENDS?
QUIVER
PAT
RODA?
RODA! YOU TOO?
GOOD GIRL...
LICK
ROO
SNORT
UUUH... UUUH...
WAAAA...
WAAAA...

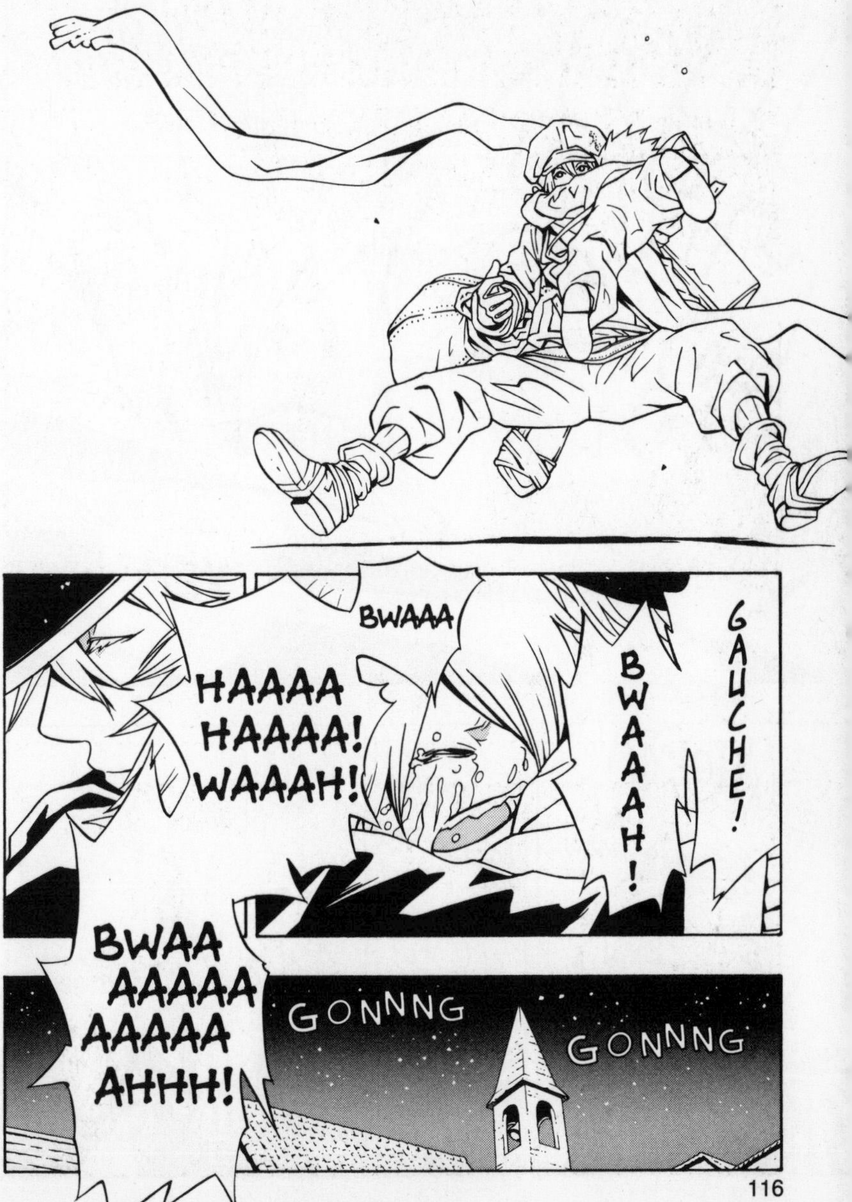
GAUCHE!
BWAAAAH!
BWAAA
HAAAA HAAAA! WAAAH!
GONNNG
GONNNG
BWAA AAAAA AAAAA AHHH!

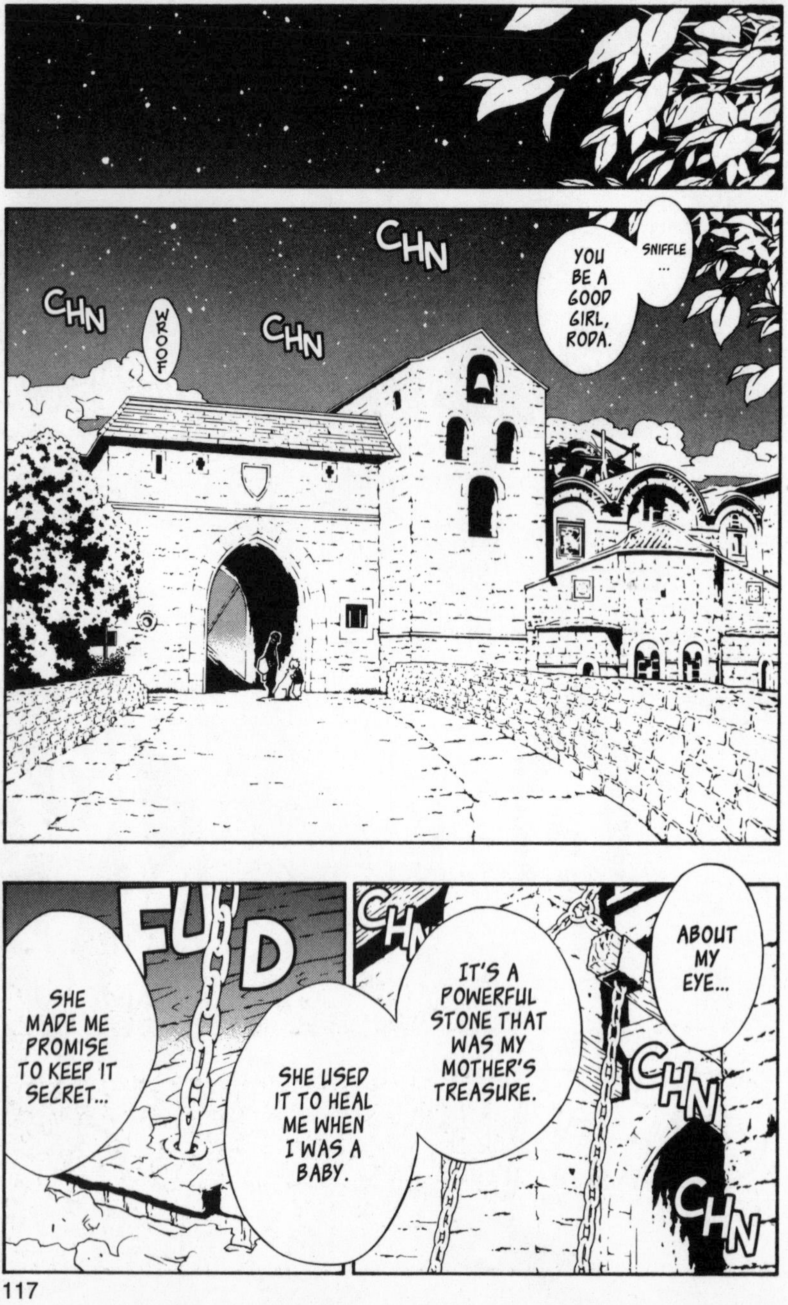
SNIFFLE...
YOU BE A GOOD GIRL, RODA.
CHN
CHN
WROOF
CHN
ABOUT MY EYE...
IT'S A POWERFUL STONE THAT WAS MY MOTHER'S TREASURE.
CHN
CHN
CHN
SHE USED IT TO HEAL ME WHEN I WAS A BABY.
SHE MADE ME PROMISE TO KEEP IT SECRET...
FUD

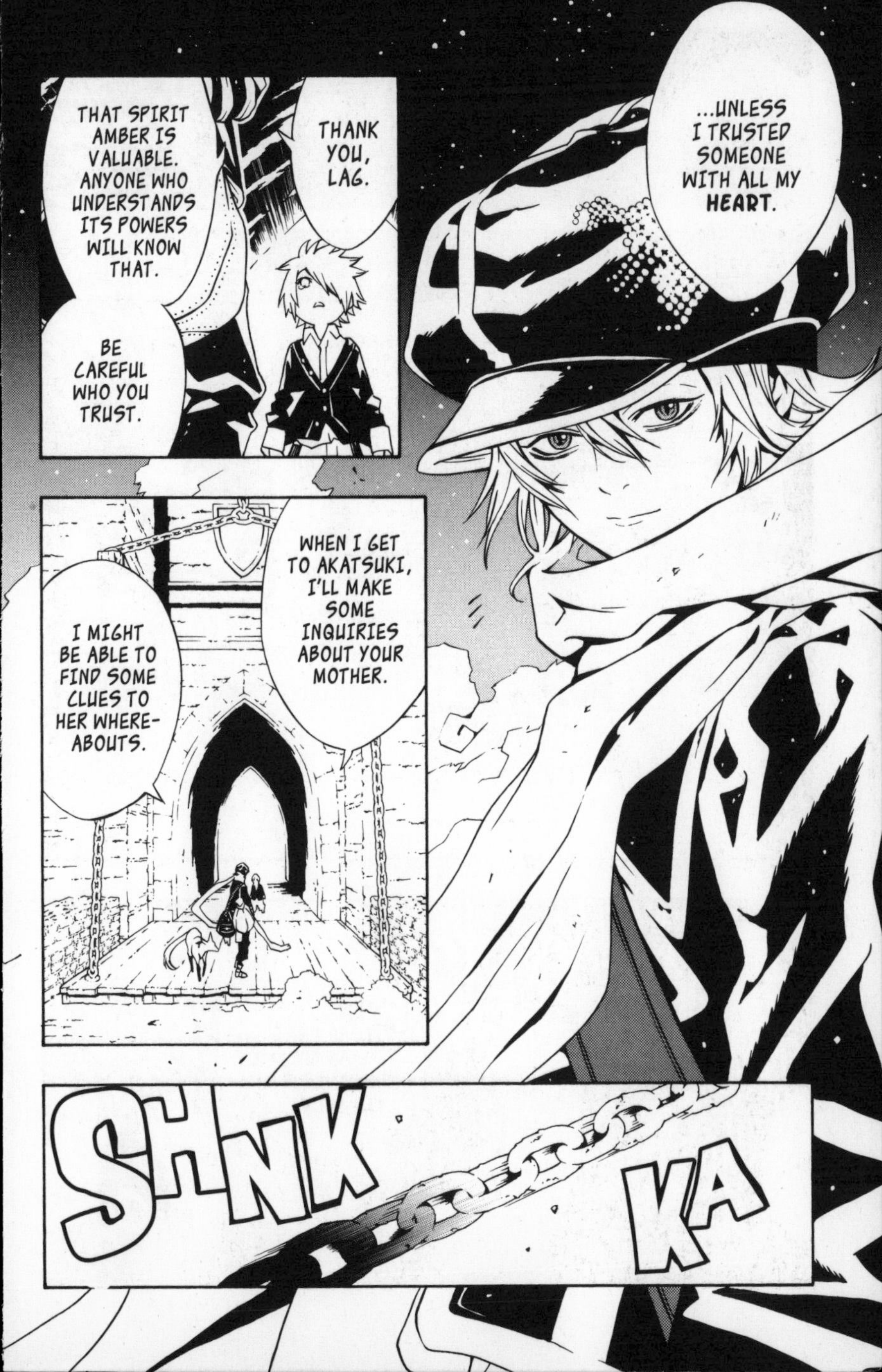
...UNLESS I TRUSTED SOMEONE WITH ALL MY **HEART**.
THANK YOU, LAG.
THAT SPIRIT AMBER IS VALUABLE. ANYONE WHO UNDERSTANDS ITS POWERS WILL KNOW THAT.
BE CAREFUL WHO YOU TRUST.
WHEN I GET TO AKATSUKI, I'LL MAKE SOME INQUIRIES ABOUT YOUR MOTHER.
I MIGHT BE ABLE TO FIND SOME CLUES TO HER WHERE-ABOUTS.
KA
SHNK

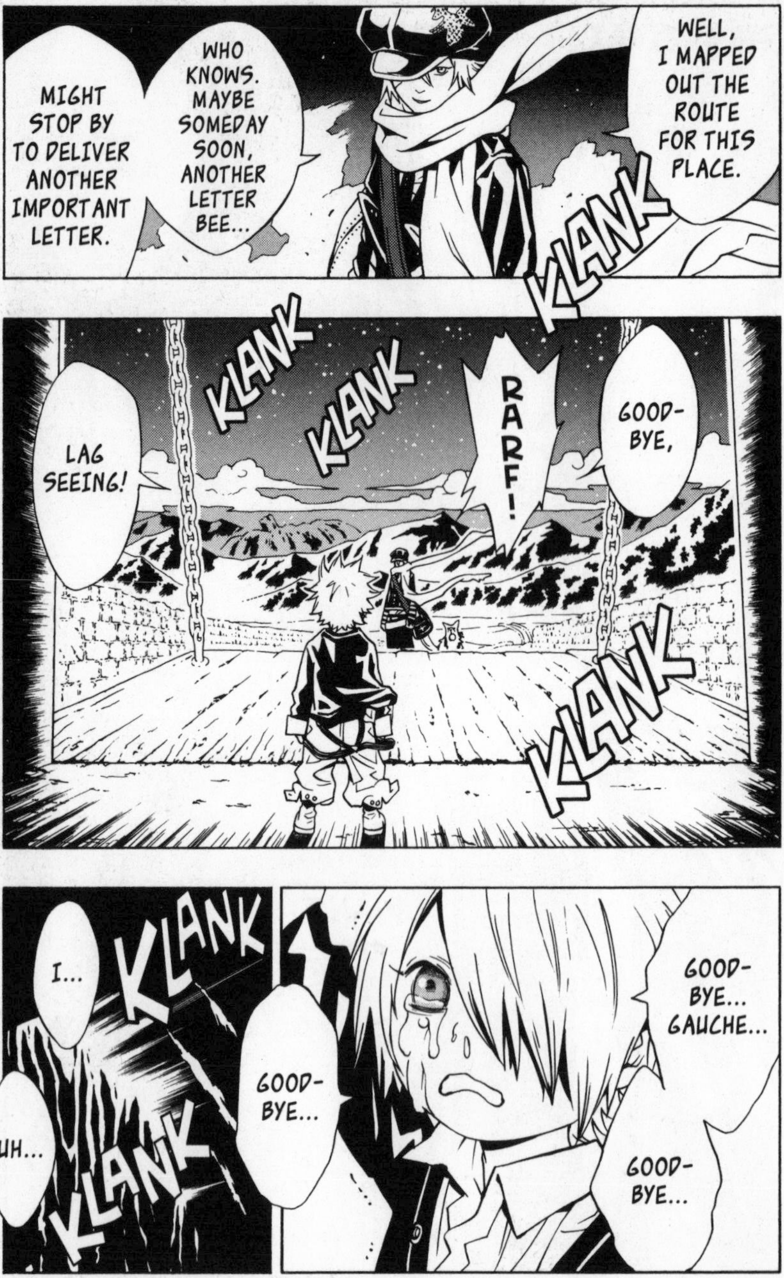
WELL, I MAPPED OUT THE ROUTE FOR THIS PLACE.
KLANK
WHO KNOWS. MAYBE SOMEDAY SOON, ANOTHER LETTER BEE...
MIGHT STOP BY TO DELIVER ANOTHER IMPORTANT LETTER.
GOOD-BYE,
RARF!
KLANK
KLANK
KLANK
LAG SEEING!
GOOD-BYE... GAUCHE...
GOOD-BYE...
GOOD-BYE...
KLANK
I...
UH...
KLANK

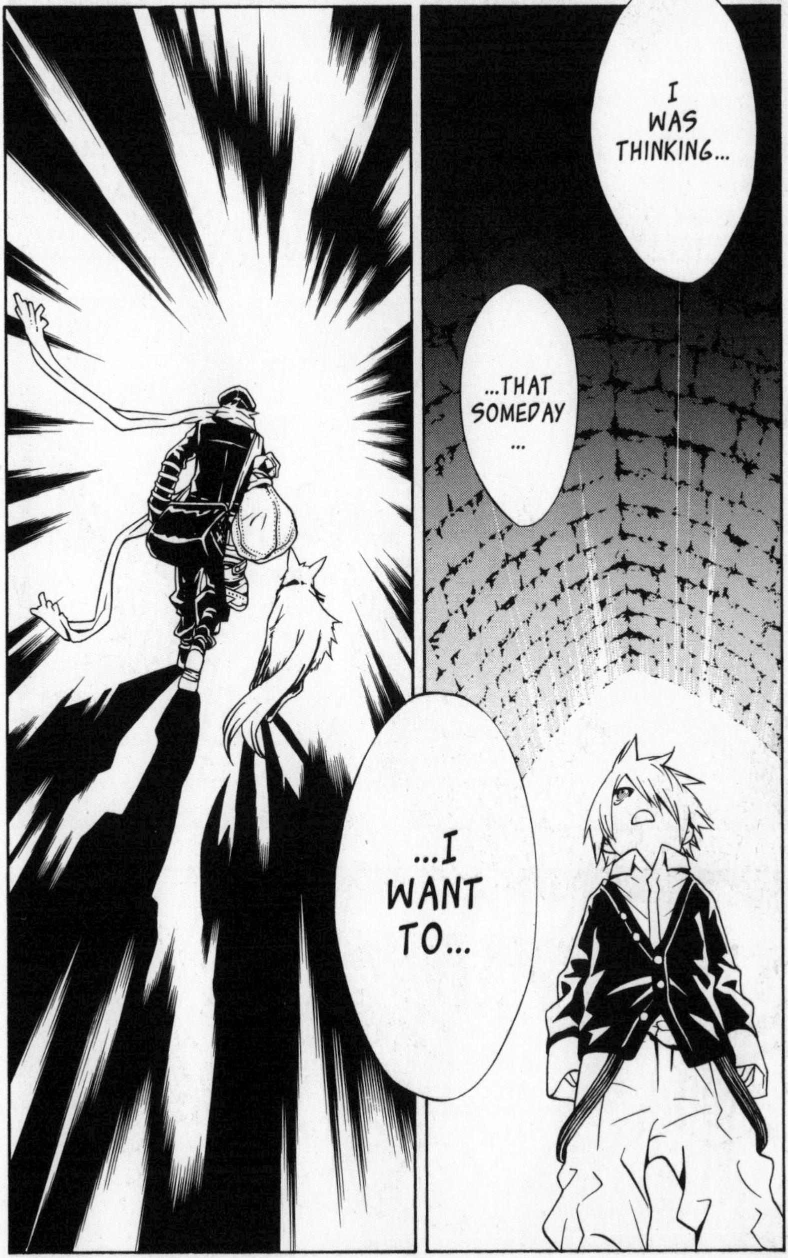
I WAS THINKING...
...THAT SOMEDAY...
...I WANT TO...

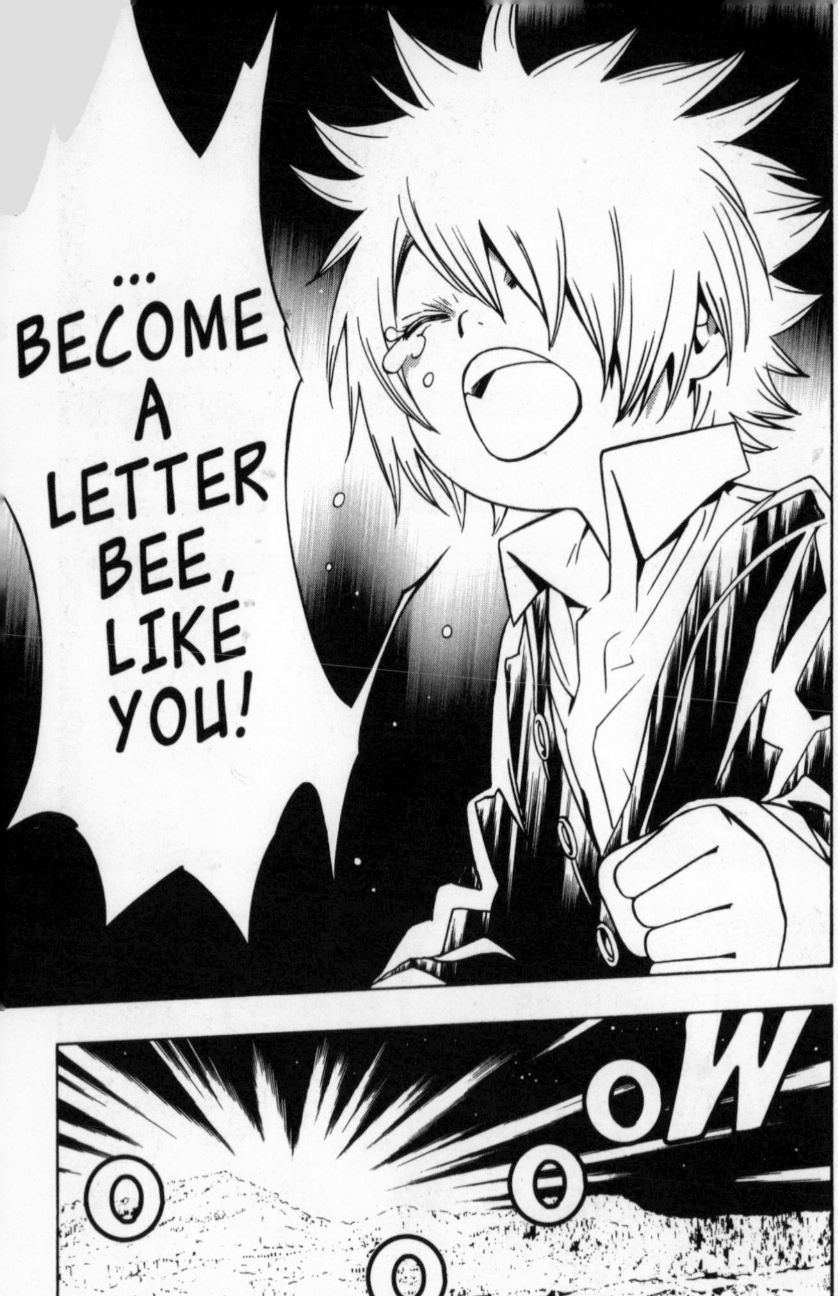
...BECOME A LETTER BEE, LIKE YOU!
OOOOW

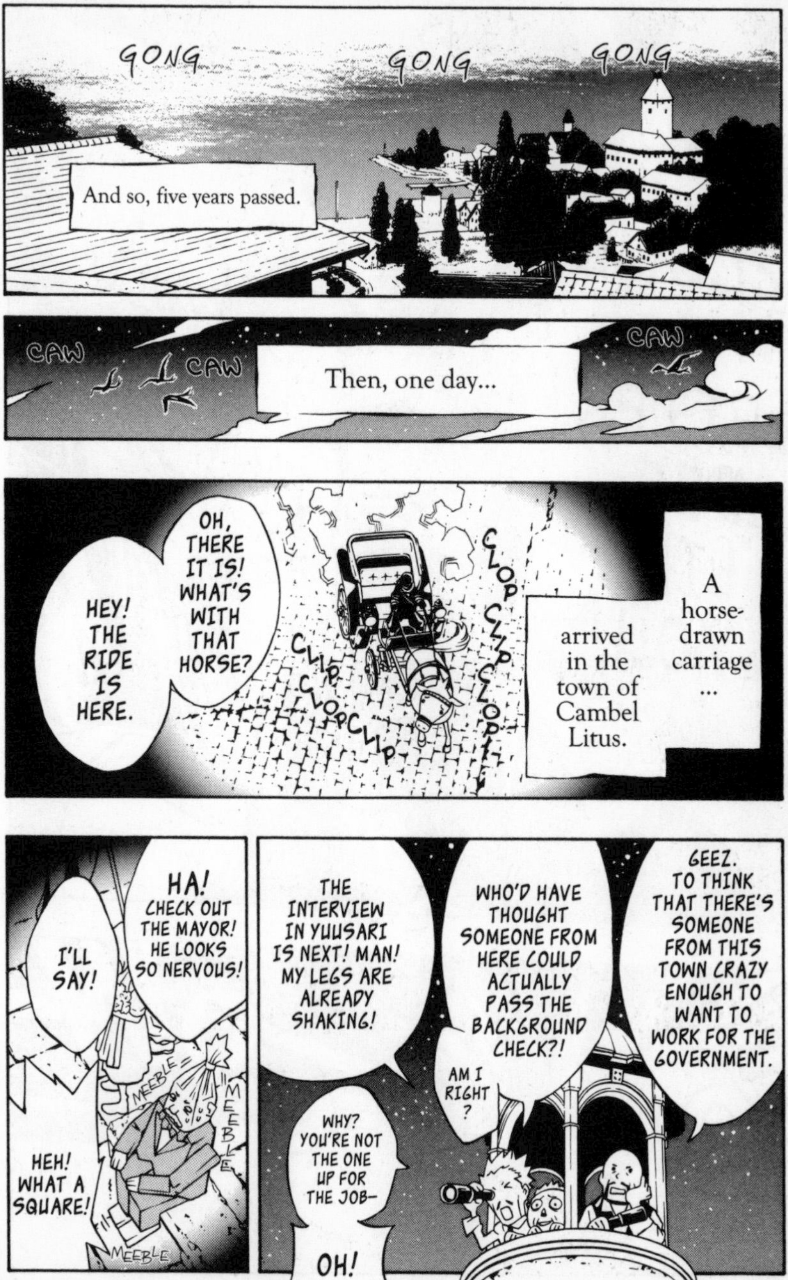
GONG GONG GONG
And so, five years passed.
CAW CAW CAW
Then, one day...
A horse-drawn carriage...
arrived in the town of Cambel Litus.
CLOP CLIP CLOP
CLIP CLOP CLIP
OH, THERE IT IS! WHAT'S WITH THAT HORSE?
HEY! THE RIDE IS HERE.
GEEZ. TO THINK THAT THERE'S SOMEONE FROM THIS TOWN CRAZY ENOUGH TO WANT TO WORK FOR THE GOVERNMENT.
WHO'D HAVE THOUGHT SOMEONE FROM HERE COULD ACTUALLY PASS THE BACKGROUND CHECK?!
AM I RIGHT?
THE INTERVIEW IN YUUSARI IS NEXT! MAN! MY LEGS ARE ALREADY SHAKING!
WHY? YOU'RE NOT THE ONE UP FOR THE JOB—
OH!
HA! CHECK OUT THE MAYOR! HE LOOKS SO NERVOUS!
I'LL SAY!
MEEBLE MEEBLE
HEH! WHAT A SQUARE!
MEEBLE

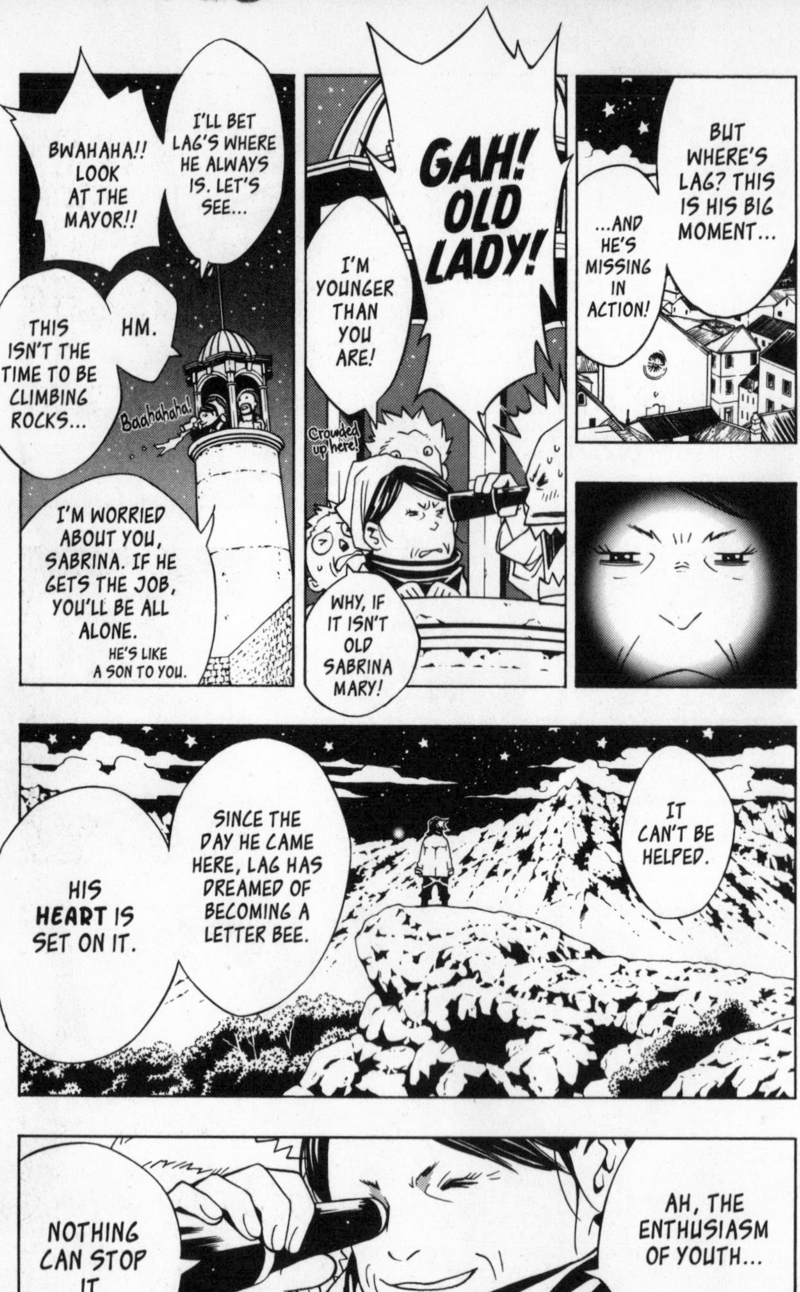
BUT WHERE'S LAG? THIS IS HIS BIG MOMENT...
...AND HE'S MISSING IN ACTION!
GAH! OLD LADY!
I'M YOUNGER THAN YOU ARE!
Crowded up here!
WHY, IF IT ISN'T OLD SABRINA MARY!
I'LL BET LAG'S WHERE HE ALWAYS IS. LET'S SEE...
BWAHAHA!! LOOK AT THE MAYOR!!
HM.
THIS ISN'T THE TIME TO BE CLIMBING ROCKS...
Baahahaha!
I'M WORRIED ABOUT YOU, SABRINA. IF HE GETS THE JOB, YOU'LL BE ALL ALONE.
HE'S LIKE A SON TO YOU.
IT CAN'T BE HELPED.
SINCE THE DAY HE CAME HERE, LAG HAS DREAMED OF BECOMING A LETTER BEE.
HIS **HEART** IS SET ON IT.
AH, THE ENTHUSIASM OF YOUTH...
NOTHING CAN STOP IT.

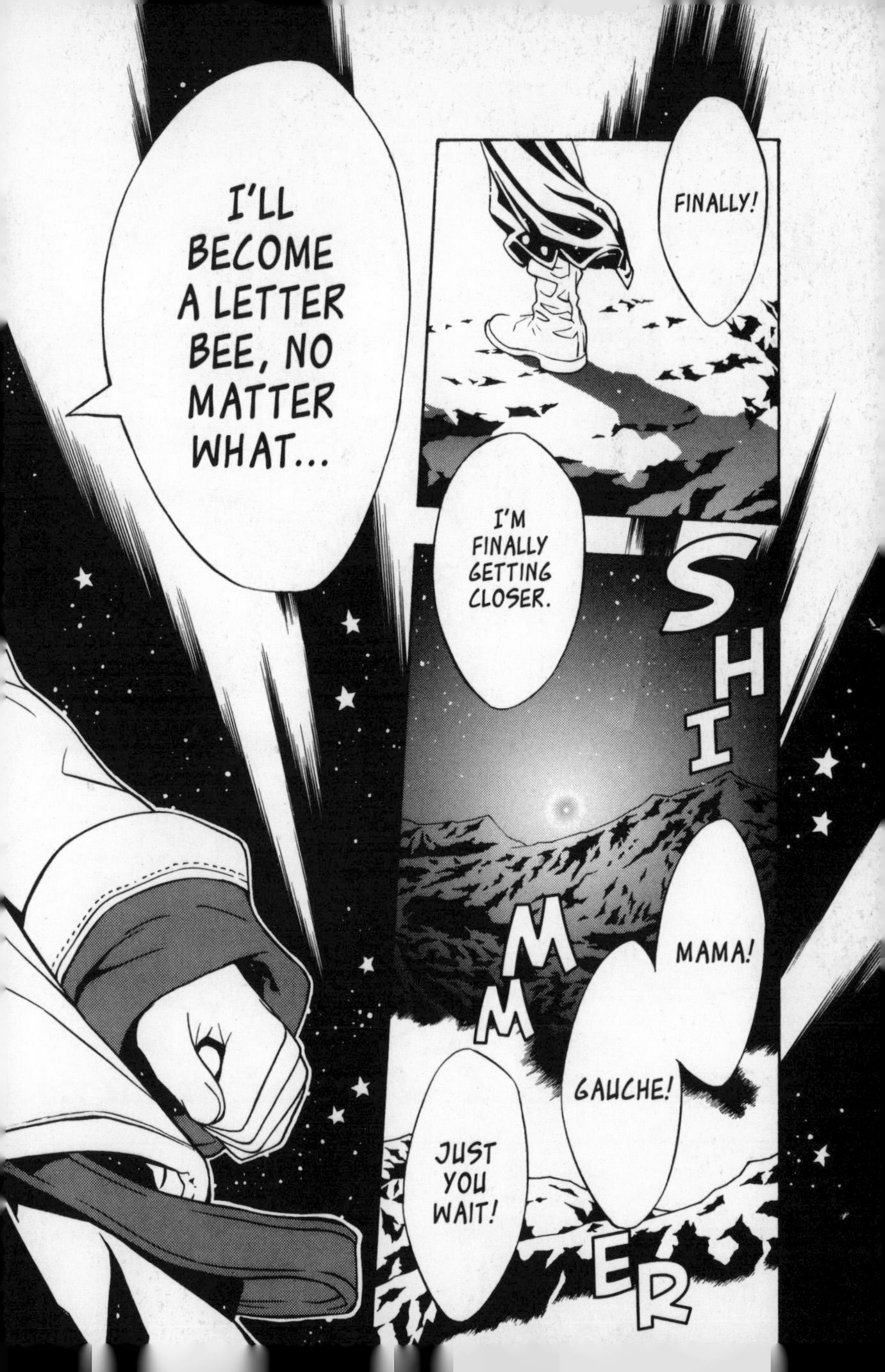
FINALLY!
I'M FINALLY GETTING CLOSER.
SHIMMER
MAMA!
GAUCHE!
JUST YOU WAIT!
I'LL BECOME A LETTER BEE, NO MATTER WHAT...

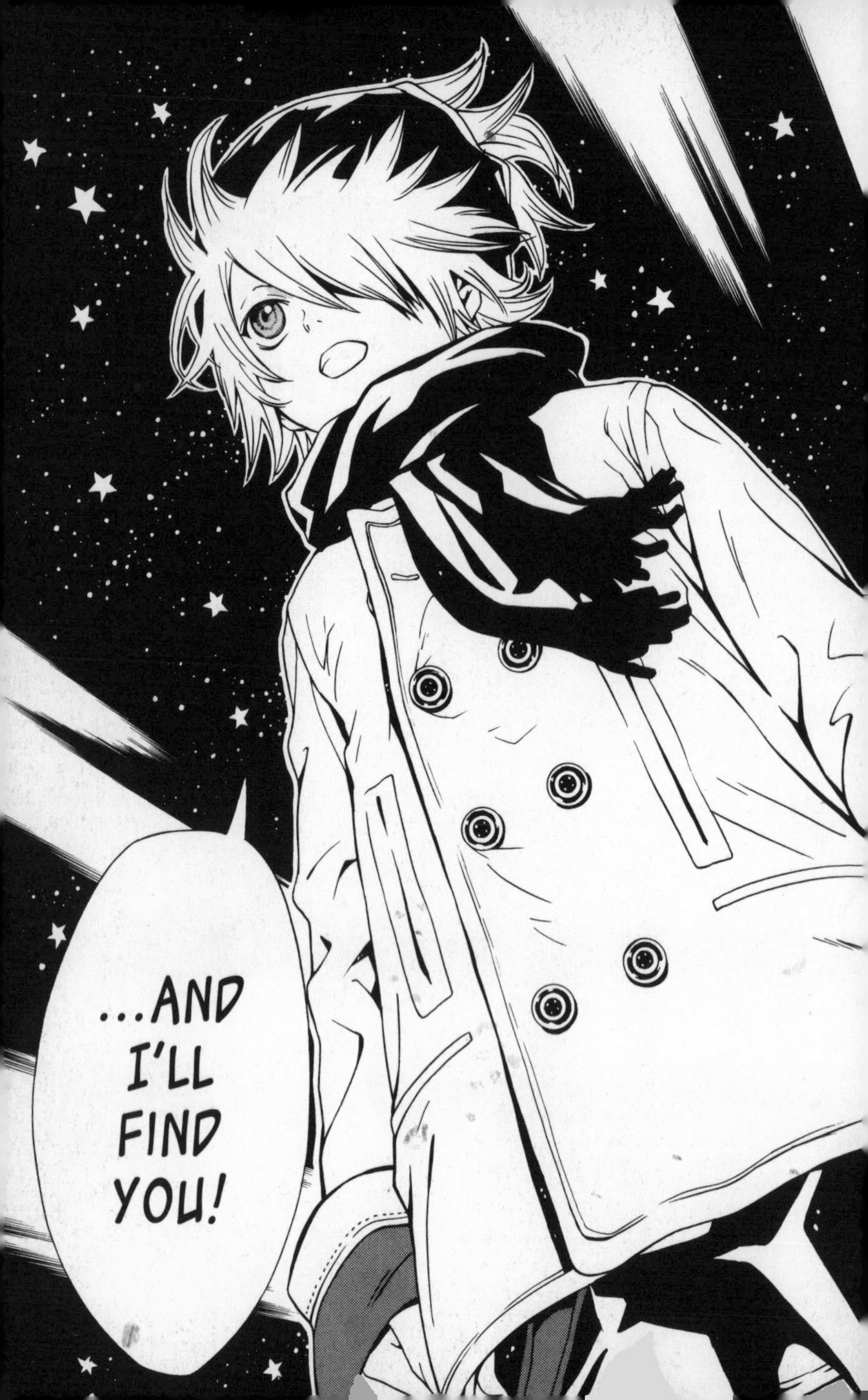
...AND I'LL FIND YOU!

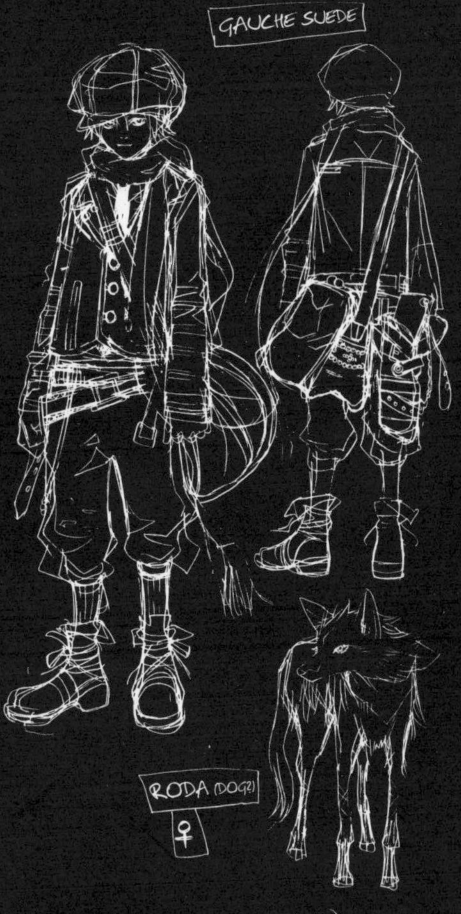
GAUCHE SUEDE
RODA (DOG?)
♀

Lag Seeing ラグ・シーイング

Lag

1. Rag/old cloth. (ラグ)
2. *Lagrima*, Spanish for "teardrop." (ラグリマ)
3. *Lugh*, from Celtic mythology. (ルー) (ルーグ)

The sun god of the Tuatha Dé Danann (or "people of the goddess Danu"), god of light.

Seeing

1. To see. (シーイング)

A word that evokes the experience of stars twinkling in the sky.

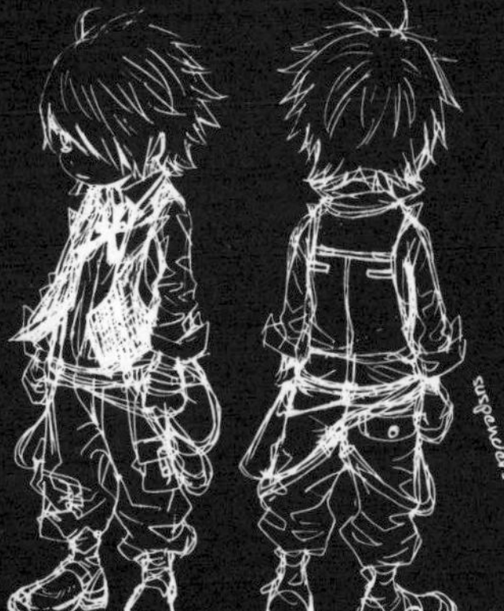
suspenders

CHAPTER 2: Crybaby Boy, Letter Girl

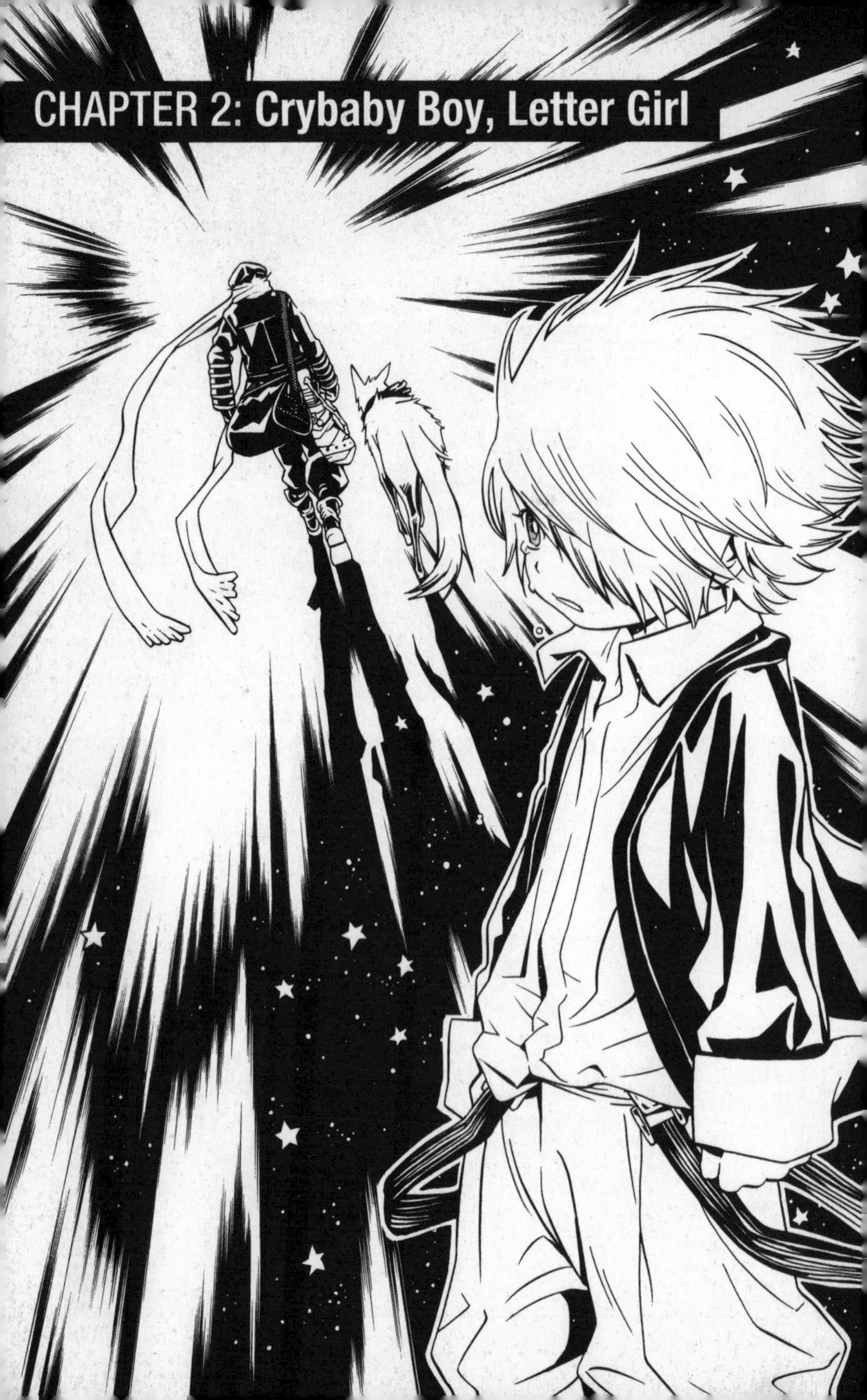

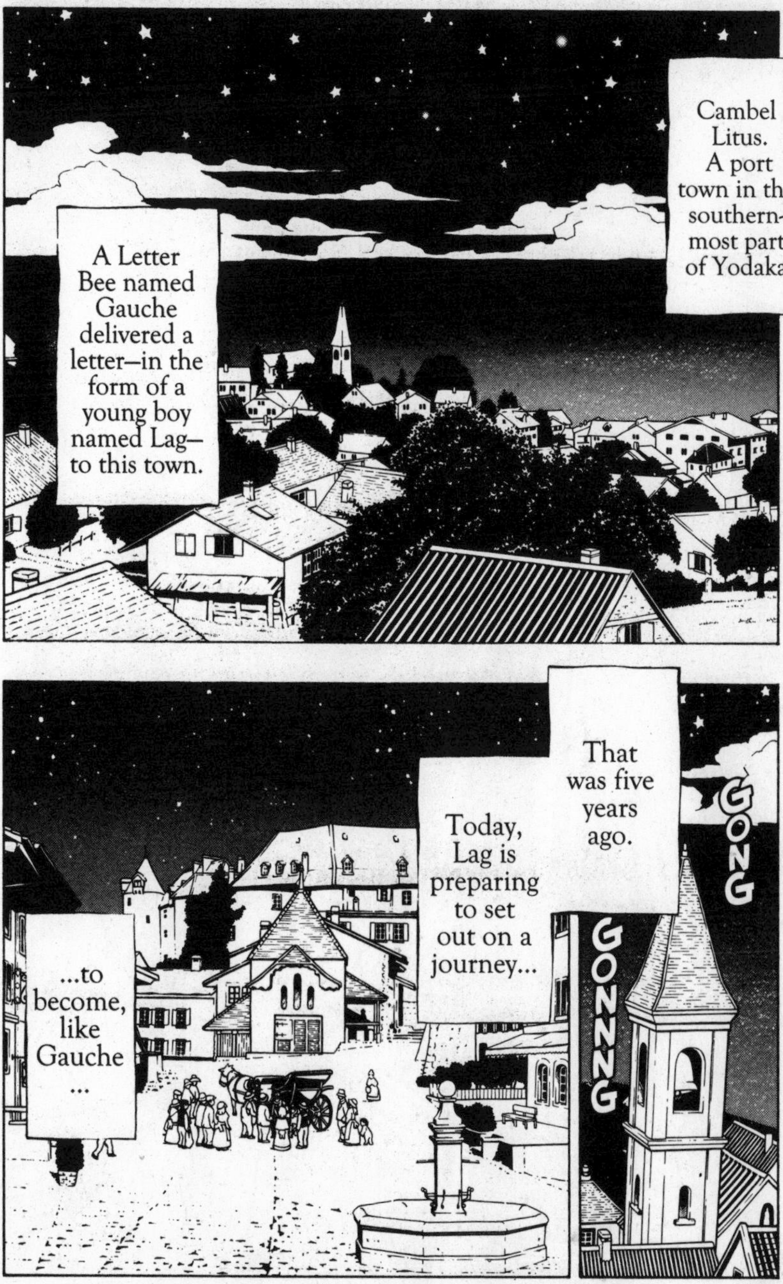

Cambel Litus. A port town in the southernmost part of Yodaka.
A Letter Bee named Gauche delivered a letter—in the form of a young boy named Lag—to this town.
That was five years ago.
GONG
GONNNG
Today, Lag is preparing to set out on a journey...
...to become, like Gauche...

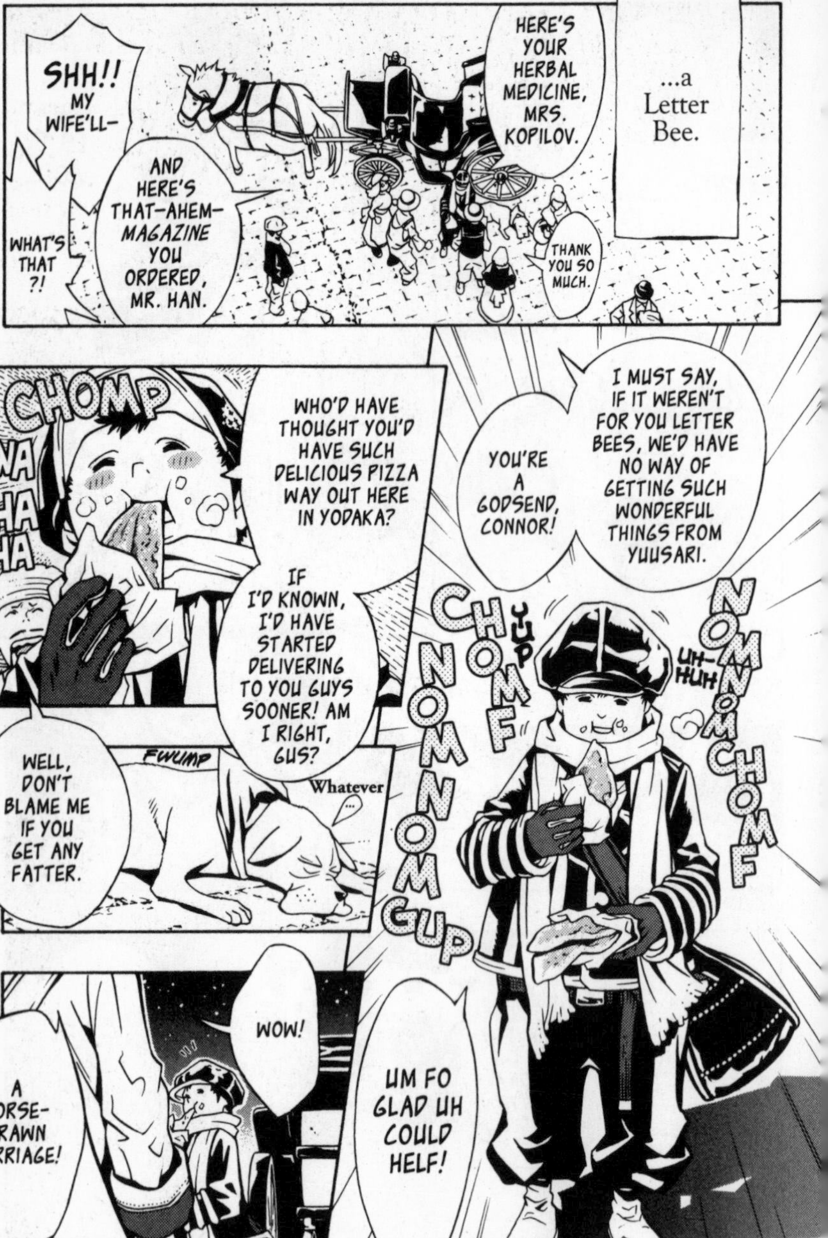
...a Letter Bee.
HERE'S YOUR HERBAL MEDICINE, MRS. KOPILOV.
THANK YOU SO MUCH.
SHH!! MY WIFE'LL—
AND HERE'S THAT—AHEM—MAGAZINE YOU ORDERED, MR. HAN.
WHAT'S THAT?!
I MUST SAY, IF IT WEREN'T FOR YOU LETTER BEES, WE'D HAVE NO WAY OF GETTING SUCH WONDERFUL THINGS FROM YUUSARI.
YOU'RE A GODSEND, CONNOR!
NOMNOMCHOMF
UH-HUH
CHOMF
YUP
NOMNOMNOMGUP
UM FO GLAD UH COULD HELF!
CHOMP
WHO'D HAVE THOUGHT YOU'D HAVE SUCH DELICIOUS PIZZA WAY OUT HERE IN YODAKA?
IF I'D KNOWN, I'D HAVE STARTED DELIVERING TO YOU GUYS SOONER! AM I RIGHT, GUS?
WA HA HA
FWUMP
Whatever
...
WELL, DON'T BLAME ME IF YOU GET ANY FATTER.
WOW!
A HORSE-DRAWN CARRIAGE!

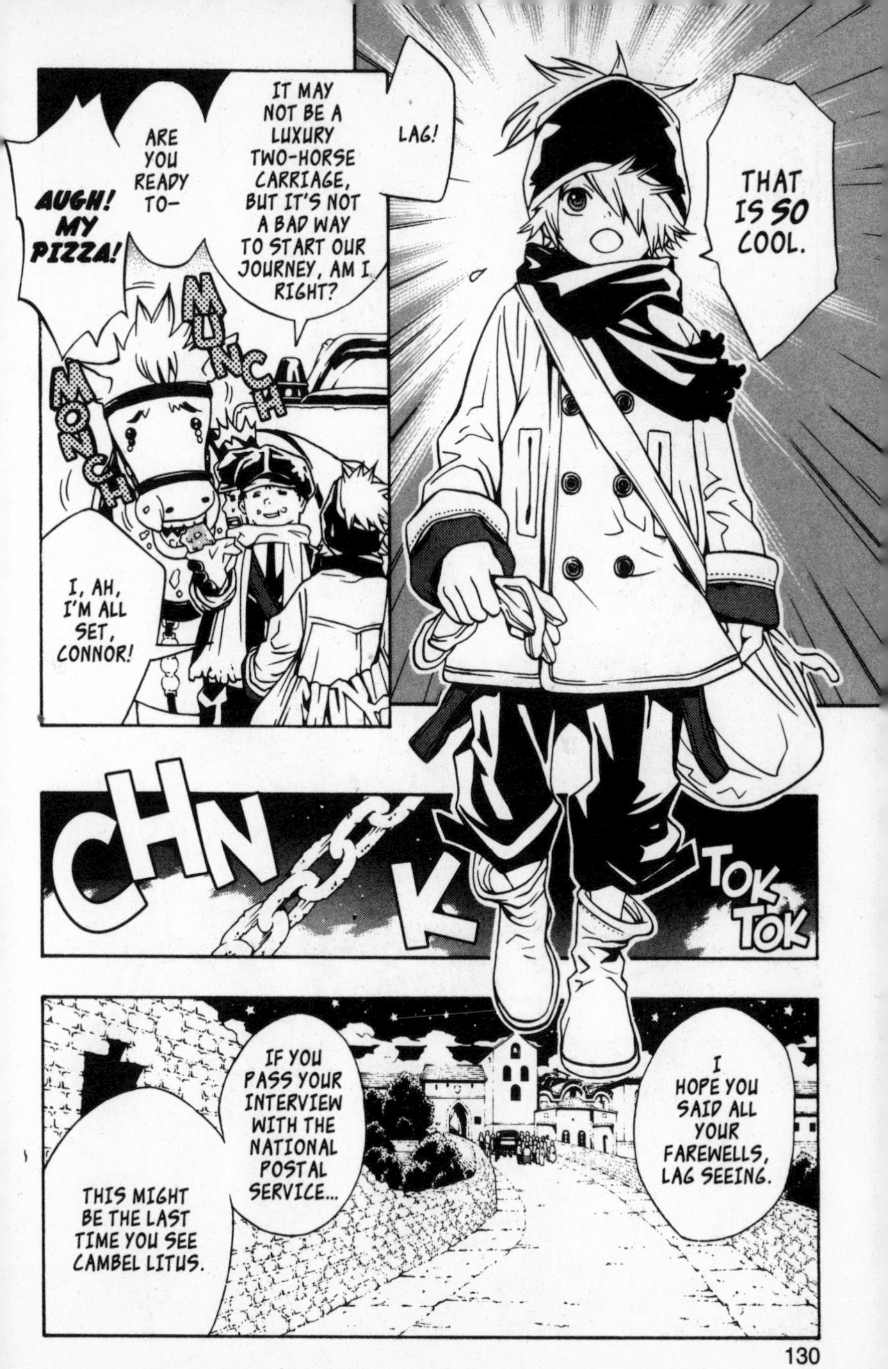

THAT IS SO COOL.
LAG!
IT MAY NOT BE A LUXURY TWO-HORSE CARRIAGE, BUT IT'S NOT A BAD WAY TO START OUR JOURNEY, AM I RIGHT?
ARE YOU READY TO—
AUGH! MY PIZZA!
MUNCH
MONCH
I, AH, I'M ALL SET, CONNOR!
TOK TOK
CHN
K
I HOPE YOU SAID ALL YOUR FAREWELLS, LAG SEEING.
IF YOU PASS YOUR INTERVIEW WITH THE NATIONAL POSTAL SERVICE...
THIS MIGHT BE THE LAST TIME YOU SEE CAMBEL LITUS.

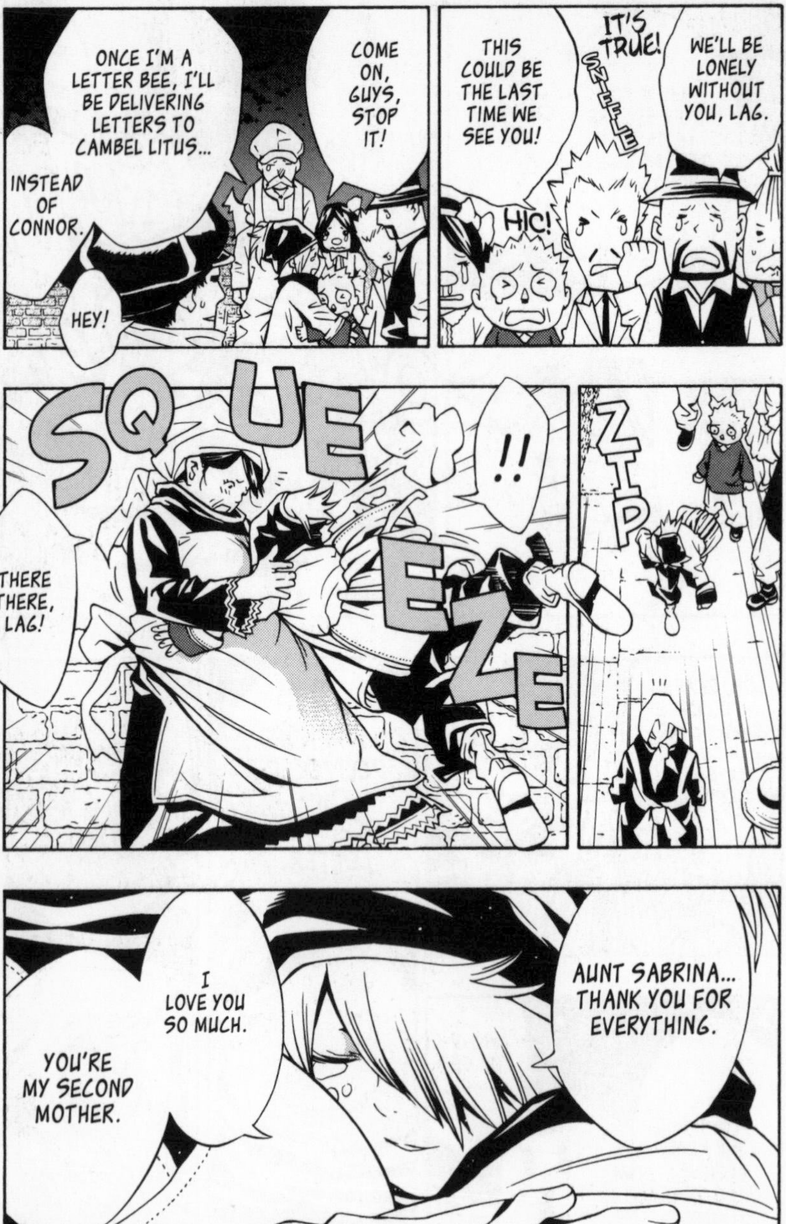
WE'LL BE LONELY WITHOUT YOU, LAG.
IT'S TRUE!
SNIFFLE
THIS COULD BE THE LAST TIME WE SEE YOU!
HIC!
COME ON, GUYS, STOP IT!
ONCE I'M A LETTER BEE, I'LL BE DELIVERING LETTERS TO CAMBEL LITUS...
INSTEAD OF CONNOR.
HEY!
ZIP
!!
SQUEEZE
THERE THERE, LAG!
AUNT SABRINA... THANK YOU FOR EVERYTHING.
I LOVE YOU SO MUCH.
YOU'RE MY SECOND MOTHER.

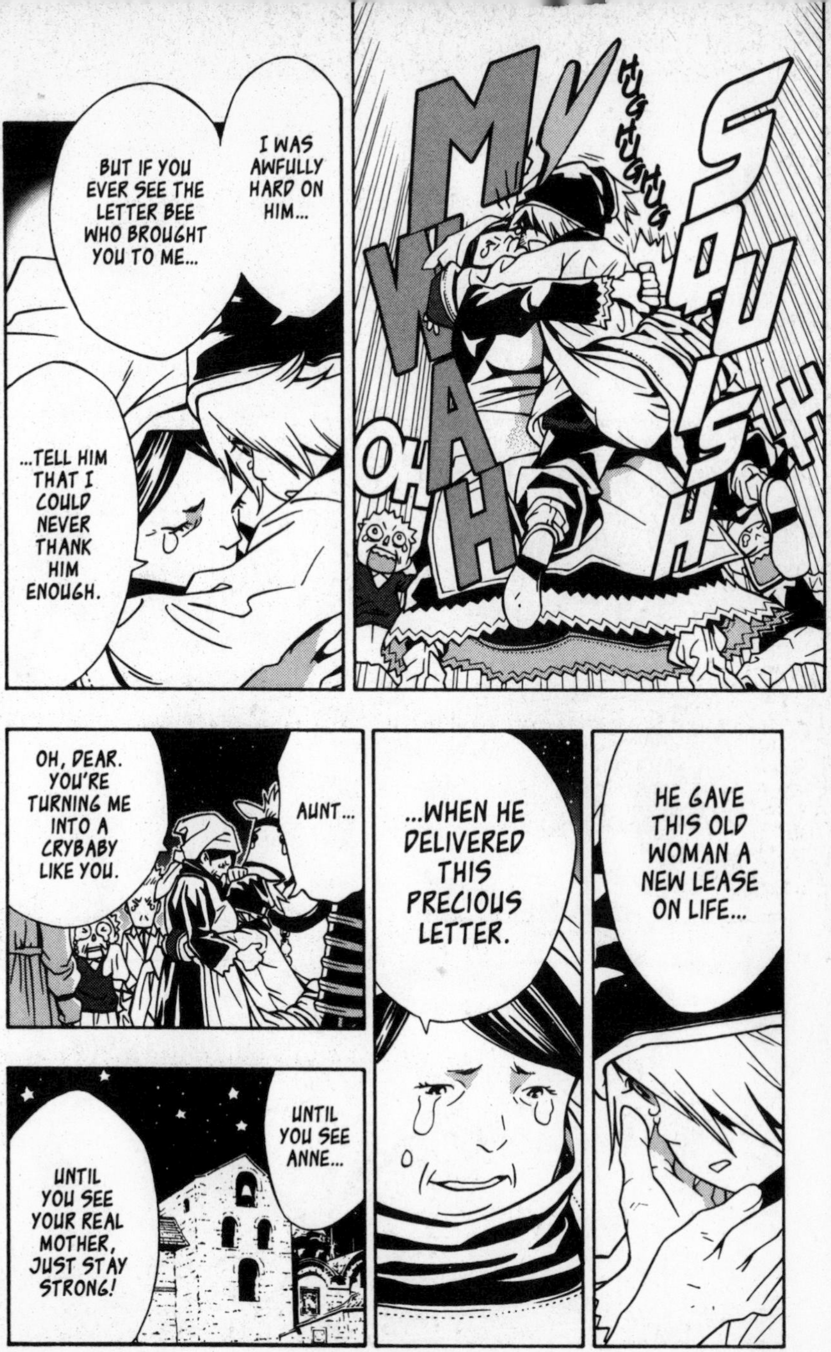
SQUISH
HUG HUG HUG
MWAH
OH
I WAS AWFULLY HARD ON HIM...
BUT IF YOU EVER SEE THE LETTER BEE WHO BROUGHT YOU TO ME...
...TELL HIM THAT I COULD NEVER THANK HIM ENOUGH.
HE GAVE THIS OLD WOMAN A NEW LEASE ON LIFE...
...WHEN HE DELIVERED THIS PRECIOUS LETTER.
AUNT...
OH, DEAR. YOU'RE TURNING ME INTO A CRYBABY LIKE YOU.
UNTIL YOU SEE ANNE...
UNTIL YOU SEE YOUR REAL MOTHER, JUST STAY STRONG!

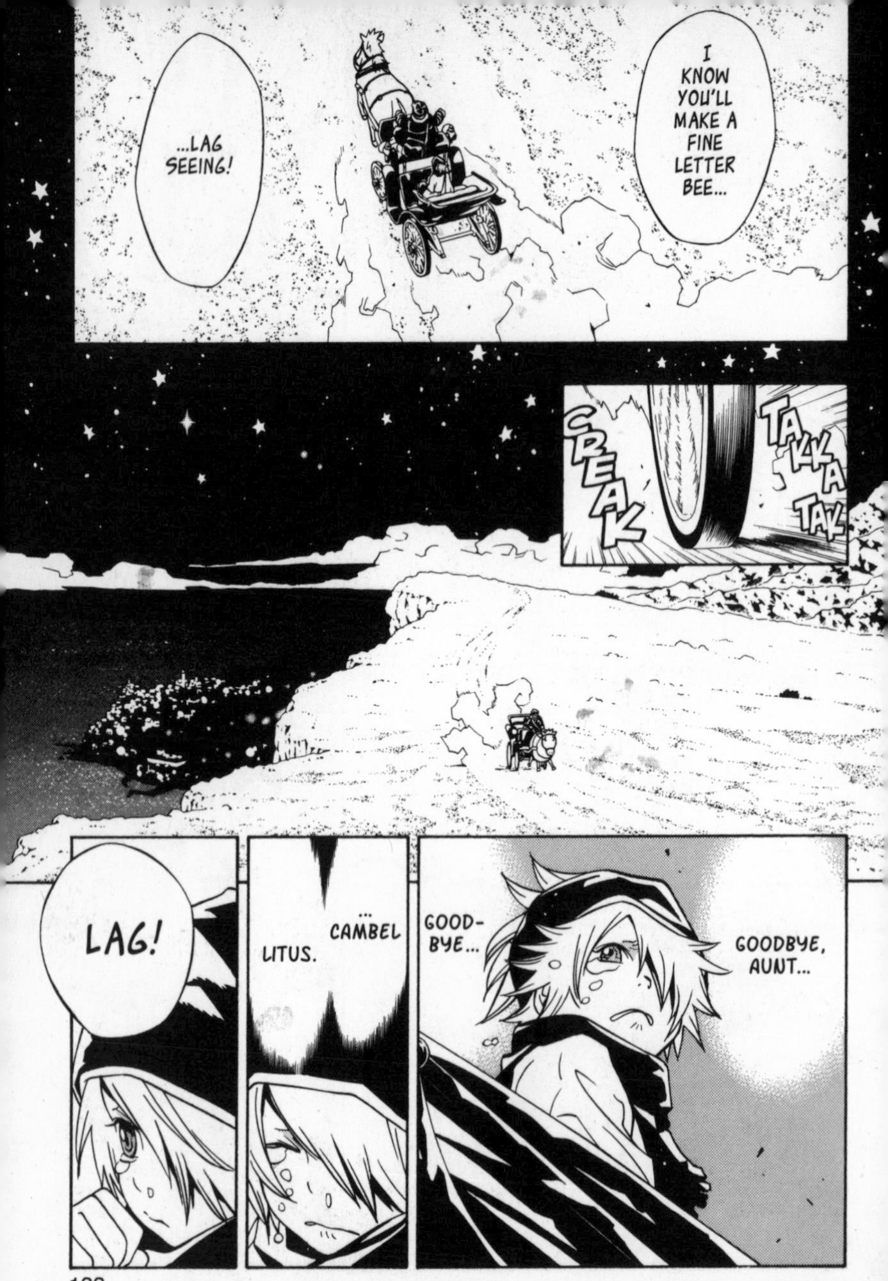
I KNOW YOU'LL MAKE A FINE LETTER BEE...
...LAG SEEING!
TAKKATAK
CREAK
GOODBYE, AUNT...
GOOD-BYE...
...CAMBEL
LITUS.
LAG!

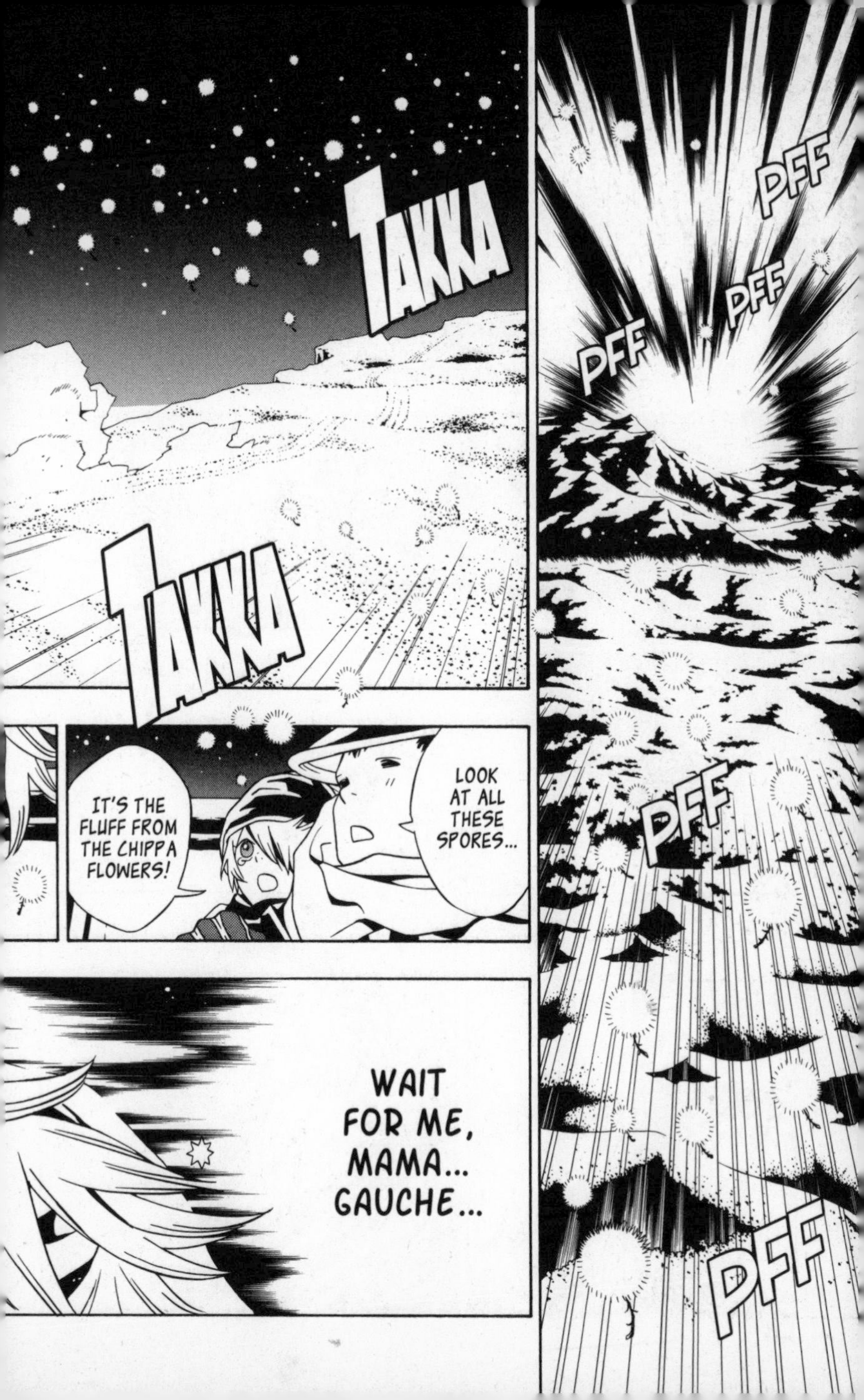

PFF
PFF
PFF
PFF
PFF
TAKKA
TAKKA
LOOK AT ALL THESE SPORES...
IT'S THE FLUFF FROM THE CHIPPA FLOWERS!
WAIT FOR ME, MAMA... GAUCHE...

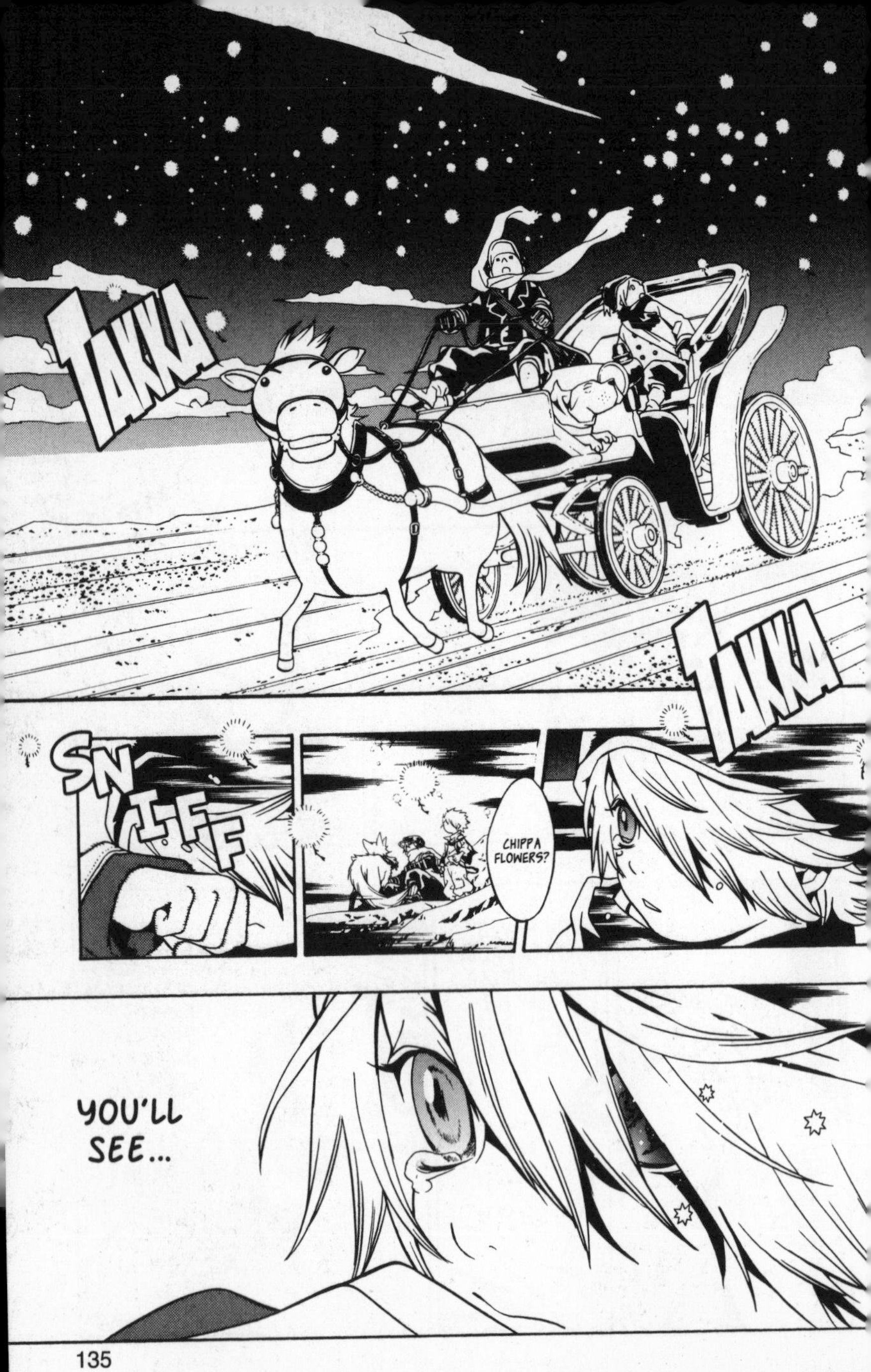
TAKKA
TAKKA
CHIPPA FLOWERS?
SNIFF
YOU'LL SEE...

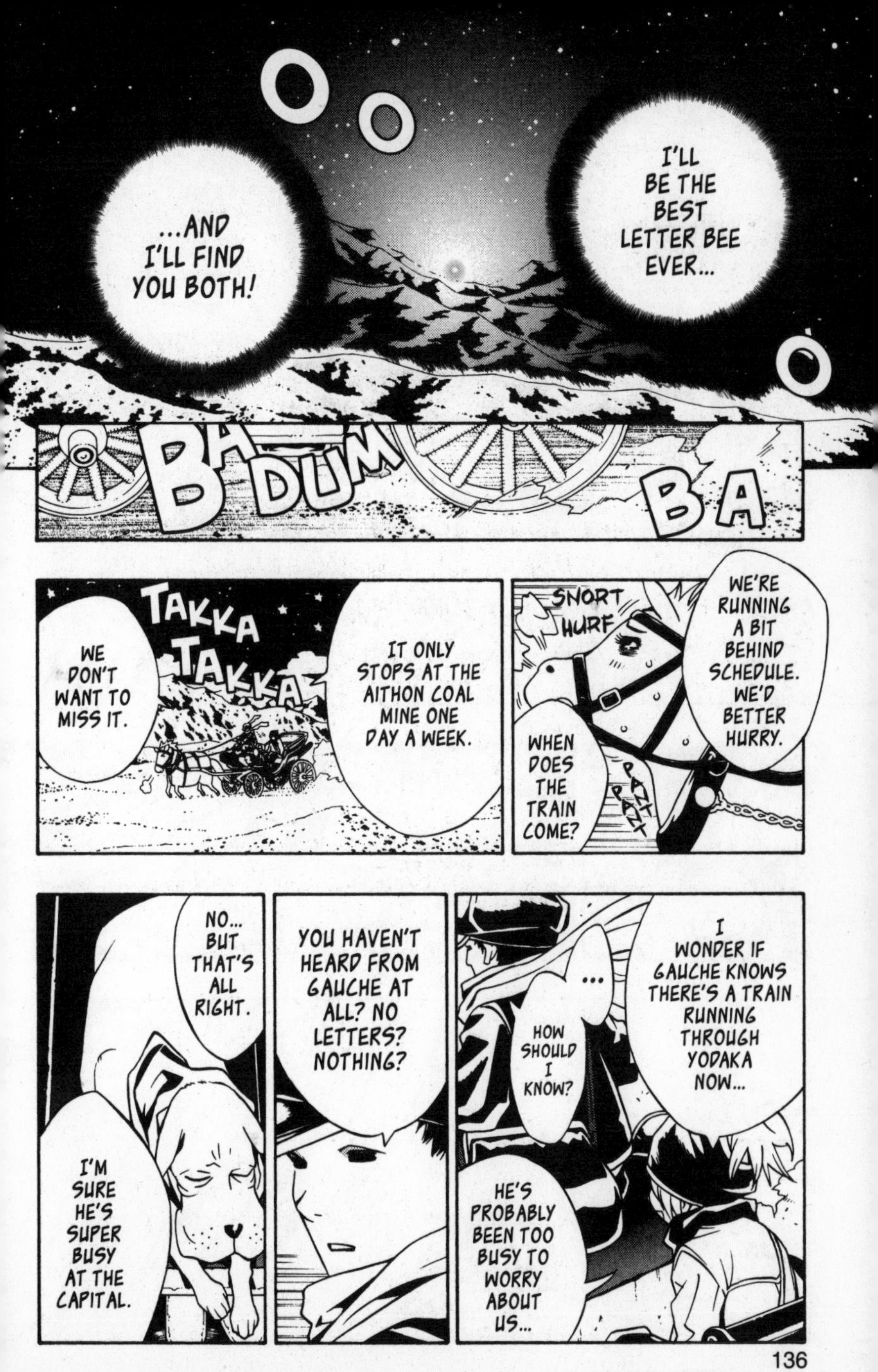

I'LL BE THE BEST LETTER BEE EVER...
...AND I'LL FIND YOU BOTH!
BA DUM
BA
WE'RE RUNNING A BIT BEHIND SCHEDULE. WE'D BETTER HURRY.
SNORT HURF
WHEN DOES THE TRAIN COME?
PANT PANT
IT ONLY STOPS AT THE AITHON COAL MINE ONE DAY A WEEK.
TAKKA TAKKA
WE DON'T WANT TO MISS IT.
I WONDER IF GAUCHE KNOWS THERE'S A TRAIN RUNNING THROUGH YODAKA NOW...
...
HOW SHOULD I KNOW?
HE'S PROBABLY BEEN TOO BUSY TO WORRY ABOUT US...
YOU HAVEN'T HEARD FROM GAUCHE AT ALL? NO LETTERS? NOTHING?
NO... BUT THAT'S ALL RIGHT.
I'M SURE HE'S SUPER BUSY AT THE CAPITAL.

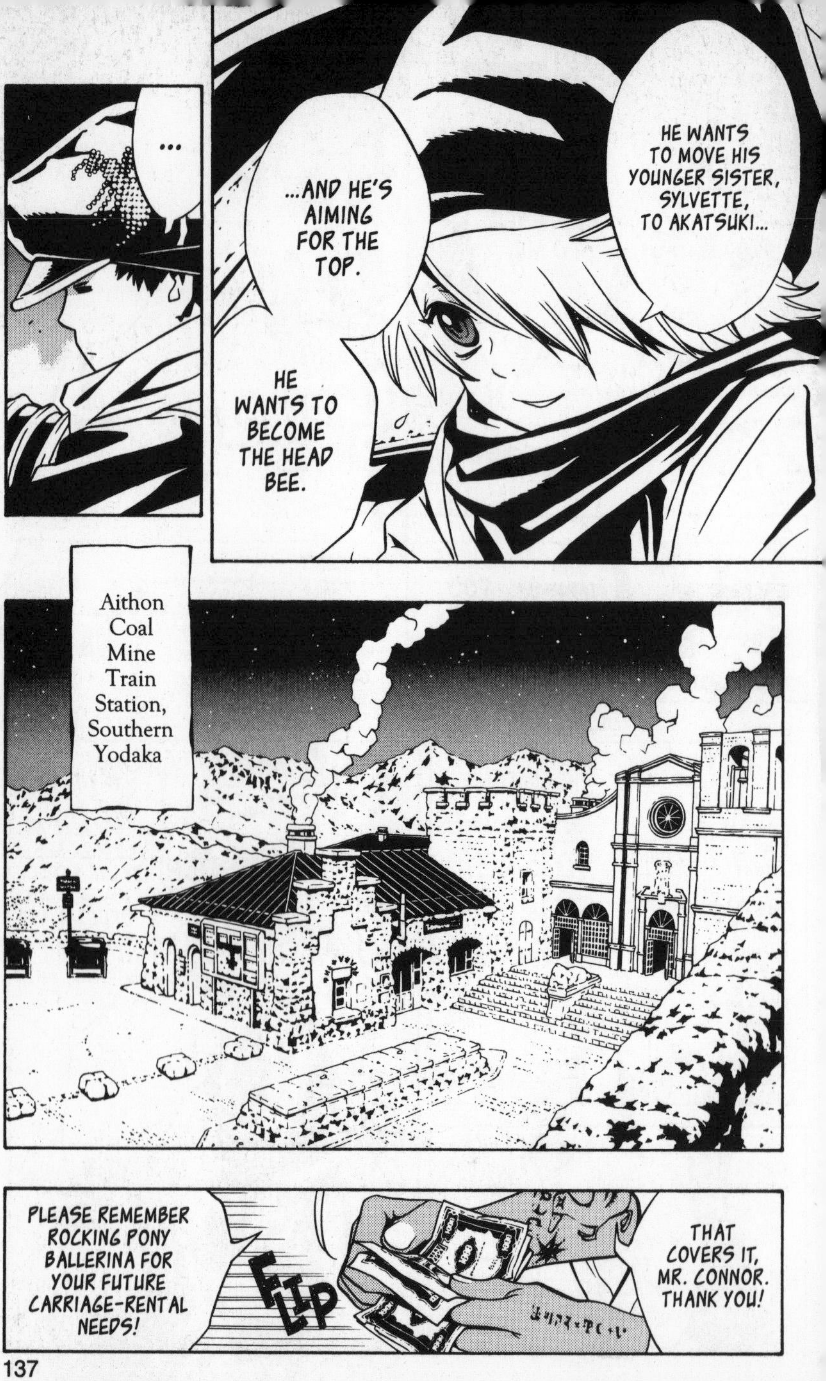
HE WANTS TO MOVE HIS YOUNGER SISTER, SYLVETTE, TO AKATSUKI...
...AND HE'S AIMING FOR THE TOP.
HE WANTS TO BECOME THE HEAD BEE.
...
Aithon Coal Mine Train Station, Southern Yodaka
THAT COVERS IT, MR. CONNOR. THANK YOU!
FLIP
PLEASE REMEMBER ROCKING PONY BALLERINA FOR YOUR FUTURE CARRIAGE-RENTAL NEEDS!

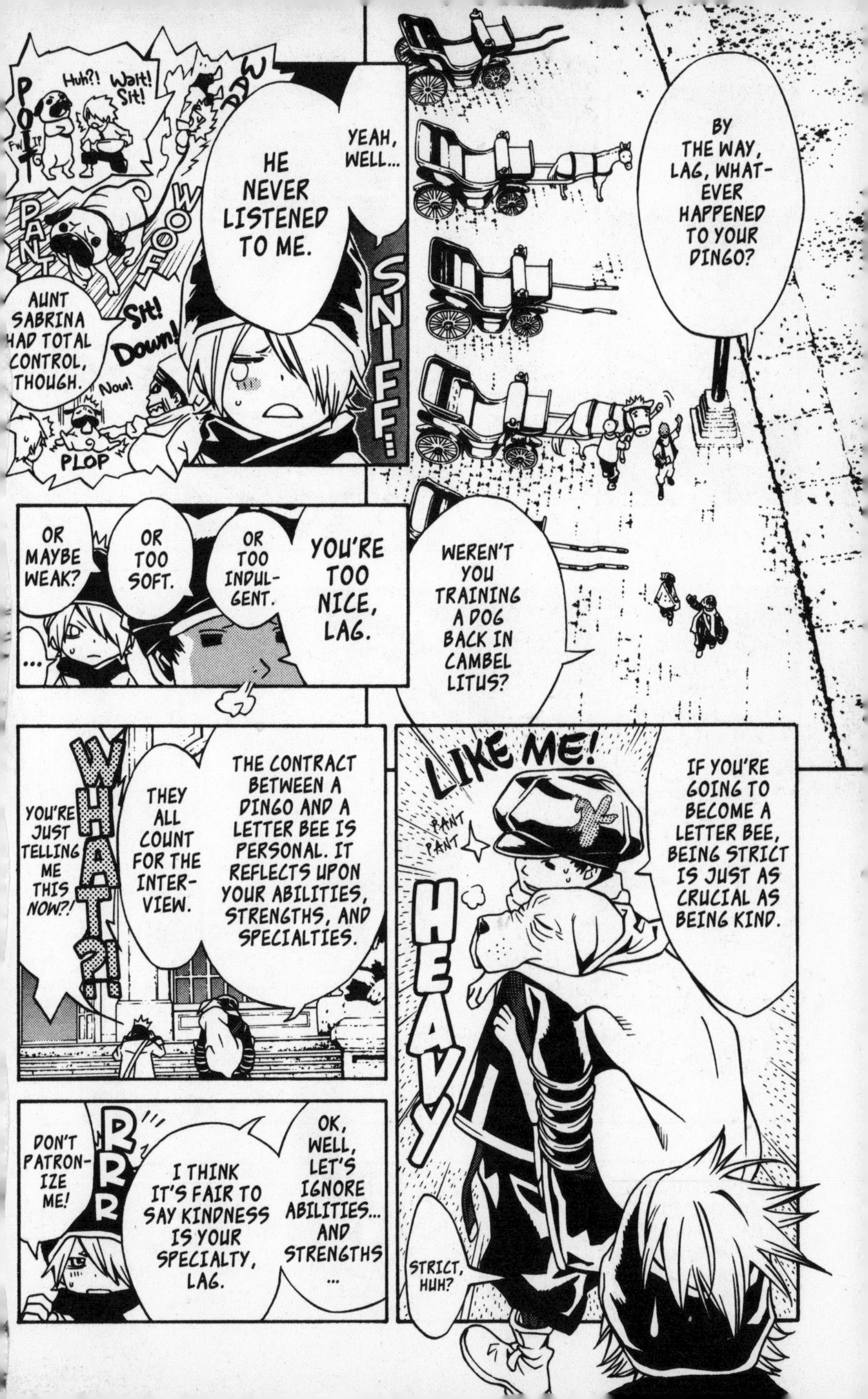
BY THE WAY, LAG, WHATEVER HAPPENED TO YOUR DINGO?
WEREN'T YOU TRAINING A DOG BACK IN CAMBEL LITUS?
YEAH, WELL...
HE NEVER LISTENED TO ME.
SNIFF...
PAW
Wait! Sit!
Huh?!
POIT
FWIP
WOOF
PANT
AUNT SABRINA HAD TOTAL CONTROL, THOUGH.
Sit! Down!
Now!
PLOP
YOU'RE TOO NICE, LAG.
OR TOO INDULGENT.
OR TOO SOFT.
OR MAYBE WEAK?
...
IF YOU'RE GOING TO BECOME A LETTER BEE, BEING STRICT IS JUST AS CRUCIAL AS BEING KIND.
LIKE ME!
PANT PANT
HEAVY
STRICT, HUH?
THE CONTRACT BETWEEN A DINGO AND A LETTER BEE IS PERSONAL. IT REFLECTS UPON YOUR ABILITIES, STRENGTHS, AND SPECIALTIES.
THEY ALL COUNT FOR THE INTERVIEW.
WHAT?!
YOU'RE JUST TELLING ME THIS NOW?!
OK, WELL, LET'S IGNORE ABILITIES... AND STRENGTHS...
I THINK IT'S FAIR TO SAY KINDNESS IS YOUR SPECIALTY, LAG.
RRR
DON'T PATRONIZE ME!

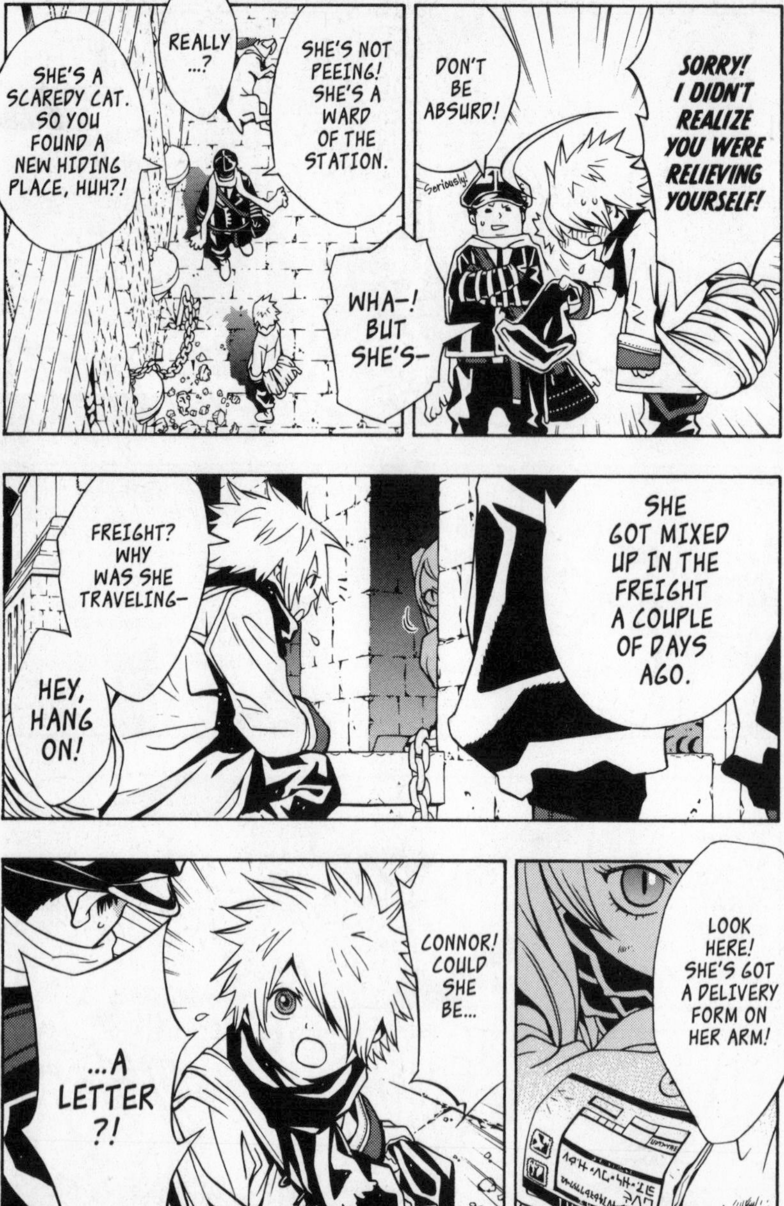
SORRY! I DIDN'T REALIZE YOU WERE RELIEVING YOURSELF!
DON'T BE ABSURD!
Seriously!
WHA-! BUT SHE'S-
SHE'S NOT PEEING! SHE'S A WARD OF THE STATION.
REALLY ...?
SHE'S A SCAREDY CAT. SO YOU FOUND A NEW HIDING PLACE, HUH?!
SHE GOT MIXED UP IN THE FREIGHT A COUPLE OF DAYS AGO.
FREIGHT? WHY WAS SHE TRAVELING-
HEY, HANG ON!
LOOK HERE! SHE'S GOT A DELIVERY FORM ON HER ARM!
CONNOR! COULD SHE BE...
...A LETTER ?!

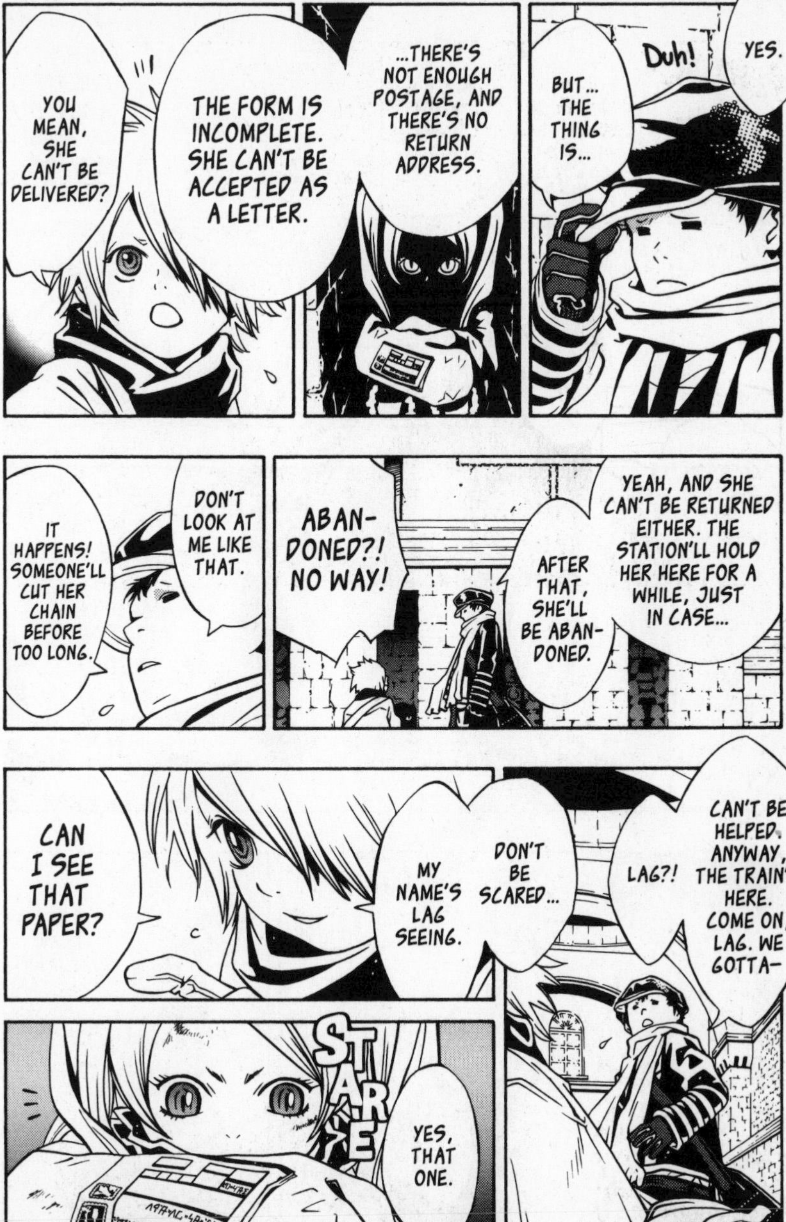
YES.
Duh!
BUT... THE THING IS...
...THERE'S NOT ENOUGH POSTAGE, AND THERE'S NO RETURN ADDRESS.
THE FORM IS INCOMPLETE. SHE CAN'T BE ACCEPTED AS A LETTER.
YOU MEAN, SHE CAN'T BE DELIVERED?
YEAH, AND SHE CAN'T BE RETURNED EITHER. THE STATION'LL HOLD HER HERE FOR A WHILE, JUST IN CASE...
AFTER THAT, SHE'LL BE ABANDONED.
ABANDONED?! NO WAY!
DON'T LOOK AT ME LIKE THAT.
IT HAPPENS! SOMEONE'LL CUT HER CHAIN BEFORE TOO LONG.
CAN'T BE HELPED. ANYWAY, THE TRAIN'S HERE. COME ON, LAG. WE GOTTA-
LAG?!
DON'T BE SCARED...
MY NAME'S LAG SEEING.
CAN I SEE THAT PAPER?
STARE
YES, THAT ONE.

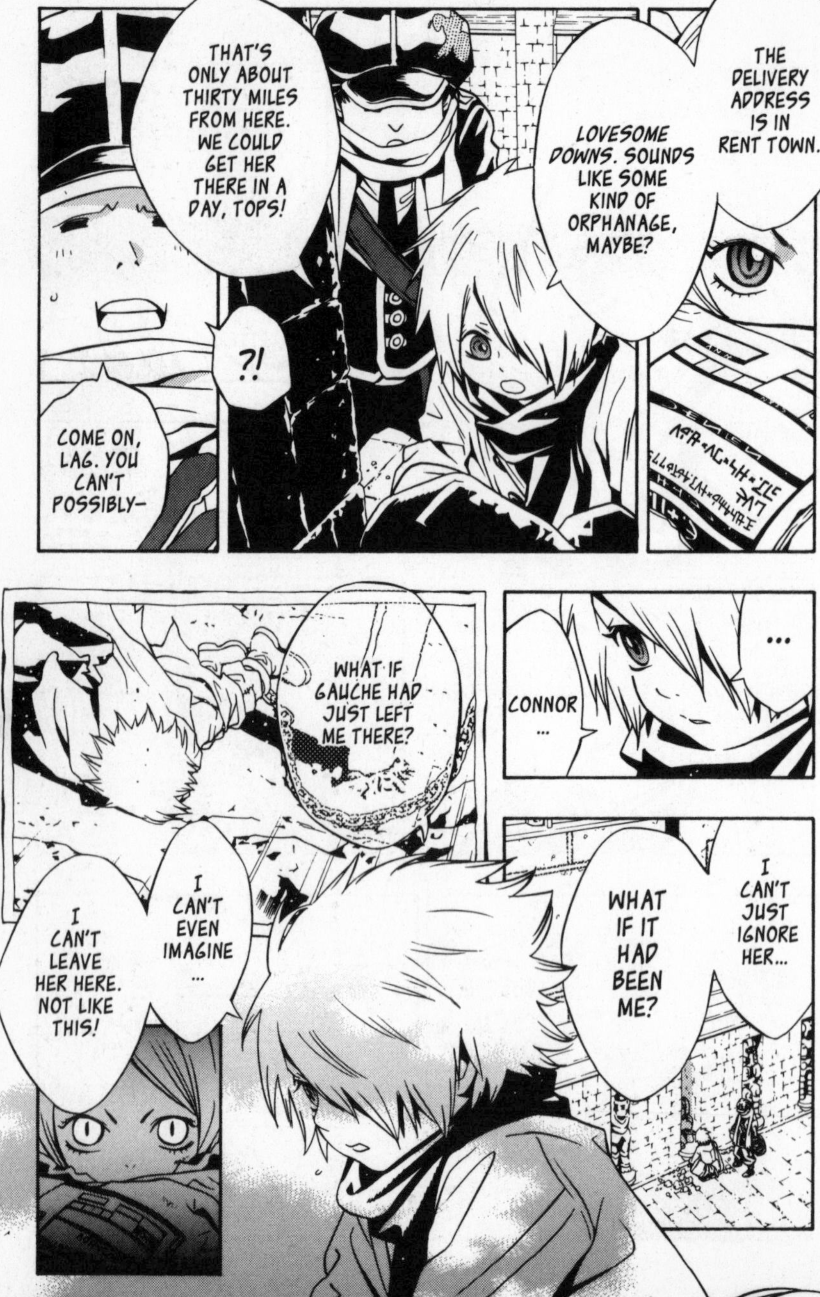
THE DELIVERY ADDRESS IS IN RENT TOWN.
LOVESOME DOWNS. SOUNDS LIKE SOME KIND OF ORPHANAGE, MAYBE?
THAT'S ONLY ABOUT THIRTY MILES FROM HERE. WE COULD GET HER THERE IN A DAY, TOPS!
?!
COME ON, LAG. YOU CAN'T POSSIBLY—
...
CONNOR ...
WHAT IF GAUCHE HAD JUST LEFT ME THERE?
I CAN'T JUST IGNORE HER...
WHAT IF IT HAD BEEN ME?
I CAN'T EVEN IMAGINE ...
I CAN'T LEAVE HER HERE. NOT LIKE THIS!

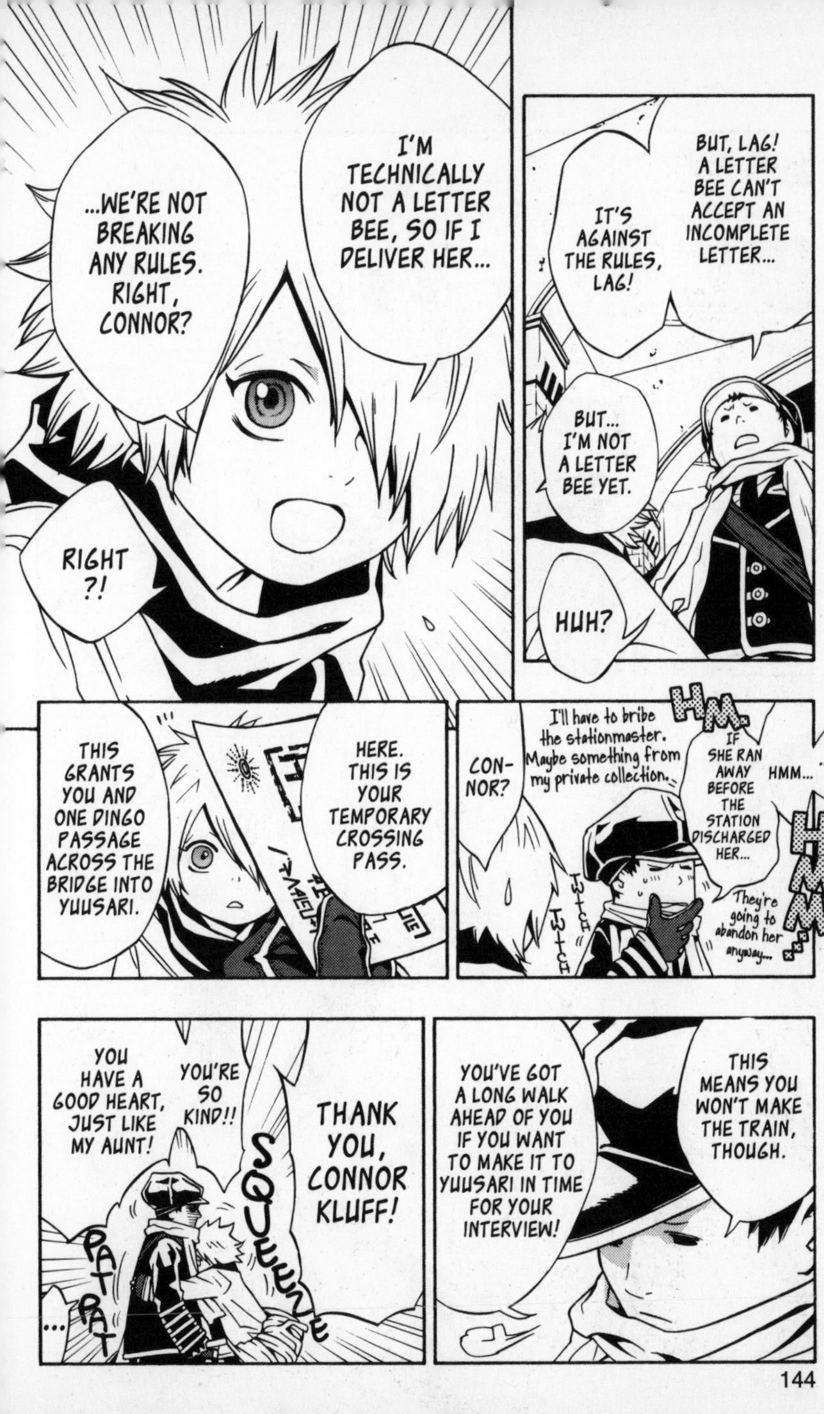
BUT, LAG! A LETTER BEE CAN'T ACCEPT AN INCOMPLETE LETTER...
IT'S AGAINST THE RULES, LAG!
BUT... I'M NOT A LETTER BEE YET.
HUH?
I'M TECHNICALLY NOT A LETTER BEE, SO IF I DELIVER HER...
...WE'RE NOT BREAKING ANY RULES. RIGHT, CONNOR?
RIGHT?!
HM.
...
IF SHE RAN AWAY BEFORE THE STATION DISCHARGED HER...
HMM...
I'll have to bribe the stationmaster. Maybe something from my private collection.
CON-NOR?
HMM...
They're going to abandon her anyway...
TWITCH TWITCH
HERE. THIS IS YOUR TEMPORARY CROSSING PASS.
THIS GRANTS YOU AND ONE DINGO PASSAGE ACROSS THE BRIDGE INTO YUUSARI.
THIS MEANS YOU WON'T MAKE THE TRAIN, THOUGH.
YOU'VE GOT A LONG WALK AHEAD OF YOU IF YOU WANT TO MAKE IT TO YUUSARI IN TIME FOR YOUR INTERVIEW!
THANK YOU, CONNOR KLUFF!
SQUEEEEZE
YOU'RE SO KIND!!
YOU HAVE A GOOD HEART, JUST LIKE MY AUNT!
PAT PAT
...

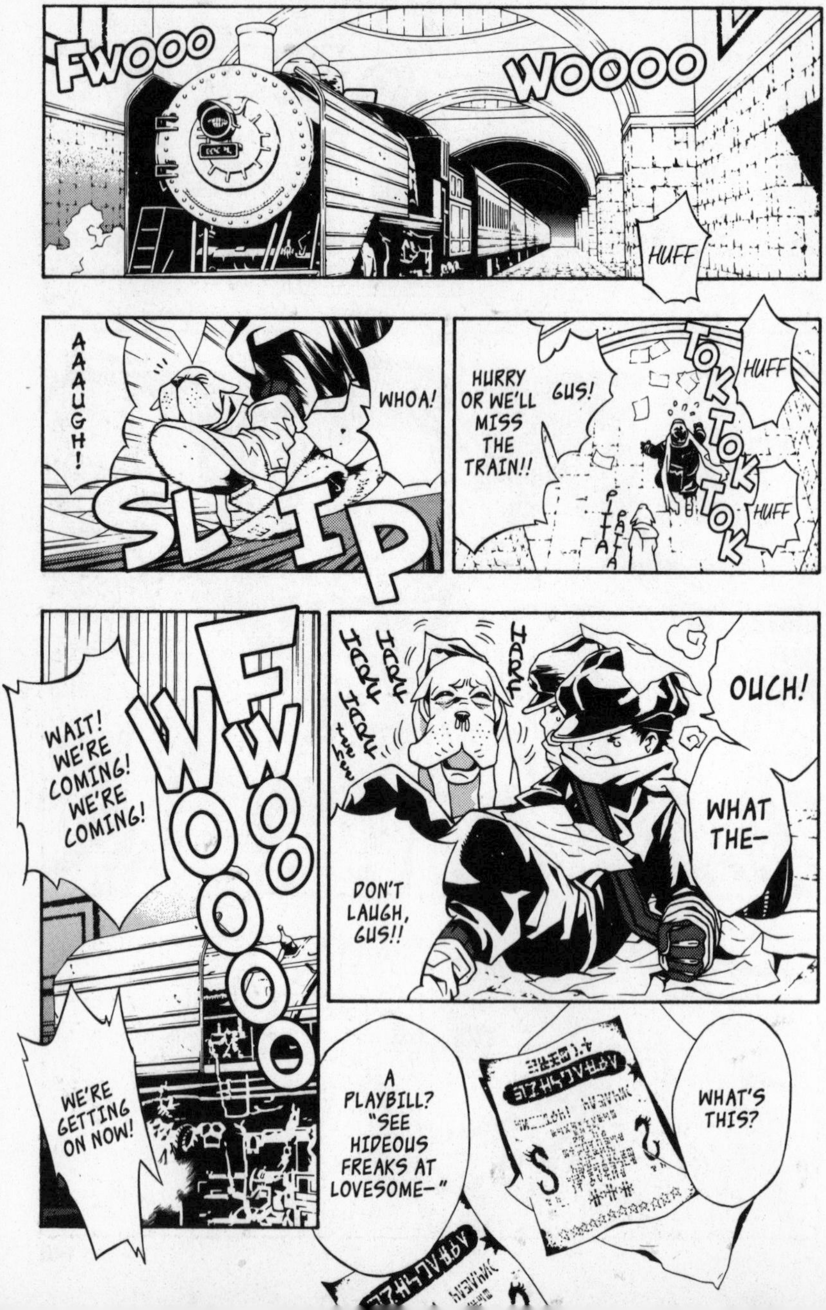
FWOOO WOOOO
HUFF
TOK TOK TOK
HUFF
HUFF
GUS!
HURRY OR WE'LL MISS THE TRAIN!!
PAPAPA
WHOA!
AAAAUGH!
SLIP
OUCH!
HARF HARF HARF HARF
WHAT THE—
DON'T LAUGH, GUS!!
WHAT'S THIS?
A PLAYBILL? "SEE HIDEOUS FREAKS AT LOVESOME—"
FWOOOOOO
WAIT! WE'RE COMING! WE'RE COMING!
WE'RE GETTING ON NOW!

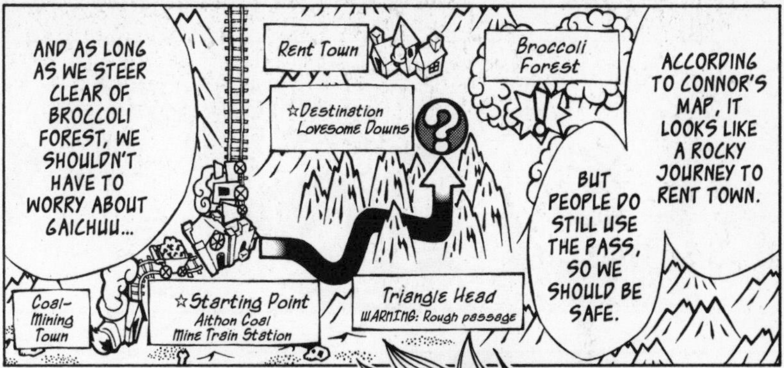
ACCORDING TO CONNOR'S MAP, IT LOOKS LIKE A ROCKY JOURNEY TO RENT TOWN.
BUT PEOPLE DO STILL USE THE PASS, SO WE SHOULD BE SAFE.
Broccoli Forest
Rent Town
☆Destination Lovesome Downs
Triangle Head
WARNING: Rough passage
☆Starting Point
Aithon Coal Mine Train Station
Coal-Mining Town
AND AS LONG AS WE STEER CLEAR OF BROCCOLI FOREST, WE SHOULDN'T HAVE TO WORRY ABOUT GAICHUU...

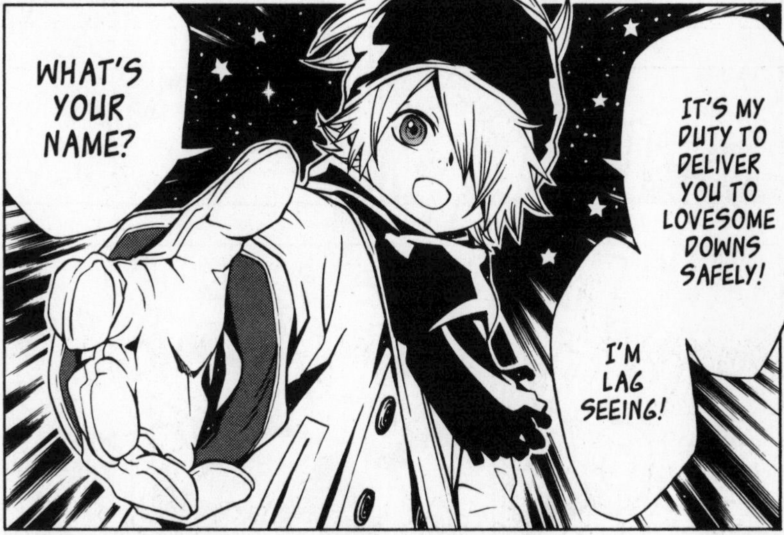
IT'S MY DUTY TO DELIVER YOU TO LOVESOME DOWNS SAFELY!
I'M LAG SEEING!
WHAT'S YOUR NAME?

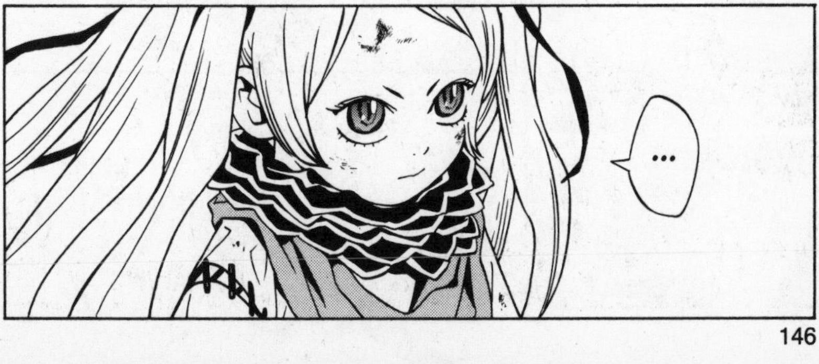
...

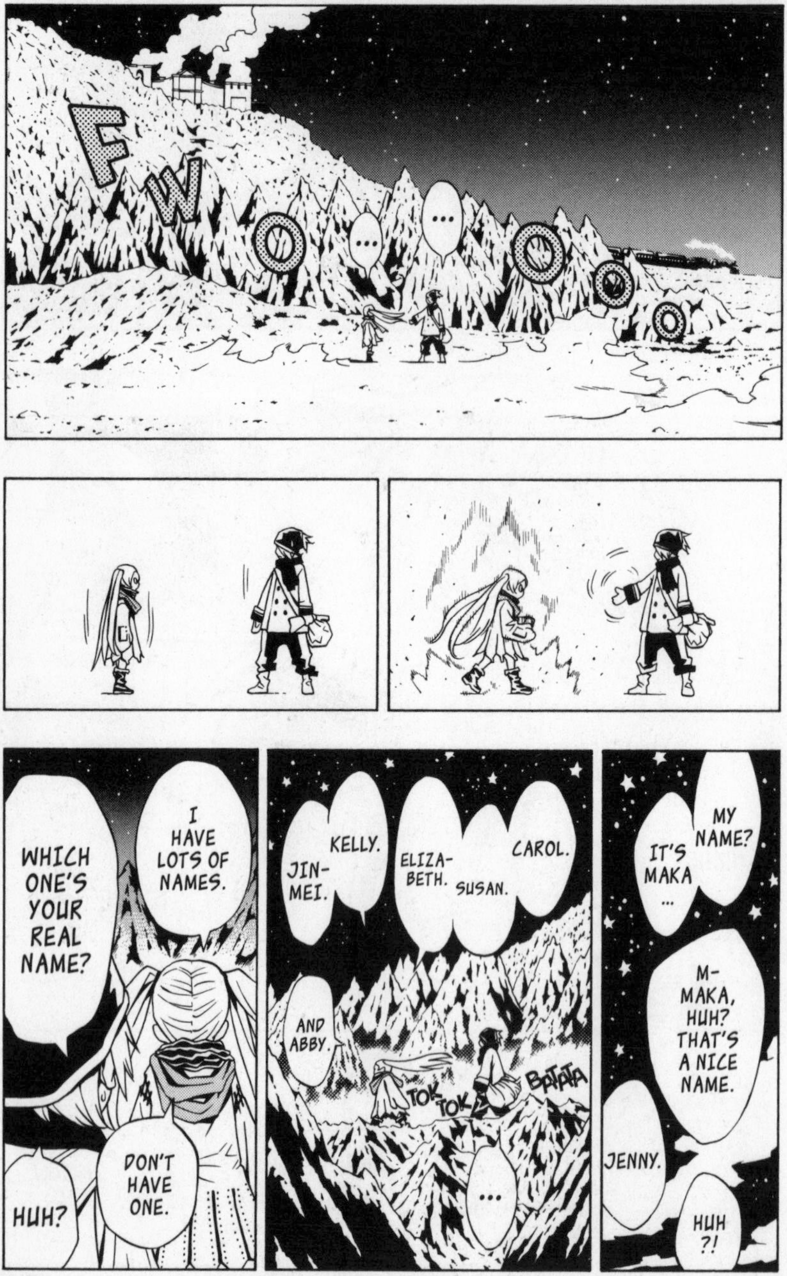
...
...
FWOOOOO
MY NAME?
IT'S MAKA ...
M-MAKA, HUH? THAT'S A NICE NAME.
JENNY.
HUH ?!
CAROL.
SUSAN.
ELIZA-BETH.
KELLY.
JIN-MEI.
AND ABBY.
BATATA
TOK TOK
...
I HAVE LOTS OF NAMES.
WHICH ONE'S YOUR REAL NAME?
DON'T HAVE ONE.
HUH?

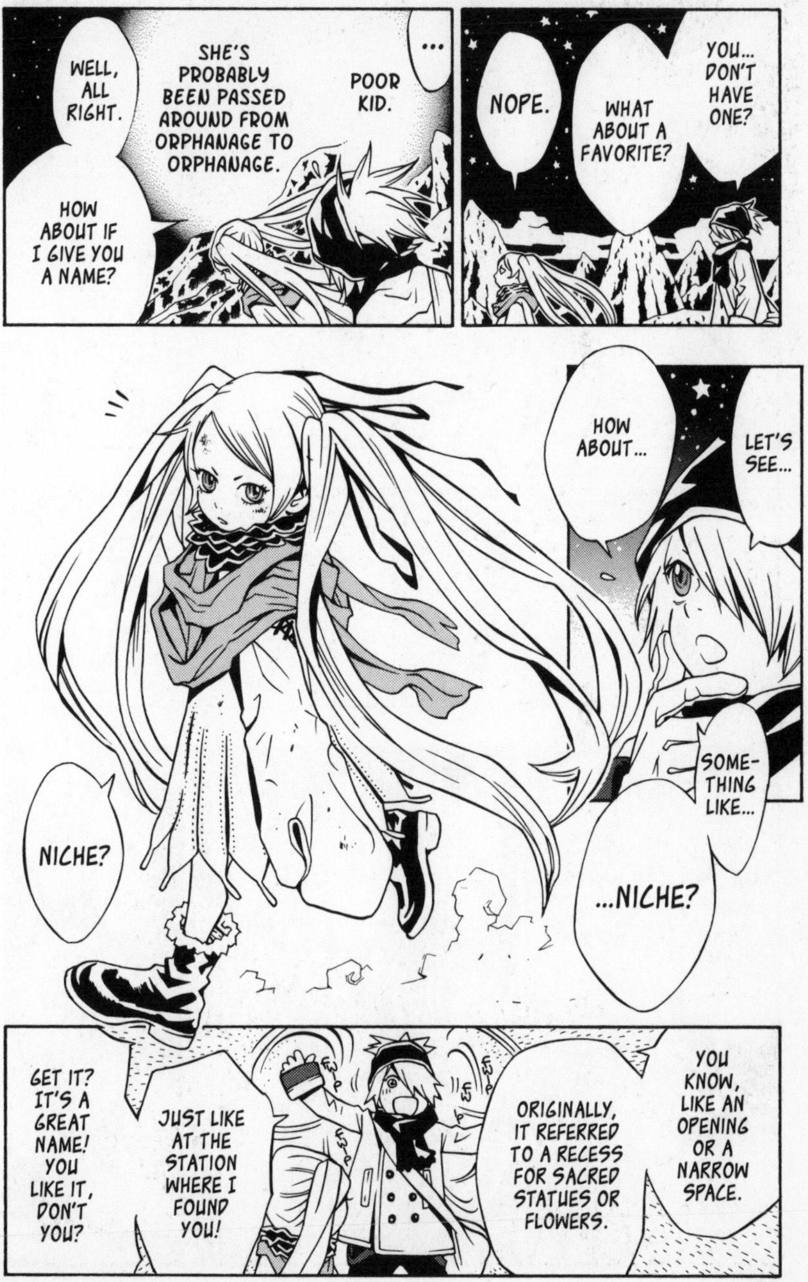
YOU... DON'T HAVE ONE?
WHAT ABOUT A FAVORITE?
NOPE.
...
POOR KID.
SHE'S PROBABLY BEEN PASSED AROUND FROM ORPHANAGE TO ORPHANAGE.
WELL, ALL RIGHT.
HOW ABOUT IF I GIVE YOU A NAME?
LET'S SEE...
HOW ABOUT...
SOME-THING LIKE...
...NICHE?
NICHE?
YOU KNOW, LIKE AN OPENING OR A NARROW SPACE.
ORIGINALLY, IT REFERRED TO A RECESS FOR SACRED STATUES OR FLOWERS.
JUST LIKE AT THE STATION WHERE I FOUND YOU!
GET IT? IT'S A GREAT NAME! YOU LIKE IT, DON'T YOU?

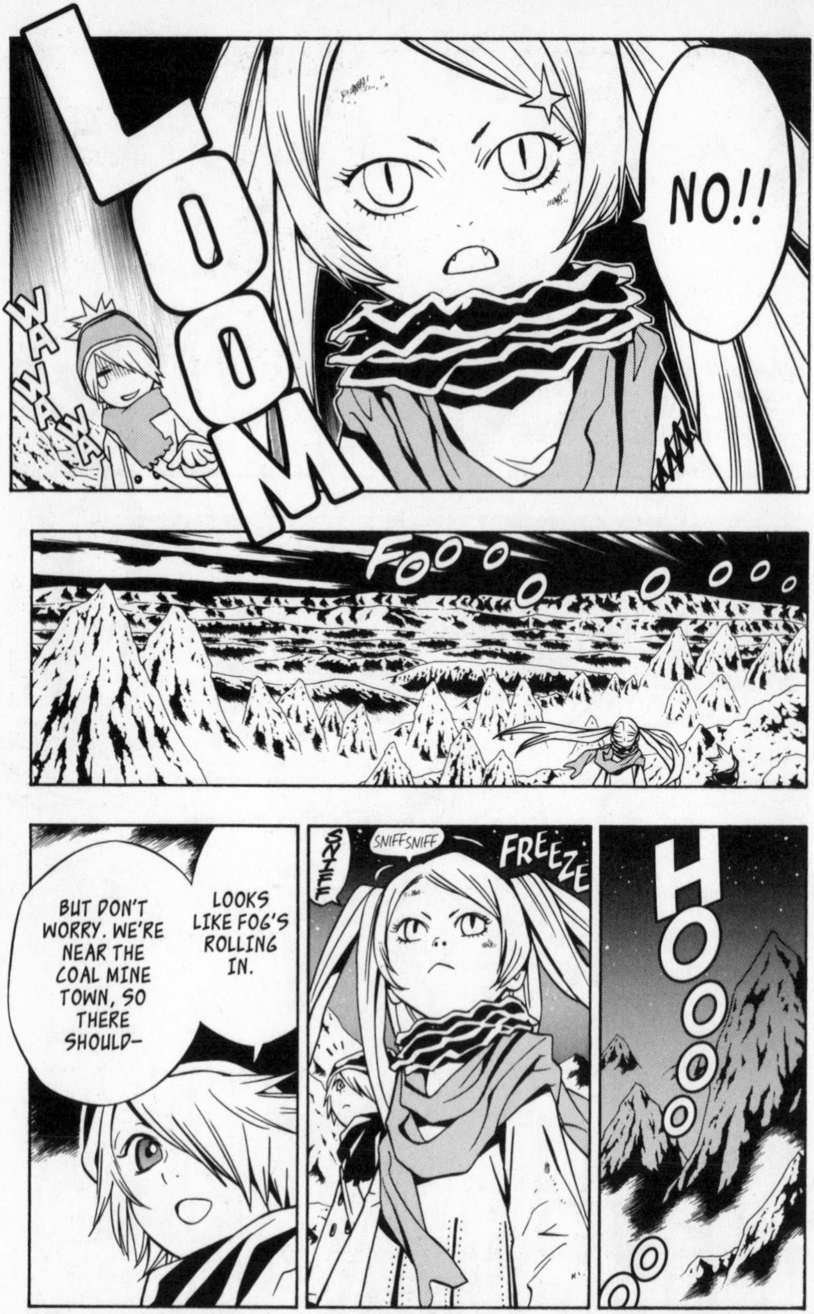
NO!!
LOOOM
WAWAWAWA
FOOOOOOOOO
HOOOOOOOO
FREEZE
SNIFFSNIFF
SNIFF
LOOKS LIKE FOG'S ROLLING IN.
BUT DON'T WORRY. WE'RE NEAR THE COAL MINE TOWN, SO THERE SHOULD—

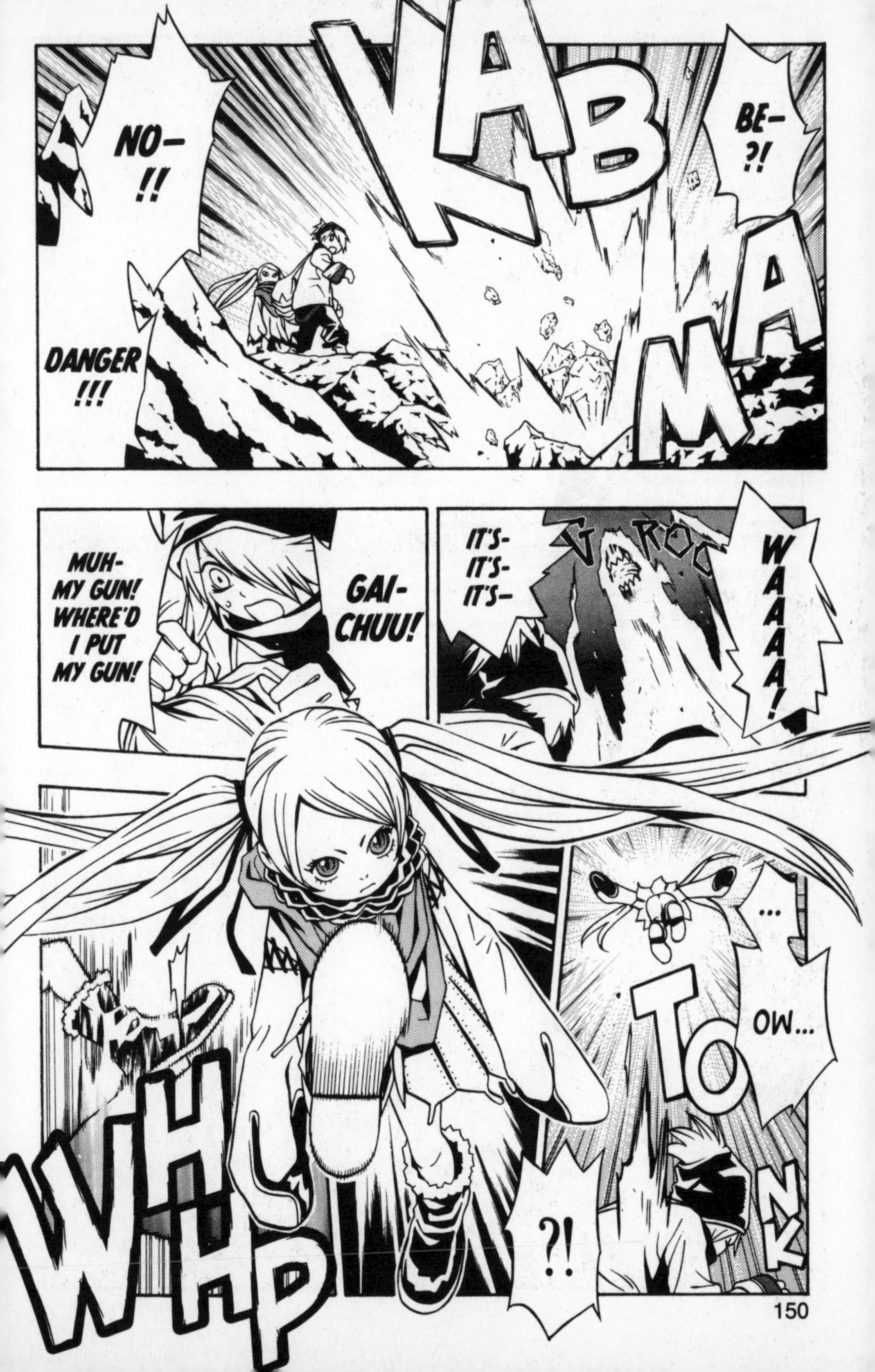
BE- ?!
KABAMA
NO- !!
DANGER !!!
WAAAAA!
IT'S- IT'S- IT'S-
GAI-CHUU!
MUH- MY GUN! WHERE'D I PUT MY GUN!
...
OW...
TONK
?!
WHU
WHP

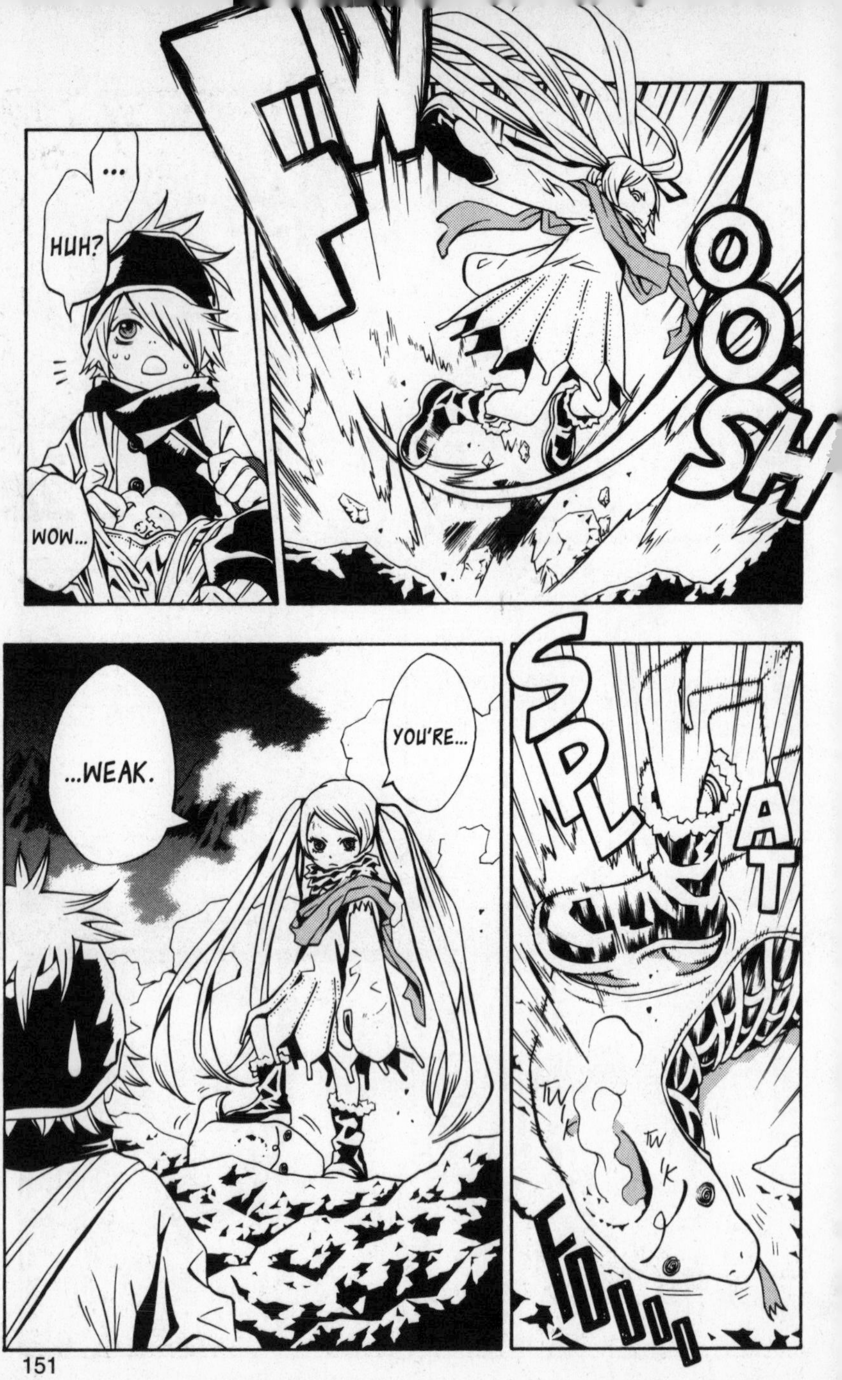
FWOOOSH
...
HUH?
WOW...
SPLAT
TWIK
TWIK
FOOOOO
YOU'RE...
...WEAK.

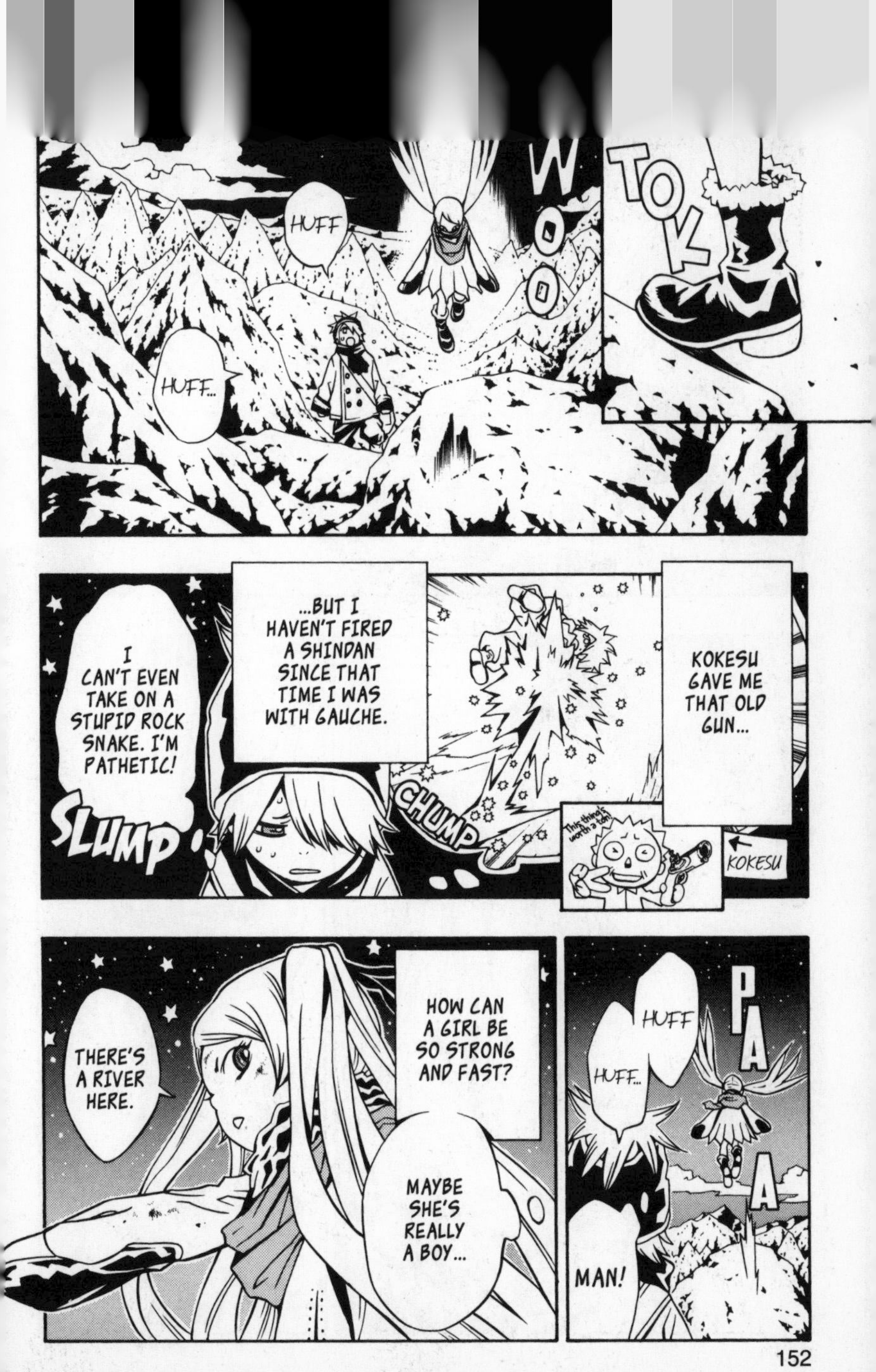
TOK
WOO
HUFF
HUFF...
KOKESU GAVE ME THAT OLD GUN...
This thing's worth a ton!
KOKESU
CHUMP
...BUT I HAVEN'T FIRED A SHINDAN SINCE THAT TIME I WAS WITH GAUCHE.
I CAN'T EVEN TAKE ON A STUPID ROCK SNAKE. I'M PATHETIC!
SLUMP
PA
A
HUFF
HUFF...
MAN!
HOW CAN A GIRL BE SO STRONG AND FAST?
MAYBE SHE'S REALLY A BOY...
THERE'S A RIVER HERE.

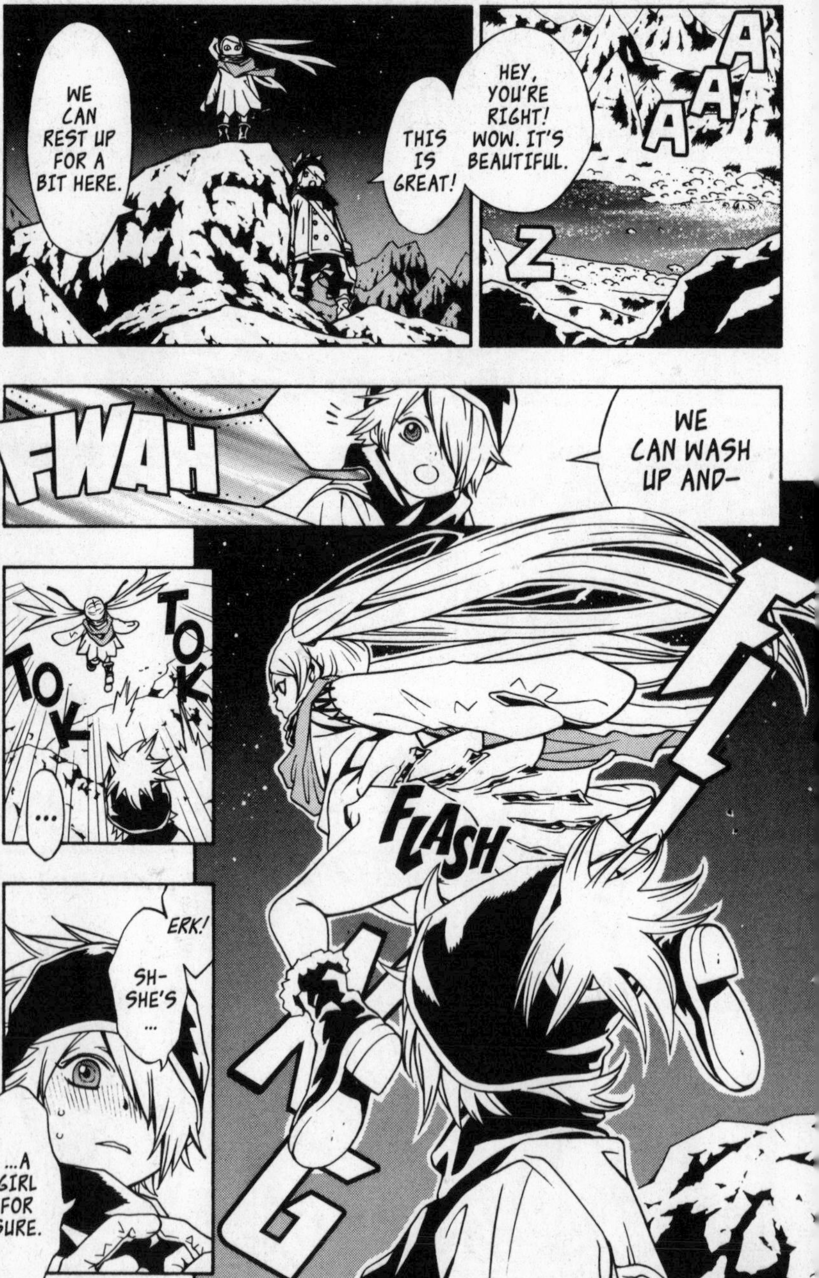

AAAA
Z
HEY, YOU'RE RIGHT! WOW. IT'S BEAUTIFUL.
THIS IS GREAT!
WE CAN REST UP FOR A BIT HERE.
WE CAN WASH UP AND–
FWAH
FLASH
FLING
TOK TOK
...
ERK!
SH-SHE'S ...
...A GIRL FOR SURE.

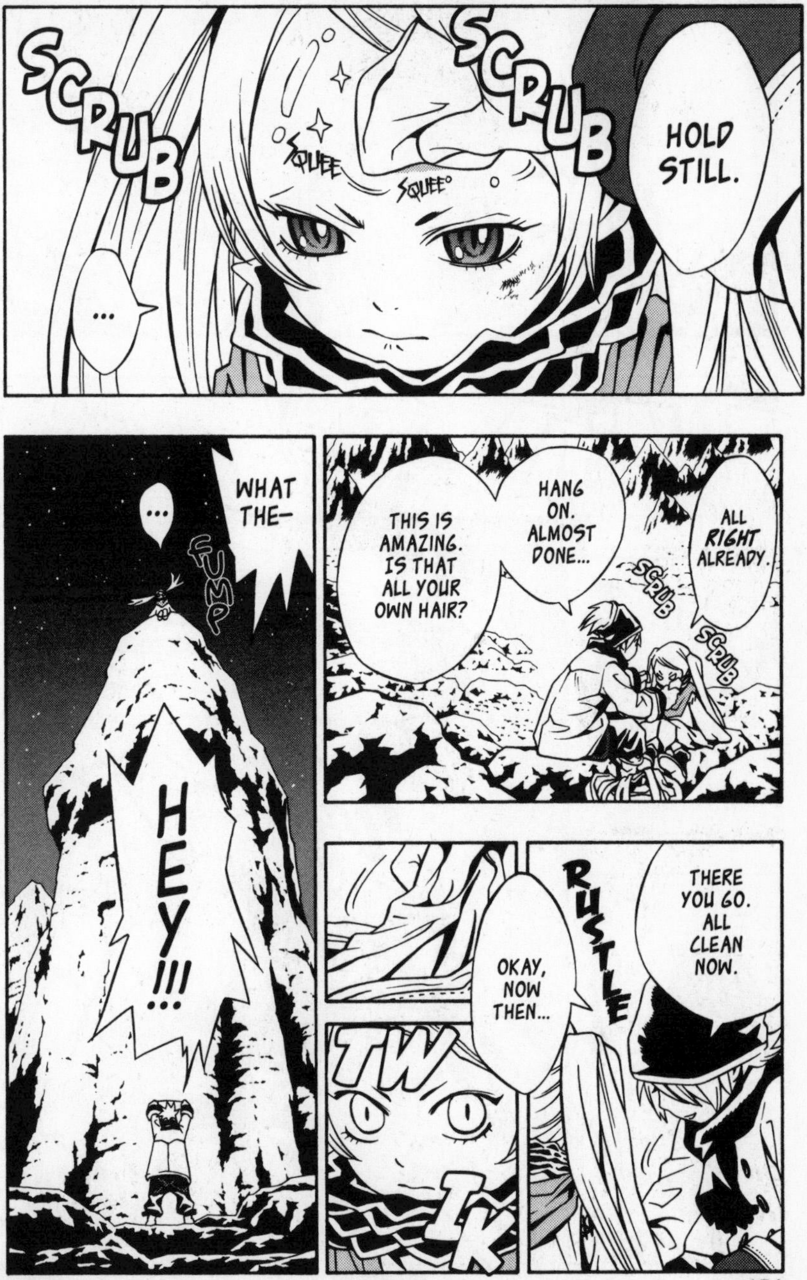
HOLD STILL.
SCRUB
SCRUB
SQUEE
SQUEE
...
ALL RIGHT ALREADY.
SCRUB
SCRUB
HANG ON. ALMOST DONE...
THIS IS AMAZING. IS THAT ALL YOUR OWN HAIR?
THERE YOU GO. ALL CLEAN NOW.
RUSTLE
OKAY, NOW THEN...
TWIK
WHAT THE—
...
FUMP
HEY!!!

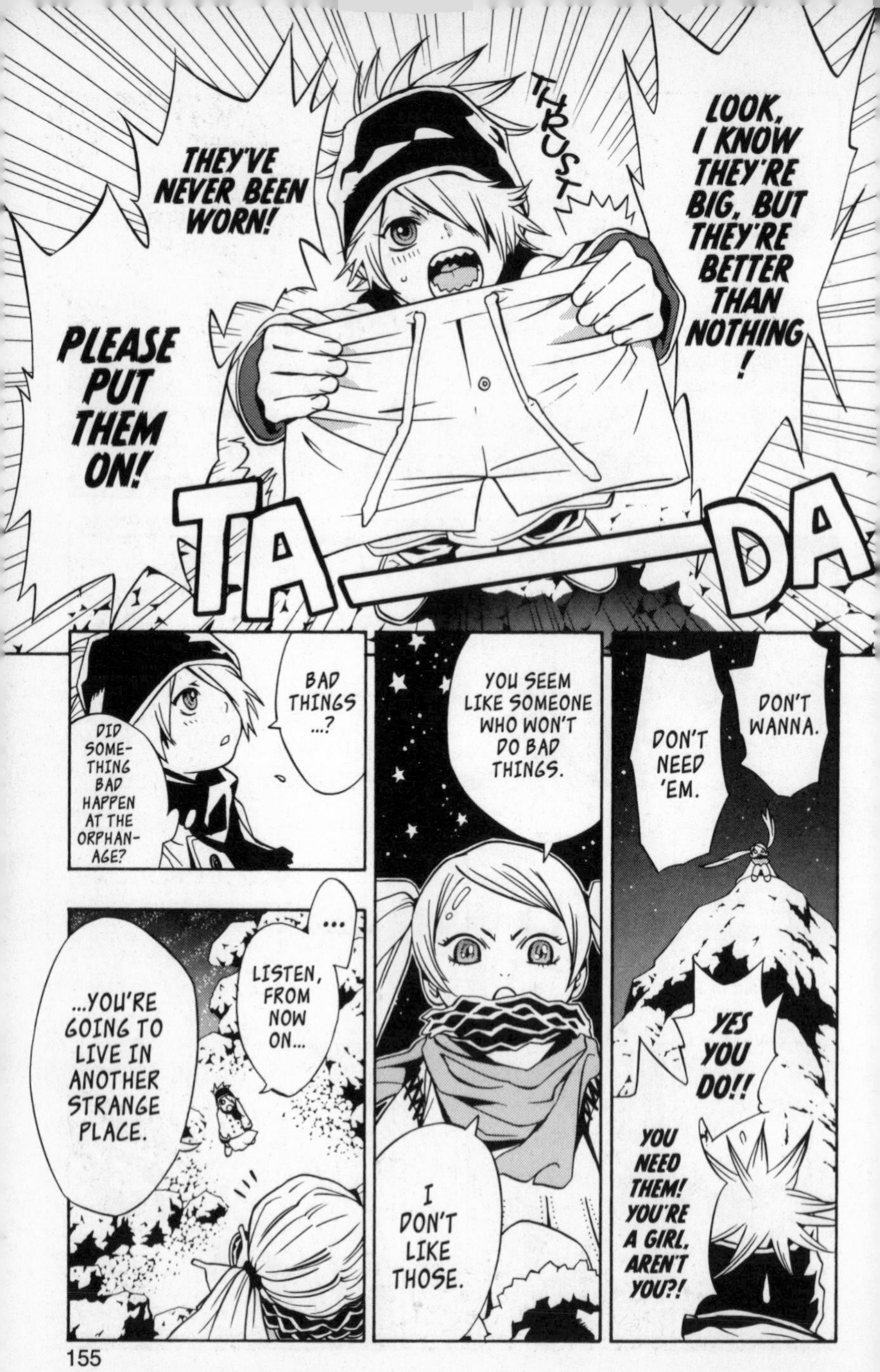
LOOK, I KNOW THEY'RE BIG, BUT THEY'RE BETTER THAN NOTHING!
THRUST
THEY'VE NEVER BEEN WORN!
PLEASE PUT THEM ON!
TA—DA
DON'T WANNA.
DON'T NEED 'EM.
YES YOU DO!!
YOU NEED THEM! YOU'RE A GIRL, AREN'T YOU?!
YOU SEEM LIKE SOMEONE WHO WON'T DO BAD THINGS.
I DON'T LIKE THOSE.
BAD THINGS ...?
DID SOMETHING BAD HAPPEN AT THE ORPHANAGE?
...
LISTEN, FROM NOW ON...
...YOU'RE GOING TO LIVE IN ANOTHER STRANGE PLACE.

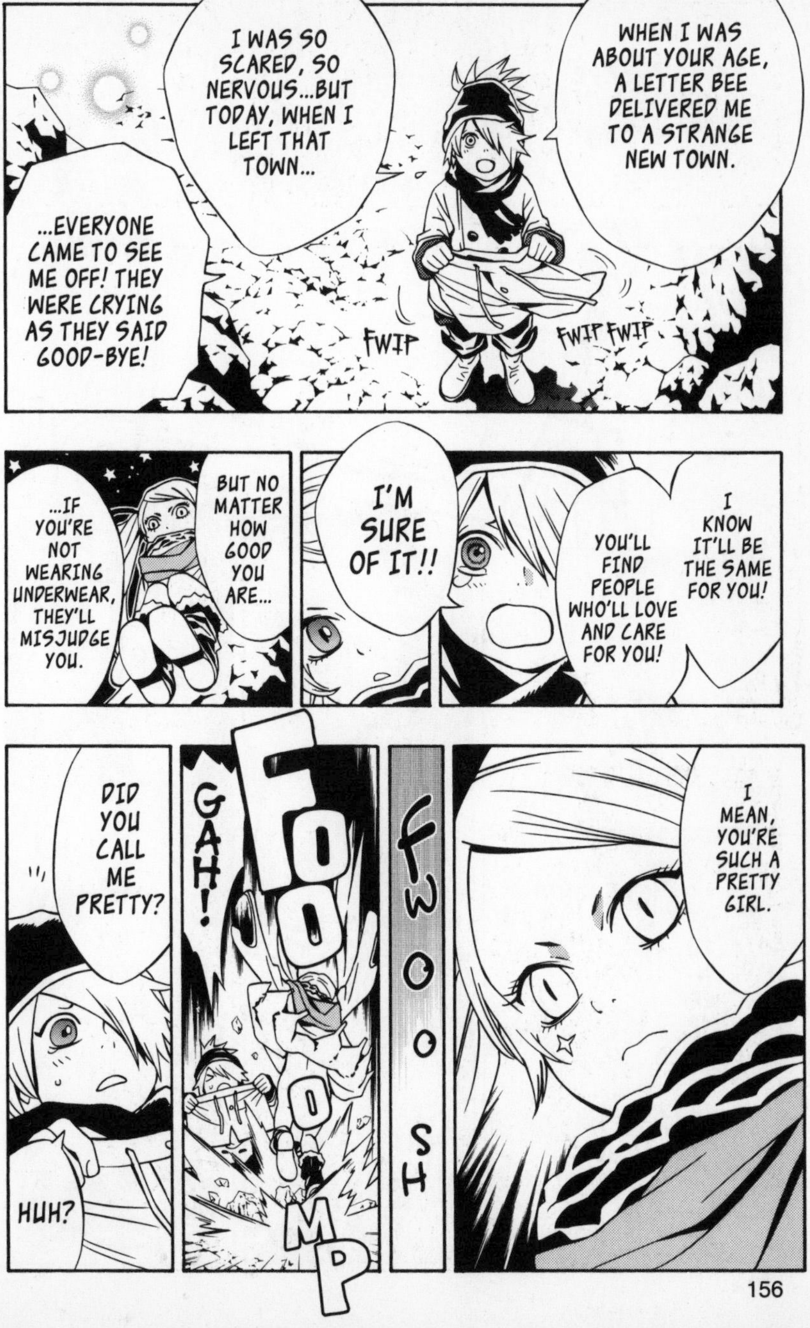
WHEN I WAS ABOUT YOUR AGE, A LETTER BEE DELIVERED ME TO A STRANGE NEW TOWN.
I WAS SO SCARED, SO NERVOUS...BUT TODAY, WHEN I LEFT THAT TOWN...
...EVERYONE CAME TO SEE ME OFF! THEY WERE CRYING AS THEY SAID GOOD-BYE!
FWIP FWIP
FWIP
I KNOW IT'LL BE THE SAME FOR YOU!
YOU'LL FIND PEOPLE WHO'LL LOVE AND CARE FOR YOU!
I'M SURE OF IT!!
BUT NO MATTER HOW GOOD YOU ARE...
...IF YOU'RE NOT WEARING UNDERWEAR, THEY'LL MISJUDGE YOU.
I MEAN, YOU'RE SUCH A PRETTY GIRL.
FWOOOSH
FOOOOMP
GAH!
DID YOU CALL ME PRETTY?
HUH?

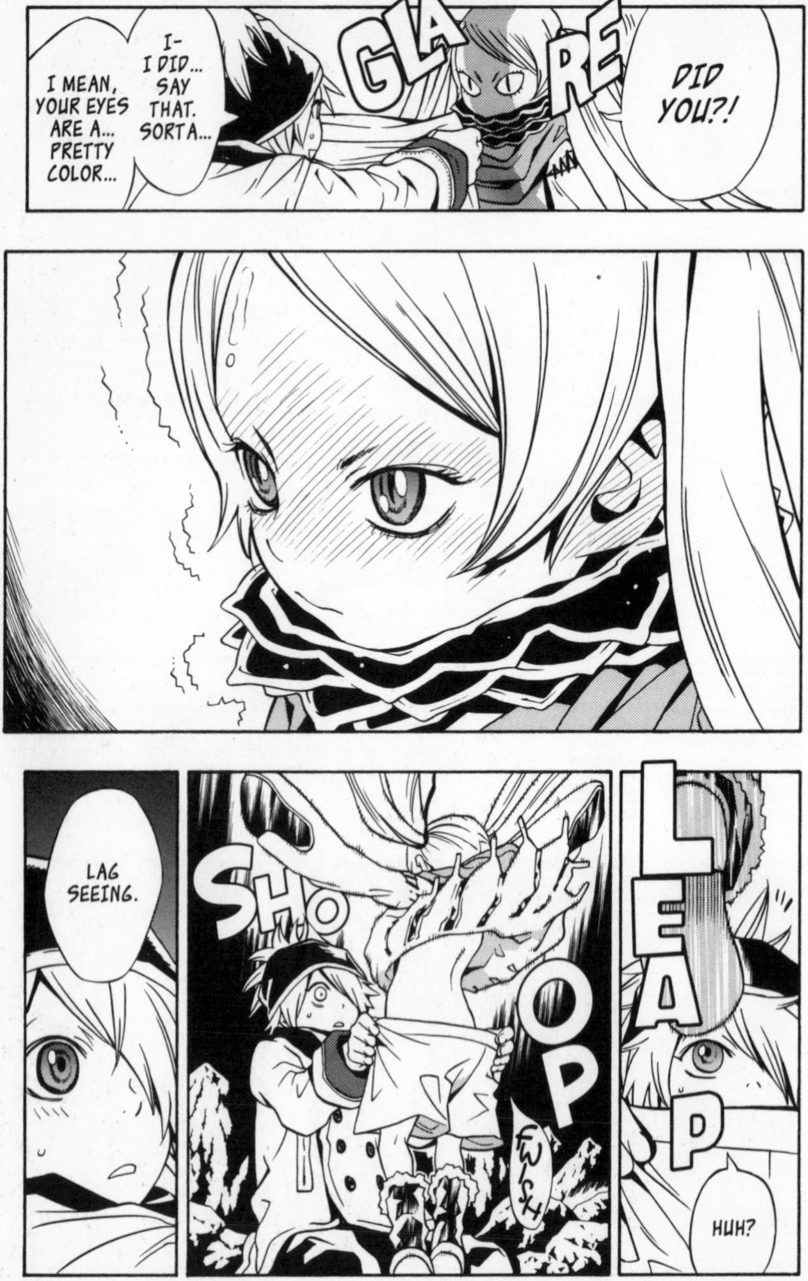
DID YOU?!
GLARE
I- I DID... SAY THAT. SORTA...
I MEAN, YOUR EYES ARE A... PRETTY COLOR...
LEAP
HUH?
SHOOP
FWISH
LAG SEEING.

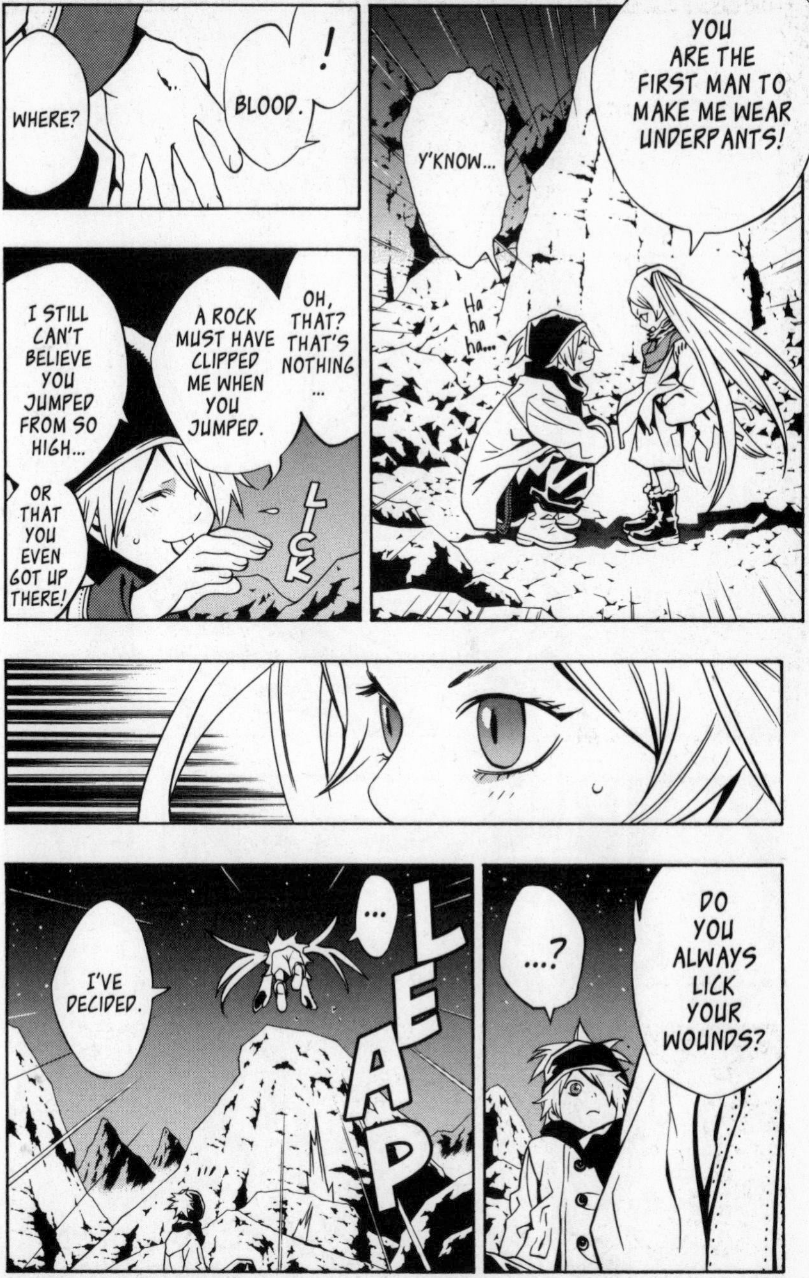
YOU ARE THE FIRST MAN TO MAKE ME WEAR UNDERPANTS!
Y'KNOW...
Ha ha ha...
!
BLOOD.
WHERE?
OH, THAT? THAT'S NOTHING ...
A ROCK MUST HAVE CLIPPED ME WHEN YOU JUMPED.
I STILL CAN'T BELIEVE YOU JUMPED FROM SO HIGH...
LICK
OR THAT YOU EVEN GOT UP THERE!
DO YOU ALWAYS LICK YOUR WOUNDS?
...?
...
LEAP
I'VE DECIDED.

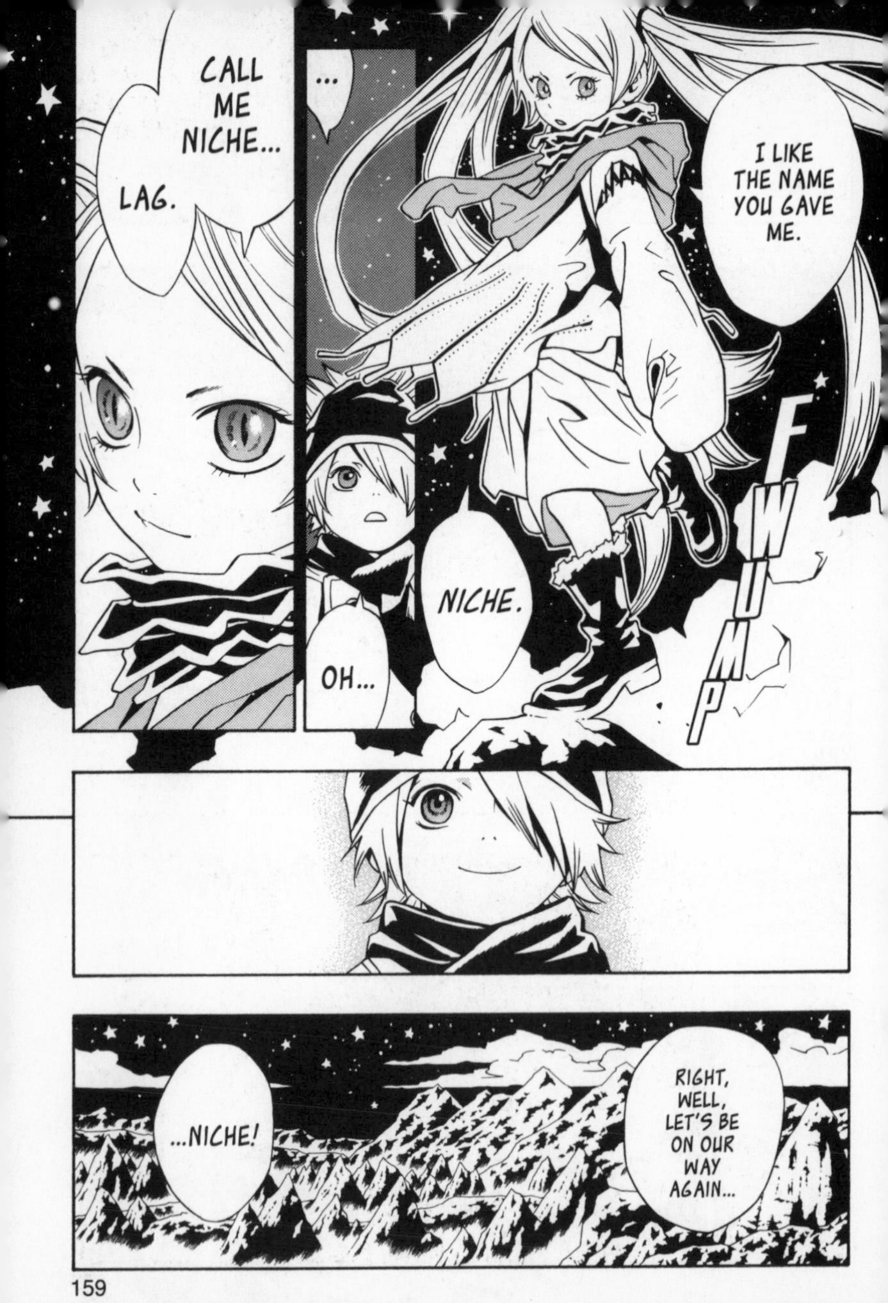
I LIKE THE NAME YOU GAVE ME.
FWUMP
NICHE.
...
OH...
CALL ME NICHE...
LAG.
RIGHT, WELL, LET'S BE ON OUR WAY AGAIN...
...NICHE!

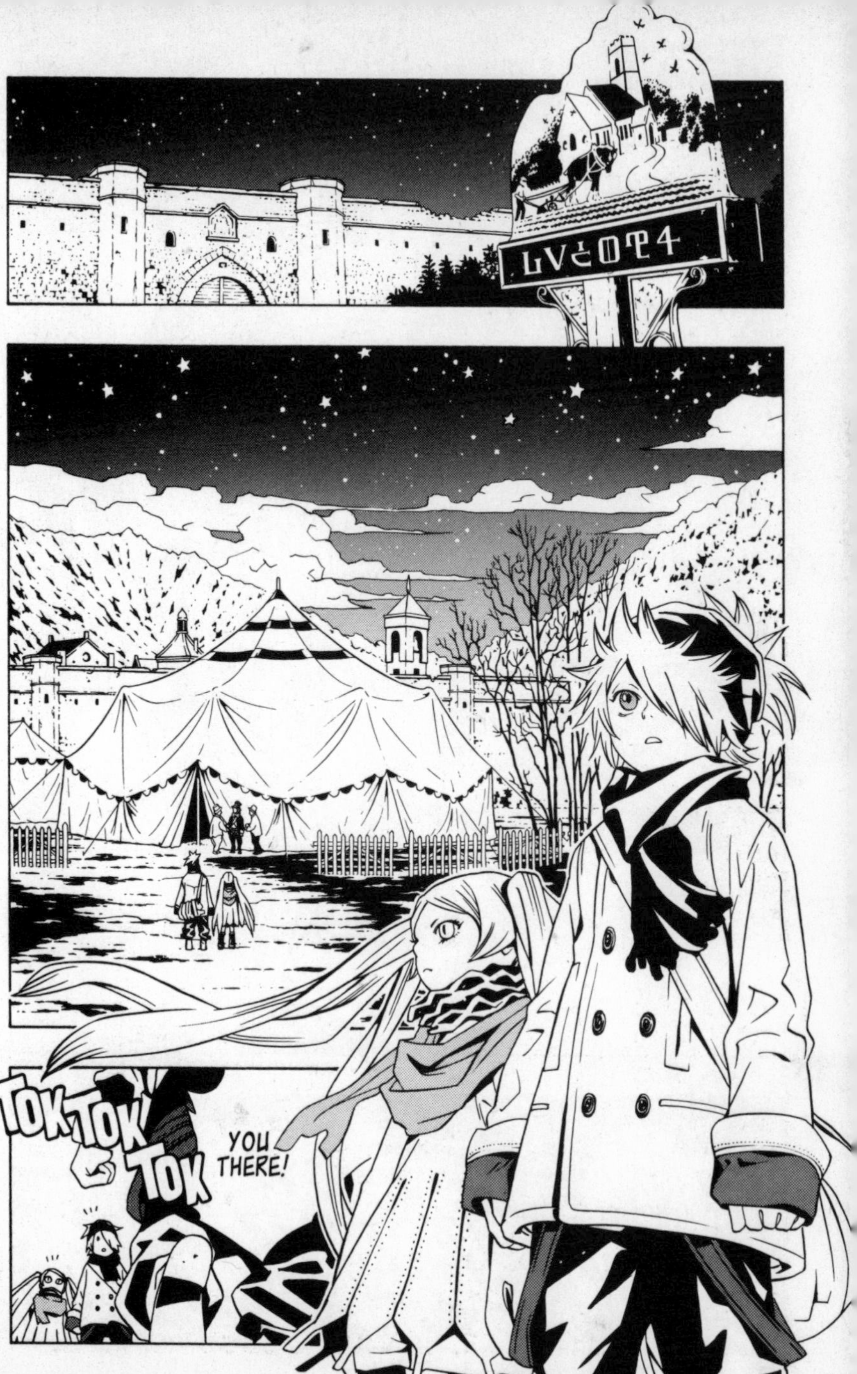
TOK TOK TOK
YOU THERE!

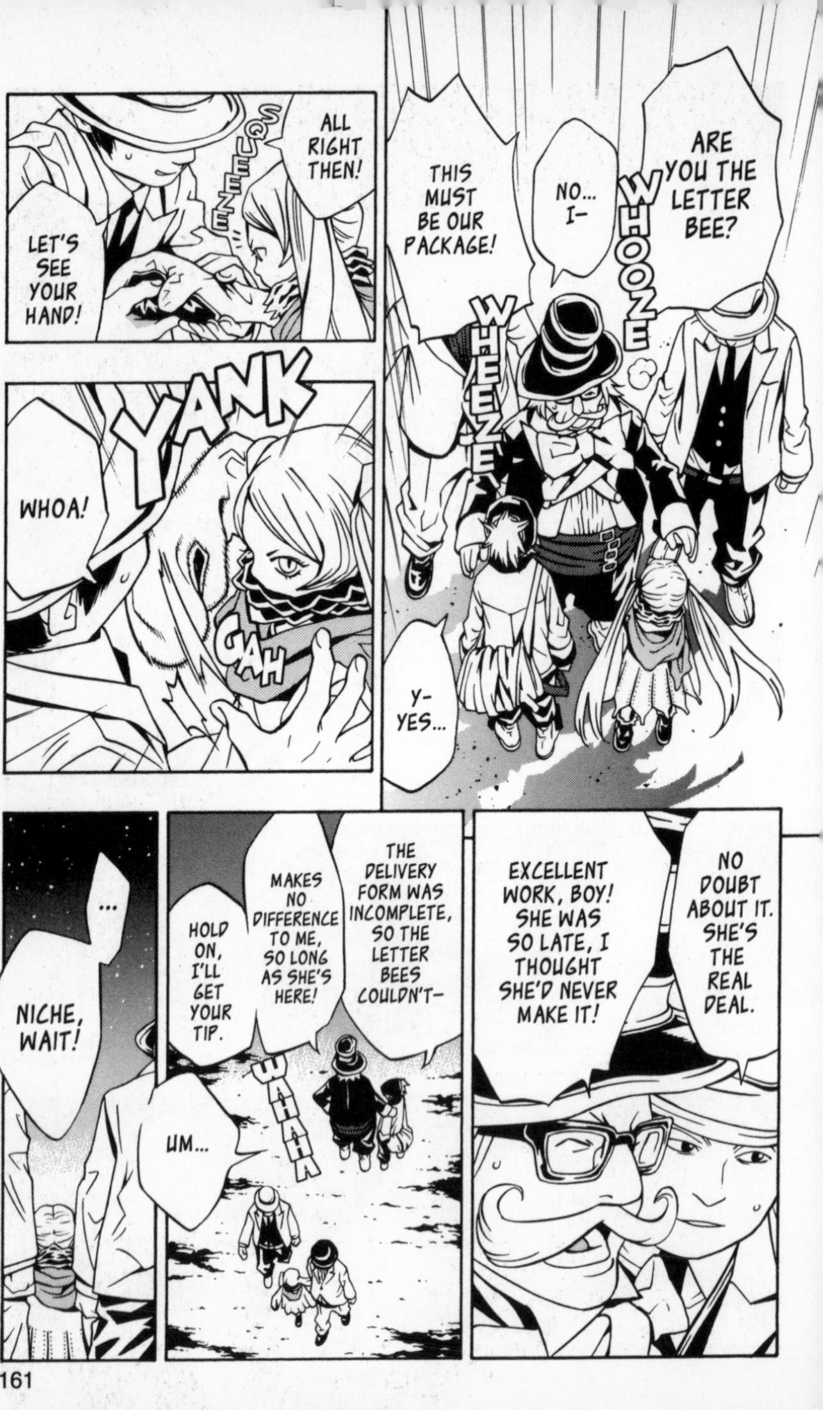
ARE YOU THE LETTER BEE?
WHOOZE
NO... I–
THIS MUST BE OUR PACKAGE!
WHEEZE
Y-YES...
ALL RIGHT THEN!
SQUEEZE
LET'S SEE YOUR HAND!
YANK
WHOA!
GAH
NO DOUBT ABOUT IT. SHE'S THE REAL DEAL.
EXCELLENT WORK, BOY! SHE WAS SO LATE, I THOUGHT SHE'D NEVER MAKE IT!
THE DELIVERY FORM WAS INCOMPLETE, SO THE LETTER BEES COULDN'T–
MAKES NO DIFFERENCE TO ME, SO LONG AS SHE'S HERE!
HOLD ON, I'LL GET YOUR TIP.
WAHAHAHA
UM...
...
NICHE, WAIT!

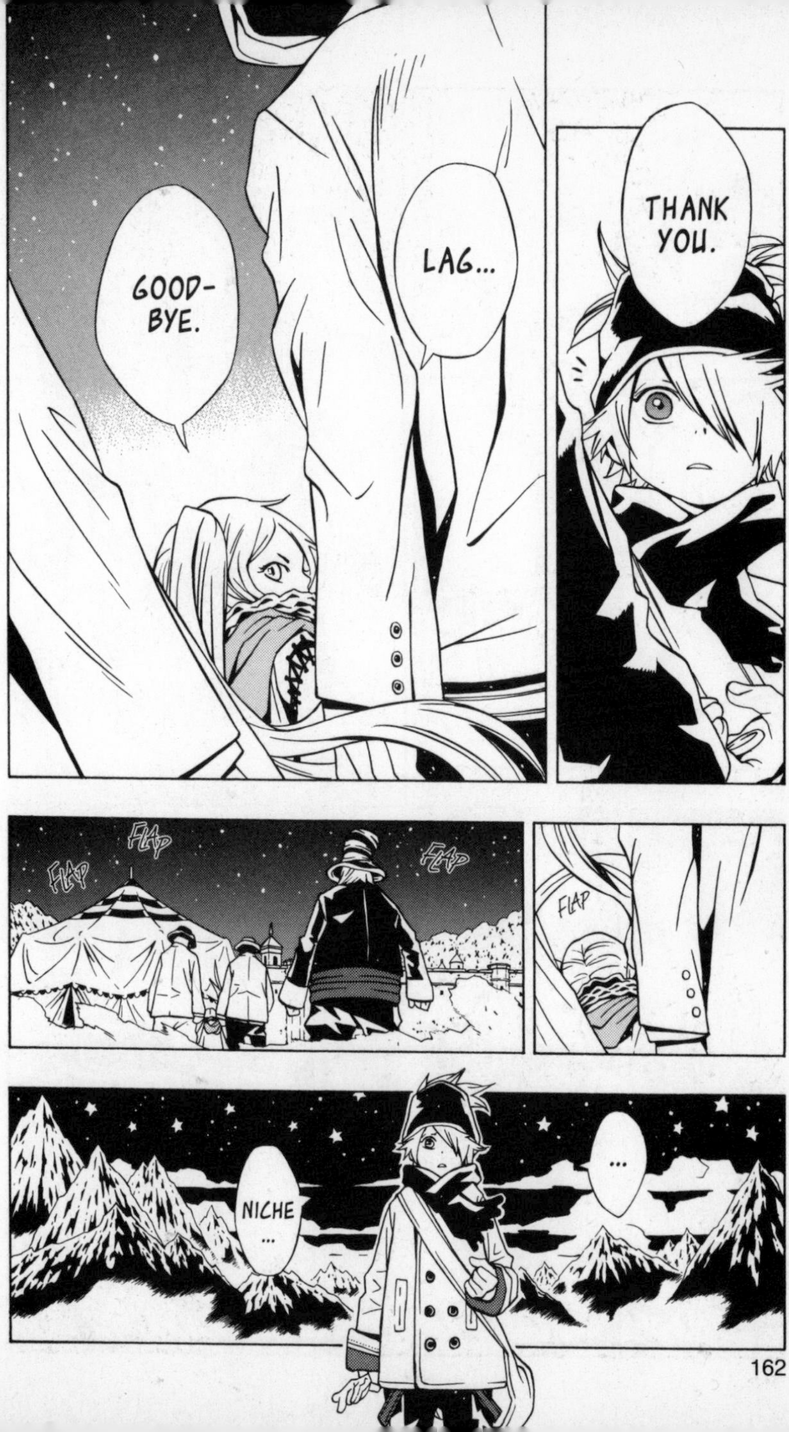
THANK YOU.
LAG...
GOOD-BYE.
FLAP
FLAP
FLAP
FLAP
...
NICHE ...

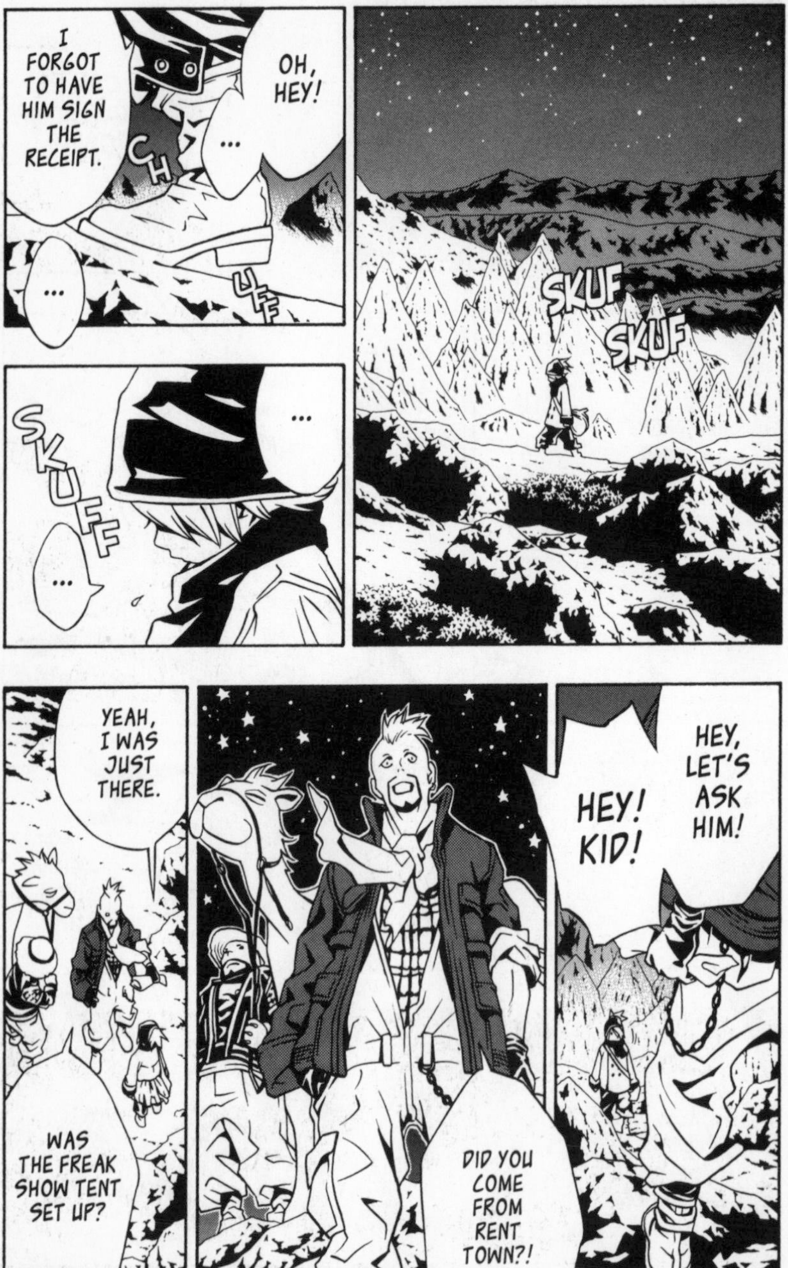
SKUF
SKUF
OH, HEY!
I FORGOT TO HAVE HIM SIGN THE RECEIPT.
...
CH
UFF
...
...
SKUFFF
...
HEY, LET'S ASK HIM!
HEY! KID!
DID YOU COME FROM RENT TOWN?!
YEAH, I WAS JUST THERE.
WAS THE FREAK SHOW TENT SET UP?

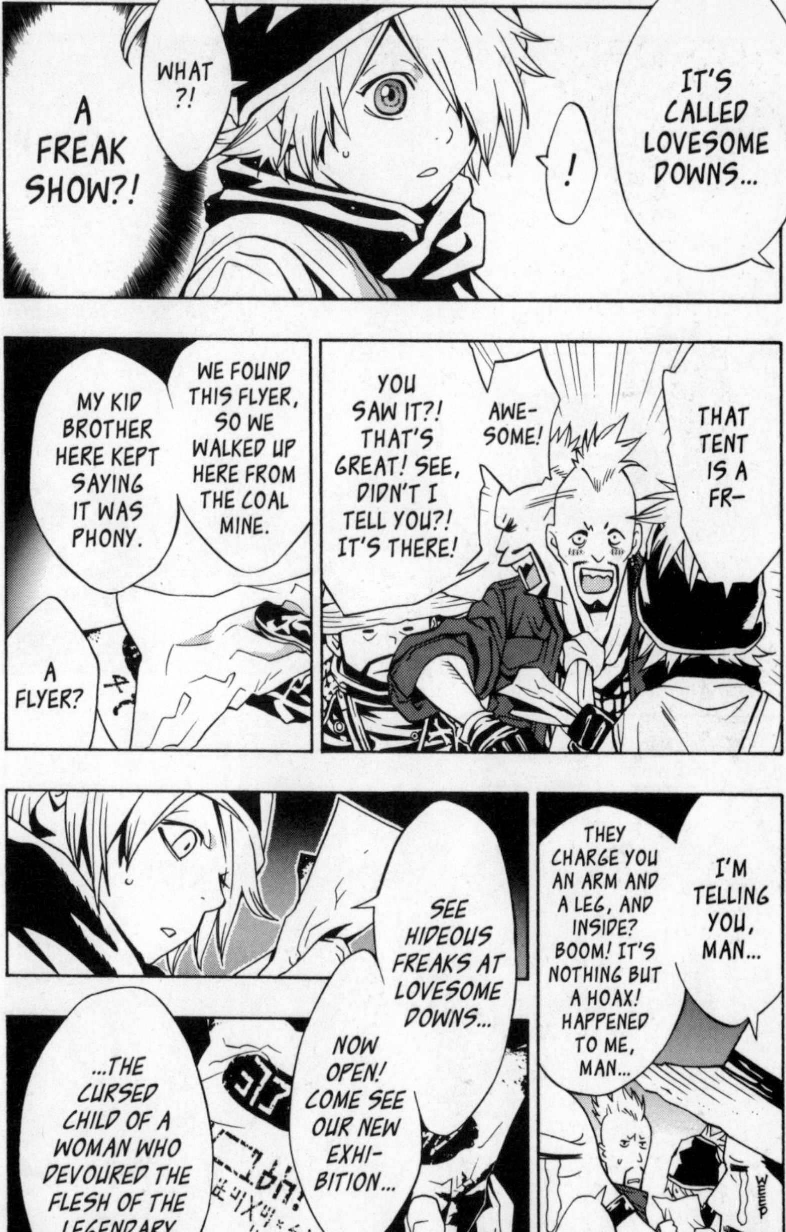
IT'S CALLED LOVESOME DOWNS...
!
WHAT?!
A FREAK SHOW?!
THAT TENT IS A FR-
AWE-SOME!
YOU SAW IT?! THAT'S GREAT! SEE, DIDN'T I TELL YOU?! IT'S THERE!
WE FOUND THIS FLYER, SO WE WALKED UP HERE FROM THE COAL MINE.
MY KID BROTHER HERE KEPT SAYING IT WAS PHONY.
A FLYER?
I'M TELLING YOU, MAN...
THEY CHARGE YOU AN ARM AND A LEG, AND INSIDE? BOOM! IT'S NOTHING BUT A HOAX! HAPPENED TO ME, MAN...
WEEP
AW, QUITCHER CRYIN'!
SEE HIDEOUS FREAKS AT LOVESOME DOWNS...
NOW OPEN! COME SEE OUR NEW EXHI-BITION...
...THE CURSED CHILD OF A WOMAN WHO DEVOURED THE FLESH OF THE LEGENDARY MAKA!

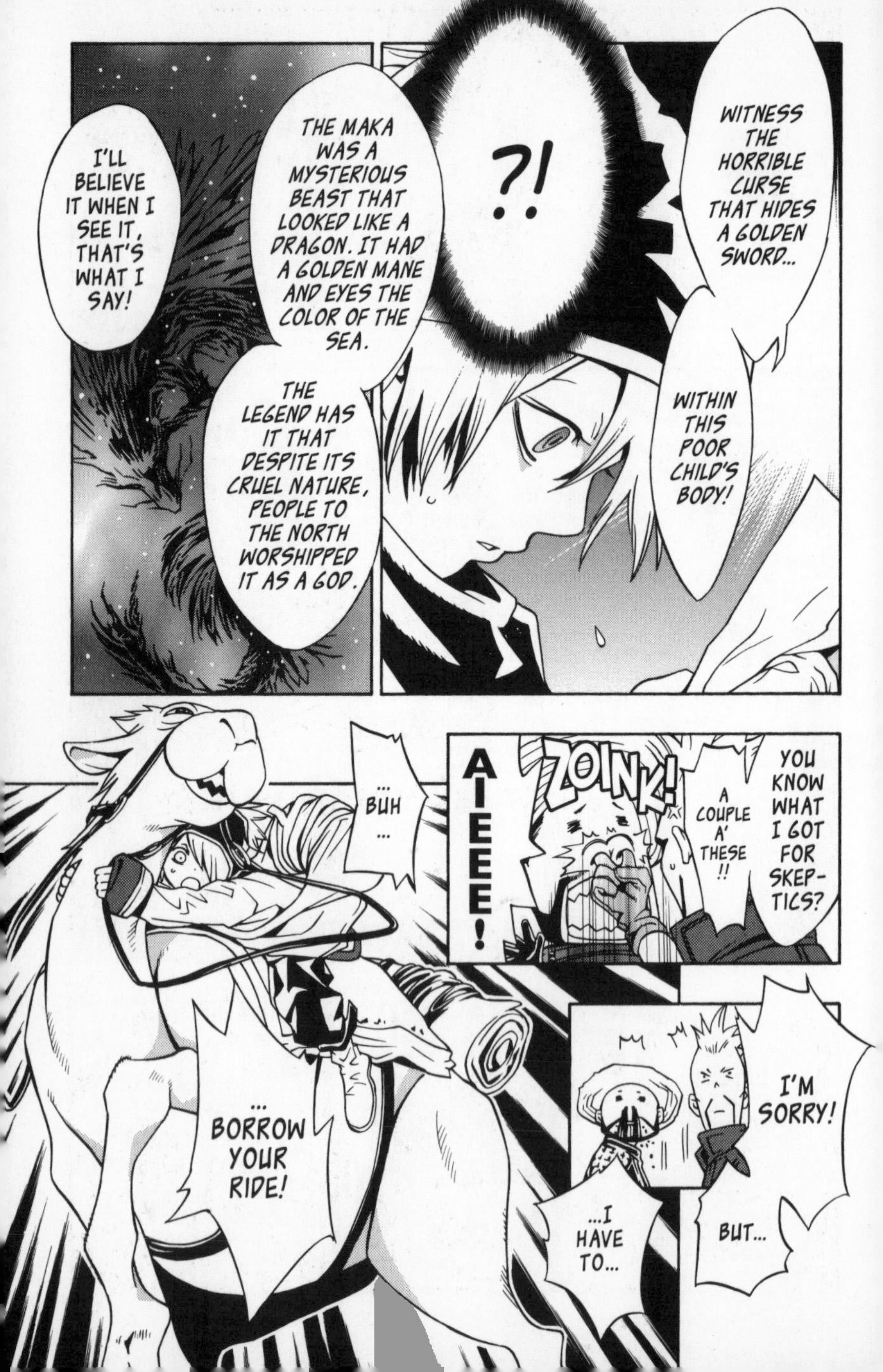
WITNESS THE HORRIBLE CURSE THAT HIDES A GOLDEN SWORD...
?!
WITHIN THIS POOR CHILD'S BODY!
THE MAKA WAS A MYSTERIOUS BEAST THAT LOOKED LIKE A DRAGON. IT HAD A GOLDEN MANE AND EYES THE COLOR OF THE SEA.
THE LEGEND HAS IT THAT DESPITE ITS CRUEL NATURE, PEOPLE TO THE NORTH WORSHIPPED IT AS A GOD.
I'LL BELIEVE IT WHEN I SEE IT, THAT'S WHAT I SAY!
YOU KNOW WHAT I GOT FOR SKEP-TICS?
A COUPLE A' THESE !!
ZOINK!
AIEEE!
I'M SORRY!
BUT...
...I HAVE TO...
...BUH...
...BORROW YOUR RIDE!

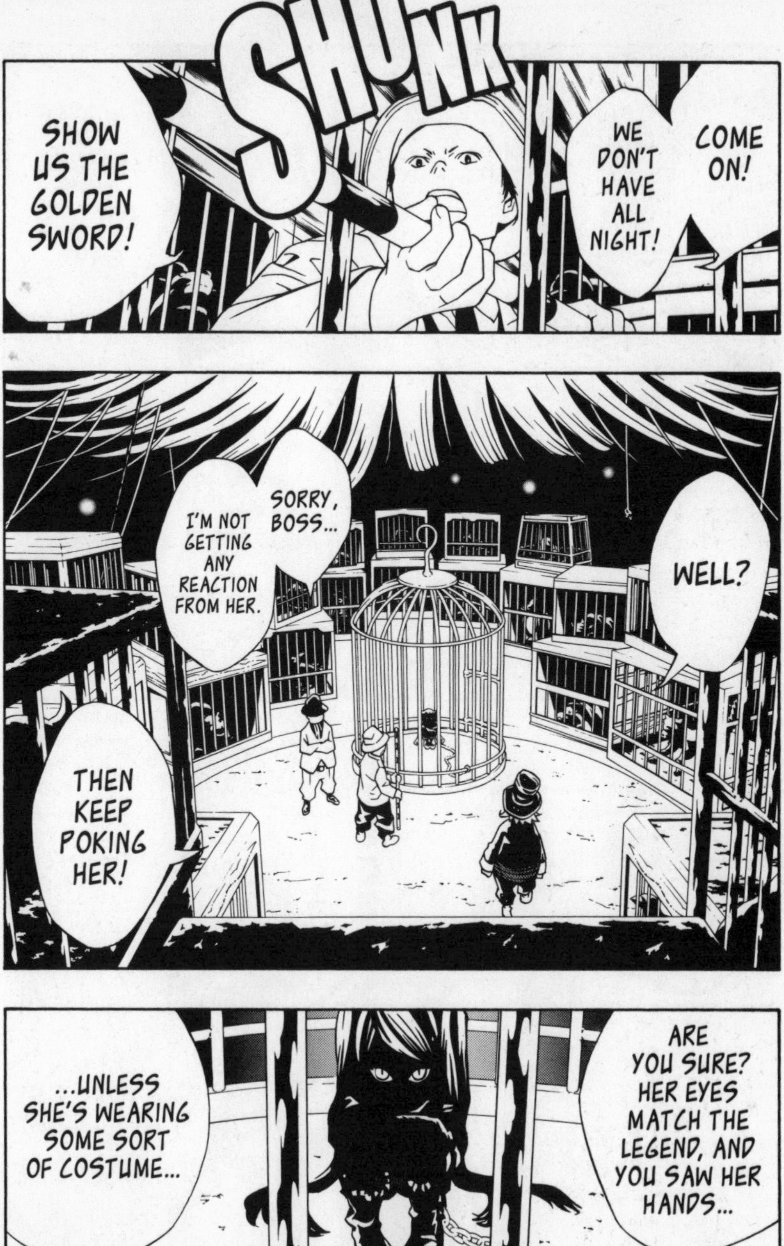
SHUNK
COME ON!
WE DON'T HAVE ALL NIGHT!
SHOW US THE GOLDEN SWORD!
WELL?
SORRY, BOSS...
I'M NOT GETTING ANY REACTION FROM HER.
THEN KEEP POKING HER!
ARE YOU SURE? HER EYES MATCH THE LEGEND, AND YOU SAW HER HANDS...
...UNLESS SHE'S WEARING SOME SORT OF COSTUME...

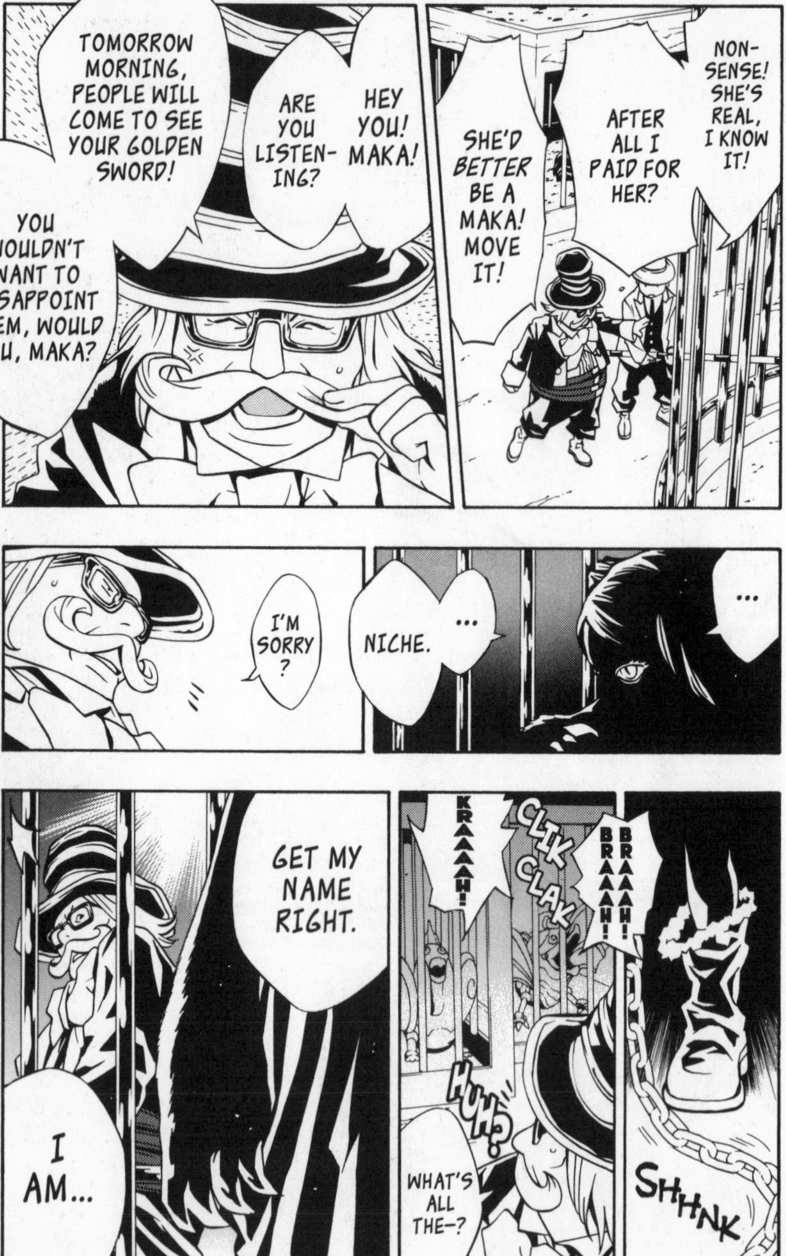
NON-SENSE! SHE'S REAL, I KNOW IT!
AFTER ALL I PAID FOR HER?
SHE'D BETTER BE A MAKA! MOVE IT!
HEY YOU! MAKA!
ARE YOU LISTEN-ING?
TOMORROW MORNING, PEOPLE WILL COME TO SEE YOUR GOLDEN SWORD!
YOU WOULDN'T WANT TO DISAPPOINT THEM, WOULD YOU, MAKA?
...
...
NICHE.
I'M SORRY?
BRAAAAH!
BRAAAAH!
SHHNK
CLIK CLAK
KRAAAAH!
HUH?
WHAT'S ALL THE-?
GET MY NAME RIGHT.
I AM...

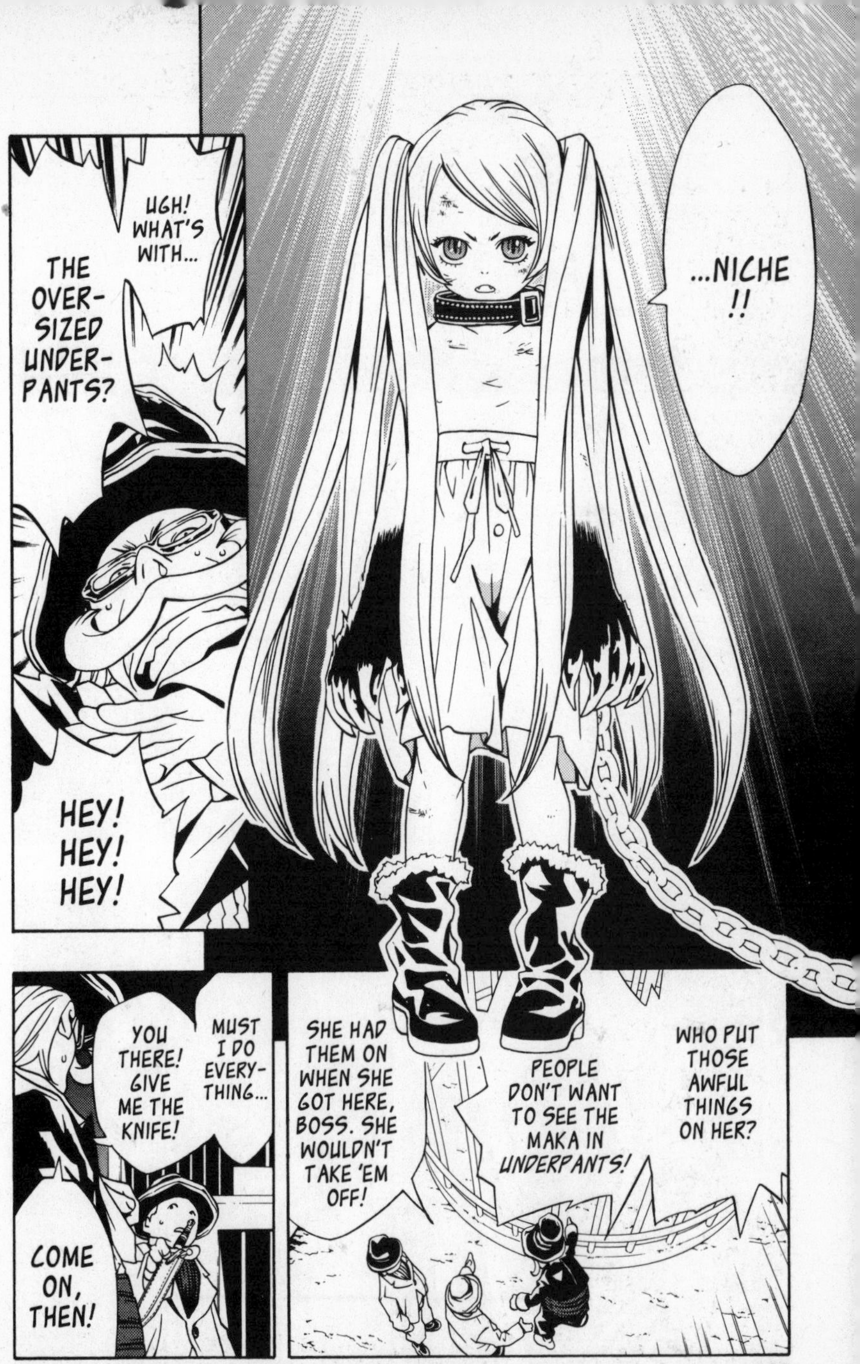
...NICHE !!
UGH! WHAT'S WITH...
THE OVER-SIZED UNDER-PANTS?
HEY! HEY! HEY!
WHO PUT THOSE AWFUL THINGS ON HER?
PEOPLE DON'T WANT TO SEE THE MAKA IN UNDERPANTS!
SHE HAD THEM ON WHEN SHE GOT HERE, BOSS. SHE WOULDN'T TAKE 'EM OFF!
MUST I DO EVERY-THING...
YOU THERE! GIVE ME THE KNIFE!
COME ON, THEN!

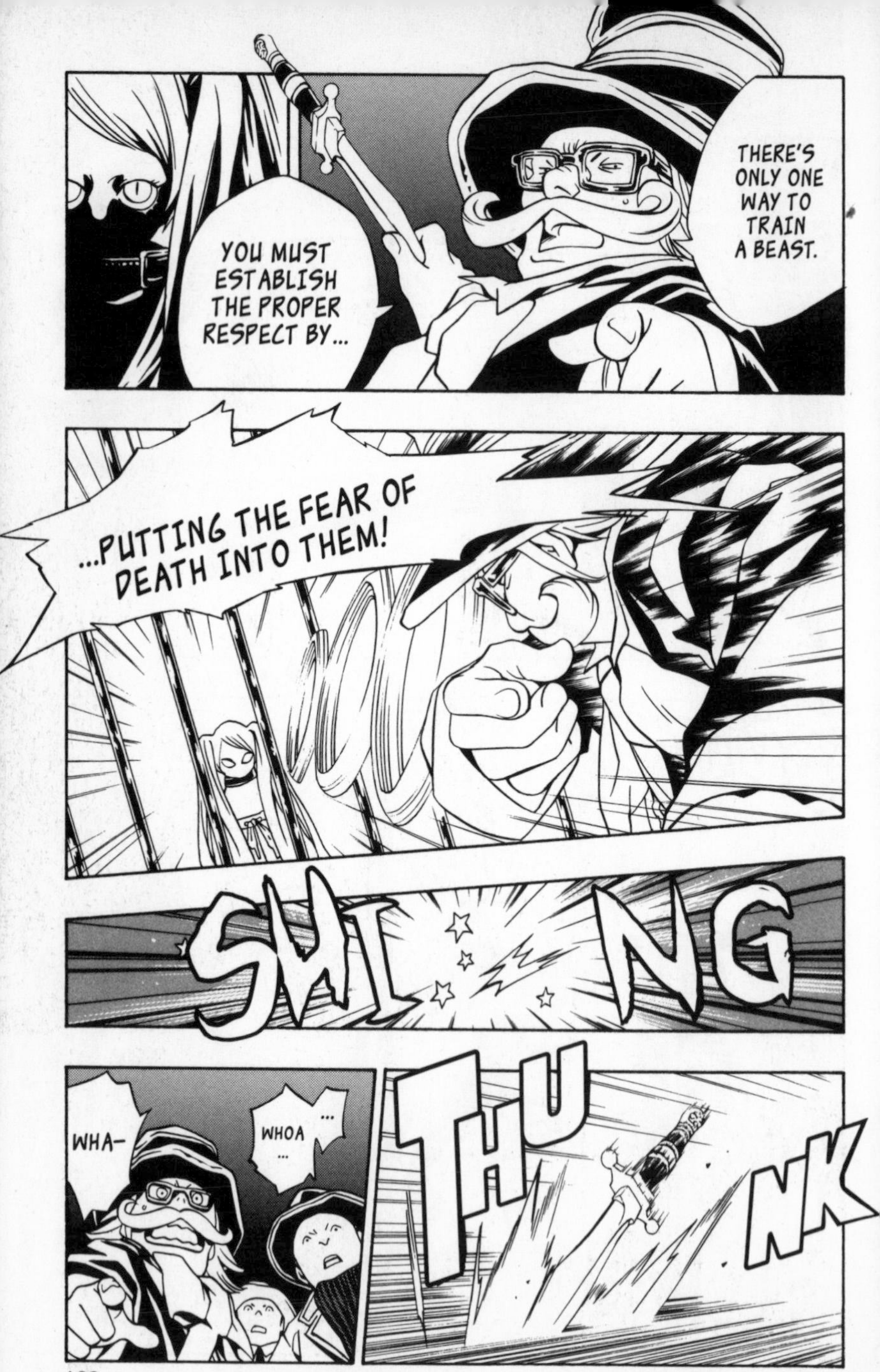
THERE'S ONLY ONE WAY TO TRAIN A BEAST.
YOU MUST ESTABLISH THE PROPER RESPECT BY...
...PUTTING THE FEAR OF DEATH INTO THEM!
SWI NG
THU NK
... WHOA ...
WHA-

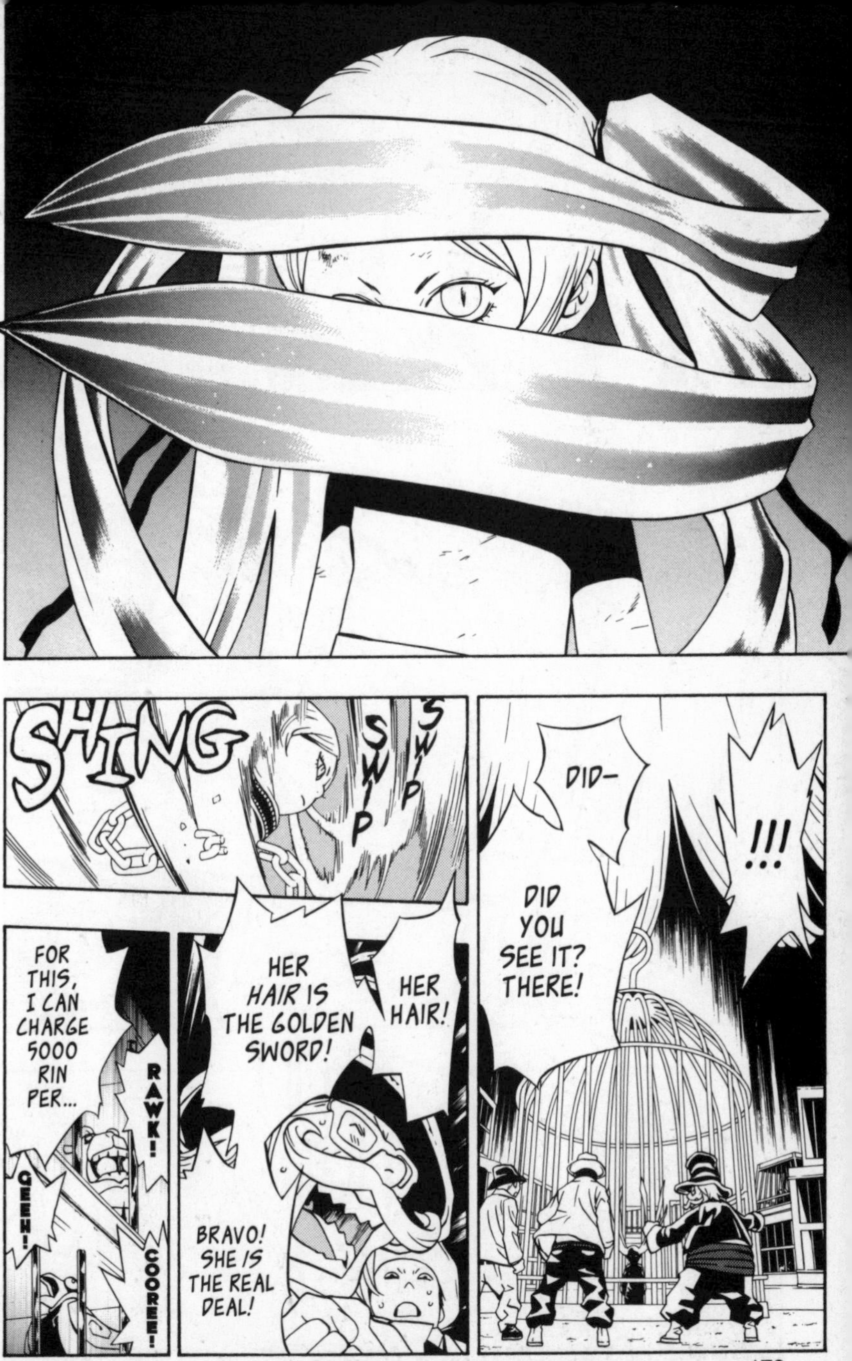
DID-
!!!
DID YOU SEE IT? THERE!
SWIP SWIP
SHING
HER HAIR!
HER HAIR IS THE GOLDEN SWORD!
BRAVO! SHE IS THE REAL DEAL!
FOR THIS, I CAN CHARGE 5000 RIN PER...
RAWK!
GEEH!
COOREEE!

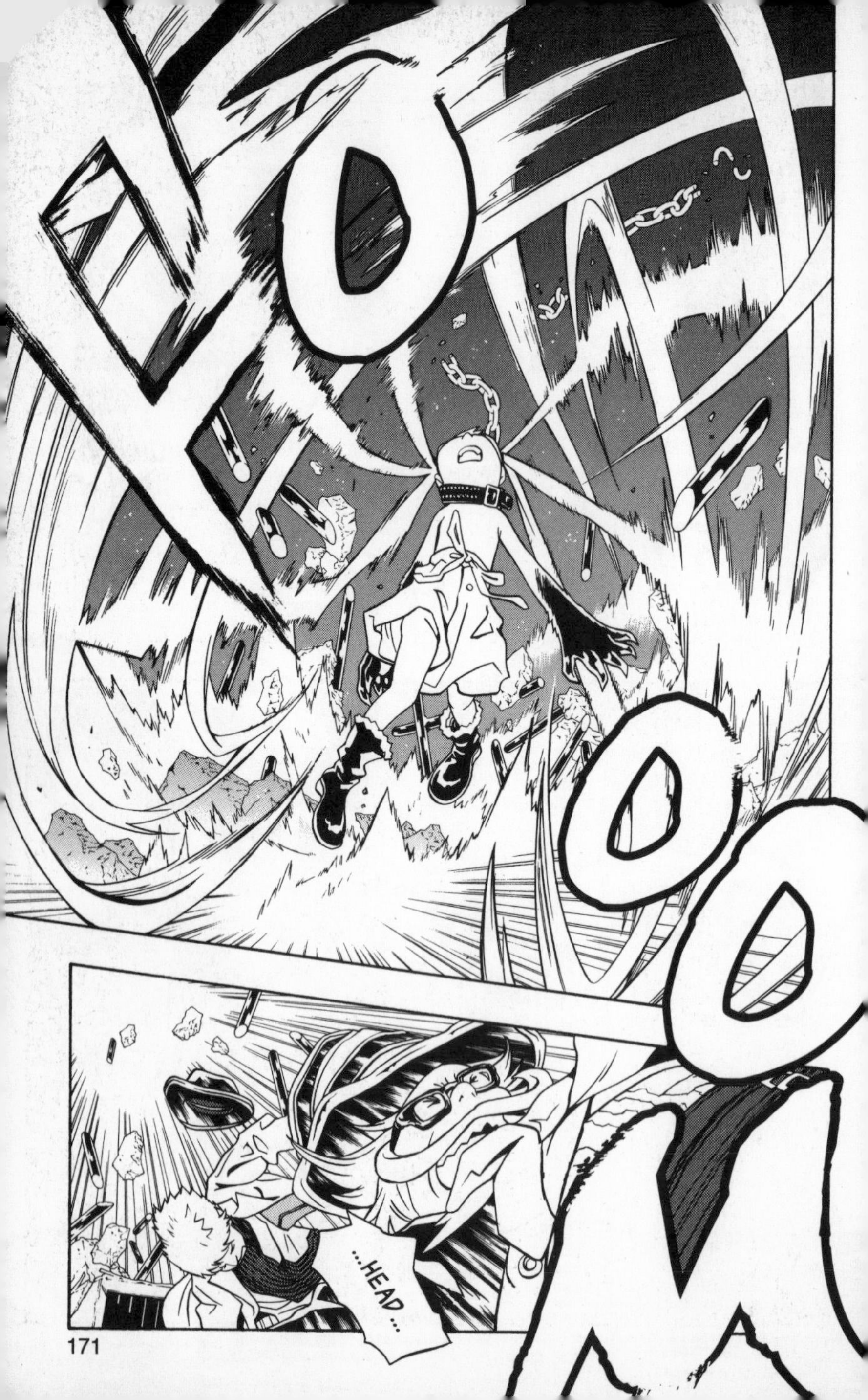
...HEAD...

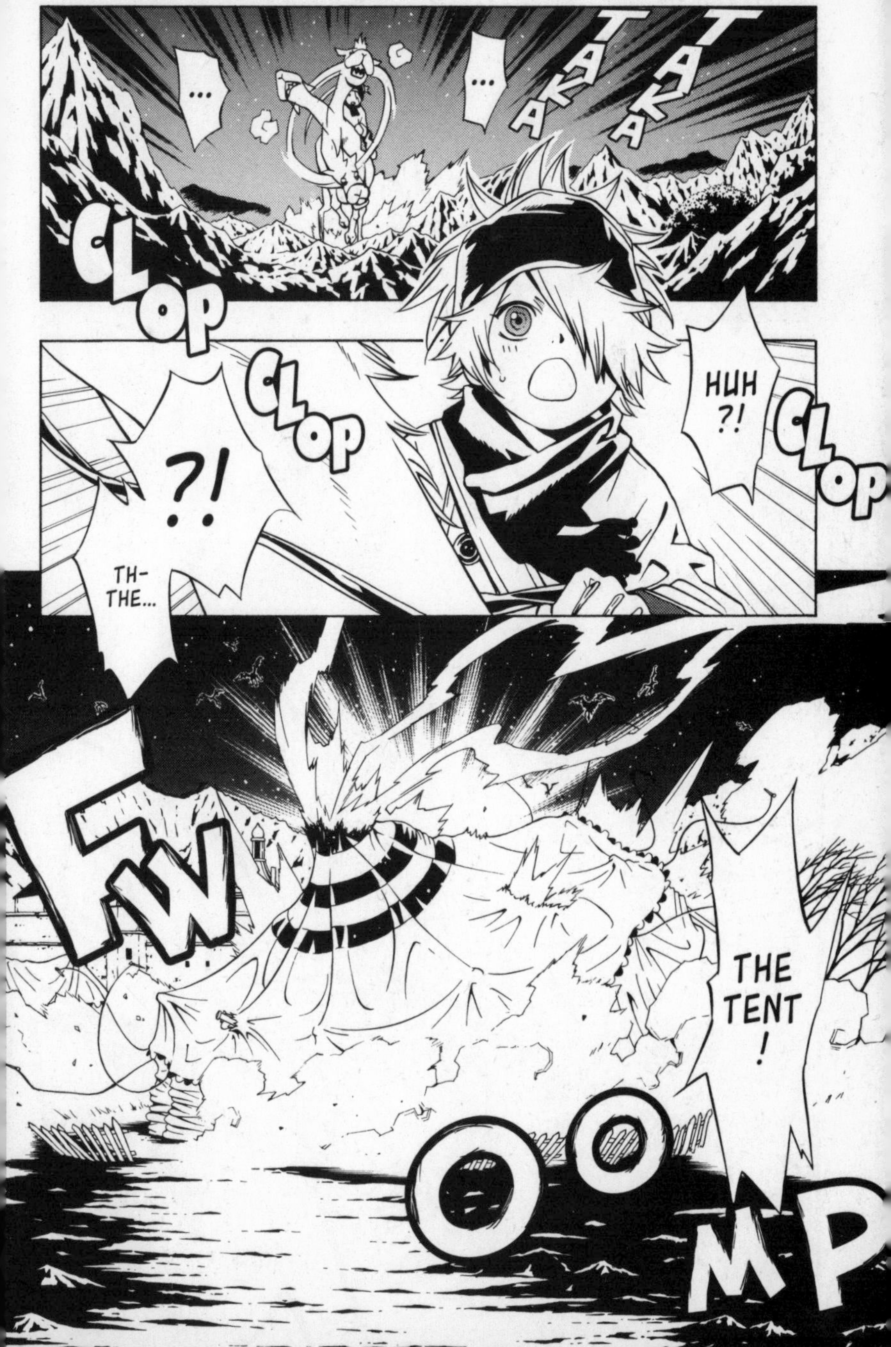
TAKA TAKA
...
...
G
G
CLOP
CLOP
HUH ?!
CLOP
CLOP
?!
TH- THE...
THE TENT!
FWOOOMP

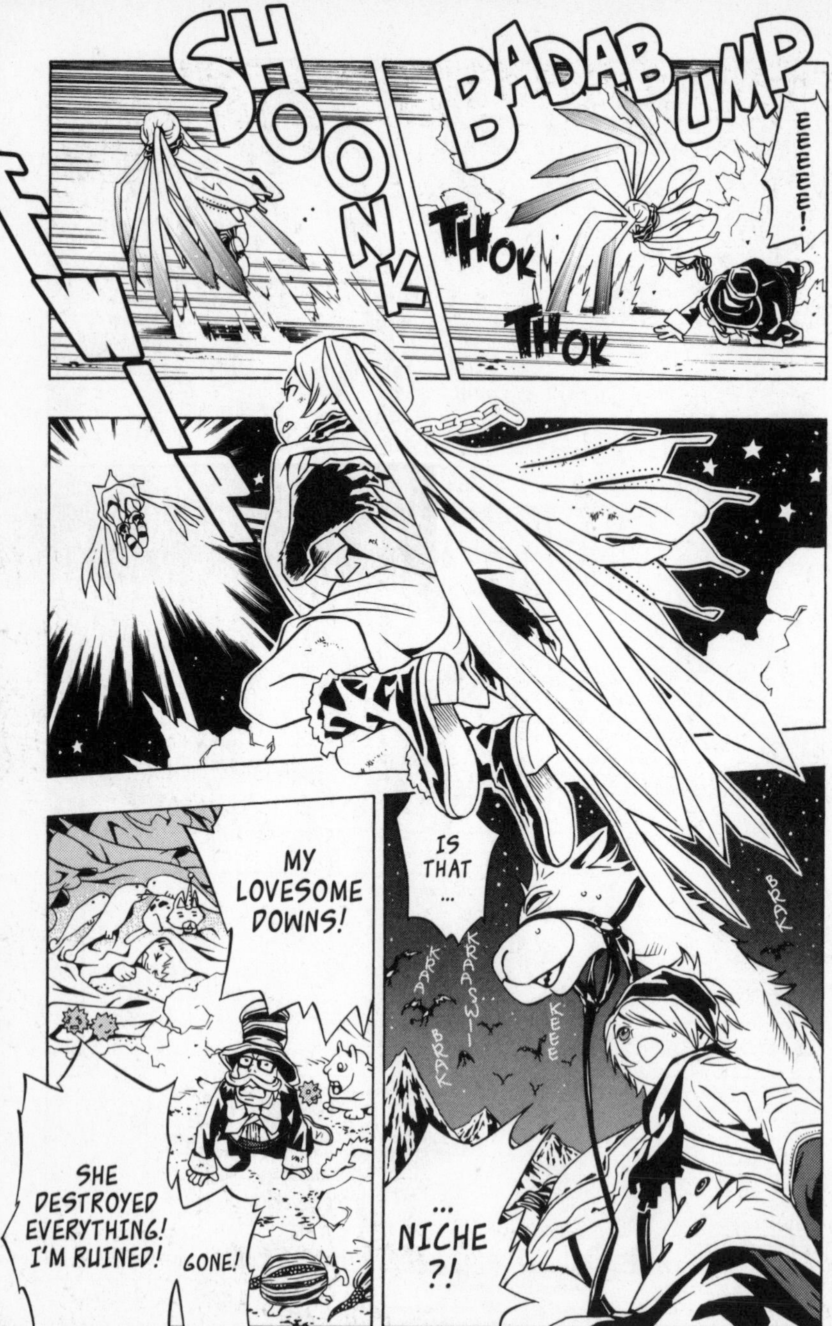
BADABUMP
EEEEEE!
THOK
THOK
SHOOONK
FWHIP
IS THAT ...
BRAK
KRASWII
KRAA
KEEE
BRAK
... NICHE ?!
MY LOVESOME DOWNS!
SHE DESTROYED EVERYTHING! I'M RUINED!
GONE!

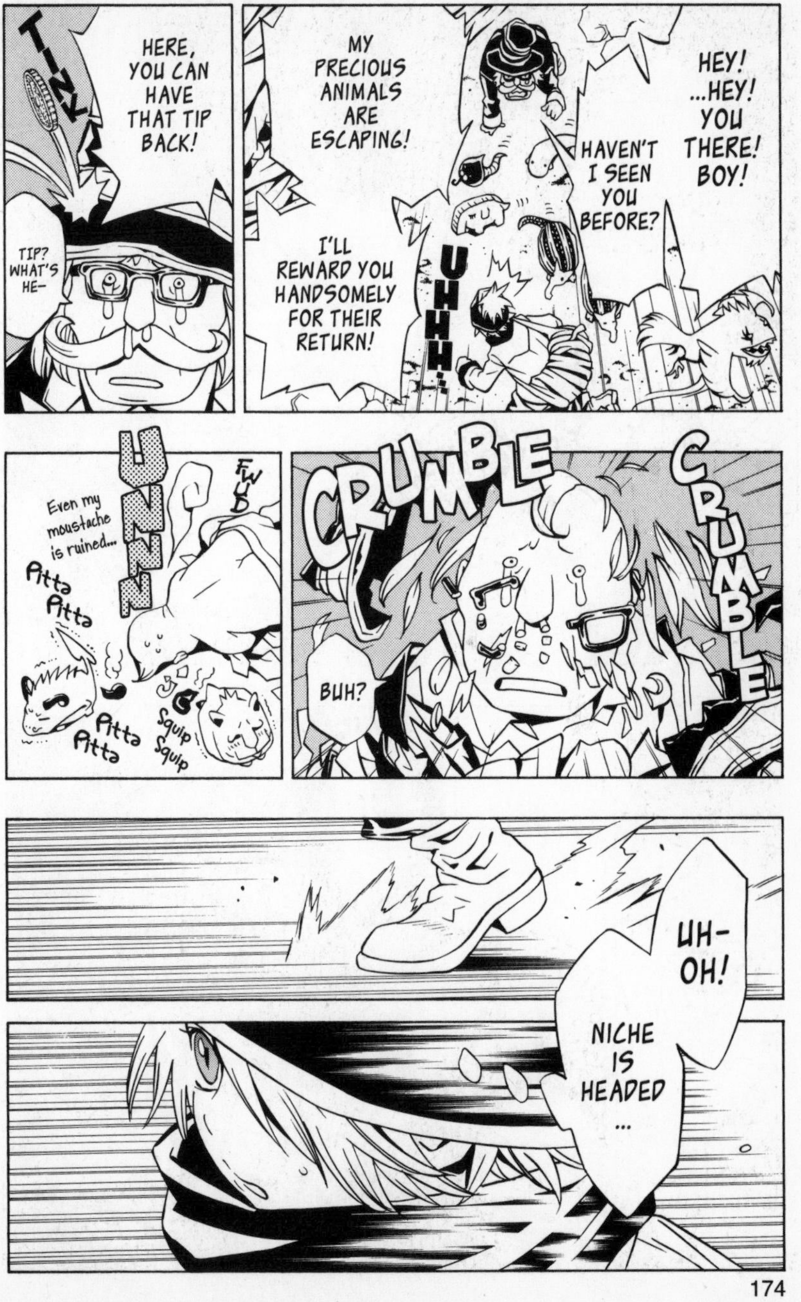

HEY! ...HEY! YOU THERE! BOY!
HAVEN'T I SEEN YOU BEFORE?
MY PRECIOUS ANIMALS ARE ESCAPING!
I'LL REWARD YOU HANDSOMELY FOR THEIR RETURN!
UHHH..
TINK
HERE, YOU CAN HAVE THAT TIP BACK!
TIP? WHAT'S HE–
CRUMBLE
CRUMBLE
BUH?
FWUD
UNNN
Even my moustache is ruined...
Pitta Pitta
Squip Squip
Pitta Pitta
UH-OH!
NICHE IS HEADED ...

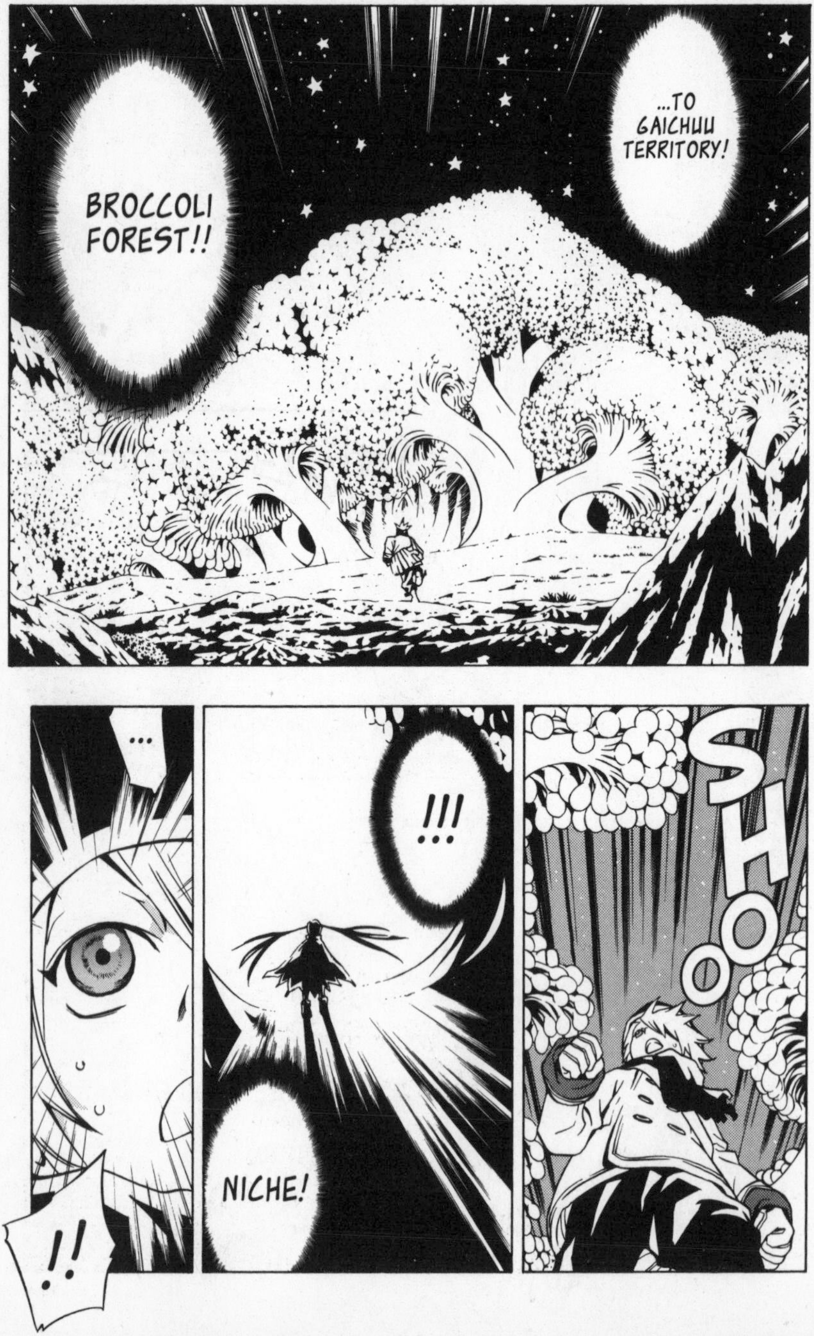
...TO GAICHUU TERRITORY!
BROCCOLI FOREST!!
SHOOO
!!!
NICHE!
...
!!

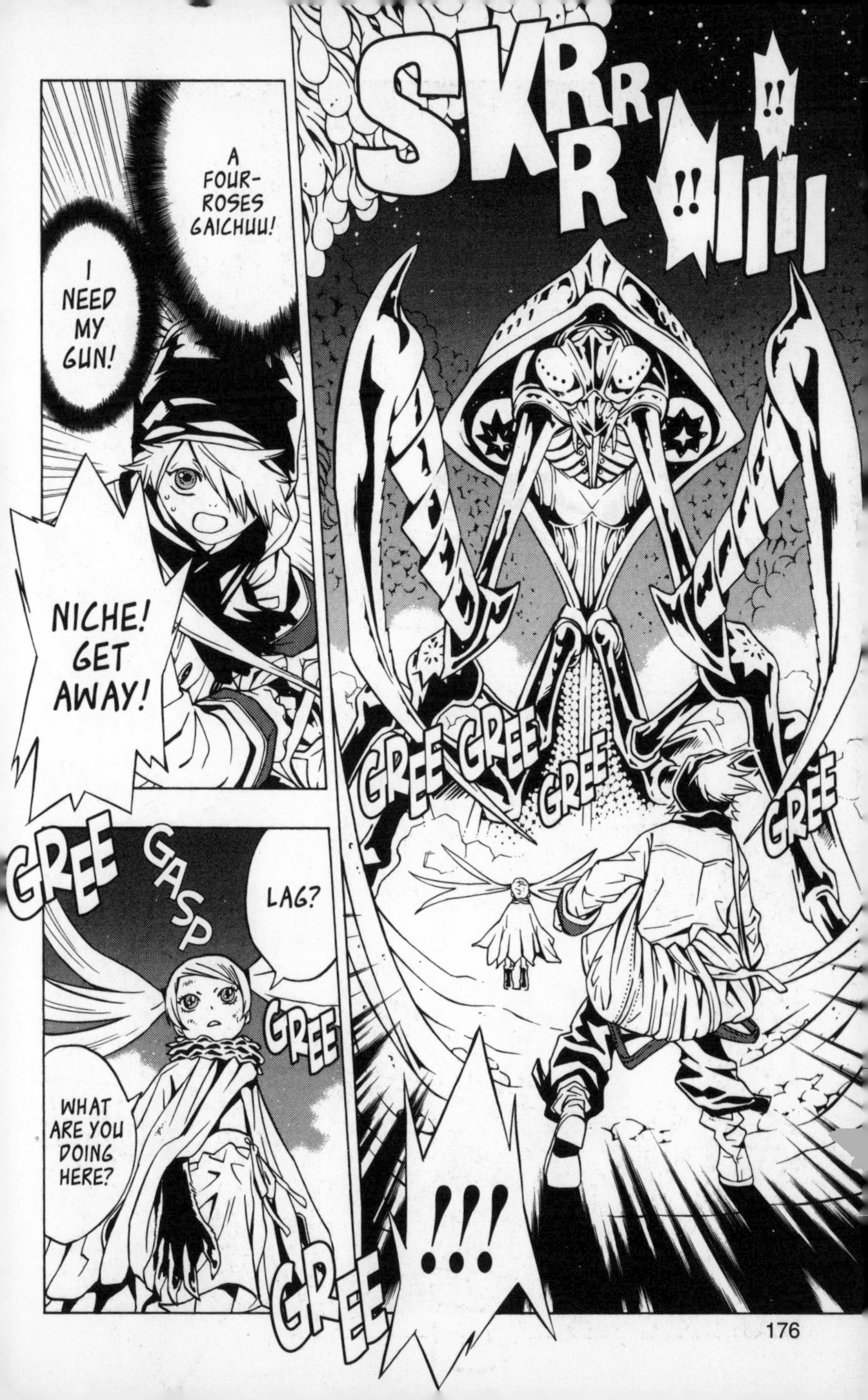
SKRRRIIII
!!
!!
GREE
GREE
GREE
GREE
GREE
!!!
A FOUR-ROSES GAICHUU!
I NEED MY GUN!
NICHE! GET AWAY!
GREE
GASP
LAG?
GREE
WHAT ARE YOU DOING HERE?

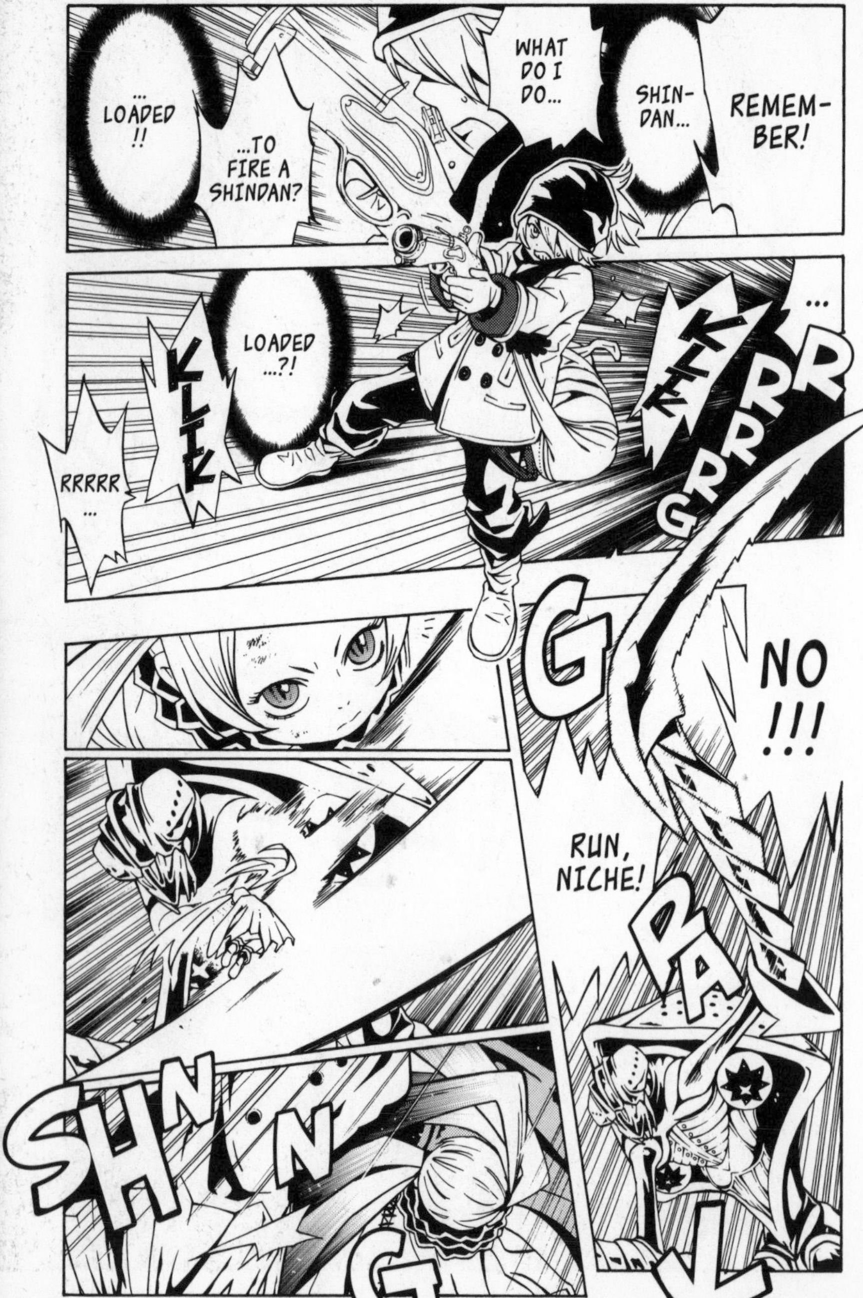
REMEMBER!
SHINDAN...
WHAT DO I DO...
...TO FIRE A SHINDAN?
...LOADED!!
...
KLIK
RRRRG
LOADED...?!
KLIK
RRRRR...
G
NO!!!
RUN, NICHE!
RA
K
SHNNG

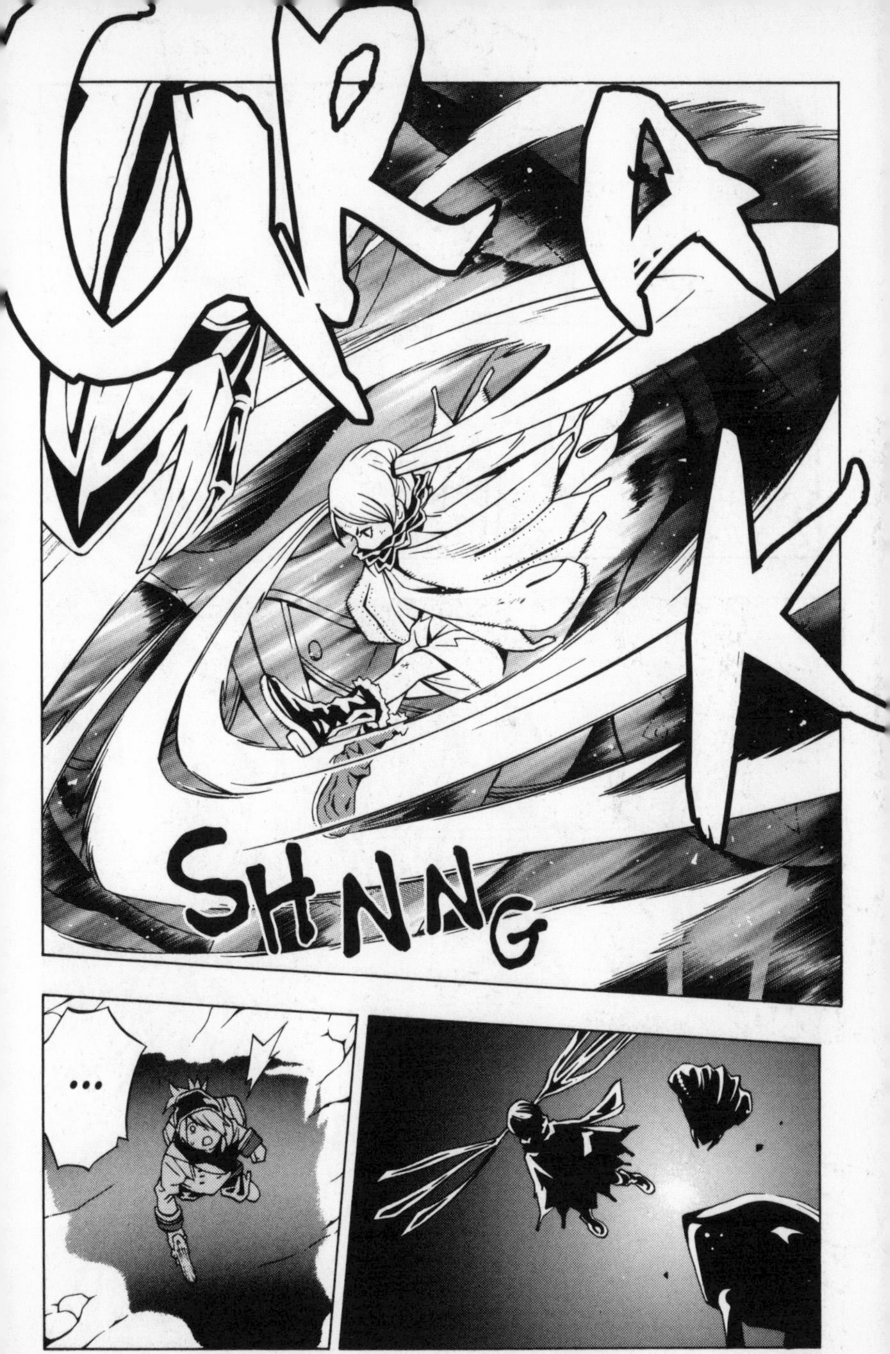
CRACK
SHNNG
...

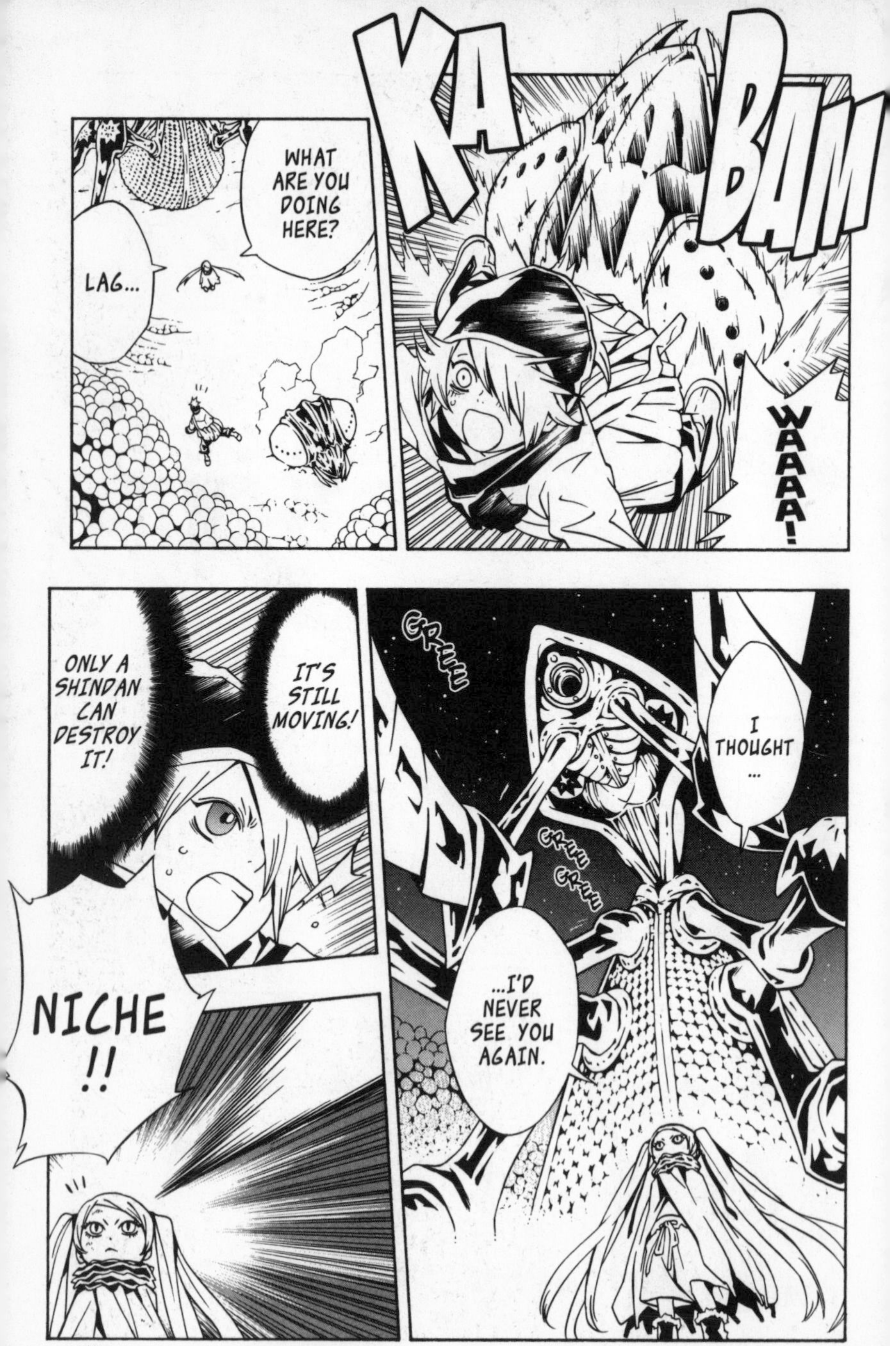
KA BAM
WAAAAA!
WHAT ARE YOU DOING HERE?
LAG...
I THOUGHT ...
...I'D NEVER SEE YOU AGAIN.
IT'S STILL MOVING!
ONLY A SHINDAN CAN DESTROY IT!
NICHE !!

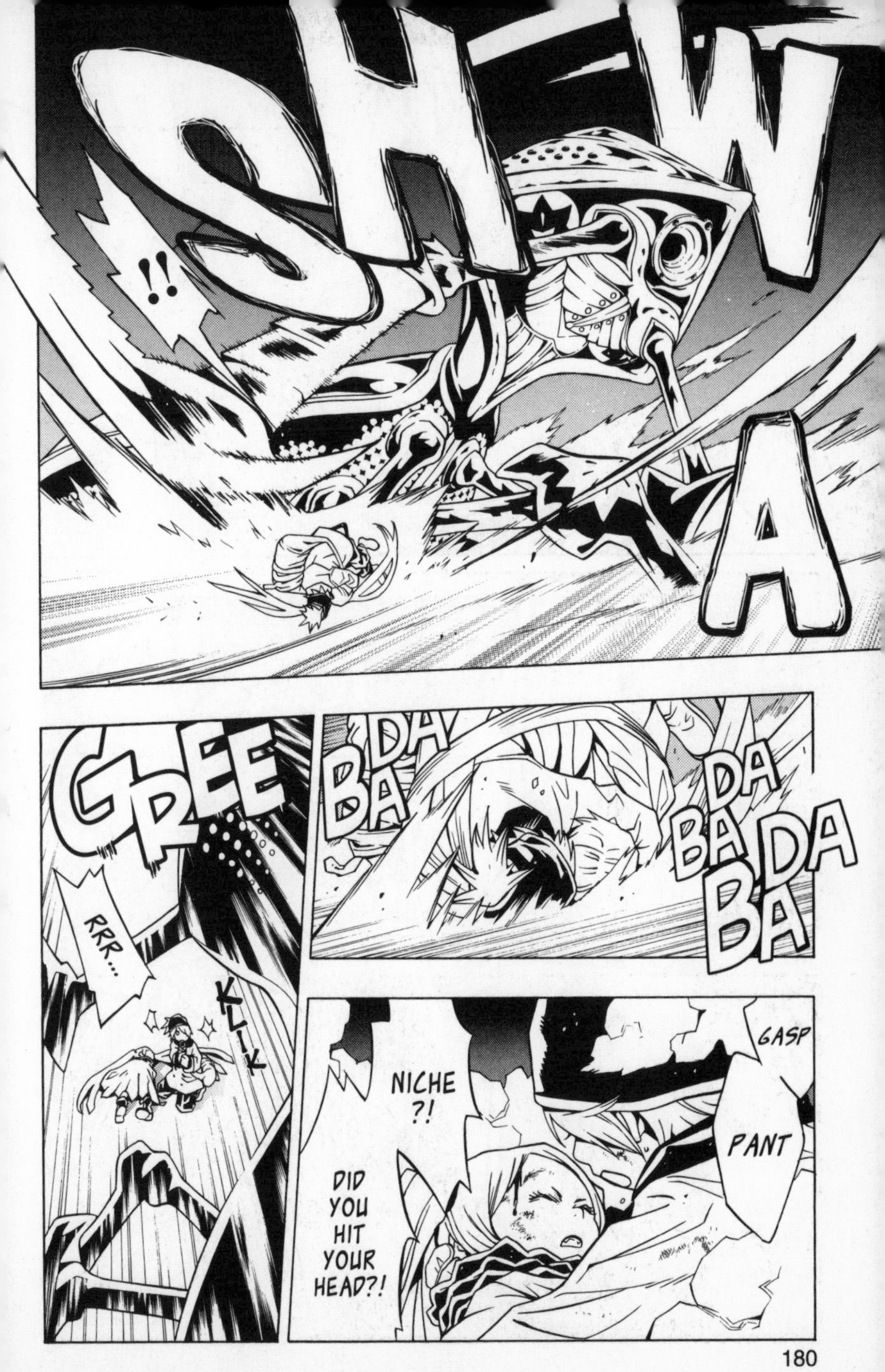
SHEWA
!!
DADA BADADA BABA
GASP
PANT
NICHE?!
DID YOU HIT YOUR HEAD?!
GREE
RRR...
KLIK

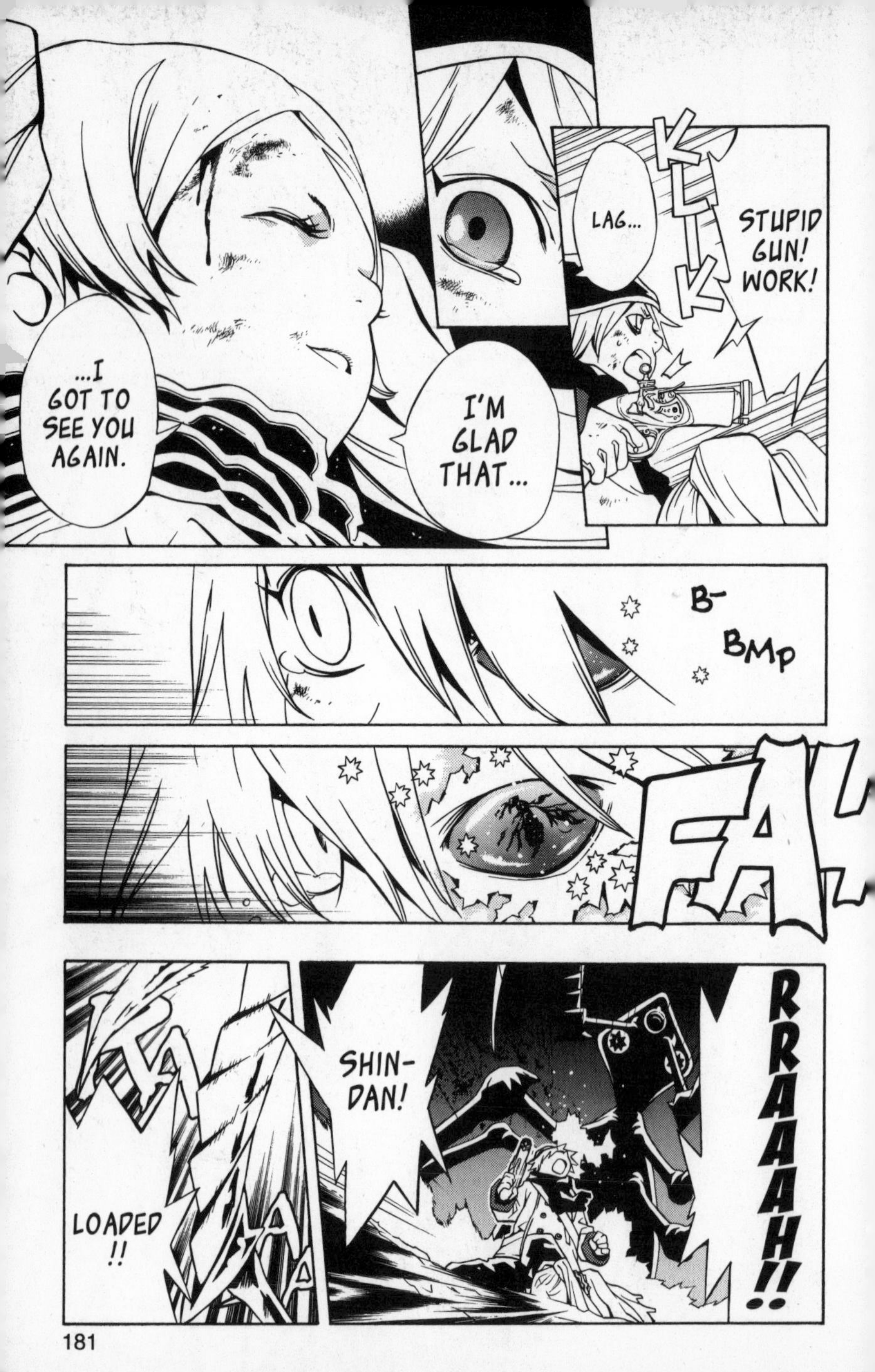
LAG...
KLIK
STUPID GUN! WORK!
I'M GLAD THAT...
...I GOT TO SEE YOU AGAIN.
B-BMP
FA!
RRAAAAH!!
SHIN-DAN!
LOADED !!

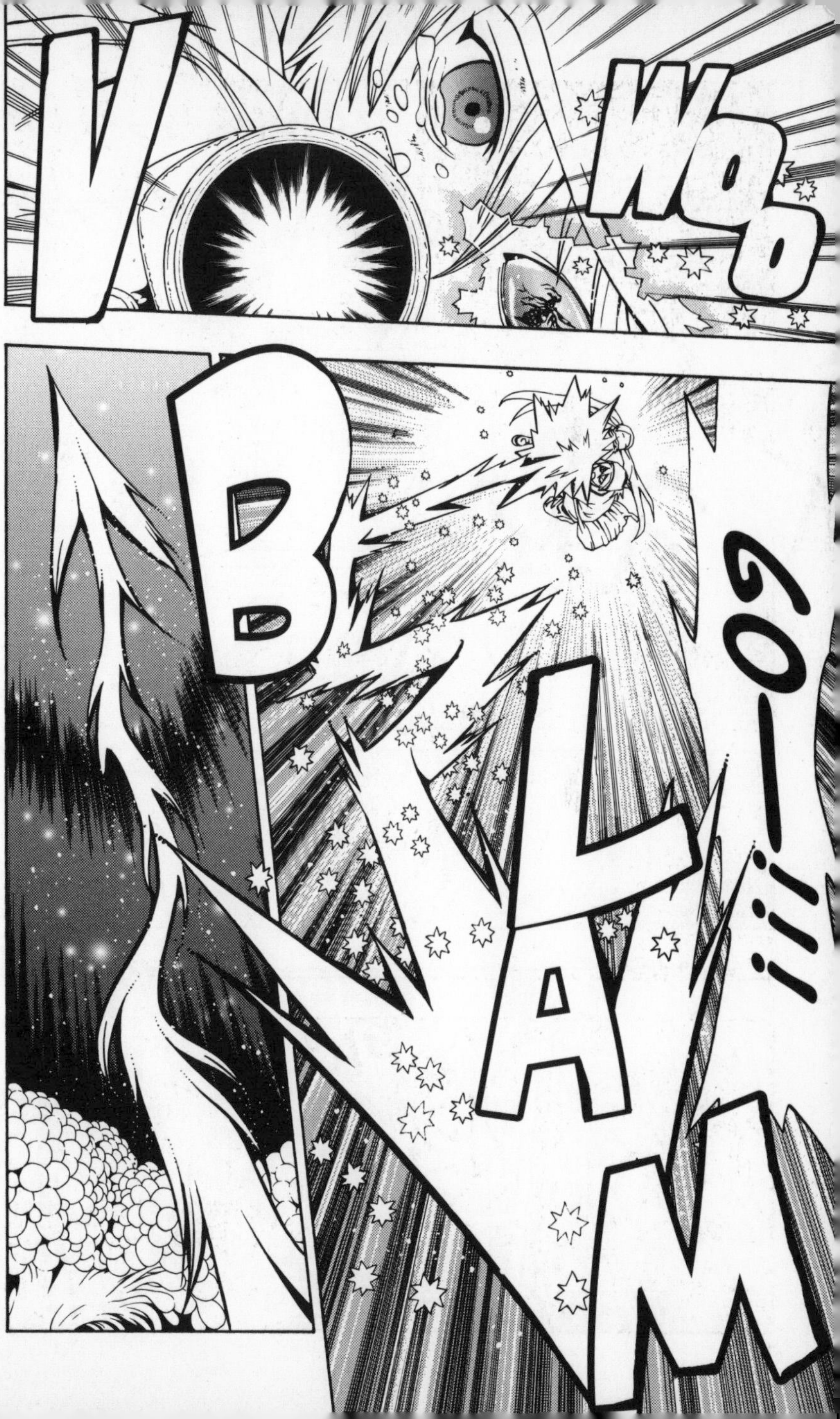

V
WOB
BLAM
GO—!!!

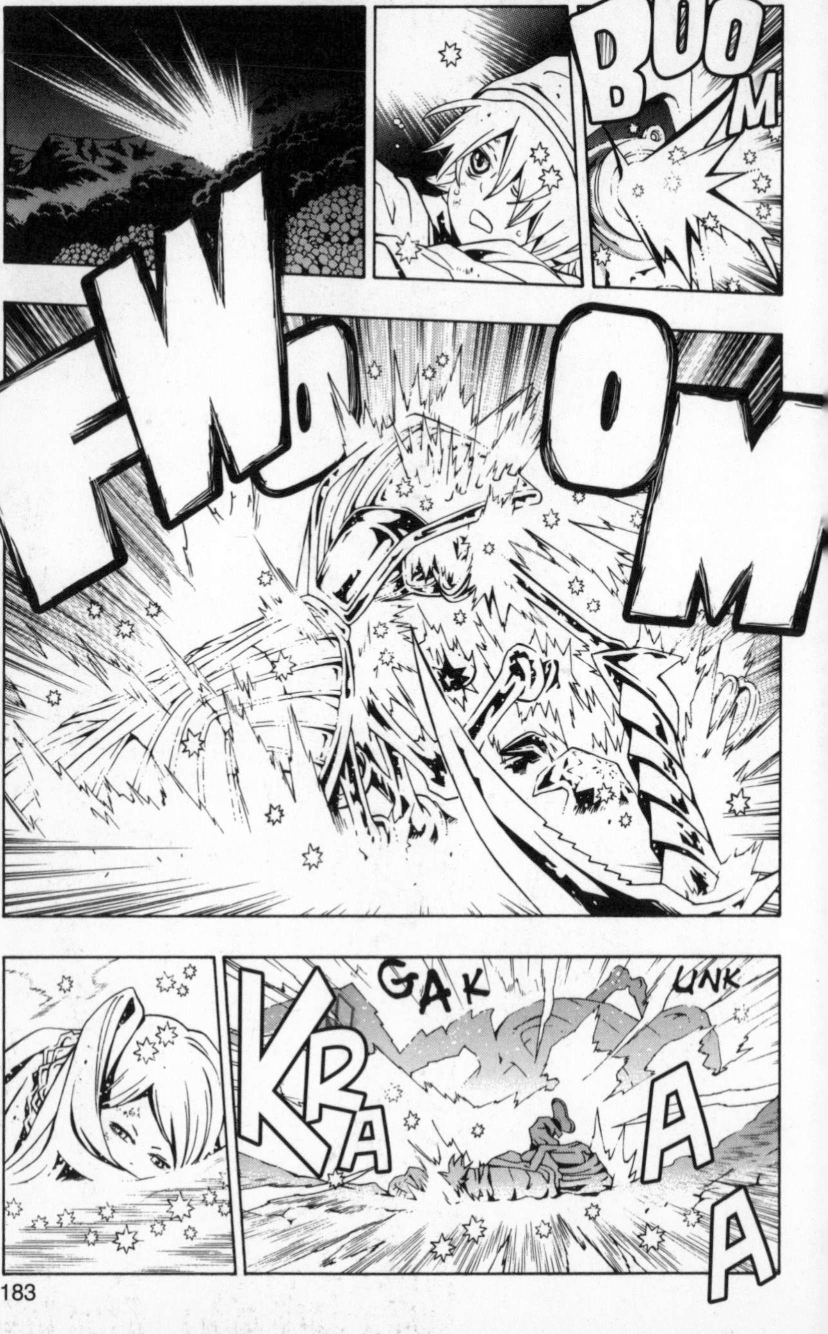
BOOM
FWOOM
KRAAA
GAK UNK

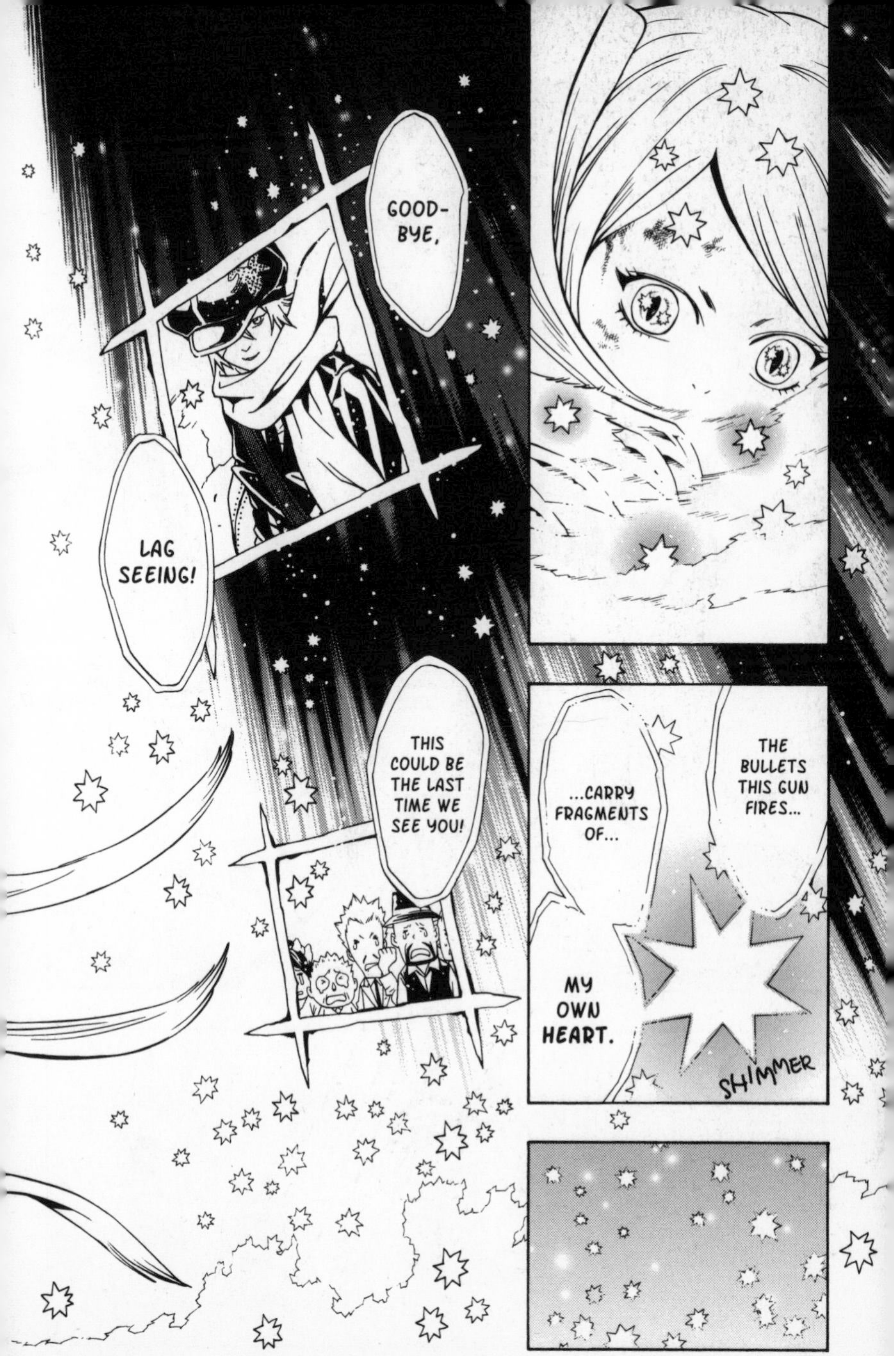
THE BULLETS THIS GUN FIRES...
...CARRY FRAGMENTS OF...
MY OWN HEART.
SHIMMER
GOOD-BYE,
LAG SEEING!
THIS COULD BE THE LAST TIME WE SEE YOU!

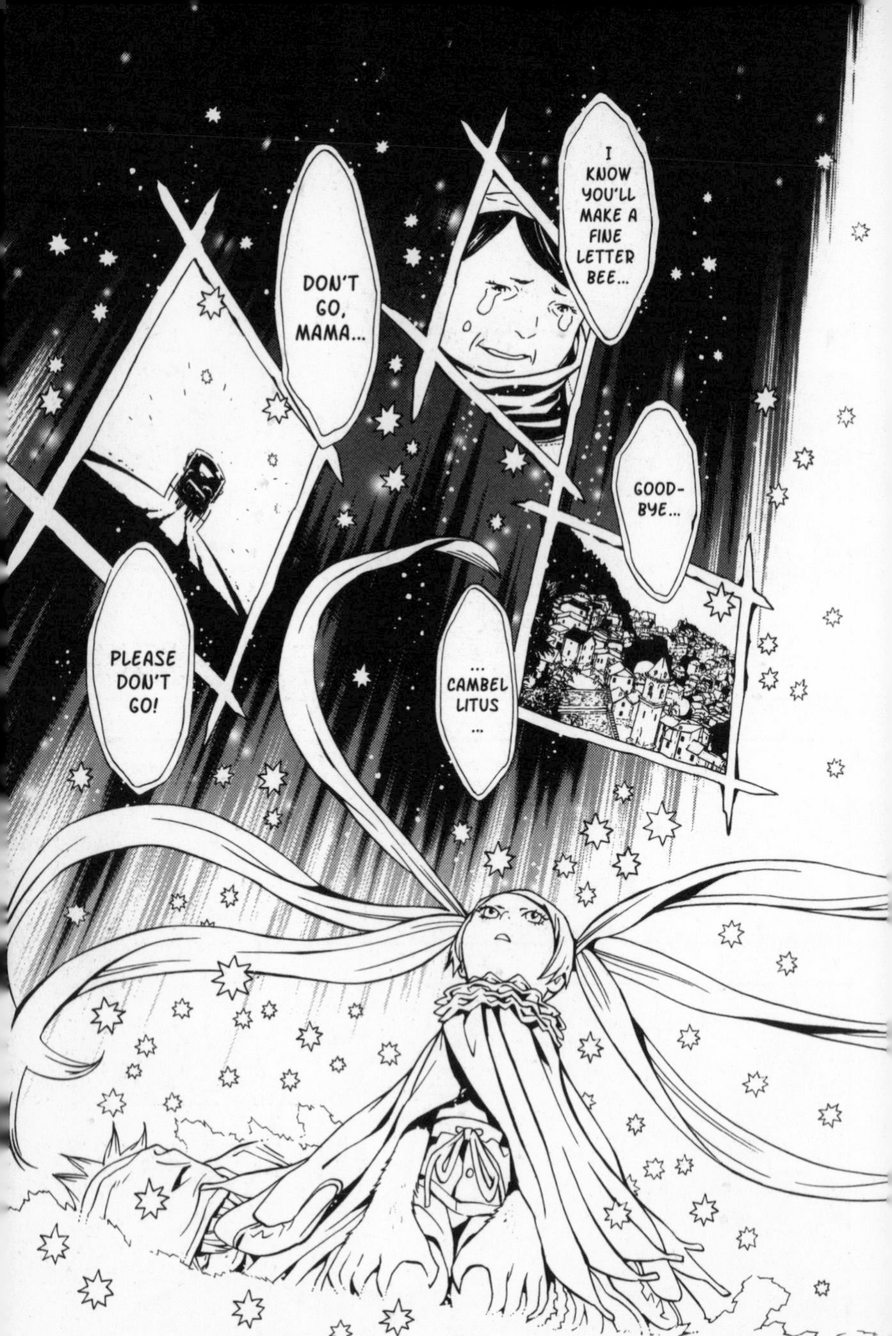
I KNOW YOU'LL MAKE A FINE LETTER BEE...
DON'T GO, MAMA...
GOOD-BYE...
...CAMBEL LITUS...
PLEASE DON'T GO!

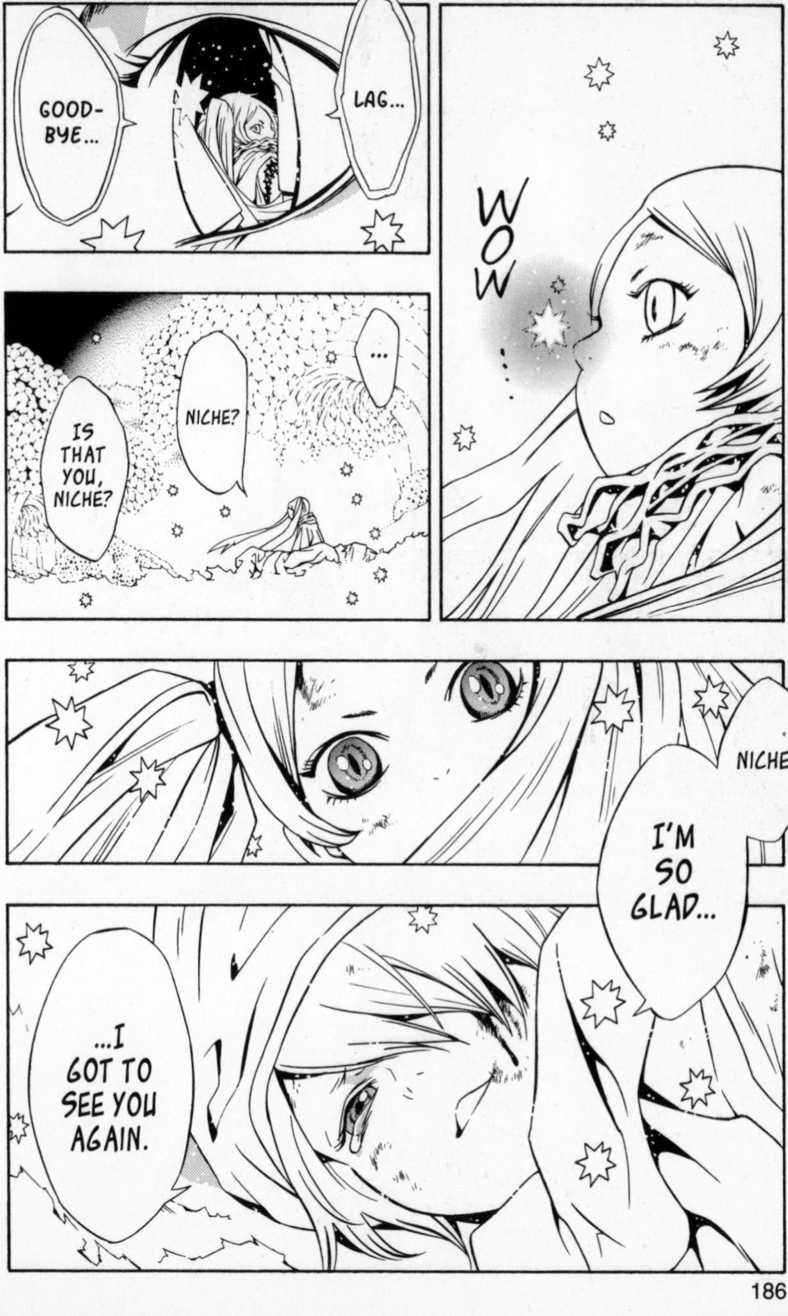
WOW...
LAG...
GOOD-BYE...
...
NICHE?
IS THAT YOU, NICHE?
NICHE...
I'M SO GLAD...
...I GOT TO SEE YOU AGAIN.

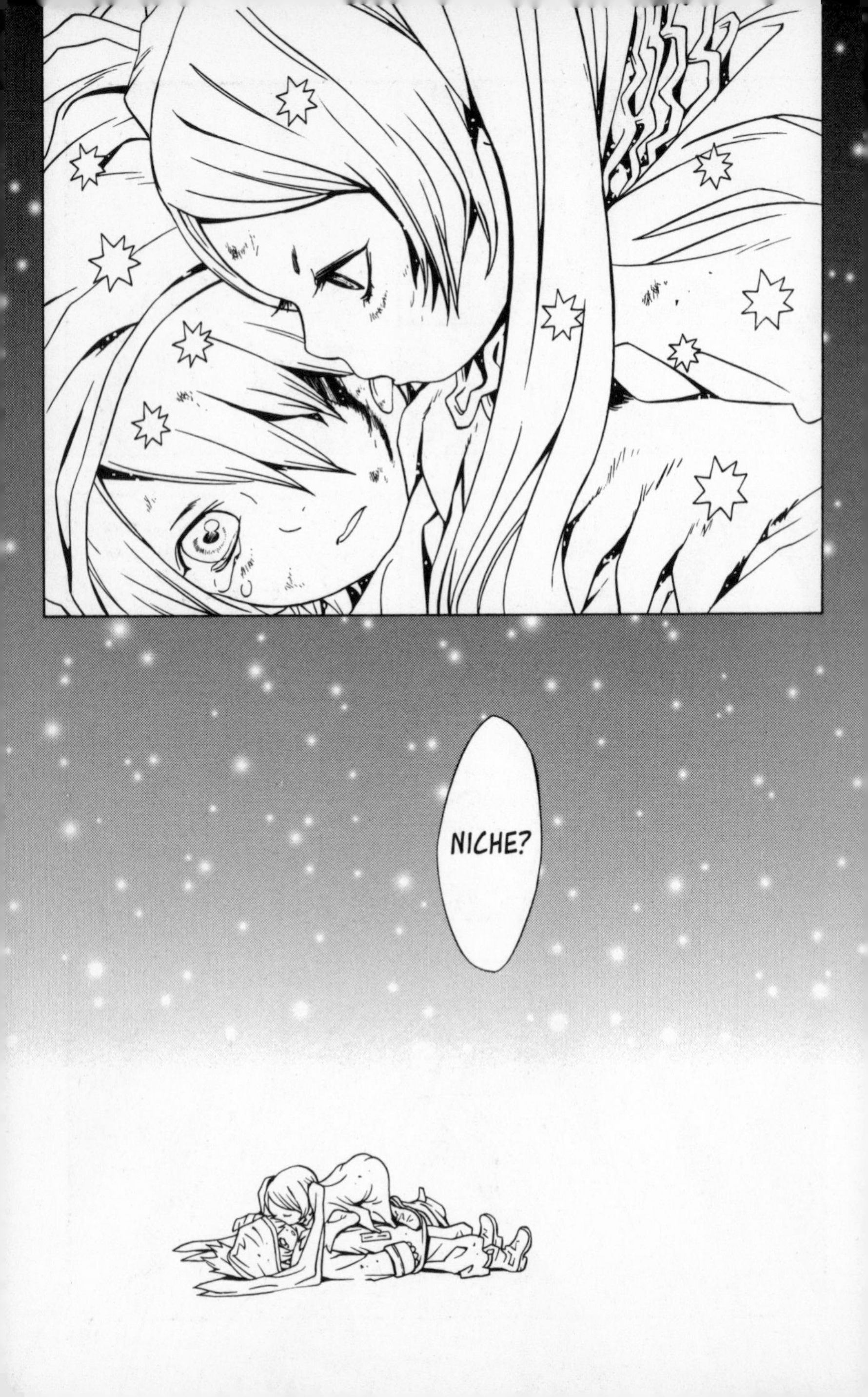
NICHE?

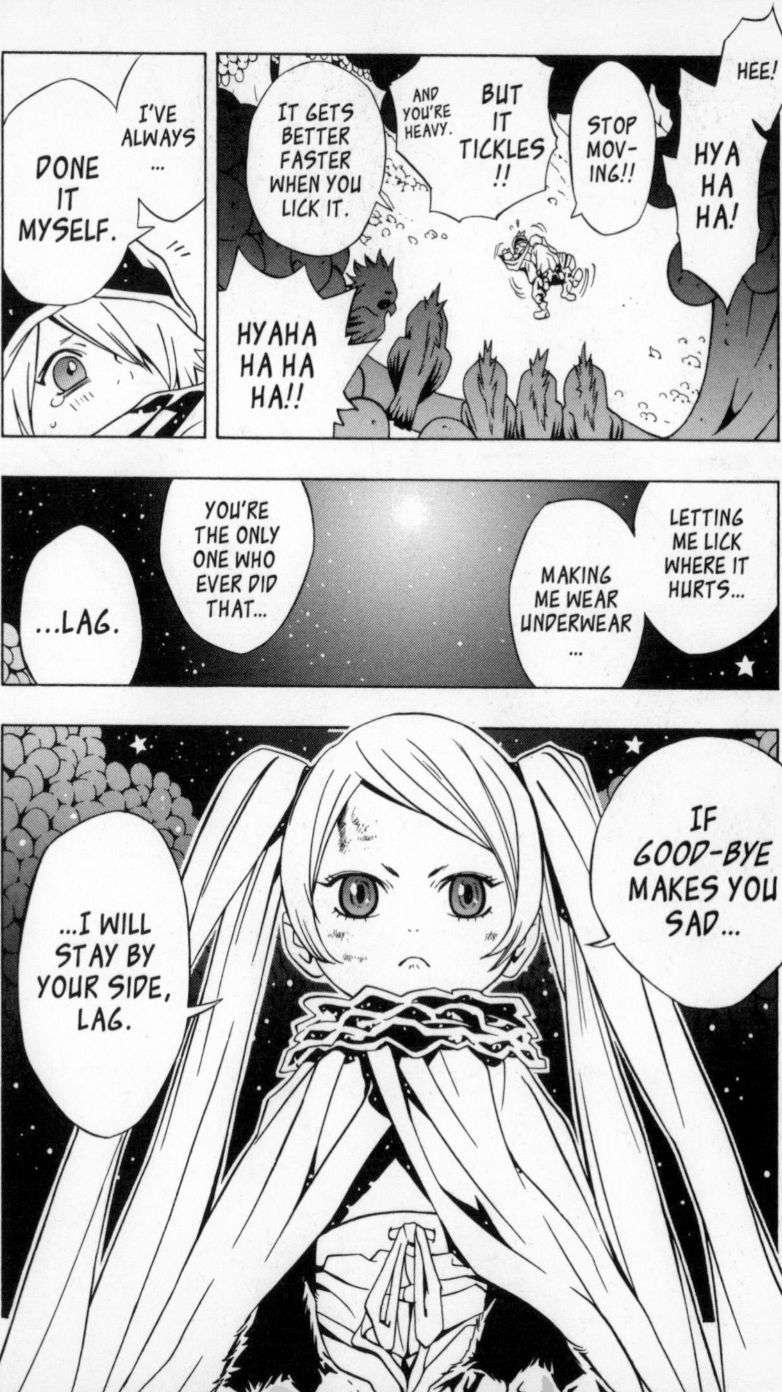
HEE!
HYA HA HA!
STOP MOV-ING!!
BUT IT TICKLES!!
AND YOU'RE HEAVY.
IT GETS BETTER FASTER WHEN YOU LICK IT.
HYAHA HA HA HA!!
I'VE ALWAYS ...
DONE IT MYSELF.
LETTING ME LICK WHERE IT HURTS...
MAKING ME WEAR UNDERWEAR ...
YOU'RE THE ONLY ONE WHO EVER DID THAT...
...LAG.
IF GOOD-BYE MAKES YOU SAD...
...I WILL STAY BY YOUR SIDE, LAG.

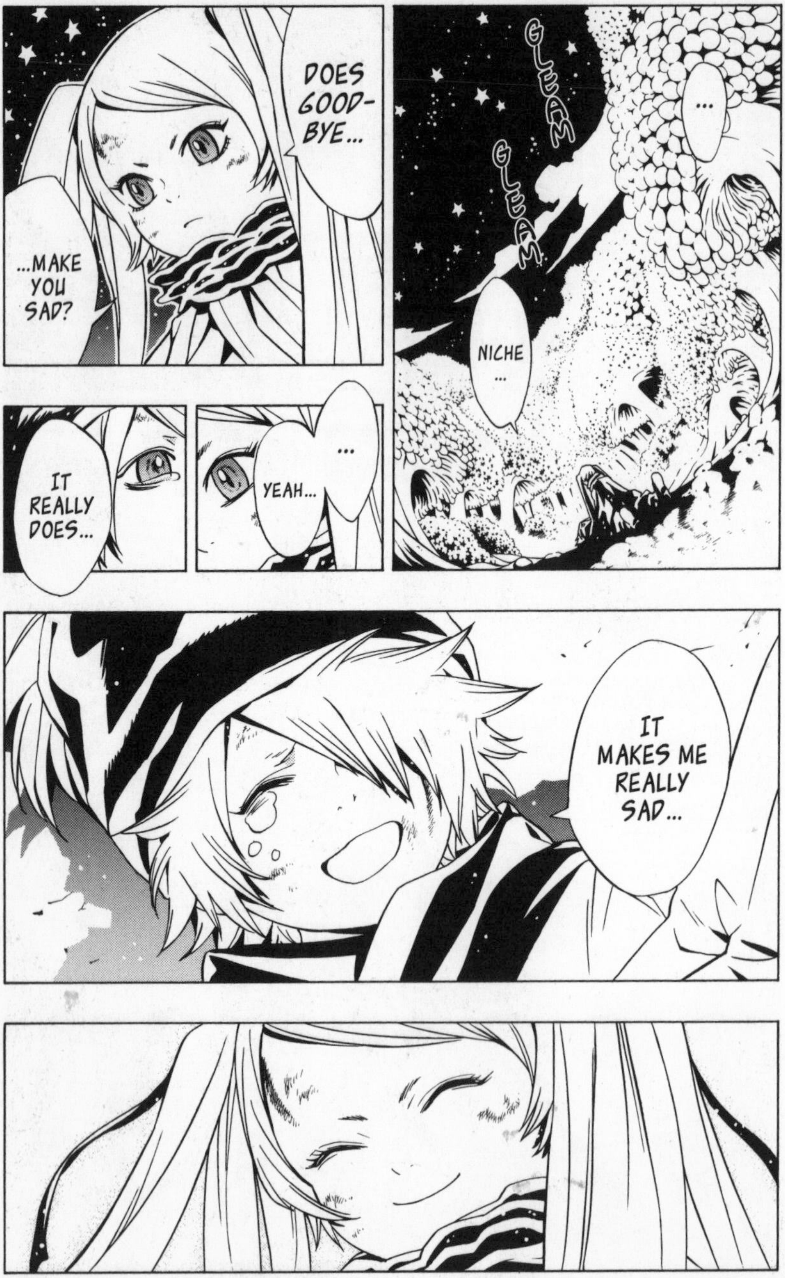
...
GLEAM
GLEAM
NICHE...
DOES GOODBYE...
...MAKE YOU SAD?
...
YEAH...
IT REALLY DOES...
IT MAKES ME REALLY SAD...

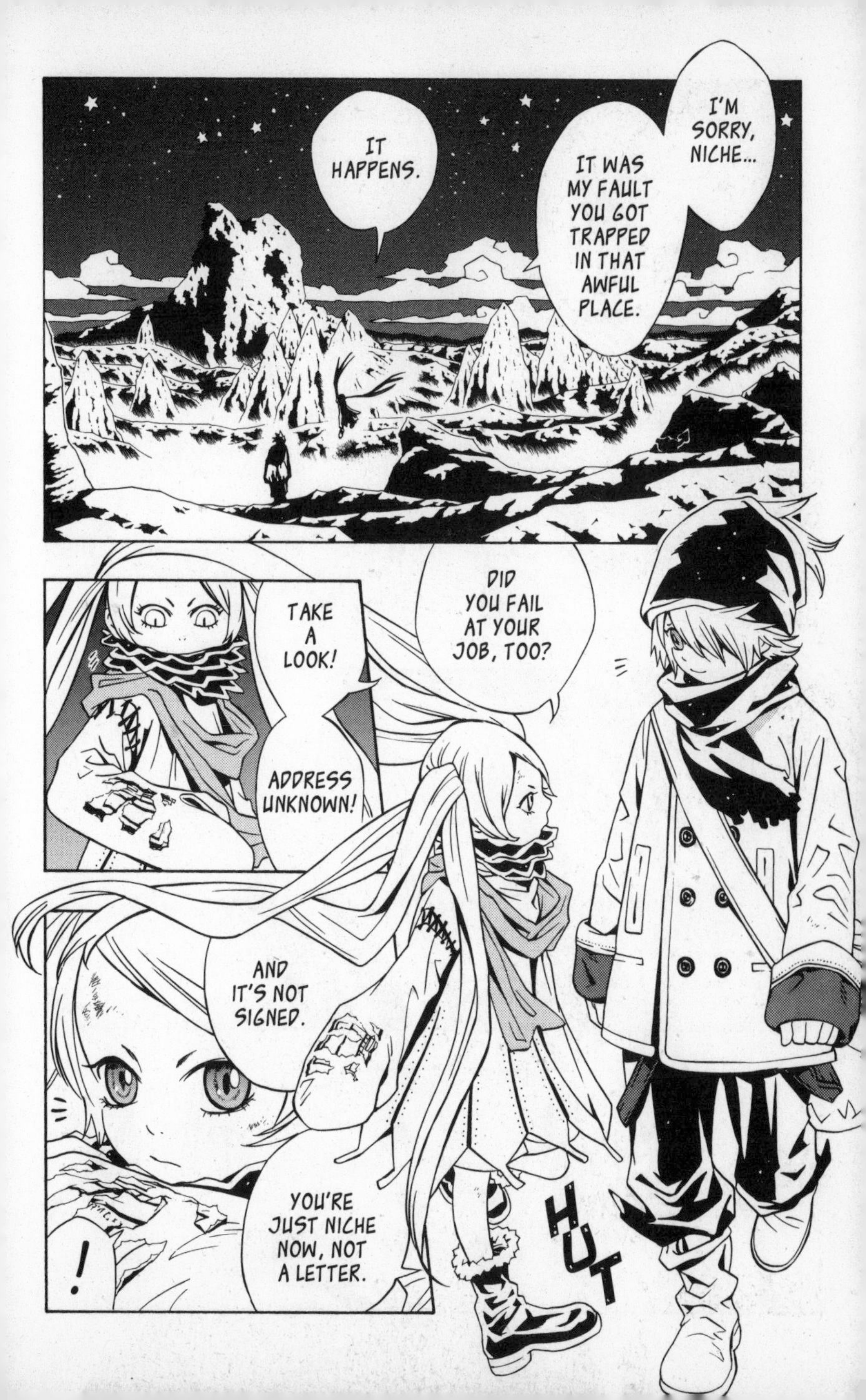
I'M SORRY, NICHE...
IT WAS MY FAULT YOU GOT TRAPPED IN THAT AWFUL PLACE.
IT HAPPENS.
DID YOU FAIL AT YOUR JOB, TOO?
HUT
TAKE A LOOK!
ADDRESS UNKNOWN!
AND IT'S NOT SIGNED.
YOU'RE JUST NICHE NOW, NOT A LETTER.
!

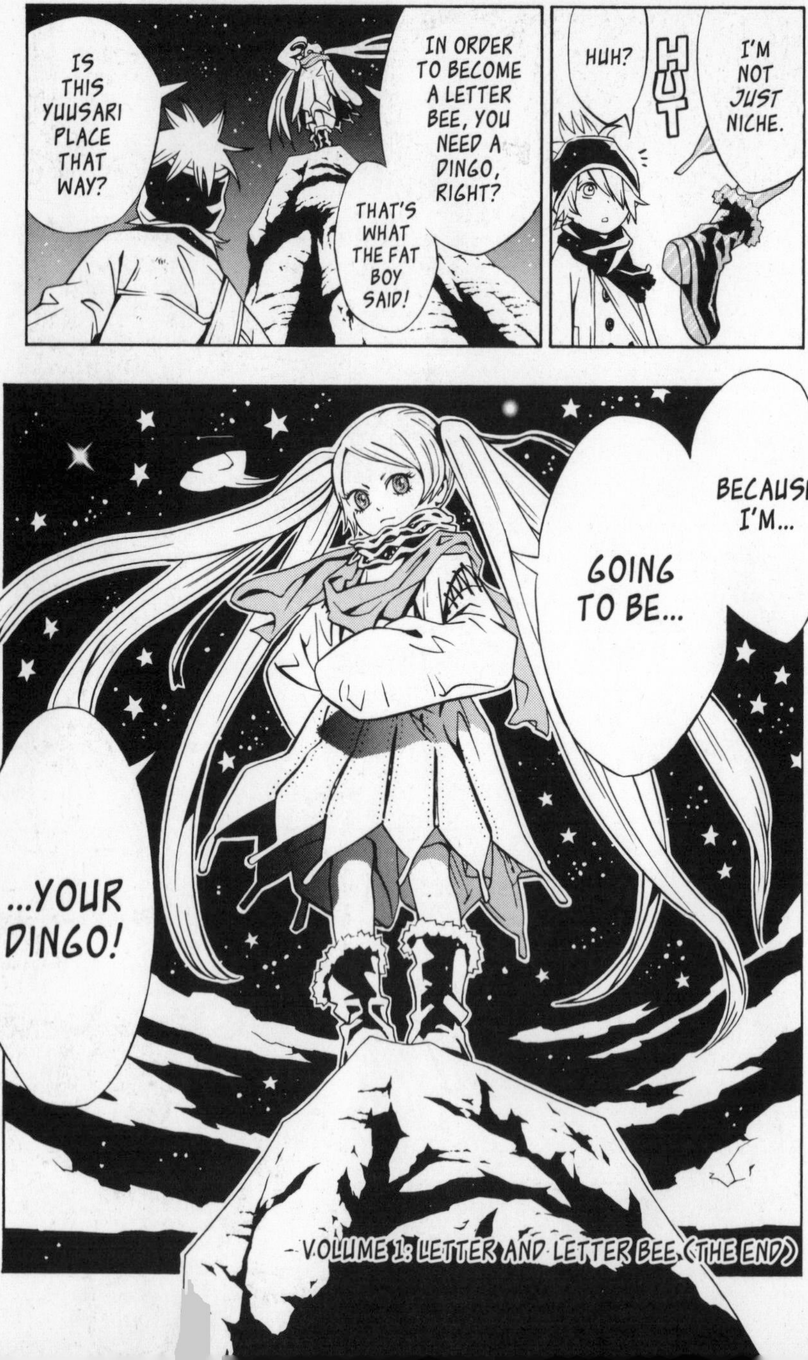
I'M NOT JUST NICHE.
HUT
HUH?
IN ORDER TO BECOME A LETTER BEE, YOU NEED A DINGO, RIGHT?
THAT'S WHAT THE FAT BOY SAID!
IS THIS YUUSARI PLACE THAT WAY?
BECAUSE I'M...
GOING TO BE...
...YOUR DINGO!
VOLUME 1: LETTER AND LETTER BEE (THE END)

Dr. Thunderland's Reference Desk

My name is Dr. Thunderland, but you can call me Professor Thunderland. I haven't made an appearance in the main story—yet. (Have I appeared in another manga? Absolutely not!*) I work at the Letter Bee Hive, researching all manner of phenomena pertaining to Amberground. Today's lecture covers the beginning to Chapter 2. Take your seats, everybody, let's begin...

*Dr. Thunderland appeared in "Pez and Dr. Thunderland," which ran in volume 3 of the color manga anthology *Robot*.

■ AMBERGROUND (AG)

Surrounded by ocean on four sides, Amberground is called "the land of perpetual night." Here, various ethnicities live in a chaotic state. The nation is divided by caste into three river-bound districts: Akatsuki, Yuusari, and Yodaka. Passage between districts occurs via government-regulated bridges.

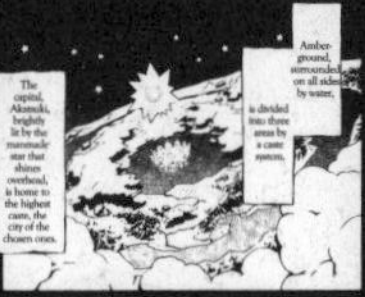
Amberground, surrounded on all sides by water,
is divided into three areas by a caste system,
The capital, Akatsuki, brightly lit by the manmade star that shines overhead, is home to the highest caste, the city of the chosen ones.

Crossing from Yodaka into Yuusari requires a government-issued Crossing Pass. Only the few who clear a very high security level are granted the Capital Crossing Pass, which is required to enter Akatsuki.

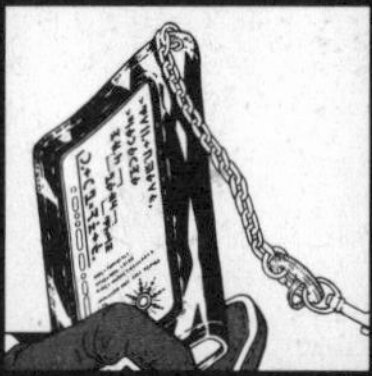

■ DISTRICTS OF AMBERGROUND

Akatsuki:

The capital of Amberground. Access is strictly limited. A Capital Crossing Pass is required for entry, and it is restricted to the holder only—even the holder's family cannot easily obtain clearance. Only the elite call Akatsuki home.

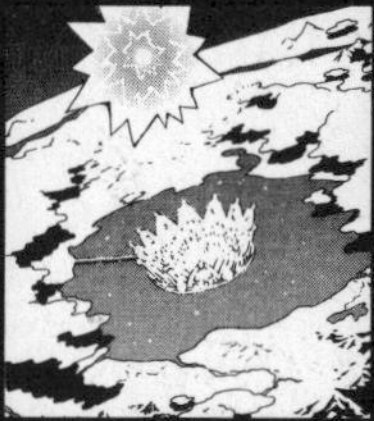

Yuusari:

This district is populated by the middle caste. The central office of the Amberground National Postal Service, known as the Beehive, is here. I live here as well! Or at least, I'm supposed to...

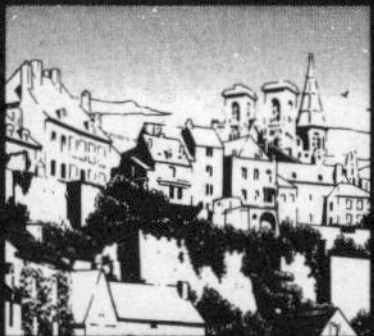

Yodaka:

This is the stage for the current volume. The citizens here are the lowest caste of Amberground. Yodaka's mountains, plains, and deserts are infested with Gaichuu. Most people work in agriculture or fishing, but heavy government taxes take most of the profit, leaving some families with barely enough food. Illegal fishing and smuggling rings are rumored to bring some prosperity to Yodaka's coasts.

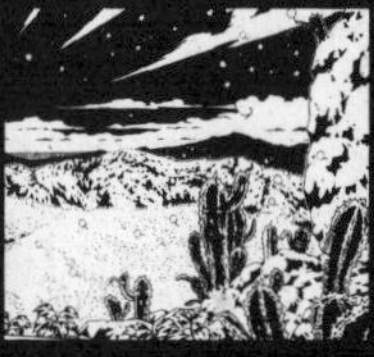

■ ARTIFICIAL SUN

The night may be endless in Amberground, but the capital of Akatsuki enjoys a simulated daylight under a small, man-made sun. In Yuusari, this sun casts a perpetual twilight. In Yodaka, the light is no brighter than a full moon.

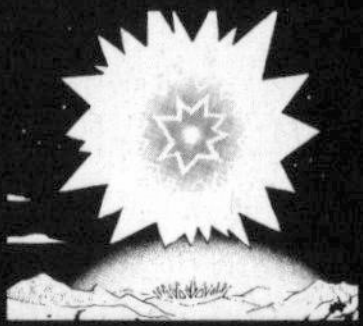

■ GAICHUU

These giant insect-like beasts are covered in armor. They prefer the dark regions of Amberground—specifically Yuusari and Yodaka. There are countless species, each with different shapes and abilities. Most scholars consider Gaichuu too mindless to be evil, although they do attack humans quite often, lured by the energy of *heart*. Perhaps, in ages past, they possessed some will or intelligence in search of some unknown thing... Well, that's the theory, at any rate. My theory, I mean. Still working on the details... Anyway, in fulfillment of his duties, a Letter Bee cannot avoid fighting these Gaichuu. To destroy them, one must penetrate the armor with *heart*, and that is no easy task.

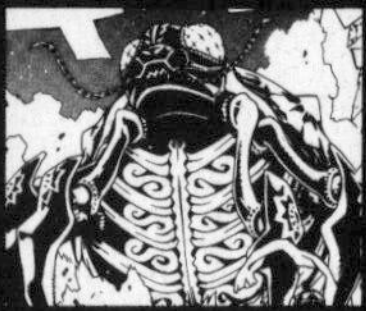

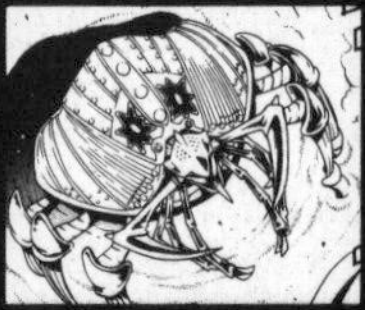

■ SPIRIT AMBER

In place of the sun's warming energy, Amberground is sustained by Spirit Amber, a natural source of energy that has lain buried underground for eons. Even in far-off Yodaka, which receives very little light, crops flourish because of the geothermal heat generated by buried Spirit Amber. It also preserves Amberground's magnetic field. Because the Spirit Amber lies so deep underground, mining operations are costly. [*continued on page 196*]

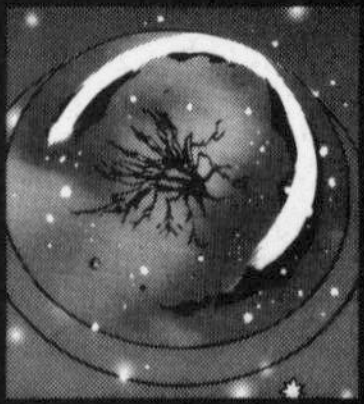

The government conducts the mining of this resource, and details are known only to those directly involved in the operation.

Seirei is name for the spiritual energy of the natural world. This energy finds a ready host in tiny insects. When these so-called spirit insects fall into tree resin to form amber, the *seirei* they carry is preserved. The government supplies the Letter Bees with Spirit Amber, which Letter Bees use to fuel their weapons and enhance their *heart*.

■ SHINDAN AND SHINDANJUU

Letter Bees use a variety of weapons and tools in concert with their *heart* to protect themselves from Gaichuu. One item, the Shindan, is a bullet made from a fragment of a Letter Bee's *heart*. Spirit Amber is inserted into the Shindanjuu—a kind of "*heart* gun"—and serves as the catalyst to form the Shindan. Letter Bee Gauche Suede once said, "The Shindan only appears as a bullet—but it's actually *heart*. Even though it's not live ammunition, we still load the cartridge to help control the concentration of *heart* and the power of the Shindan." The Shindan is a powerful weapon indeed, but it has its risks. Using too much *heart* can lead to a dangerous fatigue. The Shindan can also aid in recovery from illness or injury, and it has many other uses. The qualities of the *heart* differ from person to person.

Route Map

Finally, I am including a map created by the fine people at the Lonely Goatherd Map Station, whose shop is in Nocturne Hood in central Yuusari.

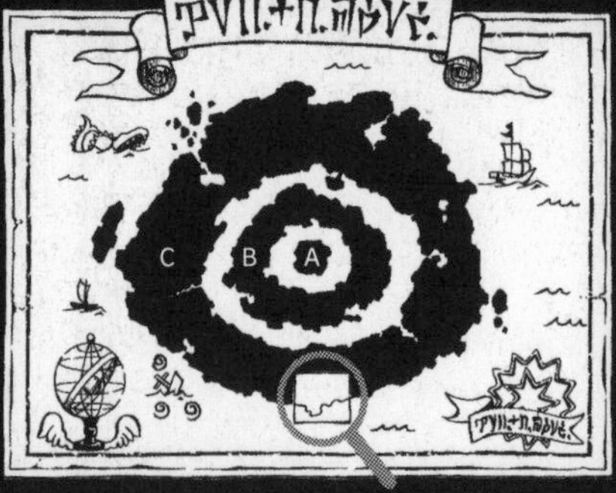
C
B
A

A: Akatsuki B: Yuusari C: Yodaka

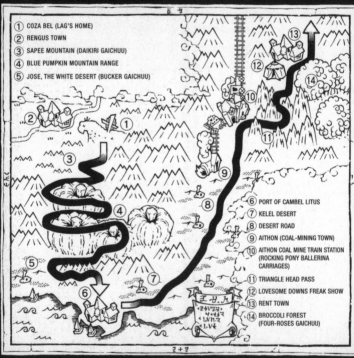

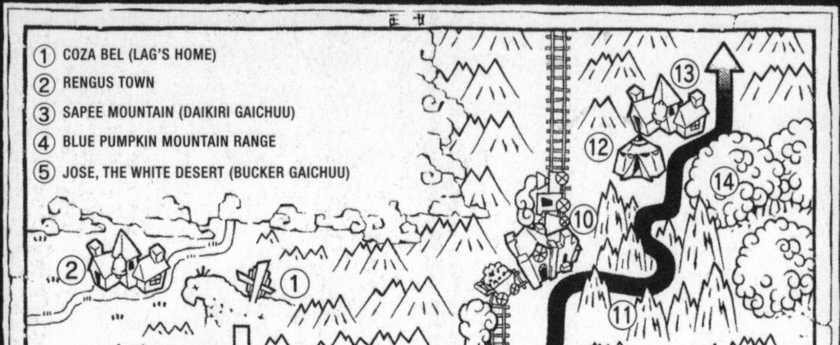
1 COZA BEL (LAG'S HOME)
2 RENGUS TOWN
3 SAPEE MOUNTAIN (DAIKIRI GAICHUU)
4 BLUE PUMPKIN MOUNTAIN RANGE
5 JOSE, THE WHITE DESERT (BUCKER GAICHUU)
6 PORT OF CAMBEL LITUS
7 KELEL DESERT
8 DESERT ROAD
9 AITHON (COAL-MINING TOWN)
10 AITHON COAL MINE TRAIN STATION (ROCKING PONY BALLERINA CARRIAGES)
11 TRIANGLE HEAD PASS
12 LOVESOME DOWNS FREAK SHOW
13 RENT TOWN
14 BROCCOLI FOREST (FOUR-ROSES GAICHUU)

How was the lesson? Remember, we've only just scratched the surface today. Amberground is full of mysteries, and the journey has only just begun. I'm sure much more will come up in our story—and, of course, I'm sure I'll see you all for volume 2. Bah! What a pain! I have much more important things to do, you know. And when do I get to make my appearance in the manga?!

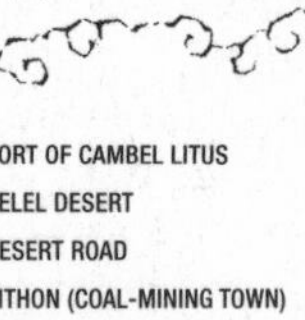

Tegami Bachi
LETTER · BEE

Volume 1

SHONEN JUMP Manga Edition
This manga contains material that was originally published in
English in SHONEN JUMP #75–78.

English Adaptation/Rich Amtower
Translation/JN Productions
Touch-up and Lettering/Annaliese Christman
Design/Frances O. Liddell
Editor/Daniel Gillespie

Printed in the U.S.A.

Published by VIZ Media, LLC
P.O. Box 77010
San Francisco, CA 94107

10 9 8 7 6 5 4 3
First printing, September 2009
Third printing, October 2011

In the next volume...

Lag and Niche are on the way to Yuusari for
Lag's final interview with the Letter Bees when they
stop in a town known as the Dead End, full of people
desperate to cross over to Yuusari. A friendly boy
shows them to an inn. He's so friendly that they don't
notice when he steals their crossing pass!

Plus, a mysterious man expresses a keen interest in
acquiring "the child of Maka." Watch out, Niche!

**Continue the journey through the strange land of
Amberground in volume 2! Available Now!**

The World's Greatest Manga Now available on your iPad

Full of FREE previews and tons of new manga for you to explore

From legendary manga like *Dragon Ball* to *Bakuman*, the newest series from the creators of *Death Note*, the best manga in the world is now available on the iPad through the official VIZ Manga app.

- **Free App**
- **New content weekly**
- **Free chapter 1 previews**

SHONEN JUMP
NARUTO
THE MOVIE SHIPPUDEN
-Bonds- 絆

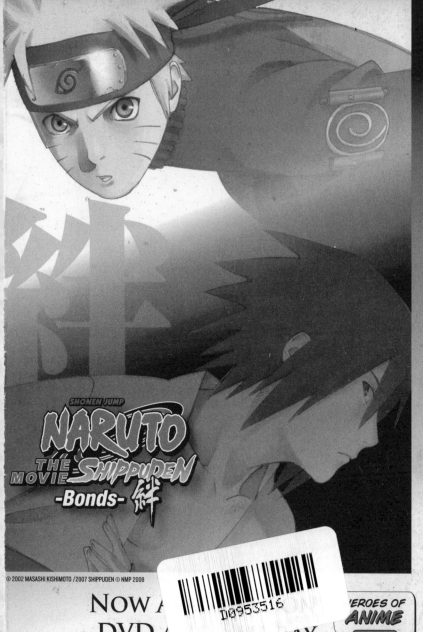

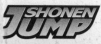